M A S T E R I N G
ITALIAN
HEAR IT • SPEAK IT • WRITE IT • READ IT

Developed for the
FOREIGN SERVICE INSTITUTE,
DEPARTMENT OF STATE

Stephen Zappala

BARRON'S

Cover design by Milton Glaser, Inc.

This edition published in 1996 by Barron's Educational Series, Inc.

The title of the original course is *Italian—Programmed (Volume 1)*

This course was developed for the Foreign Service Institute, Department of State by Stephen Zappala.

All inquiries should be addressed to:
Barron's Educational Series, Inc.
250 Wireless Boulevard
Hauppauge, New York 11788

Paper Edition

International Standard Book No. 0-8120-2222-X

A large part of the text of this book is recorded on the accompanying tapes, as follows:

Units 1, 2, 3	Tape 1A
Units 4, 5	Tape 1B
Units 6, 7	Tape 2A
Units 8, 9	Tape 2B
Units 10, 11 (part)	Tape 3A
Units 11 (part), 12	Tape 3B
Units 13, 14	Tape 4A
Unit 15	Tape 4B
Units 16, 17(part)	Tape 5A
Units 17 (part), 18 (part)	Tape 5B
Units 18 (part), 19 (part)	Tape 6A
Units 19 (part) 20 (part)	Tape 6B
Unit 20 (part)	Tape 7A
Unit 21	Tape 7B
Unit 22 (part)	Tape 8A
Units 22 (part), 23 (part)	Tape 8B
Units 23 (part), 24 (part)	Tape 9A
Units 24 (part), 25	Tape 9B
Unit 26 (part)	Tape 10A
Units 26 (part), 27 (part)	Tape 10B
Units 27 (part), 28 (part)	Tape 11A
Unit 28 (part)	Tape 11B
Unit 29 (part)	Tape 12A
Units 29 (part), 30	Tape 12B

On the tapes selected statements about Italy and its culture adapted from:
Learn Italian the Fast and Fun Way by Marcel Danesi
Italian at a Glance by Mario Costantino.

PRINTED IN THE UNITED STATES OF AMERICA

19   18   17   16   15   14   13

CONTENTS

Unit 5

Unit 6

Unit 7

Unit 8

Unit 9

Unit 12

Unit 13

Unit 17

Unit 18

Unit 19

Unit 20

Unit 21

—Something in Progress or in Existence
at the Time of Utterance 1) a single, durative
event (frames 45–46) 2) the events leading
to a punctual act (frames 47–51) 3) a series

consisting of the repetition of an event
(frame 57) 4) a plan or schedule for
something to happen in the future (frame 58)

Unit 22

Unit 23

Unit 24

Unit 26

Unit 27

Unit 28

Unit 29

Unit 30

PREFACE

Mastering Italian is part of a series of language courses being presented by Barron's Educational Series, Inc. This course is intended for the serious language student who wishes to speak Italian fluently. The course book and accompanying tapes present Italian as a spoken language, emphasizing pronunciation and verbal comprehension.

This course was developed by the Foreign Service Institute of the Department of State to train government officers who needed to speak Italian fluently. In addition to being an excellent choice for those who wish to teach themselves Italian, this course can be of great value studying it in school and wishes to achieve greater fluency.

Innovative features of this text include (1) the emphasis on concept understanding (Units 4, and 31) and (2) new analyses for Italian of intonation (Units 5, 6, 7), and "double" consonants (Unit 25) and "gender words" (Units 22 and 29).

The course was designed by Stephen Zappala, Chairman of Italian in the Department of Romance Languages. Egle Camozzo, instructor in Italian, was the author's chief consultant who also wrote many of the drill sentences, narratives and dialogs, especially in Units 21–30. In addition, she reviewed and edited all materials and made many useful suggestions. Additional suggestions came from other members of the FSI Italian teaching staff who also reviewed the text.

The original recordings were made in the studio of the FSI Language Laboratory with the technical assistance of Jose M. Ramirez. The voicing was done by Egle Comozzo, Emilia Francini, Giovanni Salvo, and Mr. Zappala.

FOREWORD

Organization

This volume is designed to introduce you to spoken Italian. It covers virtually the entire sound-system of the language and introduces the basic grammatical categories (Gender, Number, Unit Noun Markers, Person, Tense). Although verb forms are for the most part limited to the Present tense, a few other forms including Past tense and Future tense forms are also presented and practiced. The vocabulary and structure in this volume allows for participation in such situations as talking on the telephone, ordering a meal, discussing daily activities, requesting or telling someone to do something.

This volume consists of thirty units. A RECAPITULATION of the major points presented is found after Units 10, 15, 20, 25, and 30.

Vocabulary lists are at the end of the volume.

The thirty units of this volume are in a programmed format. This means that information is presented and practiced in very small steps. The steps are numbered and referred to as "frames." A unit may have as few as 27 frames (Unit 2) or as many as 117 frames (Unit 29). Because of the programmed format, the material is self-instructional and requires the use of a tape recorder.

While going through the frames, the student not only receives information about the language but also is expected to do certain drills, oral and written. At the end of the frames of each unit, one or more tests appear. Some require the use of a tape recorder; others do not. Answers to all the tests are given at the end of each unit.

Approach and Methodology

The learning process on the part of the student involves:

1) observation of individual examples
2) memorization of new vocabulary items
3) assimilation of information pertaining to the examples
4) repetition practice (drills)
5) the opportunity to make analogies (i.e., practice in trying to be creative).

An important distinction between "meaning" and "translation" permeates this course. Although in this programmed course it was deemed practical to present new vocabulary items with an English translation, the student quickly finds that one word may have many translations and that the real meaning of a foreign item is arrived at *not* through a translation but by seeing how it is used in different situations. "Thought translation" exercises appear throughout the text and are designed purposely to force the student to use only what has been presented to convey an idea, rather than to try to translate individual words. This concept is elaborated on Unit 4.

Prior Knowledge of Grammar

This course presumes no prior knowledge of any grammar on the part of the student. Grammatical terms are explained as they are introduced and students should learn them as they get them. Also in this text are some new grammatical terms that appear in no other Italian text. These are not intended to confuse, but to help students understand how Italian works without worrying about how any other language, including English, works.

Some Prior Knowledge of Italian

For the student who begins this course with some knowledge of Italian, it is recommended that he or she begin from the beginning and move very rapidly until he or she reaches something new. A quick self-check may be made by doing the end-of-unit tests.

Technical Instructions

A tape recorder is required for listening to the frames and many of the end-of-unit tests. Through Unit 12, the tape closely follows what is on the printed page. From Unit 13 on, however, frame comments, explanations, and questions are *not* normally recorded. These should be read carefully *before* turning on the recorder and listening to examples and/or frame responses.

Certain frames require a response of a particular kind. Such frames begin with an asterisk "*." Immediately at the end of such a frame you are to stop the tape (if necessary) and, unless told to do otherwise, give the response. Then start the tape again and listen. The correct response is provided on the tape either as part of the same frame or in the frame that follows. The taped response lets you know whether you are in fact learning what has been designed for you to learn. If your response was wrong, you should go back on the tape and repeat what you did not learn.

```
Tape 1A
```

UNIT 1

Code for English Sound-Types

/a/ = the vowel of *ah*
/æ/ = the vowel of *man*
/ə/ = the final vowel of *sofa*

---

1. Listen to the following Italian vowel, which we will call vowel No. 1.
   /A/ (2)

2. Here is an English vowel.
   /a/ (2)

3. Here is Italian vowel No. 1 followed by the English.
   /A/ + /a/ (2)

*4. Which is the Italian vowel, x or y?
   /A/ + /a/ (2)
     x   y

5. Here is another English vowel.
   /æ/ (2)

6. Here is Italian vowel No. 1 followed by the English.
   /A/ + /æ/ (2)
     x   y

*7. Which is the Italian vowel, x or y?
   /æ/ + /A/ (2)
     x   y

8. Here is another English vowel.
   /ə/ (2)

9. Here is Italian vowel No. 1 followed by the English.
   /A/ + /ə/ (2)

*10. Are both of these Italian vowel No. 1?
   /a/ + /A/ (2)

*11. Are both of these Italian vowel No. 1?
   /A/ + /ə/ (2)

*12. Are both of these Italian vowel No. 1?
   /A/ + /A/ (2)

*13. Which is Italian, x, y or z?
   /a/ + /A/ + /æ/ (2)
    x   y   z

*14. Which is it now, x, y or z?
   /ə/ + /a/ + /A/ (2)
    x   y   z

*15. Which is it now x, y or z?
   /æ/ + /A/ + /ə/ (2)
    x   y   z

*16. Are these three all Italian vowel No. 1?
   /A/ + /A/ + /a/ (2)

*17. Are these three all Italian vowel No. 1?
   /A/ + /A/ + /A/ (2)

*18. Does the following syllable contain vowel No. 1?
   /MAN/ (2)

*19. Does the following syllable contain vowel No. 1?
   /mæn/ (2)

*20. Does the following?
   /DA/ (2)

*21. What about this one?
   /də/ (2)

*22. Is the following Italian vowel No. 1?
   /ə/ (2)

23. So far, vowel No. 1 has been presented as a rather short, "clipped" sound. A longer version of vowel No. 1 would be the following.
   /Ā/ (2)

24. This is the short vowel No. 1 followed by the long vowel No. 1.
   /A/ /Ā/ (2)

*25. Which is the short vowel, x or y?
   /Ā/ /A/ (2)
    x   y

*26. Are the following three all short?
   /Ā/ /A/ /A/ (2)

*27. Are these three all short?
/A/ /A/ /A/ (2)

* * * * *

28. Now listen to the girl's name spelled A-m-a-n-d-a, first pronounced in English, then pronounced in Italian.
/əmǽndə/ /AMÁNDA/ (2)

29. Notice that the vowel sounds in the Italian pronunciation are all vowel No. 1.
/AMÁNDA/

*30. Are they all the short vowel No. 1?
/AMÁNDA/

*31. Which vowel in the word sounds a little *longer* than the other two—the first, the second, or the third?
/AMÁNDA/

*32. Which vowel in the word sounds a little *louder* than the other two—the first, the second, or the third?
/AMÁNDA/

33. That vowel which is relatively loud in an utterance is usually said to be STRESSED, and the other vowels are called UNSTRESSED.

*34. Which vowel is stressed in the following?
/AMÁNDA/

*35. Is this stressed vowel longer than the unstressed vowels in the word?
/AMÁNDA/

36. Most speakers of Standard Italian tend to make stressed vowels a little longer than unstressed vowels, although this tendency seems to be less strong in Northern Italy than in the rest of Italy.

* * * * *

37. The following is an Italian syllable. Listen closely.
(da) (da) (da)

38. The sound-type represented by the letter *d* in Italian is a sound-type not normally heard in English. Said with an American accent, the Italian syllable just given would sound like:
/də/ (3)

39. Here is the Italian followed by the English:

     /DA/ /də/ (2)

40. The basic difference between the Italian consonant and the English one has to do with the position of the tongue in the mouth. Whereas in English the letter *d* usually represents a sound-type made by having the front part of the tongue touch the *gum ridge behind the upper teeth*, in Italian the same letter usually stands for a sound-type made by having the front part of the tongue touch the *upper teeth.*

41. A sound made by having the front part of the tongue touch the upper teeth is sometimes referred to as a DENTAL sound. The symbol /D/ will be used here to represent this particular dental sound.

42. Have your tongue touch your upper teeth and repeat the Italian syllable. (The "X" that appears after some parentheses means that you are to repeat what you hear after what is indicated by each pair of parentheses.)

     /DA/ (2)

43. Now repeat the word *Amanda*, remembering that the /D/ is dental, and that all the vowels are the same—vowel No. 1.

     /AMÁNDA/ (3)

*44. As you have seen, vowel No. 1 is represented in Italian by what letter?

TEST

(answers not recorded)

Indicate by "yes" or "no" whether the utterances you hear are Italian or not.
Each utterance will be heard twice. To test yourself cover the letters and words
given and just listen. Then check your answers and review if necessary.

1) /A/ (2)
2) /æ/ (2)
3) /A/ (2)
4) /A/ (2)
5) /də/ (2)
6) /a/ (2)
7) /da/ (2)
8) /DA/ (2)
9) /AMÁNDA/ (2)
10) /əmǽndə/ (2)

TEST ANSWERS

1) yes
2) no
3) yes
4) yes
5) no
6) no
7) no
8) yes
9) yes
10) no

UNIT 2

Code for English Sound-Types

/u/ = the vowel of *put*
/k/ = the consonant of *coo*
/s/ = the consonant of *so*

---

1. Listen to the following Italian vowel, which we will call vowel No. 2.
   /U/ (2)

2. Here is an English vowel.
   /u/ (2)

3. Here is Italian vowel No. 2 followed by the English.
   /U/ /u/ (2)

*4. Which is the Italian vowel, x or y?
   /u/ /U/ (2)
      x   y

5. Now listen to the short vowel No. 2 followed by the long vowel No. 2.
   /U/ /Ū/ (2)

*6. Which is the short vowel, x or y?
   /U/ /Ū/ (2)
      x   y

*7. Are the following three all short?
   /U/ /U/ /U/ (2)

*8. Are these three all short?
   /U/ /Ū/ /U/ (2)

9. Vowel No. 2 should be pronounced with the mouth relatively closed, and the lips in a rounded position. Because the lips are rounded it is referred to as a ROUNDED vowel. Round your lips and repeat vowel No. 2 as you hear it.
   /U/ (2)

* * * * *

10. Now repeat the following syllable containing vowel No. 2.
    /LU/ (2)

*11. Here is another Italian syllable. Does it contain vowel No. 1 or vowel No. 2?

/KA/ (2)

12. The Italian syllable you just heard begins with a consonant sound something like the initial consonant of the English word "key." Listen to the Italian syllable followed by its English counterpart.

/KA/ /ka/ (2)

*13. Are the following all Italian syllables?

/KA/ /KA/ /KA/ (2)

*14. Are the following all Italian syllables?

/KA/ /KA/ /ka/ (2)

*15. Which is Italian, x or y?

/KA/ /ka/ (2)
   x   y

16. The difference between the Italian consonant you have been hearing (which we will represent as /K/) and the English consonant has to do with a characteristic of certain sound in English which is absent in Italian. Certain English sounds are pronounced with a puff of air, which should be avoided in Italian. A consonant pronounced with such a puff of air is called ASPIRATED. Italian consonants should *never* be ASPIRATED.

17. Repeat the following Italian syllable, represented *ca*. Remember that the consonant is *not* aspirated.

(ca)X (ca)X (ca)X

18. This unaspirated sound-type is very much like the second consonant heard in the English word "scar."

19. If you listen carefully, you can hear a difference in the pronunciation of the sound-types represented by the letter *c* in the following two English words: "car"– "scar."

20. In the word "car," the sound-type in question is aspirated, but in the word "scar" it is *not* aspirated. Listen again.

(car) (scar) (car) (scar)

21. The Italian /K/ is, therefore, more like the consonant represented by the letter *c* in "scar" than like the initial consonant of "car." It is, in other words, *not aspirated*. To pronounce it, try *thinking* of an initial /s/ before uttering the /K/.

22. Now repeat again.
    (ca)X   (ca)X   (ca)X

*　*　*　*　*

23. Now say the Italian name that corresponds to the English *Luke*. It is spelled
    L-u-c-a.
    (Luca)X   (Luca)X   (Luca)X

*24. What have we been calling the following vowel sound?
    /U/ (2)

*25. Is Italian vowel No. 2 stressed in the following name?
    /LÚKA/ (2)

*26. What letter is used in Italian to represent vowel No. 2?

27. Repeat the two names you have learned so far.
    (Amanda)X   (Luca)X   (Amanda)X   (Luca)X

TEST A

(not recorded)

Use the following five words to fill in the blanks:

aspirated	short
dental	stressed
rounded	

1) Vowel No. 2 is a_____vowel.

2) The first vowel in the name *Luca* and the second vowel in the name *Amanda* are_____.

3) Both the first and the last vowels in the name *Amanda* are_____.

4) The letter *d* in Italian usually represents a_____consonant.

5) Italian consonants are normally not_____.

TEST B

(answers not recorded)

Indicate by "yes" or "no" whether the utterances you hear are Italian or not. Each utterance will be heard twice. To test yourself cover the letters and words given and just listen. Then check your answers and review if necessary.

1) /U/
2) /U/
3) /u/
4) /ə/
5) /A/
6) /KA/
7) /lu/
8) /LÚKA/
9) /lúwkə/
10) /AMÁNDA/

TEST A   ANSWERS

1) rounded
2) stressed
3) short
4) dental
5) aspirated

TEST B   ANSWERS

1) yes	3) no	5) yes	7) no	9) no
2) yes	4) no	6) yes	8) yes	10) yes

UNIT 3

Code for English Sound-Types

/i/ = the vowel of *bit*

1. Listen to the following Italian vowel, which we will call vowel No. 3.
    /I/ (2)

2. Here is an English vowel.
    /i/ (2)

3. Here is Italian vowel No. 3 followed by the English.
    /I/ /i/ (2)

*4. Which is the Italian vowel, x or y?
    /I/ /i/ (2)
      x   y

5. Now listen to the short vowel No. 3 followed by the long vowel No. 3.
    /I/ /Ī/ (2)

*6. Which is the short vowel, x or y?
    /Ī/ /I/ (2)
      x   y

*7. Are the following three all short?
    /I/ /Ī/ /I/ (2)

*8. Are these three all short?
    /I/ /I/ /I/ (2)

9. To pronounce vowel No. 3 correctly, make your lips tense by pulling your mouth back tightly as if to produce a forced grin. Keep your mouth relatively closed. Repeat after the model.
    /I/ (3)

10. The following syllable contains vowel No. 3. Listen and repeat.
    /MI/ (2)

*11. Does the following syllable contain vowel No. 3?
    /NI/ (2)

*12. What about this one?
    /ni/ (2)

*13. And this one?

/TI/ (2)

* * * * *

14. The Italian syllable you just heard begins with a consonant sound something like the initial consonant of the English word "tea." Listen to the Italian syllable followed by its English counterpart.

/TI/ /tiy/ (2)

*15. Are the following all Italian syllables?

/TI/ /TI/ /tiy/ (2)

*16. Are the following all Italian syllables?

/TI/ /TI/ /TI/ (2)

*17. Which is Italian, x or y?

/tiy/ /TI/ (2)
  x   y

18. There are two main differences between the Italian consonant you have been hearing and the English consonant.

19. Like the English consonant sound heard in "do," the English consonant of "tea" is made by having the front part of the tongue touch the *gum ridge behind the upper teeth*. Listen to the following English word.

(tea) (tea) (tea)

20. The Italian consonant heard in frames No. 13 through No. 17 and represented here as /T/, is usually made like the Italian /D/ by having the front part of the tongue touch the *upper teeth*.

*21. What is such a sound called?

*22. Is the English consonant in "tea" normally dental?

* * * * *

23. Now listen carefully to the English word "tea."

(tea) (tea) (tea)

24. The English consonant in this word is followed by a puff of air. Listen again.

    (tea) (tea) (tea)

*25. Therefore, the English consonant in the word "tea" is said to be what?

*26. Are Italian consonants normally aspirated?

*27. Therefore, is the Italian /T/ aspirated?

*28. Is the following statement true or false?
    "Unlike the English consonant in "tea," the Italian /T/ is normally dental
    and not aspirated."

29. The unaspirated /T/, though normally dental, is very much like the sec-
    ond consonant heard in the English word "star."

30. If you listen carefully, you can hear a difference in the pronunciation of the
    sound-types represented by the letter *t* in the following two English
    words: "tar" – "star."

31. In the word "tar" the sound-type in question is aspirated, but in the word
    "star" it is *not* aspirated. Listen again.

    (tar) (star) (tar) (star)

32. The Italian /T/ is, therefore, more like the consonant represented by the
    letter *t* in "star" than like the initial consonant of "tar." It is, in other words,
    not aspirated. To pronounce it, try *thinking* of an initial /s/ before uttering
    the /T/.

33. Now repeat.

    (ta)X (ta)X (ta)X

34. Now try the following. Remember to avoid making a strong puff of air.
    Think of inhaling rather than exhaling.

    (ti)X (ti)X (ti)X

35. Listen again to the Italian syllable *ti* followed by the English word "tea"

    (ti) (tea) (ti) (tea)

*36. Is the following Italian or English?

    tea (2)

*37. What about this one?

/TI/ (2)

*38. And this one?

/TI/ (2)

* * * * *

39. Now listen to the girl's name spelled T-i-n-a, first pronounced in English, then pronounced in Italian.

/tíyna/   /TÍNA/

40. Now repeat the Italian version of the name, remembering that the /T/ is dental and not aspirated.

(Tina)X   (Tina)X   (Tina)X

*41. What letter is used in normal Italian spelling to represent /T/?

*42. This name contains two vowels, vowel No. 3 and vowel No. 1. Which is stressed?

/TÍNA/ (2)

*43. Which vowel is longer in this name, vowel No. 3 or vowel No. 1?

/TÍNA/ (2)

*44. What letter is used to represent vowel No. 3?

45. Repeat the three names you have learned, after the model.

(Amanda)X   (Luca)X   (Tina)X
(Amanda)X   (Luca)X   (Tina)X

TEST A

(not recorded)

Use the following items to fill in the blanks:

    dental   *vowel 2*
    not aspirated   *vowel 3*
    vowel 1

1. Of the three vowels you have learned, only _____ is rounded.

2. Unlike the first consonant in the English word "tea," both /T/ and /D/ are_____.

3. /K/, /T/, and /D/ are_____.

4. The final vowel in the name *Tina* is_____.

5. The stressed vowel in the name *Tina* is_____.

TEST B

(answers not recorded)

Indicate by "yes" or "no" whether the utterances you hear are Italian or not. Each utterance will be heard twice. To test yourself cover the letters and words given and just listen. Then check your answers and review if necessary.

  1) /I/
  2) /A/
  3) /i/
  4) /U/
  5) /tiy/
  6) /ə/
  7) /TÍNA/
  8) /nə/
  9) /TI/
10) /KA/

• End of Tape 1A •

UNIT 3

1) vowel no. 2
2) dental
3) not aspirated
4) vowel no. 1
5) vowel no. 3

TEST B   ANSWERS

1) yes
2) yes
3) no
4) yes
5) no
6) no
7) yes
8) no
9) yes
10) yes

UNIT 4

*1. Is the following sound, vowel No. 1, No. 2, or No. 3?

/A/   (2)

*2. What about this one?

/I/   (2)

*3. And this one?

/U/   (2)

*4. Is this No. 1, No. 2, No. 3, or some other vowel?

/ɛ/   (2)

5. The vowel you have just heard sounds somewhat like the first vowel sound in the English words "seven" or "seventy." Thus, we might conveniently refer to this vowel as vowel No. 7 or vowel No. 70. However, because this vowel, unlike vowels No. 2 and No. 3, is pronounced with the mouth relatively *open*, perhaps the zero digit in No. 70 can be used effectively here as a reminder of an OPEN vowel. For this reason we shall refer to it as vowel No. 70. In pronouncing it don't be afraid to open your mouth wide.

/ɛ/ (3)

* * * * *

6. The following is a syllable you have already heard.

(ca)   (ca)

7. Remember that the consonant in this syllable is not aspirated.

(ca)X   (ca)X

8. The particular consonant sound-type in question is /K/. Pronounce this consonant before vowel No. 3.

chi   (2)

9. The combination you have just made is an Italian word that signals a question asking for the identity of someone. Hence it corresponds roughly to the English question words "who" and "whom."

10. Repeat the word again, this time looking at its proper spelling.

(chi)X   (chi)X   (chi)X

11. Repeat the following syllables.

(chi)X (ca)X (chi)X (ca)X

12. Now you will hear a question in Italian asking for the identity of a third person being referred to.

Chi è? (2)

*13. This question has two vowels in it. Which of the following are they?

No. 1 and No. 2
No. 70 and No. 1
No. 3 and No. 70

14. Here is the proper spelling for this question. Repeat, while looking at the spelling. Notice that *our* units will use the special type ε for vowel No. 70 in a stressed position in a word.

(Chi è?)X (Chi è?)X (Chi è?)X

15. Notice that the question just given contains two words that sound like one, with the stress on the last vowel.

Chi è? (3)

*16. Two or more words said without any pause between them, form what may be called a BREATH GROUP. The phrase *Chi è?* has how many breath groups?

* * * * *

17. The following may be an answer to *Chi è?*, and constitutes one breath group. Imitate as closely as possible.

(è Amanda.)X (è Amanda.)X (è Amanda.)X

18. Here are three other possible answers. Listen carefully and repeat, noticing that any consonant that immediately follows the word è is pronounced strongly.

(è Luca.)X (è Tina.)X (è εva.)X
(è Luca.)X (è Tina.)X (è εva.)X

19. Repeat the following question-answer pairs.

(Chi è?)X (è Amanda.)X
(Chi è?)X (è Luca.)X
(Chi è?)X (è Tina.)X
(Chi è?)X (è εva.)X

*20. Observe the following model:
    S: Chi è ?
    R: È Amanda.

NOTE: "S" stands for "stimulus," and "R" stands for "response."

You will now be asked the question from the preceding model. Every time you hear the question, quickly give the appropriate response using the names as they appear in the following list. Your response will be confirmed each time.

Alina
Amina
Bista
Ɛva
Fina
Gina
Lɛa
Lia
Lina
Linda
Luca
Magda
Mɛna
Mina
Nɛna
Nina
Nini
Sabina
Savina
Spina
Tina

* * * * *

21. If the meaning of *Chi è?* is: "a question asking for the identity of a person being referred to," the following then are some of the ways of translating the Italian into English:

     a) Who is it?
     b) Who is she?
     c) Who is he?
     d) What's his name?
     e) What's her name?
     f) What's the name of the person being referred to?

*22. Is there only one English translation possible for the Italian *Chi è?*

*23. Do the English translations given all "mean" the same thing—that is, may they all be used interchangeably in any given situation?

*24. Do they all refer to the same specific situation?

*25. Let us now take the very specific situation in which one wishes to identify a famous man being described in a guessing game. Might one ask any of the following questions?

     Who is it?
     Who is he?
     What's his name?

*26. In a particular situation then, might two or more utterances be used to refer to the same thing?

* * * * *

27. Obviously then, the MEANING of something depends upon the situation or situations in which it is used.

28. If you know what something may be used to refer to, and how to use it in a particular situation or context, you have learned one of its MEANINGS.

29. The MEANING of an utterance like *Chi è?* may be arrived at by a definition such as "a question asking for the identity of a person being referred to," and by examples of situations in which *Chi è?* is used.

30. Sometimes a TRANSLATION of something like *Chi è?* may give one a *clue* to its MEANING, but the MEANING of something should not be confused with its TRANSLATION into another language.

31. The different translations given for *Chi è?* are different English ways of expressing what the Italian *Chi è?* refers to.

*32. Are the translations themselves MEANINGS, or are they reflections of (or clues to) MEANINGS?

                              * * * * *

33. Sometimes from a number of different translations of an utterance there is *one* that is used to reflect most of the meanings (or the primary meaning) of the individual words in the utterance. For instance, in the case of *Chi è?* perhaps the translation most usually found is "Who is it?" Such a translation is often referred to as the LITERAL TRANSLATION.

34. The English word "who" is the literal translation of the Italian word *chi.*

*35. Consequently, can you expect to find "who" in most cases in which Italians use the word *chi?*

*36. Should you expect to find "who" in *all* cases in which Italians use *chi*, and should you expect to find *chi* in all cases in which English speakers use "who"?

37. Unfortunately for the language learner it is not always easy to equate words in one language with words in another language.

38. As a consequence, it is impractical (and often misleading) for the language learner to equate words in one language with words in another language.

                              * * * * *

39. Let's suppose for a moment that Charles (a fictitious student of Italian) is the type of student who needs to equate words in one language with words in another language.

40. If "who" is the literal translation of the Italian word *chi*, Charles would expect to find *chi* in the normal Italian translation of the following two sentences:

  (a) Who did it?
  (b) He's the person who did it.

41. However, whereas *chi* may be used in the translation of (a), it is not to be used in the translation of (b).

42. It is natural for Charles to be puzzled by this fact since he has been equating "who" with *chi*.

43. On the other hand, the student who has been taught that *chi* is found in certain kinds of questions (for which the LITERAL TRANSLATION into English involves "who") should not be so puzzled.

*44. Is sentence (a) a question?

45. Obviously then you can expect *chi* in the Italian translation of (a).

*46. Is sentence (b) a question?

47. Obviously then you should not expect *chi* in the Italian translation of (b).

* * * * *

*48. Is the TRANSLATION of something the same as its MEANING?

*49. You will now be given both a TRANSLATION and a MEANING of the Italian sentence *è Amanda*. Tell which is the TRANSLATION and which is the MEANING.

  a) "A statement identifying "Amanda" as the individual being referred to.
  b) "Amanda is the one."

*50. As a consequence is it more accurate to say statement "x" or statement "y"?

  x) The Italian word *chi* means "who."
  y) The Italian word *chi* may be translated as "who."

*51. In order to learn the MEANING of something, should you pay attention to the situations and contexts in which it is used?

*52. Can English TRANSLATIONS be used as *clues* to the MEANING of an Italian word or phrase?

*53. Can you know the MEANING of something without your being able to give a TRANSLATION of it?

54. As you learn to say things in Italian, try to understand and remember the situations and contexts in which they appear. At all times try to avoid associating Italian words and phrases with English. Naturally, you will find that many times you will be associating Italian and English—this is natural for a native speaker of English —and sometimes this has to be done. However, if you consciously try to avoid making such associations you will find that you will be

a) concentrating more on the Italian way of saying things,
b) understanding Italian better, and
c) speeding up the learning process, since you will be going directly from the Italian utterance to its MEANING, without having to translate first into English in order to arrive at the MEANING.

TEST

(not recorded)

Use the following items to fill in the blanks:

> *aspirated*   *strongly pronounced*
> *breath group*   *translation*
> *dental*   *vowel No. 70*
> *literal translation*
> *meaning*
> *open vowel*
> *situations*

1) The letter *e* in Italian may represent_____.

2) Two or more words said without any pause between the words form what may be called a_____.

3) Unlike vowels No. 2 and No. 3, vowel No. 70 is an_____.

4) One may get a good clue to the meaning of an utterance by paying attention to the _____ in which it is used.

5) "It's Amanda' is the _____ of *è Amanda."*

6) "Amanda is the one" is a _____ of *è Amanda.*

7) "A statement identifying 'Amanda' as the individual being referred to" is the _____ of *è Amanda.*

8) A consonant immediately following the word *è* is_____ .

9) One big difference in the pronunciation of the English word "key" and the Italian word *chi* is that the consonant in the English word is_____, whereas the consonant in the Italian word is not.

10) The big difference in the pronunciation of the English word "tea" and the Italian word "ti" is that the consonant in the English word is aspirated and not_____, whereas the consonant in the Italian word is not aspirated and_____.
(NOTE: The same word fits in both blanks here.)

TEST ANSWERS

1) Vowel No. 70
2) breath group
3) open vowel
4) situations
5) literal translation
6) translation
7) meaning
8) strongly pronounced
9) aspirated
10) dental

UNIT 5

1. The following are two English sentences:
   a) Is it?
   b) Who is it?

*2. Are (a) and (b) questions or statements?

3. Although both (a) and (b) are questions they illustrate two different types of questions.

*4. To which question are you more likely to answer "Yes" or "No"?

*5. Which question are you likely to answer with a person's name?

6. Since question (a) is asking for a "Yes" or "No" answer, we shall call it a YES-NO QUESTION.

7. Since question (b) is asking for information other than "Yes" or "No," we shall call it an INFORMATION QUESTION.

*8. Is the following a YES-NO QUESTION or an INFORMATION QUESTION?
   "Do you smoke?"

*9. What about this one?
   "Are they leaving tomorrow?"

*10. And this one?
   "Why did they do it?"

*11. And this one?
   "Where's Joe?"

*12. And this one?
   "How are you?"

*13. And this one?
   "Have they finished yet?"

*14. And this one?
   "When is he going?"

*15. And what about the following Italian question?

    Chi è ?

16. Unlike most YES-NO QUESTIONS, INFORMATION QUESTIONS begin
    with a question word such as "Who," "What," "Why," "When," "Where,"
    "How."

*17. What is the question word in the Italian sentence *Chi è?*

                                    * * * * *

*18. Where is the stress in this question—is it on vowel No. 3 or vowel No. 70?

19. Notice that as you go from the unstressed vowel to the stressed vowel in
    this utterance there is a drop in the tone of voice, or in the pitch level.

    Chi è? (2)

20. Notice too that as the voice fades into silence the question ends on a low

    pitch level.

    Chi è? (2)

21. This drop in the pitch level as one goes from an unstressed syllable to the
    stressed syllable, and the maintenance of a low pitch level from the
    stressed syllable on are important characteristics of what will be referred to
    here as a LOW (or) STRESS-DROP INTONATION.

22. If instead of a drop in pitch level, there were a rise in pitch, the question
    would not be the one most usually heard, and would sound like:

    Chi è? (2)

*23. Which is the more usual, x or y?

    x = *Chi è?*; y = *Chi è?*

*24. Are all of the following the same?

    Chi è? (6)

25. A LOW or STRESS-DROP intonation is very common in information ques-
    tions in Italian, and it is characteristic, therefore, of what may be referred to
    as a CASUAL information question.

*26. Is the LOW or STRESS-DROP intonation that we have been talking about used to communicate anything?

*27. What have we seen it used for? In other words, what kind of utterance is communicated in the Italian example we have been hearing?

*28. Is this particular intonation is used to communicate something, may we say that the intonation has meaning?

*29. What is its meaning in the Italian example we have been hearing?

* * * * *

30. Now listen to the following question and answer :
    Chi è? è Amanda.

*31. In your opinion, are both the question and the answer said with a stress-drop intonation? Listen again.
    Chi è ? è Amanda.

32. The stressed vowel in the answer is indicated here by a line underneath the corresponding vowel letter.
    (è Amanda.)X   (è Amanda)X

33. Notice that the "drop" occurs right on the syllable with the stressed vowel.
    (è Amanda.)X   (è Amanda)X

34. When two utterances contain the same types of changes in pitch levels, they are said to have the same INTONATION PATTERN.

*35. Do both the following question and the following answer have the same intonation pattern?
    (Chi è?)X   (è Amanda.)X

36. In Italian, the same intonation pattern is common for both CASUAL INFORMATION QUESTIONS and CASUAL STATEMENTS.

*37. We have just learned another meaning for a LOW or STRESS-DROP intonation in Italian. What is it?

* * * * *

38. Now pay close attention to the intonation of the following question, asking if it is Amanda.

    È Amanda? (2)

*39. Is the intonation of this question the same as the one we used for the CASUAL INFORMATION QUESTION? Listen to it again, followed by the CASUAL INFORMATION QUESTION.

    x = *È Amanda?*; y = *È Amanda?*

*40. Is there any "drop in pitch level" in the question about Amanda?

    È Amanda? (2)

*41. Is there any "rise in pitch level" in this question?

    È Amanda? (2)

42. The stress in this question is on the vowel of *-man-*, indicated here by a line underneath the corresponding vowel letter.

    (È Am<u>a</u>nda?)X (È Am<u>a</u>nda?)X

*43. Does the "rise in pitch level" occur just as one reaches the syllable with the stressed vowel?

    (È Am<u>a</u>nda?)X (È Am<u>a</u>nda?)X

*44. Does the question seem to end on a high pitch level or a low pitch level, relatively speaking?

45. This rise in pitch level as one goes from an unstressed syllable to the stressed syllable, and the maintenance of a high pitch level from the stressed syllable on are important characteristics of what may be referred to here as a HIGH (or) STRESS-RISE INTONATION.

46. Whereas a LOW (or) STRESS-DROP INTONATION is common for a CASUAL INFORMATION QUESTION, a HIGH (or) STRESS-RISE INTO-NATION is common for a CASUAL YES-NO QUESTION.

*47. What is a common meaning for a HIGH or STRESS-RISE INTONATION in Italian?

* * * * *

48. If we were to use something resembling a musical scale to plot the sentences we have been examining, they would look like the following:

    a) casual information question

    b) casual statement

    c) casual yes-no question

*49. Listen again to the following—is it an INFORMATION QUESTION or a YES-NO QUESTION?

    È Amanda? (2)

50. If one were to reply to the preceding question in the affirmative, one could simply say: *Sì.*

*51. Listen again to this word. Is it being said with a LOW (or) STRESS-DROP INTONATION?

    Sì. (2)

52. Said with a HIGH (or) STRESS-RISE INTONATION, it would sound like:

    Sì? (2)

*53. With a HIGH (or) STRESS-RISE INTONATION, does the word indicate a question or a statement? Listen again and repeat.

    Sì? (2)

*54. Plot the word *Sì*, said as a casual statement, on the scale below.

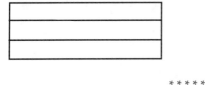

* * * * *

55. Now listen to a YES-NO QUESTION followed by *Sì* and a more complete answer. Repeat after the model, imitating as closely as possible.

(È Amanda?)X   (Sì)x   (È Amanda.)X

56. Repeat:

(È Amanda?)X   (Sì, è Amanda.)X

*57. Following the model shown, answer the questions. Your response will be confirmed each time. (Remember to pronounce strongly any consonant that immediately follows the word È.)

Model.
S: È Amanda?
R: Sì, è Amanda.

È Alina?
È Amina?
È Bista?
È Ɛva?
È Fina?
È Gina?
È Lɛa?
È Lia?
È Lina?
È Linda?
È Luca?
È Magda?
È Mina?
È Nena?
È Nini?
È Sabina?
È Savina?
È Spina?
È Tina?

*58. Now we will do the opposite. As in the model, you will hear a statement
     for which you are to ask a question.
     Model.

     S: è Amanda.
     R: Sì? è Amanda?

(the names used will be those of frame No. 57)

                              * * * * *

NOTE: The main purpose of the preceding section was simply to begin making
you aware of the importance of intonation so that you will try to imitate it as
closely as possible.

   With this end in mind we have presented only two commonly heard patterns
so far, sometimes exaggerating in order to indicate the differences more clearly
to the untrained ear.

   If a particular intonation pattern of Italian is similar to one in English accept
this as a fact, but *do not expect Italian intonation patterns to be like English!* Also, if
a particular intonation pattern exists in both English and Italian, and its meaning is similar in both languages, accept this as a fact, but *do not expect the meaning to be the same!* (What may mean cordial politeness in one language may
mean anger or displeasure in another.)The intonation patterns of a language are
many and varied, and may even differ from one region to the next.

TEST A

(not recorded)

Use the following items to fill in the blanks:

casual information question
casual statement
casual yes-no question
high intonation
high or stress-rise intonation

information other than
low intonation
low or stress-drop
  intonation
question word
"yes" or "no" answer

1) An intonation pattern characterized by a rise in pitch level as one goes from an unstressed syllable to the stressed syllable, plus the maintenance of a high pitch level from the stressed syllable on is called a_____.

2) An intonation pattern characterized by a drop in pitch level as one goes from an unstressed syllable to the stressed syllable, plus the maintenance of a low pitch level from the stressed syllable on is called a_____.

3) A high or stress-rise intonation is often indicative of a _____ in Italian.

4) 5) A low or stress-drop intonation is often indicative of a _____or a _____ in Italian.

6) A "yes-no question" is one that expects a _____.

7) An "information question" is one asking for _____ "yes" or "no."

8) An "information question" begins with a _____.

9) The word *sì*, said as a casual yes-no question, uses a _____.

10) The word *sì*, said as a casual statement, uses a _____.

TEST B

(answers not recorded)

You will hear several utterances, each said twice. Identify the kind of utterance by checking the appropriate column each time. To test yourself cover the words given and just listen.

	casual statement	casual information question	casual yes-no question
1) Chi è?			
2) è Amanda.			
3) è Amanda?			
4) Sì.			
5) è Alina?			
6) Sì?			
7) è Fina.			
8) Chi è ?			
9) è Lɛa.			
10) è Lina?			
11) Chi è?			
12) Sì.			
13) è Savina.			
14) Chi è			
15) Sì?			

• End of Tape 1B •

TEST A ANSWERS

1) high or stress-rise intonation
2) low or stress-drop intonation
3) casual yes-no question
4), 5) casual information question
   casual statement

6) "yes" or "no" answer
7) information other than
8) question word
9) high intonation
10) low intonation

TEST B ANSWERS

	casual statement	casual information question	casual yes-no question
1)		Chi è?	
2)	È Amanda.		
3)			È Amanda?
4)	Sì.		
5)			È Alina?
6)			Sì?
7)	È Fina.		
8)		Chi è?	
9)	È Lɛa.		
10)			È Lina?
11)			Chi è?
12)	Sì.		
13)	È Savina.		
14)		Chi è?	
15)			Sì?

*29. Plot ὲ *Amanda.* as a POTENTIALLY EMPHATIC statement in two ways, using a POST-STRESS-DROP intonation each time.

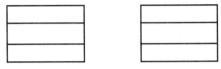

* * * * *

30. For yes-no questions there are also two kinds of POTENTIALLY EMPHAT-
IC intonations. These intonations parallel what we have seen in frame No.
29, but instead of the POST-STRESS-DROP going to the lowest pitch level
possible (as in frame No. 29), it drops only slightly for yes-no questions.
Listen to the two versions.

ὲ A-man-		man-	(2)
da		ὲ A-　da	

31. The potentially emphatic question asking if it is Amanda may thus be plot-
ted in either of the following ways:

ὲ A-man-		man-
da		ὲ A-　da

32. Repeat the CASUAL question followed by the two POTENTIALLY
EMPHATIC questions.

(ὲ Amanda?)X ( )X ( )X
(ὲ Amanda?)X ( )X ( )X

*33. Is the following question CASUAL or POTENTIALLY EMPHATIC?

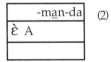

(2)

*34. What about this one?

ɛ̀ A-man-	(2)
da	

*35. And this one?

	man-	(2)
ɛ̀ A-	da	

*36. Identify the following as a CASUAL QUESTION, a CASUAL STATE-MENT, a POTENTIALLY EMPHATIC QUESTION, or a POTENTIALLY EMPHATIC STATEMENT.

	man-da	(2)
ɛ̀ A-		

*37. Do the same with this one.

ɛ̀ A-man-	
da	

*38. And with this one.

chi	
ɛ̀	

*39. And with this one.

*40. Now with this one.

*41. And with this one.

*42. And with this one.

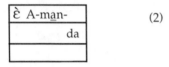   (2)

*43. And with this one.

```
        man-                 (2)
è A-        da
```

44. You will now hear a series of short dialogs. *Repeat* each line, imitating the intonation as closely as possible. You should review this section many times until you feel at ease with these intonations.

    I. speaker A: Chi è? (casual information question)
       speaker B: È Amanda. (casual statement)
              A: È Amanda? (potentially emphatic yes-no question)
              B: Sì. È Amanda. (potentially emphatic statements)

    II.
              A: È Amanda? (casual yes-no question)
              B: Sì. È Amanda. (casual statements)
              A: Sì? È Amanda? (potentially emphatic yes-no questions)
              B: Sì. È Amanda. (potentially emphatic statements)

III.   A: Chi è? (casual information question)
     (no answer, so...) Chi è? (potentially emphatic information question)
              B: è Tina. (potentially emphatic statement)
              A: Sì? (potentially emphatic yes-no question)
              B: Sì. (potentially emphatic statement)

IV.   A: è Tina. (casual statement)
              B: Sì? è Tina? (casual yes-no questions)
              A: Sì. è Tina. (potentially emphatic statements)

TEST A

(not recorded)

Use the following items to fill in the blanks:
information questions
post-stress-drop intonation
potentially emphatic
statements
yes-no questions

1) An intonation pattern characterized by either (a) *no change* in pitch level or
   (b) *a rise* in pitch level as one goes from an unstressed syllable to the stressed
   syllable, plus a *drop* in pitch level right after the stressed syllable is called
   a_____.

2) A post-stress-drop intonation is often indicative of a _____utterance
   in Italian.

3) & 4) The post-stress-drop goes to the lowest pitch level possible
   for_____and_____.

5) The post-stress-drop does *not* go to the lowest pitch level possible
   for_____.

TEST B

(answers not recorded)

You will hear 20 utterances, each said twice. Identify the kind of utterance by checking two columns for each one—one check identifying the utterance as "casual" or "potentially emphatic," and the second check identifying the utterance as a "statement," an "information question," or a "yes-no question." To test yourself cover the words and just listen.

	casual	potentially emphatic	statement	information question	yes-no question
1) Chi è?					
2) Sì.					
3) Sì?					
4) è Luca.					
5) è Gina?					
6) Sì?					
7) è Lina.					
8) Chi è?					
9) Chi è?					
10) Sì.					
11) Sì?					
12) è Lea.					
13) è Amanda?					
14) è Bista?					
15) Sì?					
16) Sì.					
17) Chi è?					
18) Chi è?					
19) è Tina.					
20) è Tina?					

TEST A   ANSWERS

1) post-stress-drop intonation.
2) potentially emphatic
3), 4) statements
        information questions
5) yes-no questions

TEST B   ANSWERS

	casual	potentially emphatic	statement	information question	yes-no question
1) Chi è?	X			X	
2) Sì.	X		X		
3) Sì?	X				X
4) È Luca.		X	X		
5) È Gina?	X				X
6) Sì?		X			X
7) È Lina.	X		X		
8) Chi è ?		X		X	
9) Chi è ?	X			X	
10) Sì.		X	X		
11) Sì?		X			X
12) È Lea.		X	X		
13) È Amanda?		X			X
14) È Bista?	X				X
15) Sì?		X			X
16) Sì.		X	X		
17) Chi è?	X			X	
18) Chi è?		X		X	
19) È Tina.	X		X		
20) È Tina?	X				X

UNIT 7

1. You have now learned three kinds of intonation patterns—a LOW or STRESS-DROP intonation, a HIGH or STRESS-RISE intonation, and a POST-STRESS-DROP intonation.

*2. If the first two patterns are indicative of CASUAL utterances, what is the POST-STRESS-DROP intonation indicative of?

3. In addition to these three patterns, there is a fourth type that is heard in Italian in both INFORMATION QUESTIONS and YES-NO QUESTIONS.

4. Because this fourth type usually suggests greater *personal involvement* or greater *self-interest* than the other three patterns, we will say that it is indicative of an INTERESTED utterance.

5. This fourth type of intonation may be divided into two sub-types.

6. Sub-type No. 1 has a *low stressed syllable* followed by a *rise in pitch level* as one goes from the STRESS NUCLEUS* to the end of the utterance.

examples:

chi ↑		è A-	da	↑		è	ta
ὲ ↑		man-		sì ↑		A-ga-	

*The STRESS NUCLEUS means the stressed syllable plus any non-final unstressed syllable(s).

7. Sub-type No. 2 has a *high stressed syllable* followed by first a *drop in pitch level* on or leading to the last syllable and then a *rise in pitch level* as the voice fades into silence.

examples:

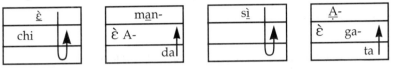

8. Looking at the diagrams of frame No. 6, repeat after the model.
   (Chi è̠?)X (È Am̠anda?)X (Sì̠?)X (È A̠gata?)X

9. Now look at the diagrams of frame No. 7 and repeat after the model.
   (Chi è̠?)X (È Am̠anda?)X (Sì̠?)X (È A̠gata?)X

*10. What is a meaning of the intonations we have been hearing in frames No. 8 and No. 9?

* * * * *

11. Repeat the following CASUAL INFORMATION QUESTION followed by the INTERESTED INFORMATION QUESTION of sub-type No. 1.

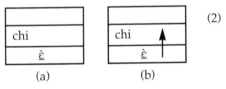

(2)

(a)   (b)

12. Repeat the following CASUAL INFORMATION QUESTION followed by the INTERESTED INFORMATION QUESTION of sub-type No. 2.

(2)

(a)   (b)

*26. What about this one?

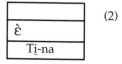

(2)

*27. And this one?

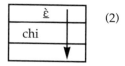

(2)

*28. And this one?

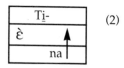

(2)

*29. What about this one?

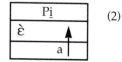

(2)

* * * * *

30. The consonant you just heard in the preceding example is one that had not been presented earlier. It is a sound very much like the second consonant heard in the English word "spy."

31. If you listen carefully, you can hear a difference in the pronunciation of the sounds represented by the letter *p* in the following two English words "par"–"spar".

32. In the word "par," the letter *p* stands for an aspirated sound-type, but in the word "spar" there is no aspiration. Listen again.

   (par) (spar) (par) (spar)

33. The Italian /P/ is, therefore, more like the sound-type represented by the letter *p* in "spar" than like the initial consonant of "par." It is, in other words, *not aspirated*.

34. Occurring after the word è, it, like any other initial consonant following è, is strongly pronounced. Repeat the question of frame No. 29.

(è Pia?)X (è Pia?)X

35. In order not to release a strong puff of air when making the /P/, you might try (as you were told to do for /T/ in Unit 3) thinking of inhaling rather than exhaling.

(pi)X (pi)X (pi)X

36. Listen now to the Italian syllable *pi* followed by the English word "pea."

(pi) (pea) (pi) (pea)

*37. Is the following Italian or English?

/PI/ (2)

*38. What about this one?

"pea" (2)

*39. And this one?

/PA/ (2)

UNIT 7

(not recorded)

The 20 diagrams below illustrate the various intonation patterns you have heard so far. Label each diagram as one of the following:

casual information question
potentially emphatic information question
interested information question
casual yes-no question
potentially emphatic yes-no question
interested yes-no question
casual statement
potentially emphatic statement

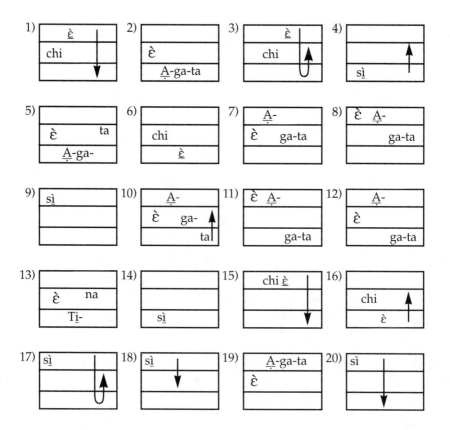

TEST B

(answers not recorded)

You will hear 20 utterances, each said three times. Identify the kind of utterance by checking two columns for each one—one check identifying the utterance as "casual," "potentially emphatic," or "interested," and the second check identifying the utterance as a "statement," an "information question," or a "yes-no question."

	casual	potentially emphatic	interested	statement	information question	yes-no question
1)						
2)						
3)						
4)						
5)						
6)						
7)						
8)						
9)						
10)						
11)						
12)						
13)						
14)						
15)						
16)						
17)						
18)						
19)						
20)						

• **End of Tape 2A** •

TEST A   ANSWERS

1) potentially emphatic information question
2) casual statement
3) interested information question
4) interested yes-no question
5) interested yes-no question
6) casual information question
7) potentially emphatic yes-no question
8) potentially emphatic yes-no question
9) casual yes-no question
10) interested yes-no question
11) potentially emphatic statement
12) potentially emphatic statement
13) interested yes-no question
14) casual statement
15) potentially emphatic information question
16) interested information question
17) interested yes-no question
18) potentially emphatic yes-no question
19) casual yes-no question
20) potentially emphatic statement

TEST B   ANSWERS

	casual	potentially emphatic	interested	statement	information question	yes-no question
1)		X		X		
2)		X				X
3)		X			X	
4)	X					X
5)	X				X	
6)	X			X		
7)			X			X
8)		X		X		
9)	X			X		
10)			X			X
11)			X		X	
12)		X		X		
13)			X			X
14)		X				X
15)		X				X
16)		X			X	
17)	X					X
18)			X			X
19)			X		X	
20)			X			X

Tape 2B

UNIT 8

*1. Is the following sound, vowel No. 1, No. 2, No. 3, or No. 70?

è (2)

*2. What about this one?

a (2)

*3. And this one?

u (2)

*4. And this one?

i (2)

*5. Is this one of the four vowels you have studied or some other vowel?

ɔ (2)

6. The vowel you have just heard sounds somewhat like the first vowel sound heard in the English word "forty." It is pronounced with the mouth relatively *open* and *rounded*. Thus, a convenient name for this vowel might be vowel No. 40, and the zero digit in No. 40 can be used effectively here as a reminder of an OPEN vowel. In pronouncing it make sure that your mouth is kept *open* and *rounded* throughout the production of the sound.

ɔ (2)

*7. Of the five Italian vowels you have now heard, two are pronounced with the lips in a rounded position and may therefore be called ROUNDED vowels. Which are these two ROUNDED vowels?

* * * * *

8. The following is a syllable you have already heard.

(na)X   (na)X

9. The consonant sound-type in this syllable will be named /N/. Pronounce this consonant before vowel No. 40.

(the Italian word *nɔ*) (2)

10. The combination you have just made is an Italian word. Its meaning is the opposite of *sì*.

11. Repeat the word, this time looking at its proper spelling. Notice that our units will use the special type ɔ for vowel No. 40 in a stressed position in a word.

    (nɔ)X   (nɔ)X   (nɔ)X

*12. In both spelling and meaning, this word should remind you of the English word *no*. Is the following word Italian or English?

    (nɔ)   (2)

*13. Which of the following is Italian, a, b, or c?

    ("no")   ("no")   (nɔ)   (2)
       a   b   c

14. Repeat the Italian again, remembering to round your lips and to *keep them rounded* throughout the production of the sound.

    (nɔ)X   (nɔ)X   (nɔ)X

15. Repeat the following casual question-answer pairs. Remember that any consonant that immediately follows the word *è* is pronounced strongly.

    (è Amanda?)X   (Sì, è Amanda.)X
    (è Luca?)X   (Sì, è Luca.)X
    (è Tina?)X   (Sì, è Tina.)X
    (è Ɛva?)X   (Sì, è Ɛva.)X
    (è Lɔla?)X   (Sì, è Lɔla.)X

*16. Notice that the first vowel in this last name, *Lɔla*, is now a familiar one. What is it?

17. The questions of frame no. 15 were yes-no questions followed by an affirmative *Sì* answer. Now repeat the following question-answer pairs in which the immediate answer is a negative *Nɔ*. What follows the *Nɔ* is extra information. Imitate the intonations as closely as possible.

casual	potentially emphatic
(è Amanda?)X	(Nɔ. è Luca.)X
(è Luca?)X	(Nɔ. è Tina.)X
(è Tina?)X	(Nɔ. è Ɛva.)X
(è Ɛva?)X	(Nɔ. è Lɔla.)X
(è Lɔla?)X	(Nɔ. è Amanda.)X

*18. If someone points to a picture of Tina and asks *è Amanda?*, what may you answer and what extra information may you give in accordance with frame No. 17?

*19. However, the question *è Tina?* in reference to a picture of Tina, should evoke what response?

*20. You will now be asked a series of questions about the identity of someone. Each time you give a positive or a negative answer as in frames No. 18 or No. 19 respectively, according to the names that follow. Your response will be confirmed every time.

   (1) Amanda
   (2) Cɔla
   (3) Lɔla
   (4) Ɛva
   (5) Nina
   (6) Amanda
   (7) Alina
   (8) Magda
   (9) Cɔla
  (10) Lia

* * * * *

21. Listen to the following question-answer pairs in which the answer begins with a negative *Nɔ* and is followed by a negative statement. Notice that the consonant immediately following the word *nɔ* is strongly pronounced:

  è Amanda?   Nɔ, non è Amanda.
  è Luca?   Nɔ, non è Luca.
  è Tina   Nɔ, non è Tina.
  è Ɛva?   Nɔ, non è Eva.
  è Lɔla?   Nɔ, non è Lola.

*22. The negative statement contains a new word. What is it?

*23. The function of this new word is to negate *the meaning of what follows*. Thus, if *è Amanda* translates as "It's Amanda," what is a translation of *Non è Amanda?*

24. Whereas in ordinary conversation the word *nɔ* may occur alone as a short answer to a question, the word *non* never does, and must be followed by something. A simple way of defining the difference between these two words is to say that *nɔ* is a stressed word that occurs before a pause (represented in writing by a punctuation mark of some kind), but *non* is normally an unstressed word that does not occur before a pause.

25. Listen again to the following question-answer pairs and repeat, paying close attention to both the intonation and the major stress in the negative statement.

casual	potentially emphatic
(È Amanda?)X	(Nɔ, non è Amanda.)X
(È Luca?)X	(Nɔ, non è Luca.)X
(È Tina?)X	(Nɔ, non è Tina.)X
(È Ɛva?)X	(Nɔ, non è Ɛva.)X
(È Lɔla?)X	(Nɔ, non è Lɔla.)X

*26. In the negative statements following the word *nɔ*, where does the major stress occur?

*27. You will now be asked a series of questions about the identity of someone. Each time, give a complete response following the *Sì* or *Nɔ* that is given. Use an affirmative statement after *Sì* and a negative statement after *Nɔ*. Your response will be confirmed each time.

(1) È Alina? Sì
(2) È Amina? Sì
(3) È Bista? Nɔ
(4) È Fina? Nɔ
(5) È Lina? Sì
(6) È Linda? Nɔ
(7) È Mɛna? Sì
(8) È Mina? Nɔ
(9) È Nɛna? Nɔ
(10) È Cɔla? Sì

* * * * *

28. Up until now you have been asked only one kind of yes-no question—an affirmative one. For example, *È Amanda?*

29. The following is a negative yes-no question—*Non è Amanda?*

*30. Notice that here the major stress occurs in the same place as in the corresponding negative statement. Where does the major stress occur? Listen again: *Non è Amanda?*

31. A normal response to the question Non è Amanda? may be one of the following:

    Sì, è Amanda.
    Nɔ, non è Amanda.
    Nɔ. è Lɔla.

*32. Are these the same responses that one might hear in answer to the affirmative question: *è Amanda?*

*33. According to what has been said in this unit, is the following question-answer sequence normal in Italian?

    Non è Amanda?   Sì, non è Amanda.

34. Accordingly, here is a definition of *sì*—"a word indicating that the affirmative counterpart of a given question is true."

35. Similarly, the word *nɔ* indicates that the *negative* counterpart of a given question is true.

*36. Applying the meanings given in frames No. 34 and No. 35, fill in the blanks with *Sì* or *Nɔ* in the following questionanswer pairs:

    (1) è Nini?_____, è Nini.
    (2) è Sabina?_____, è Sabina.
    (3) è Savina?_____. è Ɛva.
    (4) è Spina?_____, non è Spina.
    (5) è Agata?_____. Non è Linda.
    (6) Non è Cɔla?_____, è Cɔla.
    (7) Non è Lɔla?_____, è Lɔla.
    (8) Non è Amanda?_____. è Gina.
    (9) Non è Luca?_____, non è Luca.
    (10) Non è Tina?_____, non è Tina.

If necessary, repeat the preceding until you have mastered it.

* * * * *

37. We have now examined two kinds of simple yes-no questions—an affirmative one and a negative one.

38. Listen now to a third kind.

　　È Amanda, nɔ?

39. What is being expressed in this kind of question is an affirmative statement followed by a question, *nɔ?*, asking for confirmation or verification as to the validity of the statement. This type of question is sometimes called a VERIFICATION QUESTION.

40. In English, this particular verification question may be expressed as:

　　"It's Amanda, isn't it?"
　　"It's Amanda, right?"
　　"It's Amanda, isn't that correct?"

41. In Italian, a normal response to this kind of question is the same as what one might hear in answer to the simple questions:

　　È Amanda? or *Non è Amanda?*

*42. Thus, is the following question-answer sequence normal in Italian?

　　È Ɛva, nɔ?　Si, è Ɛva.

*43. Is this normal?

　　È Ɛva, nɔ?　Nɔ, non è Ɛva.

*44. Is this normal?

　　È Ɛva, nɔ?　Nɔ. è Lɔla.

TEST A

(not recorded)

Fill in the blanks with *Sì* or *Nò* in the following question-answer pairs:

1) è Alina? _____, è Alina.

2) è Lɛa _____. Non è Lɔla.

3) Non è Pia? _____, è Pia.

4) è Mina, nɔ? _____, è Mina.

5) è Nɛna, nɔ? _____. Non è Amanda.

6) è Amina? _____. è Tina.

7) Non è Lina? _____, è Lina.

8) è Pina? _____, non è Pina.

9) è Nina, nɔ? _____, non è Nina.

10) Non è Lina? _____. è Lɔla.

11) è Nini, nɔ? _____. è ɛva.

12) è Sabina, nɔ? _____. Non è Agata.

13) è Gina? _____, è Gina.

14) Non è Luca? _____. è Cɔla.

15) è Bista? _____. Non è Amanda.

16) Non è Mɛna? _____, non è Mɛna; è Linda.

17) è Savina, nɔ? _____, è Savina.

18) Non è Magda? _____, è Magda.

19) è Spina, nɔ? _____. Non è ɛva; è Spina.

20) è ɛva? _____, è Lɔla.

TEST B

(not recorded)

Match the items on the left with those on the right.

(1) a	(A) "rounded" vowels
(2) ɛ	(B) a verification question
(3) i	(C) a letter representing vowel No. 1
(4) ɔ	(D) a letter representing vowel No. 40
(5) u	(E) normally an unstressed word that does not occur before a pause
(6) vowels No. 40 and No. 70	(F) a letter representing vowel No. 70
(7) vowels No. 2 and No. 40	(G) a letter representing vowel No. 3
(8) nɔ	(H) a stressed word that occurs before a pause
(9) non	(I) "open" vowels
(10) è Lɔla, nɔ?	(J) a letter representing vowel No. 2.

UNIT 8

1) Sì	11) Nɔ
2) Sì	12) Sì
3) Sì	13) Sì
4) Sì	14) Nɔ
5) Sì	15) Sì
6) Nɔ	16) Nɔ
7) Sì	17) Sì
8) Nɔ	18) Sì
9) Nɔ	19) Sì
10) Nɔ	20) Nɔ

TEST B   ANSWERS

1) C	6) I
2) F	7) A
3) G	8) H
4) D	9) E
5) J	10) B

UNIT 9

1. Listen to the following sound.
   i (2)

*2. Is the sound you just heard a vowel?

*3. How many vowels do you hear in the following?
   /IA/

*4. How many pulse-beats did you hear?

*5. How many syllables did you hear, then?

6. Now listen carefully.
   /YA/

*7. How many syllables did you hear?

8. In this last utterance, two sounds were present, but only one syllable.
   Listen again.
   /YA/ (2)

*9. Is the first sound-type you heard in this utterance vowel No. 3?

10. For convenience, we shall represent the first sound-type in this utterance as
    /Y/.

*11. Is /Y/ a vowel if it does not constitute a syllable by itself?

*12. What do we call a sound-type similar to a vowel, but not constituting a
    syllable?

*13. Is /Y/ a semivowel?

*14. Is /I/ a semivowel?

* * * * *

15. Now listen to the following Italian name.
    Bianca (2)

*16. How many pulse-beats or syllables do you hear in this name? Listen again.
  Bianca   (2)

17. In order to represent the sound-types in this name, we will write:
  /BYÁNKA/

*18. How many vowels does the name contain?

*19. Does a vowel precede the stressed vowel?

*20. Does a semivowel precede the stressed vowel?

21. Now repeat the name, making sure that you pronounce only two syllables.
  Bianca   (2)

22. Notice that the /NK/ combination sounds very much like the ending of the English word "sunk."
  Bianca   (2)

23. Now look at the way the Italian name is actually spelled, and repeat the name again.
  (Bianca)X   (Bianca)X

*24. Is the following pronunciation Italian?
  Bianca   (2)

*25. Which of the following is Italian, a, b, or c?
  Bianca   *Bianca*   *Bianca*
    a   b   c

26. Repeat the Italian again.
  (Bianca)X   (Bianca)X

*27. If you are introduced to someone whose last name is (   ), how would you spell the name? Repeat after the model.
  Bianchi   (2)

*28. And if someone's last name is (   ), how is his name spelled? Repeat after the model.
  Fiumi   (2)

*29. If someone's last name is (   ), how is his name spelled? Repeat after the model

    Fieli   (2)

*30. Here is the name of a famous Italian wine — (   ). How is the name spelled? Repeat after the model.

    Chianti   (2)

                        * * * * *

*31. Now listen to the following utterance and tell if you hear /I/ or /Y/.

    Chi ama?   (2)

*32. What about this time?

    chiama   (2)

33. The utterances you heard in frames No. 31 and No. 32 mean two different things. Literal translations of these utterances are respectively "Who loves?" (for frame No. 31) and "he (or) she is calling" (for frame No. 32).

*34. Is this an equivalent of "Who loves?" or "He (or) She is calling"?

    chiama   (2)

*35. What about this one?

    chiama   (2)

*36. The following Italian word is an equivalent of "was spying." Does it contain /I/ or does it contain /Y/?

    spiava (2)

*37. In view of the preceding, would you say that it is important to keep /I/ and /Y/ differentiated, i.e., not to confuse the two?

*38. How is /I/ represented in Italian writing?

*39. How is /Y/ represented in the Italian word /BYÁNKA/?

40. The letter *y* is not normally used in Italian writing, and occurs rarely, mainly in words that have been borrowed from other languages. For example, *yacht, yankee.*

41. In a few words, /Y/ is represented by the letter *j*, another letter not normally used in Italian. For example, *jɔ-jɔ*.

42. However, the letter most usually used to represent /Y/ is the letter *i*.

* * * * *

43. Now listen to the semivowel /Y/ *after* a vowel.
    mai   (2)

*44. How do you think this word is spelled in Italian?
    mai   (2)

45. *Mai* is an Italian word which in *most* situations translates either the English word "never" or "ever."

*46. How many syllables do you hear in this word?
    mai   (2)

*47. How many syllables do you now hear in this, the utterance for "the Haitian woman?"
    l'haïtiana   (2)

48. In this last item the "normal" pronunciation is reflected in: /LAITYÁNA/.

49. However, in a word like *mai* in which the letter *i* is in word-final position after a vowel letter, the pronunciation may be either: /MAY/ or /MÁI/.

*50. How many syllables, then, may be heard in the pronunciation of the Italian word for "(n)ever"?

51. Because in some words it is important to keep /I/ and /Y/ differentiated, and because the Italian writing system does not do this, our units have two dots above the letter *i* next to a vowel letter in those words in which the preferred pronunciation seems to be with unstressed /I/ rather than /Y/. If the letter *i* next to a vowel letter is *not* so marked, students may for the time being follow the general rule of reading it as /Y/ in an unstressed position.

Thus:

	normal spelling	our spelling
	spïava	spïava
	l'haitiana	l'haïtiana
but,		
	Bianca	Bianca
	mai	mai

* * * * *

52. Listen to the following question and repeat.

    C'è?   (2)

53. What you just heard was a casual question asking if a particular individual or thing is in the area. Some of the translations for this utterance are:

    "Is he/she/it in?"
    "Is he/she/it around?"
    "Is he/she/it present?"
    "Is he/she/it there?"

54. Now look at the spelling and repeat.

    (C'è̠?)X   (C'è̠?)X

55. If you want to ask if a particular individual is in a given area, you may add a name. Repeat, pronouncing the first consonant of the name very strongly.

    (C'è̠ Bianca?)X   (C'è̠ Bianca?)X

*56. Translate the following sentence into Italian:

    "Is Bianca in?"

57. Here is the same question, using an INTERESTED intonation. Repeat.

    (C'è Bianca?)X   (C'è Bianca?)X

58. A complete affirmative answer is: *Sì, c'è Bianca*. Repeat, noticing that the consonant immediately following *Sì* is strongly pronounced.

    (Sì, c'è Bianca.)X   (Sì, c'è Bianca.)X

59. A short affirmative answer is: *Sì, c'è*. Repeat.

    (Sì, c'è.)X   (Sì, c'è.)

*60. Translate the following into Italian:
   "Is Bianca around?"–"Yes, she's around."

61. A complete negative answer is *Nɔ, non c'è Bianca*. Repeat, placing the major stress on *c'è*.

   (Nɔ, non c'è̱ Bianca.)X   (Nɔ, non c'è̱ Bianca.)X

62. The complete negative answer may *also* be: *Nɔ, Bianca non c'è*. Repeat, placing the major stress on *c'è̱*.

   (Nɔ, Bianca non c'è̱.)X   (Nɔ, Bianca non c'è̱)X

63. A short negative answer is: *Nɔ, non c'è*. Repeat, placing the major stress on *c'è*.

   (Nɔ, non c'è̱.)X   (Nɔ, non c'è̱.)X

*64. Translate the following into Italian:

   "Is Bianca there?"–"No, Bianca isn't here."

65. Here is the sentence for "Bianca is never in" or "Bianca is not ever in." Notice the stress on *mai*.

   Bianca non c'è ma̱i.
   Or
   Non c'è ma̱i Bianca.

*66. According to what you have observed so far, in a *question* involving *c'è*, does the name of the person usually precede *c'è* or follow *c'è*?

*67. According to what you have observed so far, in an *affirmative statement* involving *c'è* does the name of the person usually precede *c'è* or follow *c'è*?

*68. According to what you have observed so far, in a *negative statement* involving *c'è*, does it matter whether the name of the person precedes *c'è* or follows *c'è*?

69. The three preceding frames have commented on certain kinds of *frequent* word order. You should, however, expect to hear other possibilities.

* * * * *

*70. Observe the following model:

    S: C'è Bianca?
    R: Sì, c'è Bianca.

You will now be given a series of questions asking if a particular individual is in
the area. Give a complete *affirmative* response as in the model above. Your
response will be confirmed each time.

(1) C'è Amanda?   (6) C'è Cola?
(2) C'è Luca?   (7) C'è Gina?
(3) C'è Tina?   (8) C'è Lidia?
(4) C'è Lola?   (9) C'è Bista?
(5) C'è Eva?   (10) C'è l'haïtiana?

*71. Observe the following model:

    S: C'è Bianca?
    R: Nɔ, non c'è Bianca.

You will now be given a series of questions asking if a particular individual is in
the area. Give a complete *negative* response as in the model above. Your
response will be confirmed each time.

(1) C'è Alina?   (6) C'è Magda?
(2) C'è Sabina?   (7) C'è Agata?
(3) C'è Mɛna?   (8) C'è Lɛa?
(4) C'è Livia?   (9) C'è Nɛna?
(5) C'è Nini?   (10) C'è Amina?

*72. Now you will be asked one of the following kinds of questions:

    C'è Bianca?   "Is Bianca in?"
    Non c'è Bianca?   "Isn't Bianca in?"
    C'è Bianca, nɔ?   "Bianca is in, isn't she?"

Regardless of the kind of question, you are to answer either in the affirmative
(as in frame No. 70) or in the negative (as in frame No. 71), according to the
indication given. Your answer will be confirmed each time.

Questions	Answers
(1) C'è Amanda?	Sì
(2) Non c'è Alina?	Sì
(3) C'è Luca, nɔ?	Nɔ
(4) Non c'è Sabina?	Nɔ
(5) C'è Tina?	Sì
(6) C'è Magda?	Nɔ
(7) C'è Eva, nɔ?	Nɔ
(8) Non c'è Linda?	Sì
(9) C'è l'haïtiana?	Sì
(10) C'è l'haïtiana, nɔ?	Nɔ

73. You will now hear a series of short dialogs. Repeat each line, imitating as
closely as possible. You should review this section many times until you
feel at ease with each line. Note that in dialog V, the word *chi* is like *è* and
c'è in that a consonant immediately following it is normally strongly pronounced.

    I.   A: C'ɛ̱ Bianca?
        B: Sì, c'ɛ̱.

    II.   A: C'ɛ̱ Ɛva?
        B: Nɔ, non c'ɛ̱.

    III.   A: C'ɛ̱ Ɛva?
        B: Nɔ, Ɛva non c'ɛ̱; c'è Bia̱nca.

    IV.   A: C'è Bianca?
        B: Chi?
        A: Bianca!
        B: Sì, c'ɛ̱.

    V.   A: Chi c'ɛ̱?
        B: C'è Bianca.
        A: Non c'ɛ̱ Ɛva?
        B: Nɔ, Ɛva non c'ɛ̱.

    VI.   A: C'ɛ̱ Ɛva, nɔ?
        B: Nɔ, Ɛva non c'ɛ̱.
        A: Ɔh, non c'è ma̱i!

    VII.   A: C'è l'haïtiana?
        B: Nɔ, non c'ɛ̱ l'haïtiana.

TEST A

(answers not recorded)

You will hear 20 utterances, each said twice, and each containing *either* vowel
No. 3 or the semivowel /Y/. For each utterance, put a check in the appropriate
column according to whether you hear the vowel or the semivowel. To test
yourself cover the words listed and just listen.

		vowel No. 3	semivowel /Y/
1)	Bianca		✗
2)	spïava	✗	✗
3)	mai		
4)	mai	✗	✗
5)	Fiumi		✗
6)	Fiɛli		✗
7)	piana		—
8)	Chi ama?	✗	✗
9)	sɛi		
10)	ahimè	✗	✗
11)	fui		
12)	aiuta		✗
13)	chiama		✗
14)	lɛi		✗
15)	pɔi		✗
16)	sɛi	✗	
17)	vïaggia	✗	
18)	scïava	✗	
19)	mia nɔnna		✗
20)	piazza		

• **End of Tape 2B** •

TEST B

(not recorded)

Translate the following into Italian, using what has been presented to date.

1) Is Gina in? – No, she's not.

C'è Gina? No, ~~Ella~~ non c'è

2) Who's there? – Luca's there.

chi c'è? c'è Luca

3) Who is it? – It's Luca.

Chi c'è? è Luca

4) It's Bianca, isn't it? – No, it's Eva.

è Bianca, no? No, è Eva

5) Isn't Linda around? – No, she's never around.

Non c'è Linda, No, non c'è mai

6) The Haitian woman is present, isn't she? – Yes, she is.

c'è L'Haitiana, no, ~~Sì~~ Sì c'è.

7) Isn't it Lola? – Yes. It's not Lia.

Non è Lola? Sì Non è Lia

8) Is Tina here? – Yes, Tina's here.

c'è Tina? Sì c'è Tina

9) Is Luca there? – No, he isn't.

C'è Luca? No non c'è

10) Amanda's here, right? – No, Amanda's not here.

C'è Amanda, no? No, Amanda non c'è

TEST A   ANSWERS

	vowel No. 3	semivowel /Y/
1) Bianca		X
2) spïava	X	
3) mai		X
4) mai	X	
5) Fiumi		X
6) Fiɛli		X
7) piana		X
8) Chi ama?	X	
9) sɛi		X
10) ahimè	X	
11) fui		X
12) aiuta		X
13) chiama		X
14) lɛi		X
15) pɔi		X
16) sɛi	X	
17) vïaggia	X	
18) scïava	X	
19) mia nɔnna	X	
20) piazza		X

TEST B   ANSWERS

1) C'è Gina? - Nɔ, non c'è.
2) Chi c'è? - C'è Luca.
3) Chi è? - È Luca.
4) È Bianca, nɔ? - Nɔ, è Ɛva.
5) Non c'è Linda? - Nɔ, non c'è mai
6) C'è l'haïtiana, nɔ? - Sì, c'è.
7) Non è Lɔla? - Sì. Non è Lia.
8) C'è Tina? - Sì, c'è Tina.
9) C'è Luca? - Nɔ, non c'è.
10) C'è Amanda, nɔ? - Nɔ, non c'è Amanda. (or) Nɔ, Amanda non c'è.

*30. What about this time?

    la quale (2)

31. The utterances you heard in frames No. 29 and No. 30 mean different things. Literal translations of these utterances are respectively "laky" or "pertaining to a lake" (for frame No. 29) and "which" or "she who" (for frame No. 30).

*32. Is this an equivalent of "laky" or "which"?

    la quale (2)

*33. What about this one?

    lacüale (2)

*34. The following Italian word is an equivalent of "duel." Does it contain /U/ or does it contain /W/?

    düεllo (2)

*35. In view of the preceding, would you say that it is important to keep /U/ and /W/ differentiated, i.e., not to confuse the two?

*36. How is /U/ represented in Italian writing?

*37. How is /W/ represented in the Italian word /KWI/?

38. The letter *w* is not normally used in Italian writing, and occurs only rarely, mainly in words that have been borrowed from other languages. For example, *watt, Washington.*

39. The letter normally used to represent /W/ is the letter *u.*

* * * * *

40. Now listen to the semivowel /W/ *after* a vowel.

    Augusta (2)

*41. How would you spell this word in Italian?

*42. How many syllables do you hear in this name?

    Augusta (2)

*43. How many syllables do you hear in the following Italian word, the word for "fearful"?

paüroso (2)

44. Because in some words it is important to keep /U/ and /W/ differentiated and because the Italian writing system does not do this, our units have two dots above the letter *u* next to a vowel letter in those words in which the preferred pronunciation seems to be with unstressed /U/ rather than /W/. If the letter *u* next to a vowel letter is *not* so marked, students may follow the general rule of reading it as /W/ in an unstressed position.

Thus:	**normal spelling**	**our spelling**
	lacuale	lacüale
	duello	düɛllo
	pauroso	paüroso
but,		
	qui	qui
	Augusta	Augusta

* * * * *

45. Listen to the following question and repeat, remembering to pronounce the consonant following *è* very strongly

(È qui?)X (È qui?)X

46. What you just heard was a casual question asking if a particular individual or thing is *here*. The normal translation for this utterance is:

"Is he/she/it here?"

47. If you want to ask whether a particular individual is here, you may add a name. Repeat.

(È qui Augusta?)X   (È qui Augusta?)X

*48. Translate the following sentence into Italian: "Is Augusta *here?*"

49. Here is the same question, using an INTERESTED intonation. Repeat.

(È qui Augusta ?)X   (È qui Augusta?)X

50. A complete affirmative answer is: Sì, è qui Augusta. Repeat, placing the major stress on *qui*.

Sì, è qui Augusta. (2)

51. The complete affirmative answer may also be: Sì, Augusta è qu̲i̲. Repeat, placing the major stress on *qui*.

    Sì, Augusta è qu̲i̲. (2)

52. A short affirmative answer is: Sì, è; qu̲i̲. Repeat, placing the major stress on *qui*.

    Sì, è qu̲i̲. (2)

*53. Translate the following into Italian:

    "Is Augusta in this place?"– "Yes, she's here."

54. A complete negative answer is: Nɔ, non è qui Augusta. Repeat, placing the major stress on *è*.

    No, non è qui Augusta. (2)

55. The complete negative answer may also be: Nɔ, Augusta non è qui. Repeat, placing the major stress on *è*.

    Nɔ, Augusta non è qui. (2)

56. A short negative answer is: Nɔ, non è qui. Repeat, placing the major stress on *è*.

    Nɔ, non è qui. (2)

*57. Translate the following into Italian:

    "Is Augusta here?"–"No, Augusta isn't here."

58. Here is the sentence for "Augusta is never here." Notice the stress on *mai*.

    Augusta non è ma̲i̲ qui.
    or
    Non è ma̲i̲ qui Augusta.

*59. According to what you have observed so far, in a question involving *è qui,* does the name of the person usually precede *è qui* or follow *è qui?*

*60. According to what you have observed so far, in a *statement* involving *è qui,* does the name of the person usually precede or follow?

*61. In frame No. 26 you were given the opposite of *qui*. What is it?

*62. In order to ask if someone is *here* in Italian, you say: è *qui?* What would you say, then, to ask if someone is *there?*

*63. Translate the following sentence into Italian: "Is Augusta *there?"*

64. Here is the same question, using an INTERESTED intonation. Repeat.
(è lì Augusta?)X　(è lì Augusta?)X

65. If in a given sentence you wish to talk about "in that place" instead of "in this place," the word *lì* is simply used in place of *qui.*

*66. Express the following idea using lì: "Augusta is never there."

* * * * *

67. In Unit 9 you were given an expression that is used to talk about someone being in a given area. What was it?

68. A major difference between *c'è* and *è qui* or *è lì* is that the latter two expressions are preferably used whenever one is *pointing* to an area or emphasizing the idea of "here" or "there" *c'è,* on the other hand, implies no emphasis on the location and is often used as a translation of the English "is in," "is around" "is present."

* * * * *

*69. Imagine that you and a friend are looking closely at a map, and that your friend is pointing to different places and each time asking if a particular individual is in the place indicated. You will now be asked questions patterned after the model below. Reply as indicated, paying close attention to what is to be stressed. Your response will be confirmed each time. Note: A consonant immediately following the word *qui* is ordinarily strongly pronounced.

S: è qui Augusta?
R: Sì, è qui Augusta. (if an affirmative response is indicated)
(or)
R: Nɔ, non è qui Augusta. (if a negative response is indicated)

Questions	Answers
(1) è qui Amanda?	Sì
(2) è qui Luca?	Nɔ
(3) è qui Tina?	Nɔ
(4) è qui Ɛva?	Sì
(5) è qui Lɔla?	Nɔ

Questions	Answers
(6) è qui Bianca?	Sì
(7) è qui Pia?	Sì
(8) è qui Gina?	Nɔ
(9) è qui Cɔla?	Nɔ
(10) è qui Lia?	Sì

*70. Now imagine that you have moved away from the map while your friend has remained near it. This time, although your friend's questions will contain the word *qui*, your answers will contain the word *lì*. Note: A consonant immediately following the word *lì* is ordinarily strongly pronounced.

S: è qui Augusta?
R: Sì, è lì Augusta. (if an affirmative response is indicated)
(or)
R: Nɔ, non è lì Augusta. (if a negative response is indicated)

Questions	Answers
(1) è qui Amanda?	Nɔ
(2) è qui Luca?	Sì
(3) è qui Tina?	Sì
(4) è qui Ɛva?	Nɔ
(5) è qui Lɔla?	Sì
(6) è qui Bianca?	Nɔ
(7) è qui Pia?	Nɔ
(8) è qui Gina?	Sì
(9) è qui Cɔla?	Sì
(10) è qui Lia?	Nɔ

*71. With your friend still *near* the map, but yourself *away* from it, imagine your friend asking you for the name of a person who happens to be in a given area. Follow the model below, using the names indicated. Your response will be confirmed each time. Note: in this kind of situation you are expected to use *c'è*.

S: Chi c'è qui? "Who is here?"
R: C'ɛ (*name*) lì.** "(name) is there."

1) Gina		6) Savina	
2) Nini		7) l'haïtiana	
3) Mɛna		8) Bianca	
4) Nɛna		9) Augusta	
5) Magda		10) Guendalina	

**The word order may also be: *Lì c'è (name)*.

*72. Now imagine that you have been given a list of names (List A). Your friend has another list of names (List B).

List A (your list)	List B (your friend's list)
Amanda	Alina
Luca	Lia
Tina	Nina
Ɛva	Cɔla
Lɔla	Magda
Bianca	Linda
Augusta	Pia

Your friend will first ask a question involving *c'è* (as in frame No. 72 of Unit 9). If the name is on *either* list, answer: *Sì, c'è;* otherwise, answer in the negative, repeating the name at the end of your response.

Then you will be asked whether the name is either "there" (meaning on your list) or "here" (meaning on *his* list, List B) Answer according to the model, always *repeating* the name at the end of a negative response, but *omitting* it in an affirmative response.

Your responses will be confirmed each time.

model

        S: C'è Sabina?
        R: No, non c'è Sabina.

but,

        S: C'è Augusta?
        R: Sì, c'è.

S: è lì?   S: Ɛ qui?
R: Sì, è qui. | R: Nɔ, non è lì Augusta; è qui.

  (1) C'è Amina?
  (2) C'è Amanda? È lì?
  (3) C'è Alina? È lì?
  (4) Non c'è Bianca? È qui?
  (5) C'è Augusta, nɔ? È lì?
  (6) Non c'è Bista? È lì?
  (7) C'è Magda?
  (8) C'è Cɔla, nɔ? È qui?
  (9) C'è Spina, nɔ?
(10) C'è Luca? È qui?
(11) Non c'è Pia? È qui?
(12) Non c'è Linda? È lì?
(13) C'è Guendalina, nɔ?
(14) C'è Lɔla? È lì?
(15) C'è Tina, nɔ? È qui?

TEST A

(answers not recorded)

You will hear 20 utterances, each said twice, and each containing *either* vowel
No. 2 or the semivowel /W/. For each utterance put a check in the appropriate
column according to whether you hear the vowel or the semivowel. To test
yourself cover the words and just listen.

	vowel No. 2	semivowel /W/
1) gusto	✓	
2) qui		✓
3) la cui ala	✓	
4) düεllo	✓	
5) fuɔchi		✓
6) Guasti		✓
7) buɔna		✓
8) flüεnti	✓	
9) qua		✓
10) suɔi		✓
11) sostitüiva	✓	
12) Guendalina		✓
13) puɔ̀		✓
14) continua		✓
15) cospicüa	✓	
16) effεttüa	✓	
17) paüroso	✓	
18) lacüale	✓	
19) sua nɔnna	✓	
20) la quale		✓

TEST B

(not recorded)

Using what has been presented to date, translate the following into Italian.
NOTE: items within parentheses are to serve as aids to the situational meaning,
and underlined words indicate greater emphasis. Some sentences involve the
use of *c'è*, whereas other sentences involve *è qui* or *è lì*. *You should be guided in
your choice by the models given in frames No. 69, 70 and 71.*

(pointing to a spot on a map)

1) Is it here? - No, it's not there.

È qui? No, non è lì

2) Is Augusta there? - Yes, Augusta is there.

È lì Augusta? Sì, Agusta è lì

3) Bianca is in this spot, isn't she? - No, Bianca's not there; she's here.

È qui Bianca, No? No, Bianca non è lì
è qui

4) Who is *here*? -The Haitian woman is *here*.

Chi è qui? C'è l Haitiana è qui

5) Isn't Luca in that place? - No, he's not *there*.

Non è lì Luca? No, non è lì

(on the phone)

6) Is Luca there? - No, he isn't.

C'è Luca? No, non c'è

7) Is Luca *there*? - No, he's never *here*.

C'è Luca? No, non è mai qui

8) Is Gina around? - Yes, she is.

C'è Gina? Sì, c'è

9) Has Tina arrived? - Yes, she has.

C'è Tina? Sì, c'è

10) Is the Haitian woman *here*? - Yes, the Haitian woman is *here*.

È qui l Haitiana? Sì l'haitiana è qui

TEST A   ANSWERS

	vowel No. 2	semivowel /W/
1) gusto	X	
2) qui		X
3) la cui ala	X	
4) düɛllo	X	
5) fuɔchi		X
6) Guasti		X
7) buɔna		X
8) flüɛnti	X	
9) qua		X
10) suɔi		X
11) sostitüiva	X	
12) Guendalina		X
13) puɔ̀		X
14) continua		X
15) cospicüa	X	
16) effɛttüa	X	
17) paüroso	X	
18) lacüale	X	
19) sua nɔnna	X	
20) la quale		X

TEST B   ANSWERS

1) È qui? - Nɔ, non è lì.

2) È lì Augusta?—Sì, lì Augusta. (or) Sì, Augusta è lì.

3) È qui Bianca, nɔ? (or) Bianca è qui, nɔ?

   - Nɔ, non è lì Bianca; è qui! (or) Nɔ Bianca non è lì, è qui!

4) Chi c'è qui? - C'è l'haïtiana qui.

5) Non è lì Luca? - Nɔ, non è lì!

6) C'è Luca? (or) È lì Luca? - Nɔ, non c'è. (or) Nɔ, non è qui.

7) È lì Luca? - Nɔ, non è mai qui!

8) C'è Gina? - Sì, c'è.

9) C'è Tina? - Sì, c'è.

10) È qui l'haïtiana? - Sì, è qui l'haïtiana. (or)

    Sì, l'haïtiana è qui.

Meaning versus Translation (Unit 4)

The *meaning* of an utterance depends upon the situation or situations in which it is used; a *translation* is a way of rendering the meaning in a given language. Thus, one meaning for *Chi è?* is "a question asking for the identity of a person being referred to," but the following are some English translations of *Chi è?*—"Who is it?" "Who is she?" "Who is he?" "What's his name?

Nɔ versus Non (Unit 8)

Nɔ is a stressed word that occurs before a pause, but *non* is normally an unstressed word that does not occur before a pause.

Meaning of Sì and Nɔ (Unit 8)

Sì is a word indicating that the affirmative counterpart of a given question is true; *nɔ* is a word indicating that the negative counterpart of a given question is true. In other words, *sì* means agreement with an *affirmative statement; nɔ* means agreement with a *negative statement*.

INTONATION

	Casual (Unit 5)	Potentially emphatic (Unit 6)	Interested (Unit 7)
Statements (ɛ̀ Amanda)	"low" or "stress-drop" ɛ̀ A- man-da	"post-stress-drop" ɛ̀ A-man- da ɛ̀ A- man- da	(see frame No. 6 and No. 7)
Information Questions (Chi ɛ̀?)	"low" or "stress-drop" chi ɛ̀	"post-stress-drop" chi ɛ̀ → ɛ̀ chi →	chi ɛ̀ ← ɛ̀ chi ↰
Yes-No Questions (ɛ̀ Amanda)	"high" or "stress-rise" ɛ̀ A- man-da	"post-stress-drop" ɛ̀ A-man- da ɛ̀ A- man- da	ɛ̀ A- da man- ɛ̀ A- man- da ←

IDENTIFICATION SENTENCES (Units 4, 5, 6, 7, 8)

Affirmative Statements	Verification Questions	Negative Statements	Yes-No Questions	Information Questions
È Amanda. "It's Amanda."	È Amanda, nɔ? "It's Amanda, isn't it?"	Non è Amanda. "It's not Amanda."	(Non) È Amanda? "Is(n't) it Amanda?"	Chi (è) ? "Who (is he/she/it)?"

LOCATION SENTENCES INVOLVING *c'è* (Unit 9)

Affirmative Statements	Verification Questions	Negative Statements	Yes-No Questions	Information Questions
C'è. "He/she/it is around/in/there/here."	*C'è, no?* "He/she/it is around, right?"	*Non c'è (mai).* "He/she/it isn't (ever) around?"	*(Non) c'è?* "Is(n't) he/she/it around?"	*Chi c'è?* "Who is around?"
			Non c'è (mai). "Isn't he/she/it ever around?"	*Chi non c'è (mai)?* "Who isn't (ever) around?"

COMMENT: A name (e.g., *Bianca*) may either precede any of the above constructions or follow *c'è (mai)*. However, it is safer for beginning students to place a name after *c'è (mai)*, since in questions and affirmative statements this is its normal position.

Thus: *C'è Bianca.* "Bianca is around/in/there/here."
Non c'è (mai) Bianca? "Isn't Bianca (ever) around?"

LOCATION SENTENCES INVOLVING qui/lì (Unit 10)

Affirmative Statements	Verification Questions	Negative Statements	Yes-No Questions	Information Questions
È { *lì* / *qui*	È { *lì* / *qui, no?*	*Non è (mai)* { *lì* / *qui.*	*(Non) è* { *lì* / *qui?*	*Chi c'è* { *lì* / *qui?*
"He/she/it is { there / here."	"He/she/it is { there / here, right?"	"He/she/it isn't (ever) { there / here."	"Is(n't) he/she/it { there / here?"	"Who is { there / here?"
			Non è mai { *lì* / *qui?*	*Chi non c'è (mai)* { *lì* / *qui?*
			"Isn't he/she/it ever { there / here?"	"Who isn't (ever) { there / here?"

COMMENT: A name (e.g. *Augusta*) may either precede any of the above constructions or follow *qui/lì*. In yes-no questions, however, a name most frequently occurs at the end.

Thus: **È** *lì Augusta.* (or) *Augusta è lì.* "Augusta is there."
(Non) è lì Augusta? "Is(n't) Augusta there?"

C'è Augusta { *lì* / *qui*   "Augusta is { there / here."

Li }
Qui } *c'è Augusta.*

COMMENT: Use this construction in response to an information question beginning with *Chi.*

UNIT 11

1. Listen to the following sound and repeat.

   /ɔ/ (3)

*2. Because the vowel you just heard sounds somewhat like the first vowel sound heard in the English word "forty," what is the name we have given it?

   /ɔ/ (2)

3. Remember that vowel No. 40 is an OPEN vowel. Keep your mouth relatively *open* and *rounded* throughout the production of the sound.

   /ɔ/ (2)

4. Now listen to the following new sound.

   /O/ (3)

5. The vowel you just heard differs from vowel No. 40 in several ways. One difference has to do with the relative openness of the mouth. The mouth is open more for vowel No. 40 than for this vowel.

   /O/ (3)

6. As a matter of fact, the position of the mouth should be the same for this new vowel as it is for vowel No. 2. Listen to both these vowels.

   /O/ /U/ (2)

7. This new vowel you have been hearing should remind you a little of the vowel sound heard in the English word "four," though the Italian vowel is somewhat shorter. It is pronounced with the mouth relatively *closed* and *rounded*. We shall refer to this vowel from now on as vowel No. 4. It is always represented by the letter *o*. Listen carefully, but do not repeat.

   (o) (o) (o)

   * * * * *

8. Listen to the following English words.

   low   owe   Joe   go   dough

21. Conventional Italian spelling does not differentiate between vowel No. 40 and vowel No. 4. Both are represented by the letter *o*. Thus, /VÓTO/ which is a word for "void, vacuum, empty spaces" and /VÓTO/ which is the word for "grade, mark, vote, vow" are both normally represented as *voto*.

22. As can be seen from the preceding example, the difference between vowel No. 40 and vowel No. 4 is important when it is related to a difference in the meanings of words.

23. It has been found, however, that such is the case with these two vowels only when they appear in the *stressed* position of a word. In unstressed positions it is not important to make a clear distinction between the two vowel sounds, and in unstressed positions either vowel No. 4 or a vowel somewhat intermediate in quality between vowel No. 40 and vowel No. 4 is for all practical purposes perfectly acceptable.

24. Even in the stressed position of a word, however, not all speakers (whether educated or not) conform to the dictionary pronunciation of words with vowel No. 40 or vowel No. 4.

25. Thus, although the dictionary pronunciation of the word for "grade" or "vote" is /VÓTO/, some speakers do say /VÓTO/ for "grade" or "vote."

26. These units will continue to make a distinction between stressed /ɔ/ and stressed /O/ according to the dictionary pronunciation. The former will generally be represented in *ɔ* and latter *o*. In the few cases in which the Florentine and the Roman pronunciations differ, the symbol *ǒ* will be used to represent a Florentine /ɔ/ but a Roman /O/ for the same word, and the symbol *ô* will be used to represent a Florentine /O/ but a Roman /ɔ/ for the same word.

27. Thus, there is a poetic word for "uncut" or "unshaven" which would be written *intǒnso*, thereby indicating that one is likely to hear a stressed /ɔ/ in the Florentine pronunciation, but a stressed /O/ in the Roman version.

28. The word for "vogue" or "fashion" would be written *vôga* to indicate that one is likely to hear a stressed /O/ in the Florentine pronunciation, but a stressed /ɔ/ in the Roman version.

29. It is important to remember that what these units are indicating is simply a guide.

• **End of Tape 3A** •

Tape 3B

30. The following is the Florentine pronunciation of the Italian word for "yoke." Listen carefully and repeat.

    giôgo (3)

31. In this pronunciation the word for "yoke" contains a stressed vowel No. 4 followed by an unstressed vowel No. 4. Make sure that you do not add the semivowel /W/ to either of these vowel No. 4's.

    giôgo (2)

32. Now look at the way the word is spelled. Observe how *gi* before *o* stands for the consonant sound in *Gina* and that the letter *i* serves to show that the syllable here is not /GO/ *go*.

    (giôgo)X   (giôgo)X

33. Now here is the word for "sirloin." Repeat.

    (lombo)X   (lombo)X   (lombo)X

34. Now we have the word for a male "pigeon" or "dove." It is also the Italian version of "Columbus." Repeat.

    (colombo)X   (colombo)X   (colombo)X

35. If the final vowel of this word is changed to vowel No. 1, we have the word for a female "pigeon" or "dove." It is also a girl's name. Repeat.

    (colomba)X   (colomba)X   (colomba)X

36. Here are four Italian given names containing vowel No. 4. The first two are feminine names and the last two are masculine names. Repeat.

    (Colomba)X   (Tosca)X   (Gosto)X   (Noè)X

37. Now here are four Italian given names containing vowel No. 40. Again the first two are feminine names and the last two are masculine names. Repeat.

    (Lɔla)X   (Sɔnia)X   (Cɔla)X   (Tɔnio)X

38. As you have probably noticed, many feminine given names in Italian end
    in vowel No. 1. Some exceptions are *Clɛo, Saffo,* and *Nini* (a variant of
    Nina).

39. Most masculine given names in Italian end in vowel No. 4. Some excep-
    tions are *Cɔla,* which is short for *Nicɔla* (related to the English "Nicholas");
    Luca (related to the English "Luke" or "Lucas"); *Noὲ* (related to the English
    "Noah"); *Giovanni* (related to the English "John").

40. Many Italian given names have both masculine and feminine forms. In
    such cases the masculine name often ends in vowel No. 4 and the feminine
    name most usually ends in vowel No. 1.

*41. Thus, what would the masculine counterpart of *Tina* be?

*42. What would the masculine counterpart of *Augusta* be?

43. Some names, however, have *only* a masculine form or *only* a feminine form.
    There is no feminine counterpart of the masculine *Nicɔla,* for example; sim-
    ilarly, there is no masculine counterpart of the feminine *Bianca.*

*44. Translate the following model into English.
    S. C'è Aldo?
    R. Nɔ, Aldo non c'ɛ̀ ; c'è Alda.

*45. You will now hear a series of questions based on the preceding model.
    Give a complete response patterned after the model. Make sure that the
    second name you mention always ends in vowel No. 1. Your response will
    be confirmed each time.

(1) C'è Aldo?	(10) C'è Giovanni?
(2) C'è Antɔnio?	(11) C'è Lɛo?
(3) C'è Augusto?	(12) C'è Lino?
(4) C'è Dino?	(13) C'è Livio?
(5) C'è Donato?	(14) C'è Nando?
(6) C'è Fabio?	(15) C'è Nino?
(7) C'è Fausto?	(16) C'è Pino?
(8) C'è Flavio?	(17) C'è Silvio?
(9) C'è Gino?	(18) C'è Tino?

*46. From the preceding exercise you may have noticed that all the masculine names ended in vowel No. 4 except for one name. What was that name?

*47. Now you will be given a series of questions involving feminine names. Give a complete response patterned after the model of frame No. 44, but this time be very careful to make the second name that you mention end in vowel No. 4. Remember—do not add any semivowel /W/ after vowel No. 4. Your response will be confirmed each time.

(1) C'è Alda?	(10) C'è Giovanna?
(2) C'è Antɔnia?	(11) C'è Lεa?
(3) C'è Augusta?	(12) C'è Lina?
(4) C'è Dina?	(13) C'è Livia?
(5) C'è Donata?	(14) C'è Nanda?
(6) C'è Fabia?	(15) C'è Nina?
(7) C'è Fausta?	(16) C'è Pina?
(8) C'è Flavia?	(17) C'è Sylvia?
(9) C'è Gina?	(18) C'è Tina?

TEST A

(answers not recorded)

You will hear 25 utterances, each said twice. Each utterance will contain a *stressed, rounded* vowel (i.e., vowel No. 2, vowel No. 4 or vowel No. 40). For each utterance write the letter that appropriately represents the stressed vowel, as indicated below. To test yourself, cover the words listed and just listen.

vowel	letter
No. 2	u
No. 4	o
No. 40	ɔ

1) su
2) scopo   2
3) sɔ   4
                  40
4) botti   4
5) bulla   2
                  40
6) bolla   4
7) fossi   4
                  40
8) colto   40
                  4
9) mɔto   4
10) vɔlto   40
11) molta   2
12) volto   4
13) fɔssi   2
14) multa
15) voto   2
16) muto   40
17) bɔtti   2
18) butti   4
19) coi
20) scɔpo   40
21) vɔto   4 o
                  4
22) tosco   4 o
23) cɔlto
24) cui   2 o
25) tɔsco   4

TEST B

(answers not recorded)

You will hear 25 names, each said twice. Each name is spelled with the letter *o* on the end. Some of the names will be pronounced correctly with a final vowel No. 4, but others will be mispronounced because a semivowel /W/ will follow vowel No. 4. For each utterance put a check in the appropriate column according to whether the name is pronounced correctly or mispronounced.

	pronounced correctly	**mispronounced**
1) Adɔlfo		
2) Alano		
3) Aldo		
4) Alfio		
5) Alfɔnso		
6) Antɔnio		
7) Augusto		
8) Beniamino		
9) Dino		
10) Donato		
11) Ɛlio		
12) Fausto		
13) Gino		
14) Guido		
15) Lɛo		
16) Livio		
17) Nando		
18) Nino		
19) Quinto		
20) Silvio		
21) Tano		
22) Tino		
23) Ugo		
24) Clɛo		
25) Saffo		

(not recorded)

Translate the following thoughts into Italian as best you can by using *only* what has been presented to date.

1) Has Colomba arrived yet? (N.B. Do not use *qui* or *lì*!)

   C È Colomba?

2) What's the name of the person you just mentioned?

   Chi È?

3) Aldo is the one you mean, right?

   È Aldo, No?

4) You can find Silvio over there.

   Lì c È Silvio

5) You'll never find Gino around *here*!

   non è mai qui Gino!

6) May I speak to Antonio? (said on the phone)

   C È Antonio?

7) Antonio is gone.

   Antonio non c È.

8) Hasn't Nino come in yet? (N.B. Do not use *qui* or *lì*!)

   Non c È Nino?

9) Who is *here*?

   Chi c È qui?

10) He's always away.

   Non è mai qui.

TEST A   ANSWERS

1) u	6) o	11) o	16) u	21) ɔ
2) o	7) o	12) o	17) ɔ	22) o
3) ɔ	8) o	13) ɔ	18) u	23) ɔ
4) o	9) ɔ	14) u	19) o	24) u
5) u	10) ɔ	15) o	20) ɔ	25) ɔ

TEST B   ANSWERS

	pronounced correctly	mispronounced
1)	X	
2)		X
3)	X	
4)		X
5)	X	
6)	X	
7)	X	
8)	X	
9)		X
10)	X	
11)		X
12)		X
13)		X
14)	X	
15)	X	
16)		X
17)	X	
18)		X
19)		X
20)	X	
21)		X
22)	X	
23)		X
24)		X
25)	X	

TEST C   ANSWERS

1) C'è Colomba?
2) Chi? (or) Chi è?
3) È Aldo, nɔ?
4) C'è Silvio lì. (or) Lì c'è Silvio.
5) Non è mai qui Gino. (or) Gino non è mai qui.
6) C'è Antɔnio?
7) Non c'è Antɔnio. (or) Antɔnio non c'è.
8) Non c'è Nino?
9) Chi c'è qui?
10) Non c'è mai.
   (or)
   Non è mai qui. (if the meaning is "away from here")
   (or)
   Non è mai lì. (if the meaning is "away from there")

FEMININE

a	u	i	o	ɔ	ɛ
Agata*	Augusta	Alìna	Colomba	Antɔnia	Clɛo
Alda		Amina	Tosca	Lɔla	Ɛva
Amanda		Bista		Sɔnia	Lɛa
Bianca		Dina			
Donata		Fina			
Fabia		Gina			
Fausta*		Guendalina			
Flavia		Lia			
Giovanna		Lidia			
Magda		Lina			
Nanda		Linda			
Saffo		Livia			
		Mina			
		Nina			
		Nini			
		Pia			
		Pina			
		Sabina			
		Savina			
		Silvia			
		Spina			
		Tina			

MASCULINE

a	u	i	o	ɔ	ɛ
Alano	Augusto	Beniamino	Gosto	Adɔlfo	Ɛlio
Aldo	Luca	Dino		Alfɔnso	Lɛo
Alfio	Ugo	Gino		Antɔnio	Noè**
Donato		Guido		Cɔla	
Fabio		Lino		Nicɔla	
Fausto*		Livio		Tɔnio	
Flavio		Nino			
Giovanni		Pino			
Nando		Quinto			
Tano		Silvio			
		Tino			

*A dot (to be explained later) should be placed under the first vowel letter of this name to indicate the stressed vowel.

**The accent mark (to be explained later) is as much a part of the written word as the individual letters. Therefore, to omit it from this name is an error.

*17. Here are five more examples. Write what an Italian would write for each utterance.

    (   )
    (   )
    (   )
    (   )
    (   )

18. For frame No. 17 you should have written: *le, uei, uei, be, le.*

*19. Now try this test involving fifteen utterances. Write what an Italian would write for each utterance.

    (   )
    (   )
    (   )
    (   )
    (   )
    (   )
    (   )
    (   )
    (   )
    (   )
    (   )
    (   )
    (   )
    (   )
    (   )

20. For frame No. 19 you should have written: *lei, uei, bei, be, ue, le, le, ue, bei, le, ue, be, bei, uei, lei.*

   (a) If out of the fifteen utterances, you got fewer than eleven correct, you should return to frame No. 11 and review from there until you do get more than ten correct. Then proceed with frame No. 21.

   (b) If out of the fifteen utterances, you got more than ten correct, proceed with frame No. 21.

* * * * *

21. Conventional Italian spelling does not differentiate between vowel No. 70 and vowel No. 8. Both are represented by the letter *e*. Thus, /PÉSKA/ which is the word for "peach" and /PÉSCA/ which is the word for "fishing" or "load of fish" are both normally represented as *pesca*.

22. As can be seen from the preceding example, the difference between vowel No. 70 and vowel No. 8 is important when it is related to a difference in the meanings of words.

23. It has been found, however, that such is the case with these two vowels only when they appear in the *stressed* position of a word. In unstressed positions it is not important to make a clear distinction between the two vowel sounds, and in the unstressed positions either vowel No. 8 or a vowel somewhat intermediate in quality between vowel No. 70 and vowel No. 8 is for all practical purposes, perfectly acceptable.

24. Even in the stressed position of a word, however, not all speakers (whether educated or not) conform to the dictionary pronunciation of words with vowel No. 70 or vowel No. 8.

25. Thus, although the dictionary pronunciation of the word for "fishing" is /PÉSKA/, some speakers do say /PÉSKA/ for "fishing."

26. These units will continue to make a distinction between stressed /ɛ/ and stressed /E/ according to the dictionary pronunciation. The former will generally be represented ɛ and the latter *e*. In the few cases in which the Florentine and the Roman pronunciations differ, the symbol ĕ will be used to represent a Florentine /ɛ/ but a Roman /E/ for the same word, and the symbol ê will be used to represent a Florentine /E/ but a Roman /ɛ/ for the same word.

27. Thus, the word for "temple" would be written *tĕmpio* to indicate that one is likely to hear a stressed /ɛ/ in the Florentine pronunciation, but a stressed /E/ in the Roman version.

28. The word for *Elba* would be written *Êlba* to indicate that one is likely to hear a stressed /E/ in the Florentine pronunciation, but a stressed /ɛ/ in the Roman version.

29. It is important to remember that what these units are indicating is simply a guide.

* * * * *

30. The following is an Italian word for "baby." It is a French borrowing. Listen carefully and repeat.

 bébé (3)

31. This word is pronounced here with an unstressed vowel No. 8 followed by a stressed vowel No. 8. Make sure that you do not add the semivowel /Y/ to either of these vowel No. 8's.

 bébé (2)

32. Now look at the way the word is spelled. The accent marks are simply marks retained from the French spelling.

 (bébé)X (bébé)X

33. Now here is the word for "chick-pea." Repeat.

 (cece)X (cece)X (cece)X

34. Don't be surprised by the spelling *ce*. After all, the English word "cello" is spelled with *ce*. Here is the word for "cement." Repeat.

 (cemento)X (cemento)X (cemento)X

35. Here is another word that looks like its English counterpart. It is the word for "element." Repeat.

 (elemento)X (elemento)X (elemento)X

36. Here are four Italian given names containing vowel No. 8. The first two are feminine names end the last two are masculine names. Repeat.

 (Fede)X (Lena)X (Bela)X (Cecè) X

37. Now here are four Italian given names containing vowel No. 70. Again the first two are feminine names and the last two are masculine names. Repeat.

 (Lεa)X (Mεna)X (Lεo)x (Èlio)X

*38. In Unit 11 we saw that feminine given names in Italian tend to end in a certain vowel. What is this vowel?

*39. Also in Unit 11 we saw that masculine given names in Italian tend to end in a certain vowel. What is this vowel?

40. Many Italian given names, however, end in vowel No. 8. Such names may be masculine or feminine names, and there is no way to tell which is which from the spelling.

41. Here is a list, read twice, of feminine names ending in vowel No. 8. Look at the spelling for each and repeat after the model. Make sure that you do not add any semivowel /Y/ after vowel No. 8.

    (Adɛle)X   (Adɛle)X
    (Cice)X   (Cice)X
    (Clɔe)X   (Clɔe)x
    (Dafne)X   (Dafne)X
    (Ɛbe)X   (Ɛbe)X
    (Edvige)X   (Edvige)X
    (Ɛgle)X   (Ɛgle)X
    (Selɛne)X   (Selɛne)X

42. Now here is a list, read twice, of masculine names ending in vowel No. 8. As before, look at the spelling for each, and repeat after the model. Do not add any semivowel /Y/ after vowel No. 8.

    (Adone)X   (Adone)X
    (Dante)X   (Dante)X
    (Felice)X   (Felice)X
    (Leone)X   (Leone)X
    (Napoleone)X   (Napoleone)X
    (Pasquale)X   (Pasquale)X
    (Samuɛle)X   (Samuɛle)X
    (Valɛnte)X   (Valɛnte)X

*43. Observe the following model.

    S: C'è Adɛle?
    R: Nɔ, Adɛle non its; c'è Adone.

You will now hear a series of questions based on the preceding model and using the feminine names from frame No. 41. Give a complete response patterned after the model and using the masculine names (in order) from frame No. 42. Remember—do not add any semivowel /Y/ after vowel No. 8! Your response will be confirmed each time.

    (1) C'è Adɛle?   (5) C'è Ɛbe?
    (2) C'è Cice?   (6) C'è Edvige?
    (3) C'è Clɔe?   (7) C'è Ɛgle?
    (4) C'è Dafne?   (8) C'è Selɛne?

*44. Observe the following model.

> S: C'è Adone?
> R: Nọ, Adone non c'è̠; c'è Adɛle.

You will now be given a series of questions involving the masculine names from frame No. 42. Give a complete response patterned after the above model, and using the feminine names (in order) from frame No. 41. Remember again—do not add any semivowel /Y/ after vowel No. 8! Your response will be confirmed each time.

(1) C'è Adone?   (5) C'è Napoleone?
(2) C'è Dante?   (6) C'è Pasquale?
(3) C'è Felìce?   (7) C'è Samuɛle?
(4) C'è Leone?   (8) C'è Valɛnte?

TEST A

(answers not recorded)

You will hear 25 utterances, each said twice. Each utterance will contain one of three *stressed, unrounded* vowels (i e., vowel No. 3, vowel No. 8 or vowel No. 70). For each utterance write the letter that appropriately represents the stressed vowel, as indicated below. To test yourself, cover the words given and just listen.

vowel	letter
No. 3	i
No. 8	e
No. 70	ε

1) vinto

2) accɛtta

3) ɛsse

4) venti

5) mila

6) vendette

7) affɛtto

8) se

9) fisso

10) mela

11) accetta

12) vɛnto

13) legge

14) esse

15) sì

16) mena

17) mɛsse

18) affetto

19) seno

20) fesso

21) vɛnti

22) messe

23) lɛgge

24) vendɛtte

25) mina

TEST B

(answers not recorded)

You will hear 20 names, each said twice. Each name is spelled with the letter *e* on the end. Some of the names will be pronounced correctly with a final vowel No. 8, but others will be mispronounced because a semivowel /Y/ will follow vowel No. 8. For each utterance put a check in the appropriate column according to whether the name is pronounced correctly or mispronounced.

	pronounced correctly	**mispronounced**
1) Adone		
2) Dante		
3) Felice		
4) Leone		
5) Napoleone		
6) Pasquale		
7) Samuɛle		
8) Solone		
9) Ulisse		
10) Valɛnte		
11) Vitale		

* * * * *

12) Adɛle

13) Cice

14) Clɔɛ

15) Dafne

16) Ɛbe

17) Edvige

18) Ɛgle

19) Fede

20) Selɛne

• End of Tape 3B •

TEST A   ANSWERS

1) i	6) e	11) e	16) e	21) ε
2) ε	7) ε	12) ε	17) ε	22) e
3) ε	8) e	13) e	18) e	23) ε
4) e	9) i	14) e	19) e	24) ε
5) i	10) e	15) i	20) e	25) i

TEST B   ANSWERS

	pronounced correctly	mispronounced
1)		X
2)		X
3)		X
4)		X
5)	X	
6)		X
7)	X	
8)		X
9)	X	
10)	X	
11)	X	
12)		X
13)	X	
14)		X
15)	X	
16)	X	
17)	X	
18)	X	
19)		X
20)		X

PRELIMINARY NOTE

From this unit on, frame comments, explanations and questions will *not* normally be recorded. These should be read carefully *before* you turn on the recorder and listen to (a) examples, usually indicated by (   ) and/or (b) frame responses.

Tape 4A

UNIT 13

1. Listen to the following English words.
   (sun) (basis) (this)

*2. These three words have one letter in common. What is it?

*3. Does the letter s in these three words represent the same type of sound? Listen again.
   (sun)X (basis)X (this)X

4. The type of sound we have been talking about is often referred to as the "s" sound.

5. Italian has a sound-type very similar to this, which we will represent here as /S/.

* * * * *

6. If we listen carefully to the types of sounds represented by the letter s in other English words, we notice that it is not always this same type of sound.

7. Consider the English words:
   (easy) (is) (his)

*8. Does the letter s in these three words represent the same sound-type represented by the s in "sun," "basis," or "this"? Listen again.
   (easy)X (is)X (his)x

9. Italian has a sound-type very similar to that heard in "easy," "is," and "his." We will represent *this* sound-type as /$/.

* * * * *

10. Now consider these three English words.
    (sure) (sugar) (mission)

*11. Does the letter s in these three words represent the socalled "s" sound of "sun," "basis," or "this"? Listen again.
    (sure)X (sugar)X (mission)X

12. Italian has a sound-type very similar to that heard in "sure," "sugar," and "mission." We will represent *this* sound-type as /š/.

* * * * *

13. Now consider these three English words:
    (Asia) (pleasure) (vision)

*14. Does the letter *s* in these three words represent the so-called "s" sound of "sun," "basis," or "this"? Listen again.
    (Asia)X   (pleasure)X   (vision)X

15. In Tuscan, a sound-type similar to that heard in "Asia," "pleasure," and "vision" does exist, but because it is regionally limited (mainly to Tuscany), beginning students should avoid using it in Italian.

* * * * *

16. Besides these four different sound-types represented by the letter *s* in English, it might be useful to remember that in some English words the letter *s* represents no sound. Consider, for example, "island," "corps," "debris."

* * * * *

17. The letter s in Italian is most usually ased to represent either /S/ or /S/. Depending on what follows the letter *s* in a given word, three cases may be established.

*18. The first case would be the one in which *nothing* follows the letter *s*, that is, it occurs in final position in a word. Listen to the following examples and tell which occurs, /S/ or /S/.

   (gas) (bis) (autobus)

* * * * *

19. The second case is the one in which a *consonant letter* follows the letter s in a given word. Depending on the consonant letter that follows, the letter s may represent either /S/ or /Š/. An easy way to remember the rule involved here is to use the phrase "safe pact" as a reminder. The five consonants represented in this phrase can be used to remind you that the letter s in Italian *always* represents /S/ before the letters "s," "f," "p," letters representing /K/, and "t." Before all other consonant letters, s represents /Š/.

*20. Here are five Italian words. Applying the SAFE PACT rule of frame No. 19, put a cut (') above each s that represents /Š/.

   sbuca scala schifo sdɛnta sfida

21. For frame No. 20 you should have marked only the first and fourth words. Thus,

   šbuca, šdɛnta.

*22. Here are five more Italian words. Again put a cut (') above each s that represents /Š/.

   sgɛlo disgusto ɔslo smania snido

23. For frame No. 22 you should have marked every s except the *second* one in the *second* word.

*24. Now apply this same rule to the following 25 words.

spia	svaga´	splɛnde	slega´	sbianca
squalo	sfilata	sgonfio´	dismonto	disnudo´
smɛla´	svina´	esclama	slavo´	sgomento´
basso	Lisbona	sconto	sdogana´	maschio
stadio	snɔda´	fisso	spiɛga	disgɛla´

25. For frame No. 24 you should have marked only the following words: šmɛla, švaga, švina, Lišbona, šnɔda, šgonfio, šlega, dišmonto, šlavo, šdogana, šbianca, dišnudo, šgomento, dišgɛla.

* * * * *

(a) If out of the 25 words, you got fewer than 20 correct, you should return to frame No. 19 and review from there until you do get 20 or more correct. Then proceed with frame No. 26.

(b) If out of the 25 words, you got 20 or more correct, proceed with frame No. 26.

26. The third case involving the letter *s* is the one in which a *vowel letter* (*a, e, i, o, u*) follows it in a given word.

27. In this case, at the beginning of a word, only /S/ occurs. For example, *sì, Sabina, Sɔnia.*

28. For *-ss-* within a word, a strongly pronounced /S/ occurs. Thus, *Ulisse.*

29. After a consonant, /S/ occurs. Thus, *Alfɔnso, Elsa.* NOTE: A regional pronunciation (primarily Central and Southern Italian) has what sounds like /TS/ after some consonants (for example, /ALFƆNTSO/, /ÉLTSA/), but students are advised to use only /S/ in this case.

30. For *-s-* between vowel letters within a word, several possibilities exist. In the general North, /$/ occurs. In the Tuscan region, one hears some words with /$/ and others with /S/. In the rest of Italy, one generally hears /S/. Thus, for example, the following situation exists with regard to the words for "nose" and "vase."

	naso "nose"	*vaso* "vase"
Northern:	/NÁ$O/	/VÁ$O/
Tuscan:	/NÁSO/	/VÁSO/
other:	/NÁSO/	/VÁSO/

31. Better Italian dictionaries indicate the general Tuscan pronunciation with regard to *-s-* between vowel letters within a word.

32. Because the Tuscan pronunciation with regard to this matter is the most unpredictable of all, and because this course does not attempt to teach a pronunciation that is limited to Tuscan, these units will in no way mark the letter *-s-* between vowel letters.

33. Students may, therefore, choose to pronounce *either* /$/ or /S/ in this case, but they should not strive to imitate more than one model of pronunciation.

34. If one does not attempt to learn the dictionary (Tuscan) pronunciation with regard to the -s- between vowel letters within a word, perhaps the easiest rule to follow is to imitate the general Northern pronunciation, namely, /$/. The other Italian pronunciation with /S/can be dangerous, since a slightly strong pronunciation, which we will indicate here as /Ś/, can sometimes mean another word, one that would be spelled with -ss-. For example, the word for "house" or "home" spelled *casa* is in Roman pronunciation /KÁSA/, but if one says /KÁŚA/ one has pronounced the Italian word for "case" or "box," spelled *cassa*. This confusion can be avoided if one pronounces the word for "house" as /KÁ$A/, in accordance with the Northern pronunciation.

* * * * *

35. In order for the student to have simple guidelines involving the letter *s* in Italian, all he needs to know is that he *must* use /$/ Only before consonants other than the SAFE PACT consonants of frame No. 19. In other cases he may *always* use /S/, except that he can better avoid the "house"–"case" type of mistake by using /$/ for the single -s- between vowel letters within a word.

* * * * *

36. Here is a word that signals a question asking for the identity of something. Hence it corresponds roughly to the English question word "what." Listen and repeat, making sure that you do *not* add the semivowel /Y/ on the end.

    (che?)X   (che?)X   (che?)X

37. You will have noticed that the /K/ is represented here by *ch*. This should not seem so strange, since English too has words in which a corresponding type of sound is represented by *ch*. Consider, for example, the word "chemistry."

38. The question word *che* is like the question word *chi*, in that it may occur in the same position in sentences as the word *chi*.

*39. How do you say, "Who is there?" using the word *lì?*

*40. Therefore, how would you say, "What's over there?" using the word *lì?*

*41. The word *che* is like *è* and *c'è* in that any consonant immediately following it is strongly pronounced. Listen carefully and repeat.
(Che c'è lì?)X   (Che c'è lì?)X

42. Here is a word meaning "thing."
(cɔsa)X   (cɔsa)X   (cɔsa)X

43. In Italian, whenever the question word *che* appears, as in the sentence, *Che c'è lì?*, it may be replaced by the phrase the *che cɔsa*, the second word here beginning with a strongly-pronounced /K/.

*44. Therefore, how would you say, "What's over there?" using the phrase *che cɔsa?*

45. A third way of expressing the same idea as *che?* or *che cɔsa?* is by using only *cɔsa?*

*46. Therefore, what is a third way of saying, "What's over there?"

47. Although Italian has these three different ways of expressing "what?" Italians sometimes prefer one of these in a given sentence. Of the three expressions, perhaps the one that is almost always acceptable is *che cɔsa*. Therefore, unless specifically told to do otherwise, use *che cɔsa?* rather than *che?* or *cɔsa?*

* * * * *

*48. The expression *che cɔsa?* or *cɔsa?* normally loses its final vowel before the word *è*. Therefore, how would you say, "What is it?" in Italian?

49. Here is the word for "this." Repeat, making sure that you do not add the semivowel /W/ on the end:
(questo)X   (questo)X   (questo)X

50. Here is the sentence often used when asking for the identity of something. Its usual English equivalent is "What's this?" Repeat, making sure that both the second and the last words begin with a strongly-pronounced /K/:

(Che cɔs'è questo?) X   (Che cɔs'è questo?)X   (Che cɔs'è questo?)X

51. Here is a normal response to the above question, that may be used in various situations, such as when pointing to a picture of a small basket or a waste-basket. Listen carefully and repeat.

È un cestino. (3)

52. If one is pointing to a picture of a wolf, the normal response is:

È un lupo. (3)

53. Notice that each of these responses begins with /ɛWN/. Repeat each one.

È un cestino. È un lupo. (2)

54. Here is the way these sentences look. Notice that although three words are involved in each sentence, the first two words are pronounced in one syllable.

(È un cestino.)X   (È un lupo.)X
(È un cestino.)X   (È un lupo.)X

55. In Italian, when a word *ending* in a vowel letter (for example, *è*) is followed in the same breath group by a word *beginning* with a vowel letter (for example, *un*), it is normal for the two vowel letters to represent one syllable, unless special stress is involved.

(È un cestino.)X   (È un lupo.)X
(È un cestino.)X   (È un lupo.)X

56. Here are eight other possible answers to *Che cɔs'è questo?* that might be used in a word-guessing game. Listen and repeat each one.

(È un cece.)X	"It's a chick-pea."
(È un cemento.)X	"It's a (type of) cement."
(È un dɛnte.)X	"It's a tooth."
(È un giôgo.)X	"It's a yoke."
(È un naso.)X	"It's a nose."
(È un sasso.)X	"It's a stone."
(È un sofà.)X	"It's a sofa."
(È un tɔpo.)X	"It's a rat."

*57. Now you will be asked the question *Che cos' è questo?* Answer each time by using the following sentences in the order given. Your response will be confirmed each time.

    (1) È un cece.
    (2) È un cemento.
    (3) È un cestino.
    (4) È an dɛnte.
    (5) È un giôgo.
    (6) È un lupo.
    (7) È un naso.
    (8) È un sasso.
    (9) È un sofà.
   (10) È un tɔpo.

*58. You will now be asked the same question. Answer as in frame No. 57. Do so, however, by translating the following sentences. Your response will be confirmed each time.

    (1) "It's a chick-pea."
    (2) "It's a (type of) cement."
    (3) "It's a waste-basket"
    (4) "It's a tooth."
    (5) "It's a yoke."
    (6) "It's a wolf."
    (7) "It's a nose."
    (8) "It's a stone."
    (9) "It's a sofa."
   (10) "It's a rat."

* * * * *

If you did not feel comfortable with this last frame, repeat frames No. 57 and No. 58 until you know the ten utterances well. When you feel you have mastered the utterances, continue with frame No. 59.

*59. Here is the same question. Answer again by translating the following sentences. Your response will be confirmed each time.

    (1) "It's a (type of) cement."
    (2) "It's a chick-pea."
    (3) "It's a nose."
    (4) "It's a rat."
    (5) "It's a sofa."

(6) "It's a stone."
(7) "It's a tooth."
(8) "It's a waste-basket."
(9) "It's a wolf."
(10) "It's a yoke."

*60. Observe the following model.

    S: Che cɔs'è questo? (pointing to a rat)
    R: È un tɔpo.
    S: È un tɔpo?   "Is it a rat?"
    R: Sì, è un tɔpo.

You will now be asked questions as in the model above. Give a complete response patterned after the model. Your response will be confirmed each time.

(1) Che cɔs'è questo? – è un sasso? (pointing to a stone)
(2) .... è un giôgo? (pointing to a yoke)
(3) .... è un cemento? (pointing to a (type of) cement)
(4) .... è un lupo? (pointing to a wolf)
(5) .... è un naso? (pointing to a nose)
(6) .... è un cece? (pointing to a chick-pea)
(7) .... è un cestino? (pointing to a waste-basket)
(8) .... è un tɔpo? (pointing to a rat)
(9) .... è un sofà? (pointing to a sofa)
(10) .... è un dɛnte? (pointing to a tooth)

*61. Observe the following model.

    S: È un tɛpo questo? "Is this a rat?" (pointing to a rat)
    R: Sì, è un tɔpo.
(or)
    S: È un tɔpo questo? (pointing to a wolf)
    R: Nɔ, è un lupo.

You will be asked questions as in the model above. Give a complete affirmative or negative response as in the model, according to the cue given. Your response will be confirmed each time.

(1) è un cemento questo? (pointing to a (type of) cement)
(2) è un naso questo? (pointing to a nose)
(3) è un cestino questo? (pointing to a waste-basket)
(4) è un tɔpo questo? (pointing to a wolf)
(5) è un sasso questo? (pointing to a stone)
(6) è un giôgo questo? (pointing to a yoke)
(7) è un cece questo? (pointing to a tooth)
(8) è un sofà questo? (pointing to a chick-pea)
(9) è un dɛnte questo? (pointing to a rat)
(10) è un lupo questo? (pointing to a sofa)

*62. Observe the following model.

S: (student): (pointing to a rat) Che cɔs'è questo? È un tɔpo?
R: Sì, è un tɔpo.

This time you are to *initiate* the conversation by asking questions according to the cue given. Answers will always be given in the affirmative.

(1) Sì, è un cestino. (pointing to a waste-basket)
(2) Sì, è un sasso. (pointing to a stone)
(3) Sì, è un dɛnte. (pointing to a tooth)
(4) Sì, è un tɔpo. (pointing to a rat)
(5) Sì, è un cemento. (pointing to a (type of) cement)
(6) Sì, è un naso. (pointing to a nose)
(7) Sì, è un sofà. (pointing to a sofa)
(8) Sì, è un giôgo. (pointing to a yoke)
(9) Sì, è un cece. (pointing to a chick-pea)
(10) Sì, è un lupo. (pointing to a wolf)

*63. Observe the following model.

Che
S: Che cosa? } c'è lì?   "What is there over there?"
Cɔsa

(pointing to a rat)
R: Qui c'è un tɔpo.   "There is a rat here."

You will be asked questions as in the model. Give a complete response as in the model, according to the cue given. Your answer will be confirmed each time.

   (1) Che c'è lì? (pointing to a chick-pea)
   (2) Che cosa c'è lì? (pointing to a (type of) cement)
   (3) Cosa c'è lì? (pointing to a waste-basket)
   (4) Che c'è lì? (pointing to a tooth)
   (5) Che c'è lì? (pointing to a stone)
   (6) Cosa c'è lì? (pointing to a nose)
   (7) Che cosa c'è lì? (pointing to a wolf)
   (8) Cosa c'è lì? (pointing to a yoke)
   (9) Che c'è lì? (pointing to a sofa)
  (10) Che cosa c'è lì? (pointing to a rat)

TEST A

(answers not recorded)

You will hear 20 words, each said twice. For each word put a check in the appropriate column, according to whether you hear /S/ or /Š/ in the word.

	/S/	/Š/
1) abuso		
2) Asia		
3) asma		
4) basta		
5) cɔsa		
6) Mɔsa		
7) Elsa		
8) Sofịa		
9) ɔmnibus		
10) smetto		
11) sala		
12) sdegno		
13) inglese		
14) slitta		
15) Pisa		
16) Tasmania		
17) francese		
18) snɛllo		
19) uso		
20) Cɔsma		

TEST B

(answers not recorded)

You will hear 10 utterances, each said once. Translate each one into English. To test yourself cover the Italian words given and try to translate the utterances after only listening to them.

1) Che cɔs'è questo?

_____ what's ~~know~~ is this _____

2) è un giôgo.

_____ its   a   yoke _____

3) Chi è?

who's ~~what~~ is it

4) È un sasso?

its a stone

5) C'è Amanda.

~~Its around~~ amenda is around

6) Qui c'è Luca.

here is Luca Luca is here

7) Non è mai qui Nicola.

Nicola is never here

8) Cosa c'è lì?

whats over there

9) È un cestino.

its a chest

10) C'è un cemento.

There its cement

TEST A ANSWERS

	/S/	/$/		/S/	/$/
1)		X	11)	X	
2)		X	12)		X
3)		X	13)	X	
4)	X		14)		X
5)	X		15)	X	
6)		X	16)		X
7)	X		17)		X
8)	X		18)		X
9)	X		19)		X
10)		X	20)		X

TEST B ANSWERS

1) What is this?
2) It's a yoke.
3) Who is it?
4) Is it a stone?
5) Amanda is around. (or)
   .... in./.... there./.... here.

6) Here is Luca. (or) Luca is here.
7) Nicola is never here.
8) What is there over there?
9) It's a small basket. (or) It's a waste-basket.
10) There's a (type of) cement.

UNIT 14

*1. How do you say, "What's this?" in Italian?

*2. How do you say, "It's a waste-basket" in Italian?

*3. How do you say, "It's a sofa" in Italian?

4. The Italian word *sofà* is like the English word "sofa" both in sound and in meaning. This is not simply a coincidence, but happens to be so because both words have the same origin—in this case, both words come from an Arabic word. Any two words that have the same origin are called COG-NATES.

5. Italian has a large number of cognates of English words. For this reason a lot of Italian words are easily recognized by speakers of English.

*6. Here are three such words. What are the English cognates?
   (*animale*)
   (*elefante*)
   (*italiano*)

7. Now look at the spelling of these three words. Repeat.
   (animale)X   (animale)X
   (elefante)X   (elefante)X
   (italiano)X   (italiano)X

8. Notice the letter *f* in the Italian word for "elephant." This is normal. Italian never uses *ph* to represent this sound-type, that is /F/.

9. Notice, too, that the word for "Italian" is not capitalized. This, too, is normal. In Italian, nationality and regional terms are normally not capitalized except in plural phrases such as the equivalents of "the Italians," " the English," "the Romans," "the Tuscans."

10. Another important fact about the word *italiano* is that whereas it may refer to a boy or a man, it is *not* to be used as the equivalent of "Italian girl" or "Italian woman."

*11. Here is another cognate of an English word. This one is not so easily recognizable. What do you think the English cognate is?

(ospedale)X   (ospedale)X

12. Now here are three Italian words that have no commonly used English cognate:

the word for "bone" – (ɔsso)X   (ɔsso)X
the word for "man" – (uɔmo)X   (uɔmo)X
the word for "egg" – (uɔvo)X   (uɔvo)X

13. Here is the sentence for "It's an animal." Listen carefully. Do not repeat.

(è un animale.)   (è un animale.)

14. Notice that there is no pause anywhere in the sentence. Repeat, being especially careful not to pause after *un*.

(è un animale.)X   (è un animale.)X   (è un animale.)X

*15. Now think of a word-guessing game. You will be asked the question *Che cos'è questo?* Answer each time by using the following sentences in the order given. Your response will be confirmed each time. Remember—do not pause after *un:*

(1) è un animale.
(2) è un elefante.
(3) è un italiano.
(4) è un ospedale.
(5) è un ɔsso.
(6) è un uɔmo.
(7) è un uɔvo.

*16. Now you will be asked the same question. Answer as in frame No. 15. Do so, however, by translating the following sentences. Your response will be confirmed each time.

(1) "It's an animal."
(2) "It's an elephant."
(3) "It's an Italian (male)."
(4) "It's a hospital."
(5) "It's a bone."
(6) "It's a man."
(7) "It's an egg."

* * * * *

If you did not feel comfortable with the last frame, repeat frames No. 15 and No. 16 until you know the seven utterances well. When you feel you have mastered the utterances, continue with frame No. 17.

* * * * *

*17. Here is the same question. Answer again by translating the following sentences. Your response will be confirmed each time.

    (1) "It's an animal."
    (2) "It's a bone."
    (3) "It's an egg."
    (4) "It's an elephant."
    (5) "It's a hospital."
    (6) "It's an Italian (male)."
    (7) "It's a man."

* * * * *

18. Here is the Italian word for "dog." Repeat.

    (cane)X   (cane)X   (cane)X

19. Here is the sentence for "It's a dog." Listen carefully. Do not repeat.

    (È un cane.) (È un cane.)

20. Notice that the first two consonants in this sentence are /NK/. In Unit 9 it was pointed out that this combination sounds like the ending of the English word "sunk." Listen again and repeat.

    (È un cane.)X (È un cane.)X (È un cane.)X

21. The letter *n* in Italian represents a type of sound that differs according to whatever follows it. In all cases, the sound-type is one that involves the air escaping through the nose, i.e., a NASAL.

22. The first nasal in the sentences *È un cestino* and *È un animale* is really different from the first nasal in *È un cane*, despite the fact that Italians ordinarily think of them as the same.

23. The nasal before /K/ is like the nasal before /G/ (as in *Gosto*). Listen to the sentence for "It's a sweater," and repeat.

    (È un gɔlf.)X   (È un gɔlf.)X   (È un gɔlf.)X

24. The variation of /N/ that is heard before /K/ and /G/ we shall call the KEG nasal, and the letters *k* and *g* in "keg" can be used to remind one that we are referring to the variation heard before /K/ and /G/.

25. Repeat the following utterances involving the KEG nasal.

    (È un cane.)X   "It's a dog."
    (È un gɔlf.)X   "It's a sweater."
    (È un chianti.)X   "It's a (kind of) Chianti" (wine).
    (È un chimɔno.)X   "It's a kimono."
    (È un cɔno.)X   "It's a cone."
    (È un consolato.)X   "It's a consulate."
    (È un conto.)X   "It's an account." (or)
                           "It's a (hotel or restaurant) bill."

*26. You will now be asked the question *Che cɔs' è questo?* Answer each time by using the following sentences in the order given. Your response will be confirmed each time.

    (1) È un cane.
    (2) È un gɔlf.
    (3) È un chianti.
    (4) È un chimɔno.
    (5) È un cɔno.
    (6) È un consolato.
    (7) È un cɔnto.

*27. You will now be asked the same question. Answer as in frame No. 26. Do so, however, by translating the following sentences. Your response will be confirmed each time.

    (1) "It's a dog."
    (2) "It's a sweater."
    (3) "It's a (kind of) Chianti."
    (4) "It's a kimono."
    (5) "It's a cone."
    (6) "It's a consulate."
    (7) "It's an account."
    (8) "It's a (hotel or restaurant) bill."

* * * * *

If you did not feel comfortable with the last frame, repeat frames No. 25, No. 26, and No. 27 until you know the seven utterances well. When you feel you have mastered them, continue with frame No. 28.

* * * * *

*28. Here is the same question. Answer again by translating the following sentences. Your answer will be confirmed each time.

    (1) "It's an account."
    (2) "It's a (kind of) Chianti."
    (3) "It's a cone."
    (4) "It's a consulate."
    (5) "It's a (hotel or restaurant) bill."
    (6) "It's a dog."
    (7) "It's a kimono."
    (8) "It's a sweater."

* * * * *

29. Here is the Italian word for "fig." Repeat.

    (fico)X   (fico)X   (fico)X

30. Here is the sentence for "It's a fig." Listen carefully. Do not repeat.

    (È un fico.) (È un fico.)

31. Notice that the first two consonants in this sentence form the combination /NF/. The nasal before /F/ is like the nasal before /V/. In both cases one's upper teeth should touch one's bottom lip during the production of the /N/, giving what we shall call the FIVE nasal. Thus, the letters *f* and *v* in "five" can be used to remind one that we are referring to the variation of /N/ heard before /F/ and /V/.

32. Listen carefully and repeat the following utterances involving the FIVE nasal.

(È un fico.)X	"It's a fig."
(È un film.)X	"It's a film (= a movie)."
(È un fuɔco.)X	"It's a fire."
(È un vaso.)X	"It's a vase."
(È un velo.)X	"It's a veil."
(È un vino.)X	"It's a (type of) wine."
(È un voto.)X	"It's a grade (= a mark)."

*33. You will now be asked the question *Che cos'ɛ questo?* Answer each time by using the following sentences in the order given. Your response will be confirmed each time.

  (1) è un fico.
  (2) è un film.
  (3) è un fuɔco.
  (4) è un vaso.
  (5) è un velo.
  (6) è un vino.
  (7) è un voto.

*34. You will now be asked the same question. Answer as in frame No. 33. Do so, however, by translating the following sentences. Your response will be confirmed each time.
  (1) "It's a fig."
  (2) "It's a movie."
  (3) "It's a fire."
  (4) "It's a vase."
  (5) "It's a veil."
  (6) "It's a (type of) wine."
  (7) "It's a mark."

* * * * *

If you did not feel comfortable with this last frame, repeat frames No. 32, No. 33, and No. 34 until you know the seven utterances well. When you feel you have mastered them, continue with frame No. 35.

* * * * *

*35. Here is the same question. Answer again by translating the following sentences. Your response will be confirmed each time.
  (1) "It's a vase."
  (2) "It's a fire."
  (3) "It's a grade."
  (4) "It's a film."
  (5) "It's a veil."
  (6) "It's a wine."
  (7) "It's a mark."
  (8) "It's a fig."
  (9) "It's a movie."

* * * * *

36. Here is the Italian word for "male child." Repeat.
  (bambino)X (bambino)X (bambino)X

37. Here is the sentence for "It's a child." Listen carefully. Do not repeat.
    (è un bambino) (è un bambino)

38. Notice that now the *n* of *un* actually stands for /M/. Listen again and repeat.
    (è un bambino)X (è un bambino)X (è un bambino)X

39. It is normal in Italian to have /M/ (and *not* /N/) precede /B/, /M/, or /P/. Within a word, the spelling reflects this and never has the letter *n* precede *b*, *m*, or *p*. If a word *ends* in the letter *n*, however, students must remember that before an initial *b*, *m*, or *p*, the *n* represents /M/. This /M/ we shall call the BUMP nasal, and the letters *b*, *m*, and *p* in "bump" can be used to remind one that we are referring to the nasal that occurs before /B/, /M/, and /P/.

40. Listen carefully and repeat the following utterances involving the BUMP nasal.

(è un bambino.)X	"It's a (male) child."
(è un bastone.)X	"It's a cane." or "It's a stick."
(è un bɔsco.)X	"It's a wooded area (woods)."
(è un mese.)X	"It's a month."
(è un monumento.)X	"It's a monument."
(è un pane.)X	"It's a loaf of bread."
(è un pilɔta.)X	"It's a (male) pilot."
(è un poɛta.)X	"It's a (male) poet."
(è un ponte.)X	"It's a bridge."

* 41. You will now be asked the question *Che cɔs'ɛ questo?* Answer each time by using the following sentences in the order given. Your response will be confirmed each time.

    (1) è un bambino.
    (2) è un bastone.
    (3) è un bɔsco.
    (4) è un mese.
    (5) è un monumento.
    (6) è un pane.
    (7) è un pilɔta.
    (8) è un poɛta.
    (9) è un ponte.

* 42. You will now be asked the same question. Answer as in frame No. 41. Do so, however, by translating the following sentences. Your response will be confirmed each time

   (1) "It's a (male) child."
   (2) "It's a cane."
   (3) "It's a wooded area."
   (4) "It's a month."
   (5) "It's a monument."
   (6) "It's a loaf of bread."
   (7) "It's a (male) pilot."
   (8) "It's a (male) poet."
   (9) "It's a bridge."

* * * * *

If you did not feel comfortable with this last frame repeat frames No. 40, No. 41, and No. 42 until you know the nine utterances well. When you feel you have mastered them, continue with frame No. 43.

* * * * *

* 43. Here is the same question. Answer again by translating the following sentences. Your response will be confirmed each time.

   (1) "It's a bridge."
   (2) "It's a cane."
   (3) "It's a (male) child."
   (4) "It's a loaf of bread."
   (5) "It's a month."
   (6) "It's a monument."
   (7) "It's a (male) pilot."
   (8) "It's a (male) poet."
   (9) "It's a stick."
   (10) "It's a wooded area."

* * * * *

*44. Observe the following model.

   S: Che cos'ɛ questo? (pointing to an animal)
   R: È un animale.
   S: È un animale?
   R: Sì, è un animale.

You will now be asked questions as in the model above. Give a complete response patterned after the model. Your response will be confirmed each time.

   (1) Che cos'è questo? – È un animale? (pointing to an animal)
   (2) .... – È un cemento? (pointing to a (type of) cement)
   (3) .... – È un chianti? (pointing to a (kind of) Chianti)

(4) .... – è un cɔno? (pointing to a cone)
(5) .... – è un consolato?(pointing to a consulate)
(6) .... – è un elefante?(pointing to an elephant)
(7) .... – è un fico? (pointing to a fig)
(8) .... – è un film? (pointing to a film)
(9) .... – è un italiano?(pointing to an Italian man)
(10) .... – è un chimɔno? (pointing to a kimono)

* 45. Observe the following model.
     S: è un monumento questo? (pointing to a monument)
     R: Sì, è un monumento.
          (or)
     S: è un monumento questo? (pointing to a hospital)
     R: Nɔ, è un ospedale.

You will be asked questions as in the model above. Give a complete affirmative or negative response as in the model, according to the cue given. Your
response will be confirmed each time.

    (1) è un monumento questo? (pointing to a monument)
    (2) è un vaso questo? (pointing to a nose)
    (3) è un animale questo? (pointing to a hospital)
    (4) è un pɔeta questo? (pointing to a (male) pilot)
    (5) è un pilɔta questo? (pointing to a (male) poet)
    (6) è un sofà questo? (pointing to a sofa)
    (7) è un vaso questo? (pointing to a vase)
    (8) è un vɛlo questo? (pointing to a veil)
    (9) è un vino questo? (pointing to a (type of) wine)
   (10) è un uɔvo questo? (pointing to a man)

*46. Observe the following model.
     S: (student): (pointing to a dog) Che cɔs'è questo? è un cane?
     R: Sì, è un cane.

This time you are to *initiate* the conversation by asking questions according to the cue given. Answers will always be given in the affirmative.

    (1) Sì, è un cane. (pointing to a dog)
    (2) Sì, è un fuɔco. (pointing to a fire)
    (3) Sì, è un bambino. (pointing to a (male) child)
    (4) Sì, è un cestino. (pointing to a small basket)
    (5) Sì, è un ɔsso. (pointing to a bone)
    (6) Sì, è un conto. (pointing to a (hotel or restaurant) bill)
    (7) Sì, è un cece. (pointing to a chick-pea)
    (8) Sì, è un bastone. (pointing to a cane)
    (9) Sì, è un dɛnte. (pointing to a tooth)
   (10) Sì, è un uɔvo. (pointing to an egg)

*47. Observe the following model.

    Che
S: Che cɔsa ⎬ c'è lì? (pointing to a sweater)
    Cɔsa

R: Qui c'è un gɔlf.

You will be asked questions as in the model above. Give a complete response as in the model, according to the cue given. Your response will be confirmed each time.

    (1) Che cɔsa c'è lì? (pointing to a sweater)
    (2) Cɔsa c'è lì? (pointing to a grade (=a mark))
    (3) Che c'è lì? (pointing to a wooded area)
    (4) Che cɔsa c'è lì? (pointing to a yoke)
    (5) Che cɔsa c'è lì? (pointing to a month)
    (6) Che c'è lì? (pointing to a wolf)
    (7) Cɔsa c'è lì? (pointing to a loaf of bread)
    (8) Che c'è lì? (pointing to a stone)
    (9) Che cɔsa c'è lì? (pointing to a bridge)
   (10) Cɔsa c'è lì? (pointing to a rat)

NOTE: Unless you feel confident that you have mastered the drills in frames
No. 44 thru No. 47, do not continue.

*48. Observe the following model.

S: C'è un anim<u>a</u>le qui?   "Is there an animal here?" (pointing to an
                                             animal)

R: S<u>ì</u>, c'è un anim<u>a</u>le qui.   "Yes, there's an animal here."
               (or)

S: C'è un animale qui? (pointing to a monument)

R: N<u>ò</u>, non c'<u>è</u> un animale qu<u>i</u>.   "No, there isn't an animal here."

You will be asked questions as in the model above. Give a complete affirmative or negative response as in the model, according to the cue given. Your
response will be confirmed each time.

   (1) C'è un ospedale qui? (pointing to an animal)
   (2) C'è un monumento qui? (pointing to a monument)
   (3) C'è un bastone qui? (pointing to a dog)
   (4) C'è un gɔlf qui? (pointing to a sweater)
   (5) C'è un chimɔno qui? (pointing to a kimono)
   (6) C'è un uɔmo qui? (pointing to a man)
   (7) C'è un ɔsso qui? (pointing to an egg)
   (8) C'è un tɔpo qui? (pointing to a rat)
   (9) C'è un consulato qui? (pointing to a consulate)
  (10) C'è un conto qui? (pointing to a month)

TEST A

(not recorded)

In some of the following sentences the letter *n* represents /M/. Circle each such *n*.

1) È un lupo.
2) È un ɔsso.
3) È un cɔno.
4) È un vaso.
5) È un mese.
6) È un pane.
7) È un ospedale.
8) È un sofà.
9) È un bastone.
10) È un cestino.
11) È un gɔlf.
12) È un pilɔta.
13) È un naso.

14) È un monumento.
15) È un cece.
16) È un elefante.
17) È un bɔsco.
18) È un conto.
19) È un fuɔco.
20) È un bambino.
21) È un voto.
22) È un ponte.
23) È un dɛnte.
24) È un poɛta.
25) È un tɔpo.

TEST B

(answers not recorded)

You will hear ten utterances, each said once. Translate each one into English. To test yourself cover the sentences given and try to do the English translation after just listening to the Italian.

(on tape)

1) È un ospedale?

_____ Is that a hospital _____

2) È un consolato questo?

_____ Is this a consolate _____

3) Che cɔs'è questo? È un cane?

_____ whats this, a dog? _____

4) Qui c'è un voto.

_____ the grades one here _____

5) Sì, c'è un ponte qui.

_____ yes, theres a bridge here _____

6) Nɔ, non c'è un bɔsco qui.

_____ no theres no wooded area here _____

7) Cɔsa c'è lì?

_____ whats over there _____

8) C'è un golf qui?

_____ IS Vhone a Sweater here ____

9) è un animale.

_____ Its an animal ____

10) C'è un dente.

_____ Wheres a tooth ____

• **End of Tape 4A** •

TEST C

(not recorded)

Translate the following thoughts into Italian as best you can by using *only* what has been presented so far.

1) What is there over there?

_____ Che cosa c'è li? ____

2) There's a stone there.

_____ C'è un sassa li. ____

3) There's a child here.

_____ c'è un bambino goi ____

4) Is this a kimono?

_____ è un binino? ____

5) No, it's not a fig; it's an egg.

_____ No, non c'è un fico, è un uovo ____

6) It's a cane, isn't it?

_____ È un bastone, no? ____

7) Do you see a (hotel) bill there?

_____ c'è un conto li? ____

8) Is it a pilot?

_____ è un pilota? ____

9) Is there a consulate there?

_____ c'è un consolato li ____

10) No, there isn't an Italian man here.

_____ No, non c'è un Italiano goi ____

TEST A ANSWERS

Only the following sentences should be marked, as follows.

5) È (un) mese.
6) È (un) pane.
9) È (un) bastone.
12) È (un) pilota.
14) È (un) monumento.
17) È (un) bosco.
20) È (un) bambino.
22) È (un) ponte.
24) È (un) poeta.

TEST B ANSWERS

1) Is it a hospital?
2) Is this a consulate?
3) What's this? Is it a dog?
4) There's a {mark / grade} here.
5) Yes, there's a bridge here.
6) No, there isn't a wooded area here.
7) What's over there?
8) Is there a sweater here?
9) It's an animal.
10) There's a tooth.

TEST C ANSWERS

1) Che cosa c'è lì?
2) C'è un sasso lì. (or) Lì c'è un sasso.
3) C'è un bambino qui. (or) Qui c'è un bambino.
4) È un chimono?
5) No, non è un fico; è un uovo.
6) È un bastone, no?
7) C'è un conto lì?
8) È un pilota?
9) C'è un consolato lì?
10) No, non c'è un italiano qui.

UNIT 15

1. Here is a girl's name that you have already heard. Listen carefully and repeat.

   (Sɔnia)X (Sɔnia)X (Sɔnia)X

*2. Because this name is a two-syllable word, what does the letter *i* in the name represent, vowel No. 3 (i.e., /I/) or the semivowel /Y/?

3. However, if you listen carefully, you might notice that the /Y/ is not strongly pronounced, and it even sounds a little like vowel No 3.

   (Sɔnia)X (Sɔnia)X

4. This is normal in Italian whenever /N/ is followed by /Y/. The reason for it is that /N/ and /Y/ are not normally pronounced with the tongue in the same position. For the /N/, the front part of the tongue normally touches either the upper teeth or the ridge directly behind the upper teeth; for the /Y/, the front part of the tongue is normally away from the upper teeth. Thus, in going from the /N/ position to the /Y/ position, the tongue moves back in the mouth, giving the sound heard in *Sɔnia*. In the following diagram, the arrow indicates this backward movement of the tongue.

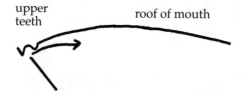

upper teeth

roof of mouth

5. Here are two other utterances with /NY/. Repeat.

   (Lavinia)X   (Lavinia)X   "girl's given name"
   (la Campania)X (la Campania)X "region in Southern Italy"

* * * * *

6. Besides the /NY/ combination, Italian has a sound-type that sounds very much like /N/ + /Y/, and yet is different. In order to make this type of sound, the front part of the tongue is normally *away* from the upper front teeth to begin with. Consequently, there is *no* backward tongue movement as described in frame No. 4.

7. In addition, this new sound-type is usually *very strongly pronounced*, thus differentiating it even further from /NY/.

8. This new sound-type, which will be represented here as /Ň/, occurs in the following utterances. Listen carefully and repeat.

(/SÓŇA/)X   (/SÓŇA/)X   "(s)he is dreaming"
(/LAVÍNA/)X   (/LAVÍNA/)X   "the vineyard"
(/LAKAMPÁŇA/)X   (/LAKAMPÁŇA/)X   "the country" (as opposed
                                                         to the "city" or "the town")

9. Notice that the distinction between /NY/ and /Ň/ is important because it is related to a difference in meaning.

10. Whereas the /NY/ combination is normally represented in Italian by *ni*, /Ň/ is normally represented by *gn*.

*11. Thus, how would /KAMPÁŇA/ be represented in normal spelling?

12. Now here are the three items of frame No. 8. Repeat each one, remembering that *gn* represents /Ň/.
    the Roman pronunciation of:

(sôgna)X   (sôgna)X
(la vigna)X   (la vigna)X
(la campagna)X   (la campagna)X

13. Remember that the symbol *ô* in *sôgna* is used in these units to indicate that one is likely to hear a stressed /O/ in the Florentine pronunciation, but a stressed /ɔ/ in the Roman version. (See Unit 11.)

14. The letters *gn* in Italian never represent the combination heard in the English words "magnificent" or "signal." The symbol *gn* always represents the nasal unit /Ň/.

*15. Here is another contrasting pair of words. Tell which one contains /NY/ and which contains /Ň/.
        Giunio   *giugno*   (2)
           a   b

16. The word *Giunio* is a boy's given name, as opposed to the word *giugno* (normally spelled with a small initial *g*) which is the word for the month of June. Listen and repeat.

   (Giunio)X   (giugno)X
   (Giunio)X   (giugno)X

17. Both /NY/ and /Ň/ may occur at the beginning of words. Listen and repeat the following.

   (niɛnte)X   (niɛnte)X   "nothing"
   (gnɔmo)X   (gnɔmo)X   "gnome"

18. Now here are the five items you have had with /NY/. Repeat carefully, remembering the backward tongue movement of frame No. 4.

   (Sɔnia)X   (Sɔnia)X
   (Lavinia)X   (Lavinia)X
   (la Campania)X   (la Campania)X
   (Giunio)X   (Giunio)X
   (niɛnte)X   (niɛnte)X

19. Now repeat the following five items, all with /Ň/. Remember that /Ň/ is strongly pronounced, and that you should start the sound by keeping the front part of the tongue *away* from the upper front teeth. the Roman pronunciation of:

   (sôgna)X   (sôgna)X
   (la vigna)X   (la vigna)X
   (la campagna)X   (la campagna)X
   (giugno)X   (giugno)X
   (gnɔmo)X   (gnɔmo)X

20. Here are the ten items from frames No. 18 and No. 19, presented in contrast. Repeat each one carefully.

   (Sɔnia)X   the Roman pronunciation of: (sôgna)X
   (Lavinia)X   (la vigna)X
   (la Campania)X   (la campagna)X
   (Giunio)X   (giugno)
   (niɛnte)X   (gnɔmo)X

*21. Now here are the same ten items presented in random order. Pronounce each one as you hear it, and write the items correctly in the space provided.

   (1) _____

   (2) _____

   (3) _____

(4) _____

(5) _____

(6) _____

(7) _____

(8) _____

(9) _____

(10) _____

22. In the preceding frame you should have written *gn* only for numbers (1), (2), (6), (8), and (9).

* * * * *

23. Listen carefully to the following and repeat.

   Betty   Eddie (4)

24. What you just heard in frame No. 23 are two common given names in English, pronounced as they ordinarily would be by a large number of speakers of American English. Notice that the two names rhyme.

   Betty   Eddie

*25. Write out these two names in English.

26. Notice again that as they are pronounced here, the two names rhyme.
   (Betty)X   (Eddie)X
   (Betty)X   (Eddie)X

27. Naturally, these names may be pronounced differently without making them rhyme. Listen and repeat *this* pronunciation.
   (Betty)X   (Eddie)X

28. The kind of pronunciation of these two names that was heard in frame No. 27 is sometimes referred to as a careful, reading pronunciation not normally heard in the everyday, colloquial speech of most Americans.

29. The pronunciation heard in frame No. 26, on the other hand, *is* normal in the colloquial speech of many Americans.

30. These different levels of pronunciation in English may conveniently be labeled here as:
    - (1) COLLOQUIAL - for the pronunciation in which "Betty" and "Eddie" rhyme, as in frame No. 26, and
    - (2) READING - for the pronunciation in which "Betty" and "Eddie" do *not* rhyme, as in frame No. 27.

31. Here are some other pairs of English utterances spelled with *t* and *d* which also rhyme in COLLOQUIAL American speech.

(latter)X	(ladder)X
(meaty)X	(needy)X
(heating)X	(heeding)X
(seating)X	(seeding)X
(waiting)X	(wading)X
(waiter)X	(wader)X
(eighty)X	(lady)X
(at it)X	(add it)X
(hit it)X	(hid it)X
(bit it)X	(bid it)X
(set it)	(said it)X
(feet up)	(feed up)X
(lit up)X	(lid up)X

32. What was heard in the last frame for each word spelled with *t* and *d* was not the consonant sound heard in the English "two" or "do" nor what was heard in the READING pronunciation of frame No. 27. You heard, instead, what is normal in COLLOQUIAL American speech—a single, quick flap of the tongue against the ridge directly behind the upper front teeth.

33. A convenient name, therefore, for the type of sound heard in this COLLO-QUIAL pronunciation is TONGUE-FLAP.

34. Repeat the following six English names as pronounced here, with the TONGUE-FLAP.

(Betty)X	(Betty)X
(Eddie)X	(Eddie)X
(Lita)X	(Lita)X
(Dotty)X	(Dotty)X
(Nedda)X	(Nedda)X
(Sadie)X	(Sadie)X

35. Let us imagine now that there are six Italians with the names listed below. Only the initial of the last name is shown here:

given name	last name	
(Bianca	B—	)X
(Ɛlio	Ɛ—	)X
(Lavinia	L—	)X
(Dina	D—	)X
(Nina	N—	)X
(Sɔnia	S—	)X

36. Notice that the fictitious last names given above sound like the items of frame No. 34. Repeat again. NOTE: *Do not* write out the last names since you have not yet been told how the TONGUE-FLAP is represented in Italian. This will be explained in a later unit.

(Bianca B—)X
(Ɛlio Ɛ—)X
(Lavinia L—)X
(Dina D—)X
(Nina N—)X
(Sɔnia S—)X

* * * * *

37. Now let us go on to something different. Repeat the following masculine given name.

(Ɛlio)X   (Ɛlio)X   (Ɛlio)X

*38. Because the name is a two-syllable word, what does the -*i*- in the name represent, vowel No. 3 (i.e., /I/) or the semivowel /Y/?

39. However, if you listen carefully, you might notice that the /Y/ is not strongly pronounced, and it even sounds a little like vowel No. 3.
(Ɛlio)X   (Ɛlio)X

40. This is normal in Italian whenever /L/ is followed by /Y/. The reason for it is that /L/ and /Y/ (like /N/ and /Y/) are not normally pronounced with the tongue in the same position. For the /L/, the front part of the tongue almost always touches either the upper teeth or the ridge directly behind the upper teeth; for the /Y/, the front part of the tongue is normally *away* from the upper teeth. Thus, in going from the /L/ position to the /Y/ position, the tongue moves back in the mouth, giving the sound heard in Ɛlio.

Here is the same diagram you saw in frame No. 4, in which the arrow indicates this backward movement of the tongue.

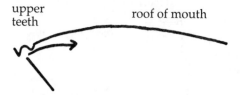

upper
teeth   roof of mouth

41. Here are some other utterances with /LY/ in them. Repeat.
    (voliamo)X   (voliamo)X   "we fly"
    (l'Emilia)X   (l'Emilia)X   (region in Northern Italy)
    (l'Italia)X   (l'Italia)X   "Italy"
    (l'ɔlio)X   (l'ɔlio)X   "the oil"

* * * * *

42. Besides the /LY/ combination, Italian has a sound-type that sounds very much like /L/ + /Y/, and yet is different. In order to make this type of sound, the front part of the tongue is normally *away* from the upper front teeth to begin with. Consequently, there is *no* backward tongue movement as described in frame No. 40.

43. Like /Ň/, this new sound-type is usually *very strongly* pronounced, thus differentiating it even further from /LY/.

44. This new sound-type, which will be represented here as /Ľ/, occurs in the following utterances. Listen carefully and repeat.
    (/VOĽÁNO/)X   (/VOĽÁNO/)X   "we want"
    (/LEMÍĽA/)X   (/LEMÍĽA/)X   "the miles'
    (/LITÁĽA/)X   (/LITÁĽA/)X   "(s)he cuts them"
    (/LɔĽO/)X   (/LɔĽO/)X   (affluent of the Po River)

45. Notice that the distinction between /LY/ and /Ľ/ is important because it is related to a difference in meaning.

46. Whereas the /LY/ combination is normally represented in Italian by *li*, /Ľ/ is normally represented by *gl* (before the letter *i*) and *gli* (elsewhere).

*47. Thus, how would /VOĽÁMO/ be represented in normal spelling?

48. Now here are the four items of frame No. 44. Repeat each one, remembering that *gli* represents /Ľ/.

(vogliamo)X	(vogliamo)X
(le miglia)X	(le miglia)X
(li taglia)X	(li taglia)X
(l'ɔglio)X	(l'ɔglio)X

49. Unlike the letters *gn*, which never represent a combination of consonant sounds, the symbol *gl* sometimes does represent a sound combination (/G/ plus /L/). It always does so before any vowel letter other than *i*, but before the letter *i* only in a small number of words. Here are a few examples.

glandola	"gland"
εgle	(feminine given name)
glεba	"clod, lump"
glɔbo	"globe"
glutine	"gluten"
anglicano	"Anglican"
negligεnte	"negligent"

50. Whereas /LY/ may occur at the beginning of a number of words /Ľ/ occurs initially only in a very limited number of cases. However, these cases occur with high frequency. Listen and repeat the following.

(liεto)X	(liεto)X	"glad"
(glielo dà)X	(glielo dà)X	"(s)he gives it to him"
(gli piace)X	(gli piace)X	"it's liked by him"

51. Now here are the five items you have had with /LY/. Repeat carefully, remembering the backward tongue movement of frame No. 40.

(l'Emilia)X	(l'Emilia)X
(l'Italia)X	(l'Italia)X
(l'ɔlio)X	(l'ɔlio)X
(εlio)X	(εlio)X
(liεto)X	(liεto)X

52. Now repeat the following five items, all with /Ľ/. Remember that /Ĺ/ is strongly pronounced, and that you should start the sound by keeping the front part of the tongue *away* from the upper front teeth.

(le miglia)X   (le miglia)X
(li taglia)X   (li taglia)X
(l'ɔglio)X   (l'ɔglio)X
(glielo dà)X   (glielo dà)
(gli piace)X   (gli piace)X

53. Here are the ten items from frames No. 51 and No. 52 presented in contrast. Repeat each one carefully.

(l'Emilia)X   (le miglia)X
(l'Italia)X   (li taglia)X
(l'ɔlio)X   (l'ɔglio)X
(ɛlio)X   (glielo da)X
(liɛto)X   (gli piace)X

*54. Now here are the same ten items presented in random order. Pronounce each one as you hear it, and write the item correctly in the space provided.

(1) _____
(2) _____
(3) _____
(4) _____
(5) _____
(6) _____
(7) _____
(8) _____
(9) _____
(10) _____

55. In the preceding frame you should have written *gli* only for numbers (2), (3), (5), (8), and (10).

56. Here are several utterances to learn. Listen and repeat.

(nome)X   (nome)X   "name, given name"
(cognome)X   (cognome)X   "surname, last name"
(none e cognome)X   (nome e cognome)X   "full name, first name and last
                                          name"
the Florentine pronunciation of: (pôsto)X
the Roman pronunciation of: (pôsto)X   "place"
(maggio)X   (maggio)X   "May"
(luglio)X   (luglio)X   "July"
(agosto)X   (agosto)X   "August"

the Florentine pronunciation of: (Bolôgna)X
Roman pronunciation of: (Bolôgna)X   "Bologna" (city in Northern Italy)

(Paglia)X   (Paglia)X ⎫
(Segni)X   (Segni)X ⎬ Italian surnames
(Vegli)X   (Vegli)X ⎭

(Giulio)X   (Giulio)X ⎫
(Emilio)X   (Emilio)X ⎭ (masculine given names)

(Giulia)X   (Giulia)X ⎫
(Emilia)X   (Emilia)X ⎭ (feminine given names)

* * * * *

*57. Observe the following model.

    S: Chi è?
    R: è Bianca B—.

You will now be asked the question *Chi è?* Answer each time by using the name given. Your response will be confirmed each time. Remember that a consonant immediately following è is normally strongly pronounced.

(1) Bianca B— ⎫
(2) ɛlio —   ⎪
(3) Lavinia L— ⎬ as in frame No. 35.
(4) Dina D—   ⎪
(5) Nina N—   ⎪
(6) Sɔnia S—   ⎭

(7) Giunio Segni
(8) Giulio Paglia
(9) Giulia Paglia
(10) Emilio Vegli
(11) Emilia Segni

NOTE: If you had trouble recalling the first six names, review this drill until you master it.

*58. Observe the following model.
    S: Nome e cognome.
    R: Nome. Bianca
       Cognome: B—

Use the full names each time as they appear in the drill of frame No. 57. Your response will be confirmed each time.

*59. Observe the following model.

>   S: Che cɔs'è? (pointing to a map of Italy)
>   R: è l'Italia. "It's Italy."

Imagine that you are looking at a rough drawing of the map of Italy. You will be asked questions as in the model above. Give a complete response as in the model, in accordance with the cue given. Your response will be confirmed each time. Remember that a consonant immediately following *è* is normally strongly pronounced.

>   (1) (pointing to Italy)
>   (2) (pointing to the region of Campania)
>   (3) (pointing to the region of Emilia)
>   (4) (pointing to Bologna)
>   (5) (pointing to the Oglio affluent of the Po River)

*60. Observe the following model.

>   S: Che cɔs'è "Bianca"?   "What is 'Bianca'?"
>   R: "Bianca" è un nome.   "'Bianca' is a name."

You will be asked twenty questions as in the model above. Give a complete response patterned after the model, but using the word *nome, cognome, pôsto,* or *mese* as the case may be. Your response will be confirmed each time.

(1) Che cɔs'è "Ɛlio"?	(11) ...."Giulia"?
(2) ...."Segni"?	(12) ...."Paglia"?
(3) ...."l'Italia"?	(13) ...."Bolôgna"?
(4) ...."giugno"?	(14) ...."Colombo"?
(5) ...."Giunio"?	(15) ...."Maggio"?
(6) ...."la Campania"?	(16) ...."Emilia"?
(7) ...."luglio"?	(17) ...."Giulio"?
(8) ...."Augusto"?	(18) ...."l'Emilia"?
(9) ...."agosto"?	(19) ...."Augusta"?
(10) ...."Emilio"?	(20) ...."Vegli"?

*61. Study the following model.

>   S: Che cɔsa fa?   "What is (s)he doing?"
>   R: Chiama.   "(S)he's calling."
>   S: Chi chiama?   "Who(m) is (s)he calling?"
>   R: Chiama Bianca.   "(S)he's calling Bianca."
>   S: Bianca chi?   "Bianca who?"
>   R: Bianca B—.   "Bianca B—."

You will now be asked questions as in the model. A space is provided after each question for your response. Answer as in the model, using the names given below. The individual responses will be confirmed each time.

(1) Che cosa fa? - Chi chiama?	– Bianca chi?	Bianca B—
(2)............	....	– Ɛlio chi?	Ɛlio—
(3)............	....	– Lavinia chi?	Lavinia L—
(4)............	....	– Dina chi?	Dina D—
(5)............	....	– Nina chi?	Nina N—
(6)............	....	– Sonia chi?	Sonia S—
(7)............	....	– Giunio chi?	Giunio Segni
(8)............	....	– Giulio chi?	Giulio Paglia
(9)............	....	– Giulia chi?	Giulia Paglia
(10)............	....	– Emilio chi?	Emilio Vegli
(11)............	....	– Emilia chi?	Emilia Segni

*62. Study the following model.

S: Che cosa fa?	"What is (s)he doing?"
R: Sôgna.	"(S)he's dreaming."
S: Che cosa sôgna?	"What is (s)he dreaming about?"
R: Sôgna l'Italia.	"(s)he's dreaming about Italy."

You will now be asked questions as above. A space is provided after each question for your response. Answer as in the model, using the items given below. The individual responses will be confirmed each time.

(1) l'Italia
(2) Bolôgna
(3) la Campania
(4) la campagna
(5) la vigna
(6) l'olio
(7) giugno (name of month)
(8) Giunio (personal name)
(9) agosto (name of month)
(10) Augusto (personal name)

*63. Study the following question-answer pairs.

      S: Che cɔsa fa?   R: Chiama.
      S: Che cɔsa fa?   R: Sôgna.
      S: Che cɔsa fa?   R: Non fa niεnte.*

*Notice that like *mai* "never," the word *niεnte* "nothing" occurs in conjunction
with *non*.

Thus: *Non c'è mai.*   "(S)he's never around."
                          "(S)he's not ever around."

Non fa *niεnte.*   "(S)he's doing nothing."
                         "(S)he's not doing anything."

NOTE: A consonant immediately following *fa* is normally strongly pronounced. Thus, *niεnte* begins with a strongly pronounced /N/ here.

You will be asked questions as above. Each time give one of the responses on the
right, according to the cue given. Your response will be confirmed each time.

      (1) (looking at a man calling someone)
      (2) (looking at a man dreaming)
      (3) (looking at a man doing nothing)
      (4) (looking at a woman calling someone)
      (5) (looking at a girl not doing anything)
      (6) (looking at a boy dreaming)
      (7) (looking at a girl dreaming)
      (8) (looking at a woman not doing anything)
      (9) (looking at a boy not doing anything)
    (10) (looking at a man calling someone)

64. Study the following model.

      S: Gli piace l'Italia?**   "Does he like Italy?"
      R: Sì, gli piace.   "Yes, he likes it. "
          (or)
      Nɔ, non gli piace.   "No, he doesn't like it."

** NOTE: Think or *gli piace* as a unit similar in force to "(it) is liked by him."
Therefore,

    Gli piace l'Italia?   corresponds closely to "Is Italy liked by him?"
    Sì, gli piace.   corresponds closely to "Yes, it is liked by him."
    Nɔ, non gli piace.   corresponds closely to "No, it is not liked by him."

You will now be asked questions as in the model above. Answer each time according to the cue given. Your response will be confirmed each time.

Question	Answer
(1) Gli piace l'Italia?	Sì
(2) ....Bianca B—?	Sì
(3) ....la campagna?	Nɔ
(4) ....Bolôgna?	Nɔ
(5) ....Giulia?	Sì
(6) ....Giulio?	Nɔ
(7) ....la vigna?	Nɔ
(8) ....Lavinia?	Sì
(9) ....Augusta?	Sì
(10) ....la Campania?	Nɔ

*65. Study the following model.

S: (student): Che cɔsa fa?	"What is he doing?"
R: Sôgna l'Italia.	"He's dreaming of Italy."
S: Gli piace l'Italia?	"Does he like Italy?"
R: Sì, gli piace l'talia.	"Yes, he likes Italy."

This time you are to initiate the conversation by asking the first question of the model. Continue the conversation as in the model. Space is provided for your two questions whieh will be confirmed each time.

(1) Sôgna l'Italia.	- Sì, gli piace l'Italia.
(2)..............Dina D—	- ....Dina D— .
(3)..............Emilia Segni.	- ....Emilia Segni.
(4)..............Bolôgna.	- ....Bolôgna.
(5)..............Sɔnia.	- ....Sɔnia.
(6)..............maggio.	- ....maggio.
(7)..............giugno.	- ....giugno.
(8)..............luglio.	- ....luglio.
(9)..............agosto.	- ....agosto.
(10)..............Augusta.	- ....Augusta.

*66. Study the following models.

    S: Ɛlio Ɛ— chiama (garbled).   "Elio E— is calling (garbled)."
    R–S: Chi chiama Ɛlio Ɛ—.   "Who(m) is Ɛlio calling?"
    R: Ɛlio Ɛ— chiama Bianca B—. "Elio E— is calling Bianca B—."
            (or)
    S: (garbled) chiama Bianca B—. "(garbled) is calling Bianca B—."
    R – S: Chi chiama Bianca B—? "Who is calling Bianca B—?"
    R: Ɛlio Ɛ— chiama Bianca B—. "Elio E— is calling Bianca B—."

You will hear a statement which is partially garbled, followed by a space. In this space ask a *chi* "who/whom"question about the garbled portion as in one of the models above. Your question will be confirmed and followed by a final response. Note that *chi* may have the force of "who" or "whom" depending on context.

(1) Lavinia L— chiama (garbled).
    ....Colomba.
(2) (garbled) chiama Amanda.
    Emilia Segni chiama Amanda.
(3) Dina D—sôgna (garbled).
    Dina D—sôgna Giulio Paglia.
(4) (garbled) sôgna Sɔnia S—.
    Emilio Vegli sôgna Sɔnia S—.
(5) (garbled) non fa niɛnte.
    Bianca B— non fa niɛnte.
(6) (garbled) non c'è.
    L'haïtiana non c'è.
(7) È (garbled).
    È Pia.
(8) Tina chiama (garbled).
    Tina chiama Lɔla.

(9) (garbled) sôgna Luca.
    Elsa sôgna Luca.
(10) (garbled) non fa mai niɛnte.
    Augusta non fa mai niɛnte.
(11) C'è (garbled) lì.
    C'è Ɛva lì.
(12) Augusto chiama (garbled).
    Augusto chiama Nina N—.
(13) (garbled) sôgna l'Italia.
    Dafne sôgna l'Italia.
(14) È (garbled)
    È Samuɛle.
(15) Non c'è mai (garbled).
    Non c'è mai Lia.

TEST A

(answers not recorded)

You will hear 20 utterances, each said twice. For each utterance put a check in
the appropriate column, according to what you hear in the utterance.

	/NY/	/Ň/
1) (Sɔnia)		
2) (Giunio)		
3) (Segni)		
4) (la Campania)		
5) (niɛnte)		
6) (la vigna)		
7) (gnɔmo)		
8) (sôgna)		
9) (la campagna)		
10) (Sɔnia)		

	/LY/	/Ľ/
11) (Paglia)		
12) (glielo dà)		
13) (l'ɔlio)		
14) (Vegli)		
15) (l'Emilia)		
16) (le miglia)		
17) (gli piace)		
18) (li taglia)		
19) (liɛto)		
20) (voliamo)		

TEST B

(answers not recorded)

You will hear 25 English utterances, each said twice. For each utterance write "yes" or "no" according to whether you hear a *tongue flap* or not.

1) Etta	10) ghetto	18) Jody
2) auto	11) attack	19) eighty
3) Betty	12) get it	20) letter
4) lady	13) steady	21) berry
5) Eddie	14) seedy	22) let it
6) Ada	15) city	23) Sara
7) Sadie	16) get out	24) ought to
8) quota	17) Nato	25) oughta
9) quota		

• **End of Tape 4B** •

TEST C

(not recorded)

Translate the following thoughts into Italian as best you can by using *only* what has been presented so far.

1) Full name.

_____ Nome é cognome _____

2) What is he doing?

_____ Che cosa fa. _____

3) He's dreaming of Italy.

_____ sogna l'Italia _____

4) He's not doing anything there.

_____ non fa niente li _____

5) He doesn't like Italy.

_____ No, non gli piace l'Italia _____

6) He doesn't like anything over there.

_____ non gli piace niente li _____

7) He likes Bianca.

_____ gli piace Bianca _____

8) Bologna doesn't appeal to him.

_____ non gli piace Bologna _____

9) What is she dreaming about?

_____ Che sogna fa cosa sogna _____

10) Nothing interests him.

no gli piace niente

11) She never calls.

non chiama mai

12) She's never in.

non c'è mai

13) There's nothing here.

non c'è niente qui

14) It's nothing.

non è niente

15) She's calling Giunio.

chiama Giunio

16) It's May.

è Maggio

17) He never dreams.

non sogna mai

18) He never dreams of the Haitian girl.

non sogna mai / dell'haitiana

19) He never dreams of anything.

non sogna mai niente

20) He never does anything.

non fa mai niente

21) Who(m) is Luca calling?

chi chiama Luca?

22) Who is calling Gina?

chi chiama Gina

23) Who is not dreaming about Italy?

chi sogna non sogna l'Italia

24) Who is never doing anything here?

chi non fa mai niente qui

25) Who is never there?

chi non c'è mai lì?

TEST A ANSWERS

	/NY/	/Ň/		/LY/	/L̆/
1)	X		11)		X
2)	X		12)		X
3)		X	13)	X	
4)	X		14)		X
5)	X		15)	X	
6)		X	16)		X
7)		X	17)		X
8)			18)		X
9)		X	19)	X	
10)	X		20)	X	

TEST B ANSWERS

1) yes	6) yes	11) no	16) yes	21) no
2) yes	7) no	12) yes	17) no	22) yes
3) no	8) yes	13) yes	18) no	23) no
4) no	9) no	14) yes	19) yes	24) no
5) yes	10) yes	15) yes	20) no	25) yes

TEST C ANSWERS

1) Nome e cognome.
2) Che cɔsa fa?
3) Sôgna l'Italia.
4) Non fa niɛnte lì.
5) Non gli piace l'Italia.
6) Non gli piace niɛnte lì.
7) Gli piace Bianca.
8) Non gli piace Bolôgna.
9) Che cɔsa sôgna?
10) Non gli piace niɛnte.
11) Non chiama mai.
12) Non c'è mai.
13) Non c'è niɛnte qui.

14) Non è niɛnte.
15) Chiama Giunio.
16) È maggio.
17) Non sôgna mai.
18) Non sôgna mai l'haïtiana.
19) Non sôgna mai niɛnte.
20) Non fa mai niɛnte.
21) Chi chiama Luca?
22) Chi chiama Gina?
23) Chi non sôgna l'Italia?
24) Chi non fa mai niɛnte qui?
25) Chi non c'è mai lì?

RECAPITULATION (Units 11–15)

Sound-Types

sound-types	written symbols	as in:	unit
VOWELS			
No. 4 (or) /O/ (closed, rounded)	o	Col<u>o</u>mba	11
No. 8 (or) /E/ (closed, unrounded)	e	F<u>ede</u>	12
CONSONANTS AND SOUND COMBINATIONS			
/B/	b	<u>b</u>am<u>b</u>ino	14
/F/	f	ele<u>f</u>ante	14
/G/	(see Unit 18)	gɔlf	14
/K/	(see Unit 18)	<u>ch</u>e, <u>chi</u>, <u>c</u>ane	14
/Ľ/	{ gl [before i]	<u>gl</u>i piace	15
	{ gli [elsewhere]	vo<u>gli</u>amo	15
/LY/	li	vo<u>li</u>amo	15
/M/	{ m	<u>m</u>ese	14
	{ n	u<u>n</u> pane	
/N/	n	ca<u>n</u>e	14
/Ň/	gn	sô<u>gn</u>a	15
/NY/	ni	Sɔ<u>ni</u>a	15
/P/	p	<u>p</u>ane	14
/S/	s	ga<u>s</u>, <u>s</u>pia, [Tuscan] na<u>s</u>o	13
/$/	s	<u>s</u>buca, [Tuscan] va<u>s</u>o	13
/V/	v	<u>v</u>ino	14

Some Spelling Features to Remember (Units 11 and 12)

The symbol ô (as in *vôga*) is used in these units to indicate a vowel that is likely to be pronounced /O/ by a Florentine, but /ɔ/ by a Roman.

The symbol ŏ (as in *intŏnso*) is used in these units to indicate a vowel that is likely to be pronounced /ɔ/ by a Florentine, but /O/ by a Roman.

The symbol ê (as in *Êlba*) is used in these units to indicate a vowel that is likely to be pronounced /E/ by a Florentine, but /ɛ/ by a Roman.

The symbol ĕ (as in *tĕmpio*) is used in these units to indicate a vowel that is likely to be pronounced /ɛ/ by a Florentine, but /E/ by a Roman.

"Safe Pact" Consonants (Unit 13)

"Safe pact" consonants are the Italian sounds that are the closest to those sounds represented by the consonant letters in the phrase SAFE PACT.

The Letter s (Unit 13)

The letter *s* in Italian always represents /$/ before consonants other than the SAFE PACT consonants. In other cases, students may always use /S/ but are advised to use /$/ for the single -*s*- between vowel letters within a word.

The Letter n (Unit 14)

The letter *n* in Italian represents a NASAL sound-type (i.e., it involves the air escaping through the nose) that differs according to whatever follows it.

> The KEG nasal: the variation of /N/ heard before /K/ and /G/.
> The FIVE nasal: the variation of /N/ heard before /F/ and /V/.
> The BUMP nasal: the nasal /M/ heard before /B/, /M/ and /P/.

The Tongue Flap (Unit 15)

The TONGUE FLAP is the consonant sound-type heard in colloquial American English within the words "Betty" and "Eddie" when these two words rhyme.

Italian Given Names (Units 11 and 12)

Most feminine given names in Italian end in /A/. Some exceptions are: Clɛo, Saffo, Nina, Adɛle. Most masculine given names in Italian end in /O/. Some exceptions are: *Cɔla, Nicɔla, Luca, Noè, Giovanni, Adone.*

Cognates (Unit 14)

Cognates are words that have the same origin, like the Italian *sofà* and the English "sofa."

Some Useful Constructions (Unit 15)

non...mai	"not...ever."
Non c'è mai.	"(S)he is { never around." / not ever around."

non.......niente	"not.........anything."
Non fa niente.	"(S)he is $\begin{cases} \text{doing nothing."} \\ \text{not doing anything."} \end{cases}$
gli piace	"It is liked by him" or "he likes it"
Gli piace l'Italia?	"Is Italy liked by him?" or
	"Does he like Italy?"
Chi chiama Elio?	$\begin{cases} \text{"Who is calling Elio?"} \\ \text{"Who(m) is Elio calling?"} \end{cases}$

IDENTIFICATION SENTENCES (Unit 13)

Affirmative Statements	Verification Questions	Negative Statements	Yes-No Questions	Information Questions
È un sofà. "It's a sofa."	*È un sofà, nɔ?* "It's a sofa, isn't it?"	*Non è un sofà.* "It's not a sofa."	*(Non) è un sofà?* "Is(n't) it a sofa?"	*Che? Cɔsa? Che cɔsa?* "What?"
			(Non) è un sofà questo? "Is(n't) this a sofa?"	*Che cɔs'è?* "What is it?"
				Che cɔs'è questo? "What is this?"

IDENTIFICATION - LOCATION SENTENCES   (Unit 13–14)

Affirmative Statements	Verification Questions	Negative Statements	Yes-No Questions	Information Questions
C'è un sofà lì. "There's a sofa there." Lì c'è un sofà.	C'è un sofà lì, nɔ? "There's a sofa there, isn't there?" Lì c'è un sofà, nɔ?	Non c'è un sofà lì. "There isn't a sofa there." Lì non c'è un sofà.	(Non) c'è un sofà lì? "Is(n't) there a sofa there?" Lì (non) c'è un sofà?	Che / Cosa / Che cosa } c'è lì? "What is there?" Lì { che / cosa / che cosa } c'è?
			(Non) c'è mai un sofà lì? "Is(n't) there ever a sofa there?" Lì (non) c'è mai un sofà?	Che / Cosa / Che cosa } non c'è (mai) lì? "What isn't (ever) there?"

UNIT 16

1. Repeat the following sentence.

   Come sta?   (2)

2. What you have just heard is the question Italians normally ask when inquiring about one's health. Thus, it is an equivalent of the English, "How is he?" or "How is she?"

3. Repeat again, this time looking at the spelling.

   (Come sta?)X   (Come sta?)X

4. A name may be added to this phrase to ask about a particular individual. Thus, for example, "How is Amanda?" may be expressed as:

   (Come sta Amanda?)X   (Come sta Amanda?)X

5. A consonant immediately following *sta* is normally strongly pronounced. Therefore, the /B/ in the following question is strongly pronounced.

   (Come sta Bianca?)X   (Come sta Blanca?)X

6. A common short answer to this question is the word for "fine." Repeat.

   (Bɛne.)X   (Bɛne.)X   (Bɛne.)X

7. Another possible short answer is the word for "fairly well" or "pretty well" Repeat.

   (Benino.)X   (Benino.)X   (Benino.)X

8. At times Italians answer by using a phrase that corresponds closely to the English "so so." Repeat.

   (Così così.)X   (Così così.)X   (Così così.)x

9. If one is not feeling well, the opposite of *bene* may be used as an equivalent of "bad" or "ill" Repeat.

   (Male.)X   (Male.)X   (Male.)X

10. A fifth possible answer is one that corresponds to the English "not bad" or "one can't complain." Repeat.

    (Non c'ɛ male.)X   (Non c'ɛ male.)X   (Non c'ɛ male.)X

11. One way to remember some of these English equivalents is to notice that:

    a) both *bene* and "fine" are four-letter words"

    b) both *così così* and "so so" are phrases consisting of a repeated item;

    c) both *non c'è male* and "not bad" or "one can't complain" contain a negative (*non* or "not").

*12. Look at the following table:

bene	benino	così così	non c'è male
Dafne	Fede	Dante	Leone
Cice	Clɔe	Felice	Bela
Elsa	Adɛle	Adone	Cecè

You will now be asked a question about the health of the different people mentioned above. Give a short answer, according to the column in which each name appears. Your response will be confirmed each time.
For example:

    S: Come sta Felice?
    R: Così così.

Questions

(1) Come sta Dafne?	(7) Come sta Cice?
(2) Come sta Adone?	(8) Come sta Fede?
(3) Come sta Bela?	(9) Come sta Elsa?
(4) Come sta Clɔe?	(10) Come sta Cecè?
(5) Come sta Dante?	(11) Come sta Adɛle?
(6) Come sta Leone?	(12) Come sta Felice?

* * * * *

13. The phrase *Come sta?* may be answered with a longer statement containing the word *sta*. This is possible with the four responses given in frames No. 6 through No. 9, but not with *Non c'è male*.
    Thus:

(Sta bɛne.)X	"(S)he is fine."
(Sta benino.)X	"(S)he is fairly well."
(Sta così così.)X	"(S)he is so so."
(Sta male.)X	"(S)he is ill."

*14. Now again using the table and the questions of frame No. 12, answer the *come sta*............ question by using *sta* wherever possible. Your response will be confirmed each time.

15. Negative answers simply use *non* as follows:

    (Non sta bɛne.)X   "(S)he is not feeling well"
    (Non sta molto bɛne.)X   "(S)he is not feeling very well."

*16. How would you ask, "Isn't he feeling well?" in Italian?

*17. Putting the name at the end of the question, how would you ask, "Isn't Luca feeling well?" in Italian?

*18. How then, would you ask, "Is Luca feeling well?" in Italian?

19. Remember that regardless of whether the question 18 phrased negatively (as in frame No. 17) or affirmatively (as in frame No. 18), the normal answer is either:

    Sì, sta bɛne.
         (or)
    Nɔ, non sta bɛne. (See Unit 8, frames 28–36)

20. Notice that in the sentences you just heard, the word *bɛne* is stressed in the affirmative response, but the word *sta* is stressed in the negative response. Listen again and repeat.

    (Sì, sta bɛne.)X   (Nɔ, non sta bɛne.)X

*21. Now once more using the table of frame No. 12, answer the *Sta.......* question affirmatively for any name mentioned in frame No. 12, but negatively for any name *not* mentioned there. Your response will be confimed each time.

Questions

(1) Sta bɛne Adɛle?	(11) Sta bɛne Fabio?
(2) Sta bɛne Aldo?	(12) Sta bɛne Dante?
(3) Sta bɛne Antɔnio?	(13) Sta bɛne Fausto?
(4) Sta bɛne Adone?	(14) Sta bɛne Flavio?
(5) Sta bɛne Augusto?	(15) Sta bɛne Gino?
(6) Sta bɛne Cice?	(16) Sta bɛne Elsa?
(7) Sta bɛne Dino?	(17) Sta bɛne Fede?
(8) Sta bɛne Clɔe?	(18) Sta bɛne Giovanni?
(9) Sta bɛne Dafne?	(19) Sta bɛne Lɛo?
(10) Sta bɛne Donato?	(20) Sta bɛne Felice?

* * * * *

22. A long answer using *sta* may have a name *precede* the whole phrase or *follow* it.

23. If the name precedes, the phrase itself may involve a STRESS-DROP (CASUAL) intonation or a POST-STRESS-DROP (POTENTIALLY EMPHATIC) intonation.

   Thus: (casual)

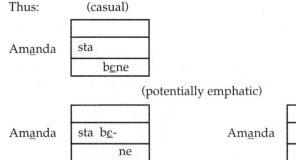

24. Repeat the following sentences that begin with a name, imitating the stress and intonation as closely as possible.

   (Amanda sta bɛne.)X
   (Luca sta benino.)X
   (Tina sta così così.)X
   (Gino sta male.)X
   (Augusta non sta molto bɛne.)X

25. If the name follows, again the phrase itself may involve a STRESS-DROP intonation or a POST-STRESS-DROP intonation, but what is characteristic about the intonation of *this* sentence is that any unstressed syllables preceding or following the last stress are on the same pitch level as the last stress.

   Thus:

Sta bɛ-

ne Amanda

26. Now repeat the following sentences, all of which end with a name. Imitate the stress and intonation as closely as possible.

(Sta bene Amanda.)X
(Sta benino Luca.)X
(Sta così così Tina.)X
(Sta male Gino.)X
(Non sta bene Bianca.)X
(Non sta molto bene Augusta.)X

*27. You will now be asked questions about the health of the six people just mentioned. Respond using the sentences of frame No. 24, but begin your answer with *Sì* or *No* whenever you are answering a YES-NO question. Your response will be confirmed each time.

(1) Sta bene Amanda?   (6) Come sta Tina?
(2) Come sta Bianca?   (7) Sta bene Augusta?
(3) Come sta Luca?   (8) Non sta molto bene Amanda?
(4) Non sta molto bene Augusta?   (9) Sta benino Luca?
(5) Sta benino Gino?   (10) Non sta bene Bianca?

*28. Proceed as in the preceding frame, but this time respond using the sentences of frame No. 26. Remember to begin your answer with *Sì* or *No* whenever you answer a YES-NO question. Your response will be confirmed each time.

(1) Sta così così Tina?   (6) Non sta benino Luca?
(2) Come sta Gino?   (7) Come sta Tina?
(3) Sta bene Bianca?   (8) Non sta bene Gino?
(4) Sta benino Augusta?   (9) Sta male Tina?
(5) Non sta bene Amanda?   (10) Sta così così Tina?

* * * * *

*29. Here are some names you learned in Unit 15. What did we call the sound-type that all of the second names have in common?

Bianca B—
Ɛlio Ɛ—
Lavinia L—
Dina D—
Nina N—
Sɔnia S—

*30. Does the following utterance contain this TONGUE-FLAP?
   "Etta"   (3)

31. The previous utterance may have reminded you of the girl's name "Etta," in English. Listen again and repeat.
   "Etta"   (3)

*32. Does the following contain the TONGUE-FLAP? Repeat.
   "oughta"   (3)

33. The previous utterance may have reminded you of the colloquial English "oughta" as in, "I oughta go." Listen again and repeat.
   "oughta"   (3)

*34. Does the following contain the TONGUE-FLAP? Repeat.
   "Oda"   (3)

35. The previous utterance may have reminded you of the girl's name "Oda" in English. Listen again and repeat.
   "Oda"   (3)

36. The previous utterance is heard in the following Italian word, that also contains /Ň/. Listen and repeat.
   sig.ª   (3)

37. Now repeat the following.
   la sig.ª   (3)

*38. How would you ask, "How is Emilia Segni?" in Italian?

39. Now repeat the following.
   Come sta la sig.ª Segni?   (3)

40. What you have just said is the equivalent of, "How is Mrs. Segni?" Repeat again, making sure that you pronounce the TONGUE-FLAP of frames No. 34 and No. 35.
   (Come sta la sig.ª Segni?)X   (Come sta la sig.ª Segni?)X
   (Come sta la sig.ª Segni?)X

41. Remember that a consonant immediately following sta is strongly pronounced. For example, the /L/ of *la.*
   (Come sta la sig. Segni?)X   (Come sta la sig.aSegni?)X

*42. Does the following contain a TONGUE-FLAP?
   /ÓRI/   (3)

43. The previous utterance may have reminded you of something that rhymes with the boy's name "Jody," in English. Listen again and repeat.
   /ÓRI/   (3)

44. Now change the stress to the second syllable.
    /ORÍ/   (3)

45. Repeat the following.
    /ORÍNA/   (3)

45. Also the following that contains /Ň/.
    sig.*na*   (3)

47. Also the following.
    la sig.*na*   (3)

48. Now the following.
    la sig.*na* Paglia   (3)

49. Now repeat the following
    Come sta la sig.*na* Paglia?   (3)

50. What you have just said is the equivalent of, "How is Miss Paglia?" Repeat again, being careful to pronounce the TONGUE-FLAP.
    (Come sta la sig.na Paglia?)X   (Come sta la sig.na Paglia?)X
    (Come sta la sig.na Paglia?)X

* * * * *

*51. How do you say, "How is Mrs. Segni?" in Italian?

52. Repeat just the last part of the previous Italian utterance beginning with /O/, remembering to pronounce the TONGUE-FLAP.
    /ORASÉŇI/   (3)

53. If now the /A/ that precedes *Segni* is so softly pronounced that a listener hardly hears it, one gets the following utterances still with the TONGUE-FLAP. Repeat.
    /ORSÉŇI/   (3)

54. Repeat the following that contains another /Ň/.
    sig. Segni   (3)

55. Now the following.
    il sig. Segni   (3)

56. Now repeat the following.

    Come sta il sig. Segni?   (3)

57. What you have just said is the equivalent of, "How is Mr. Segni?" Repeat again, being very careful to pronounce the TONGUE-FLAP.

    (Come sta il sig. Segni?)X   (Come sta il sig. Segni?)
    (Come sta il sig. Segni?)X

58. Notice that *sta* plus *il* are combined into one syllable. Repeat.

    (sta il)X   (sta il)X   (sta il)X

* * * * *

59. Now repeat the following sentences.

    (Come sta la sig.[a] Segni?)X　　　(Come sta la sig.[a] Segni?)X
    (Come sta la sig.[na] Paglia?)X　　(Come sta la sig.[na] Paglia?)X
    (Come sta il sig. Segni?)X　　　　(Come sta la sig. Segni?)X

*60. You will now be asked the above questions and others like them. Answer by placing the title and name first in your answer, and by using the cues given below. Your response will be confirmed each time.

Questions	Answers
(1) Come sta il sig. Segni?	bɛne
(2) Come sta la sig.[a] B—?	benino
(3) Come sta il sig. ɛ—?	così così
(4) Come sta la sig.[na] L—?	benino
(5) Come sta la sig.[na] D—?	non sta bɛne
(6) Come sta la sig.[a] Segni?	non sta molto bɛne
(7) Come sta la sig.[a] N—?	bɛne
(8) Come sta il sig. Paglia?	così così
(9) Come sta la sig.[na] Paglia?	non sta molto bɛne
(10) Come sta la sig.[na] S—?	male

* * * * *

61. If one does not know the name, has forgotten it, or simply does not wish to use it, it may be omitted in sentences like those of frame No. 60. In doing so, however, the man's title occurs with a final /E/ and has the force of the English "gentleman." Repeat the following question-answer pairs.

(Come sta la sig.^a?)X   (La sig.^a sta bɛne.)X
(Come sta la sig.^{na}?)X   (La sig. ^{na} sta bɛne.)X
(Come sta il sig.?)X   (Il sig. sta bɛne.)X

* * * * *

*62. You will now hear a short paragraph in Italian, read twice. The paragraph
is followed by ten questions. In the spaces below write out complete
answers to each question, making the answers longer than just one word.
After the ten questions have been read, you will hear the answers that you
should have written. Check yourself.

è giugno. Il sig. ɛ—sôgna l'Italia.
(Gli piace l'Italia.)   (2)
Lì c'è la sig.^{na} B—.

(1) è giugno?

_____Sì, è giugno_____

(2) Non è luglio?

_____No, non è luglio_____

(3) Che cɔsa fa il sig. ɛ—?

_____Sogna l'Italia_____

(4) Che cɔsa sôgna?

_____Sogna l'Italia_____

(5) Chi sôgna l'Italia?

_____Il sig E - sogna l'Italia_____

(6) Sôgna Washington il sig. ɛ—?

_____No, non sogna Washington_____

(7) Gli piace l'Italia?

_____Sì, gli piace l'Italia_____

(8) Chi c'è lì?

_____Lì c'è sogna Betty_____

(9) Lì c'è la sig.^a B—?

_____No, lì c'è la sig.^{na} Betty_____

(10) è lì la sig.^{na} B—?

_____Sì, è lì_____

TEST A

(answers not recorded)

One word in each of the following sentences begins with a strongly pronounced consonant. Underline each consonant letter that represents such a sound.

1) Chi sôgna la campagna?
2) Qui c'è il sig. Segni.
3) C'è Bianca lì?
4) È Luca, nɔ?
5) Lì c'è un vaso.
6) Sì, c'è un ospedale qui.
7) Nɔ, non c'è un cestino qui.
8) Che cɔsa fa il sig. Paglia?
9) Non fa mai niɛnte.
10) La sig.ᵃ Segni non sta bɛne.

TEST B

(answers not recorded)

You will hear a short paragraph in Italian, read twice. The paragraph is followed by twelve questions. In the spaces below write out complete answers to each question, making the answers longer than just one word. To test your understanding of spoken Italian, cover the paragraph and just listen. Then try to answer the questions.

> Qui c'è un italiano.   Nome: Giulio, cognome: Paglia.
> Non sta molto bene.
>
> Chiama Emilio Segni, un poeta. - C'è Emilio? - No,
> Emilio non c'è.

(2)

1) Chi c'è qui?
   ~~Qui Giulio Paglia~~ C'è un italiano qui

2) Chi è?
   Giulia Paglia

3) Come sta il sig. Paglia?
   Il SP non sta molto bene

4) Non sta bene?
   No, non sta molto bene

5) Chi non sta molto bene?
   Il sig Paglia non sta molto bene

6) Che cosa fa il sig. Paglia?
   Il SP chiama E-

7) Chi chiama il sig. Paglia?

8) Chi è Emilio Segni?
   ES è un Poeta

9) Chiama un poeta il sig. Paglia?

10) C'è Emilio Segni?

11) Non c'è il sig. Segni?

12) Chi non c'è?

TEST C

(not recorded)

Translate the following thoughts into Italian as best you can by using *only* what has been presented so far.

1) How is Mr. Jones feeling?

Come sta il sig Jones

2) Doesn't he feel very well?

non sta molto Bene

3) Miss Brown is so so. (referring to health)

Sig Brown sta cosi cosi

4) Is Amanda all right?

Sta Bene Amanda

5) One can't complain.

non c'è male

6) She's feeling pretty well, isn't she?

Sta Beneno, eo

7) How is Mrs. Paglia coming along? (asked of a patient in the hospital)

come sta sig a Paglia

8) The gentleman isn't well.

Il sig non sta Bene ?

9) What's the young lady's health situation?

Come sta la sign

10) The lady is ill, isn't she?

La sig sta male, no

TEST A   ANSWERS

1) Chi sôgna la campagna?
2) Qui c'è is sig. Segni.
3) C'è Bianca lì?
4) È Luca, nɔ?
5) Lì c'è un vaso.
6) Sì, c'è un ospedale qui.
7) Nɔ, non c'è un cestino qui.
8) Che cɔsa fa il sig. Paglia?
9) Non fa mai niente.
10) La sig.ª Segni non sta bɛne.

TEST B   ANSWERS

1) Qui c'è un italiano. (or) C'è un italiano qui.
2) È Giulio Paglia.
3) (Il sig. Paglia) non sta molto bɛne.
4) Nɔ, non sta (molto) bɛne.
5) Il sig. Paglia non sta molto bɛne. (or) Non sta molto bɛne il sig. Paglia.
6) (Il sig. Paglia) chiama Emilio Segni.
7) (Il sig. Paglia) chiama Emilio Segni.
8) (Emilio Segni) è un poɛta.
9) Sì, (il sig. Paglia) chiama un poɛta.
10) Nɔ, (Emilio Segni) non c'è. (or) Nɔ, non c'è (Emilio Segni).
11) Nɔ, (il sig. Segni) non c'è. (or) Nɔ, non c'è (il sig. Segni).
12) Il sig. Segni non c'è. (or) Non c'è il sig. Segni.

TEST C   ANSWERS

1) Come sta il sig. Jones?
2) Non sta molto bɛne?
3) La sig.na Brown sta così così.
4) Sta bɛne Amanda?
5) Non c'è male.
6) Sta benino, nɔ?
7) Come sta la sig.a Paglia?
8) Il sig. non sta bɛne.
9) Come sta la sig.na?
10) La sig.a sta male, nɔ?

UNIT 17

*1. How do you say, "How is (s)he?" in Italian?

*2. How do you say, "(S)he is fine" in Italian?

3. Notice that in both the question and the answer referring to the health of a third person, the same word *sta* occurs. Repeat.
   (Come sta?)X   –   (Sta bɛne.)X

4. In formal situations in Italian the question *Come sta?* may be used to refer to a person being addressed. Thus, it is also an equivalent of, "How are you?" said to one person.

* * * * *

5. Study the following question-answer pair:
   Come sta? "How are you?"   –   *Stɔ bɛne.* "I'm fine."

*6. Is *sta* found in the answer just given?

*7. What is in the answer in place of *sta?*

8. The variation in the forms *sta* and *stɔ* is a type of variation that is very common in Italian. It is a variation that corresponds to a difference in the person being referred to—*sta* refers to either the person being addressed ("you") or a third person ("he" or "she"), whereas *stɔ* refers only to the person saying *stɔ* ("I"). This type of variation is *one* of the defining characteristics of a large class of words called VERBS.

9. A verb form like *sta* or *stɔ* that shows limitations regarding the person being referred to is called a FINITE VERB.

10. It is important to note that if you are asked a question containing a verb form that refers only to a third person, the same verb form may be repeated unchanged in your answer.

Thus:

Questions		Answers
Come *sta* Amanda?	–	*Sta* bɛne.
Sta bɛne il sig. Segni?	–	Sì, *sta* bɛne.

11. However, a change is required in your answer whenever the verb form in the question refers to the person being addressed ("you") or the person speaking ("I").

Thus:

Questions		Answers
Come *sta?* "How are you?"	–	*Stɔ* bɛne.
Stɔ bɛne? "Am I well?"	–	Sì, *sta* bɛne.

12. Just as a consonant immediately following the word *sta* is strongly pronounced, so a consonant immediately following the word *stɔ* is normally strongly pronounced. Repeat the following, pronouncing a very strong /B/.

(Come sta?)X   –   (Stɔ bɛne.)X

* * * * *

*13. How do you say, "How is Mrs. Segni?" in Italian?

*14. How many words are in the Italian question of frame No. 13?

15. Now listen to the equivalent of, "How are you, Mrs. Segni?"

Come sta, sig.ᵃ Segni? (2)

*16. How many words are in the Italian question of frame No. 15?

17. In referring to a person being addressed directly, the *la* or the *il* that normally precedes a title is dropped. Compare the two lists of sentences that follow. In the "A" group one is talking *about* someones in the "B" group one is referring to the person being addressed.

A	B
(Come sta la sig.ᵃ Segni?)X	(Come sta, sig.ᵃ Segni?)X
(Come sta la sig.ⁿᵃ Paglia?)X	(Come sta, sig.ⁿᵃ Paglia?)X
(Come sta il sig. Segni?)X	(Come sta, sig. Segni?)X
(Sta bɛne il sig. Segni?)X	(Sta bɛne, sig. Segni?)X
(Come sta la sigᵃ?)X	(Come sta, sig.ᵃ?)X
(Sta bɛne la sig.ⁿᵃ?)X	(Sta bɛne, sig.ⁿᵃ?)X
(Non sta bɛne il sig?)X	(Non sta bɛne, sig.?)X
(Il sig. Segni sta bɛne?)X	(Sig. Segni, sta bɛne?)X

*18. How do you say, "How is the gentleman?" in Italian?

*19. How do you say, "How are you, sir?"

20. In referring to a woman it is normal to omit the name, as for example in: *Come sta, sig.ᵃ?* However, a man's last name, if known, should be used unless one wishes to give the force of a very formal "sir" or "the gentle-man," as in frames No. 18 and No. 19.

* * * * *

21. Listen carefully to the following.
"get Ahts"   ⎫
   (or)   ⎬   (3)
"Gidd Ahts" ⎭

*22. If someone's last name were "Ahts," which of the following ((a) or (b)) does this utterance sound like to you? Repeat it.
"get Ahts"   ⎫
   (or)   ⎬ (3)
"Gidd Ahts" ⎭
          (a) "get Ahts"
          (b) "Gidd Ahts"

23. Actually, either answer (a) or (b) in the preceding frame is correct since the utterance in question is a rapid pronunciation possible for both (a) and (b). Listen again and repeat.
"get Ahts"   ⎫
   (or)   ⎬ (3)
"Gidd Ahts" ⎭

24. The utterance you have been hearing contains the TONGUE-FLAP found in "Betty" and "Eddie."
"get Ahts"   ⎫
   (or)   ⎬ (3)
"Gidd Ahts" ⎭

25. Now repeat the following.
g———— (3)

26. You have now been given the Italian word for "Thanks" or "Thank you." Repeat carefully, noticing that, like *bene,* this word, too, ends in /E/.
g———— (3)

27. For the time being we will indicate this word as follows:
    (g————)X (g————)X (g————)X

                        * * * * *

28. Now repeat the following.
    e Lɛi?   (3)

29. Now repeat, looking at the actual spelling and noticing that the /L/ is
    strongly pronounced. This is normal for a consonant immediately following
    the word *e*.
    (*e Lɛi?*)X   (*e Lɛi?*)X   (*e Lɛi?*)X

30. Translations for the preceding are:
    "and you?"
    "and how about you?"

31. It is interesting to note that the formal word for "you," *Lɛi*, unlike its
    English counterpart is normally (though not obligatorily) spelled with a
    capital *L*, whereas English always capitalizes the word "I".

                        * * * * *

32. You will now hear a short dialog. Repeat each line, imitating as closely as
    possible. You should review this frame many times until you feel at ease
    with each line. Notice particularly that the word *g———* is said with a
    falling intonation.
    A: Come sta?
    B: Bɛne, g———, e Lɛi?
    A: Non c'è male, g———.

33. Now you are to participate in the preceding conversation; playing the part
    of (B). Answer as in the dialog. A space is provided for your part. You are to
    participate three times.

34. Now you are to play the part of (A), adding to the first line, however, the
    title with or without the name of the person you are addressing, as indicat-
    ed below. Try reading your part during the pauses provided on the tape.
    (1) A: Come sta, sig.[a]?
         B: Bɛne, g———, e Lɛi?
         A: Non c'è male, g———.

(2) A: Come sta, sig.na?
    B: Bεne, g———, e Lεi?
    A: Non c'è male, g———.

(3) A: Come sta, sig. Segni?
    B: Bεne, g———, e Lεi?
    A: Non c'è male, g———.

35. Again proceed as in the previous frame, this time trying not to read your part, but rather be guided by the cues given below.

    (1) sig.a
    (2) sig.na
    (3) sig. Segni

* * * * *

36. Repeat the following, paying special attention to the TONGUE-FLAP.
    /ÓRA/ (3)

37. Now add /NO/.
    /ÓRANO/ (3)

*38. Which of the following ((a), (b), or (c)) does this utterance sound like to you? Repeat it.
    /ÓRANO/ (3)
    (a) "oughta know"
    (b) "owed a 'no'"
    (c) "oda, no"

39. Actually, any of the three answers in the preceding frame is possible since the utterance in question contains the TONGUE-FLAP.
    /ÓRANO/ (3)

40. Now try saying the same thing in two syllables, still making the TONGUE-FLAP.
    /ÓRNO/ (3)

41. Now, thinking of the sounds in the name "Joe," say the following word that rhymes with (   ).
    /ǦÓRNO/ (3)

42. Now put /BWɔN) in front of this word.
    B.G. (3) (the Italian phrase for "good morning")

43. You have now been given the most frequently heard Italian greeting that is exchanged during the daylight hours (morning or afternoon). It is also used as a leave-taking expression very much like its English literal counterpart, "Good day."

B.G. (3) (the Italian phrase for "good morning")

44. For the time being we will indicate this expression as follows:

(B. G.)X   (B. G.)X   (B. G.)X

* * * * *

45. Repeat the following, paying special attention to the TONGUE-FLAP.

/ÉRA/ (3)

*46. Which of the following ((a) or (b)) does this utterance sound like to you? Repeat it.

/ÉRA/ (3)
    (a) "Ada"
    (b) "ate a...."

47. Actually, either of the answers in the preceding frame is correct. Repeat.

/ÉRA/   (3)

48. Now put /S/ in front of this utterance, as follows.

/SÉRA/   (3)

49. Now put /BWƆNA/ in front of this word.

B.S. (3) (the Italian phrase for "good evening")

50. You have now been given the counterpart of B.G. which is heard during the evening or late afternoon hours. Repeat.

B.S. (3)   (the Italian phrase for "good evening")

51. For the time being we will indicate this expression as follows:

(B. S.)X   (B. S.)X   (B. S.)X

* * * * *

• **End of Tape 5A** •

```
┌───────────┐
│ O ───── O │
│ Tape 5B   │
└───────────┘
```

52. You will now hear four short dialogs. Each line is followed by a pause. Repeat each line, imitating as closely as possible. Remember that the word g——— is to be pronounced with a falling intonation.

a) Sig. Vegli: B. G., sig.ª
   Sig.ª Segni: B. G., sig. Vegli. Come sta?
   Sig. Vegli: Stɔ bɛne, g———, e Lei?
   Sig.ª Segni: Non c'è male, g———.

b) Sig. Segni: B. G., sig.na
   Sig.na Paglia: B. G., sig. Segni. Come sta?
   Sig. Segni: Bɛne, g———, ɛ Lɛi?
   Sig.na Paglia: Benino, g———.

c) Sig. Paglia: B. G., sig. ɛ———.
   Sig. ɛ———: B. G., sig. Paglia. Come sta?
   Sig. Paglia: Stɔ benino, g———, e Lɛi?
   Sig. ɛ———: Così così, g———.

d) Sig.ª S———: B. S., sig.na
   Sig.na B———: B. S., sig.ª Come sta?
   Sig.ª S———: Non stɔ molto bɛne.

53. Now listen to the same dialogs said without pauses between the lines. Do not repeat.

*54. Now you will be asked eight questions on the dialogs. In the spaces below write out complete answers to each question according to the information contained in the dialogs. Make your answers longer than just one word and have each one begin with the title and name, where possible. After all the questions have been read, you will hear the answers that you should have written.

(1) Come sta il sig. Vegli?

Il sig Vegli sta bene

(2) Come sta la sig.ª Segni?

_____

(3) Sta bɛne il sig. Segni?

_Si_

(4) Non sta bɛne il sig. ɛ———?

_No_

(5) Sta benino la sig. na Paglia, nɔ?

_Si_

(6) Come sta il sig. Paglia?

il srg Paglia sta benino

(7) Sta così così is sig. ɛ——?

_____

(8) Sta bɛne la sig.ᵃ S——?

no

_____

* * * * *

55. Repeat the following question-answer pairs in which both the question and the answer refer to a third person. Notice that the verb form is the same in both the question and the answer.

Questions		Answers
(Sta bɛne?)X	"Is (s)he well?"	(Sì, sta bɛne.)X
(Chiama?)X	"Is (s)he calling?"	(Sì, chiama.)X
(Sôgna?)X	"Is (s)he dreaming?"	(Sì, sôgna.)X
(Non fa niɛnte?)X	"Isn't (s)he doing" anything?	(Nɔ, non fa niɛnte.)X
(È il sig. Segni?)X	"Is it Mr. Segni?"	(Sì, è il sig. Segni.)X

56. Now repeat the *same questions,* this time with the verb forms referring to the person being addressed. Repeat the answers here, noticing that the verb form in the answer ends in -ɔ (for one-syllable words) and -o (otherwise).

Questions		Answers
(Sta bɛne?)X	"Are you well?"	(Sì, stɔ bɛne.)X
(Chiama?)X	"Are you calling?"	(Sì, chiamo.)X
(Sôgna?)X	"Are you dreaming?"	(Sì, sôgno.)X
(Non, fa niɛnte?)X	"Aren't you doing anything?"	(Nɔ, non faccio niɛnte.)X
(È il sig. Segni?)X	"Are you Mr. Segni?"	(Sì, sôno il sig. Segni)X

57. The last two verb forms ending in -o are called IRREGULAR because they do not follow any normal or REGULAR pattern.

58. Sometimes some expressions involve other peculiarities. Repeat the first question-answer pair referring to a third person and then the same question involving "you."

Questions		Answers
(C'è?)X "Is (s)he { in there?"		(Sì, c'è.)X
(C'è?)X "Are you { in there?"		(Sì, ci sôno.)X

59. The following expressions may seem even more peculiar. Just learn them as they are given here, remembering that these expressions have a very limited use. The object of the liking here is *always* some *one* person or thing. Pronunciation note: the two-word phrases are to be pronounced as one word with the stress falling always on *piace*.

Questions		Answers
(Gli piace?)X "Does he like $\left\{ \begin{array}{l} \text{it} \\ \text{him} \\ \text{her?"} \end{array} \right.$		(Sì, gli piace.)X
(Le piace?)X "Does she like $\left\{ \begin{array}{l} \text{it} \\ \text{him} \\ \text{her?"} \end{array} \right.$		(Sì, le piace.)X
(Le piace?)X "Do you like $\left\{ \begin{array}{l} \text{it} \\ \text{him} \\ \text{her?"} \end{array} \right.$		(Sì, mi piace.)X

*60. Observe the following model.

    S: Sta bɛne?   "Are you well?"
    R: Sì, stɔ bɛne.   "Yes, I am well."

As in the model, reply in the affirmative to the questions you will now be asked about *yourself*. Your answers will be confirmed each time.

    (1) Sta bɛne?
    (2) Chiama?
    (3) Sôgna?
    (4) C'è?
    (5) Le piace l'Italia?

*61. Now reply in the negative to the following questions about yourself. Your answers will be confirmed each time.

    (1) Sta bɛne?
    (2) Chiama?
    (3) Sôgna?
    (4) È il sig. Segni?
    (5) Non c'è mai?
    (6) Non fa niɛnte?
    (7) Le piace Giulia?

*62. Now you will be asked some INFORMATION questions about yourself. Answer each time by using a verb form or verb phrase referring to yourself, together with the cues given below. Your answers will be confirmed each time.

Questions	Answers
(1) Chi è?	(Il sig. Segni)
(2) Come sta?	(bɛne)
(3) Che cɔsa fa?	(niɛnte)
(4) Chi chiama?	(Emilio)
(5) Che cɔsa sôgna?	(l'Italia)
(6) Che cɔse Le piace?	(l'Italia)

* * * * *

TEST A

(answers not recorded)

(similar to frame No. 54)

You will be asked ten questions on the dialogs of frame No. 52. In the spaces below write out complete answers to each question according to the information contained in the dialogs. Make your answers longer than just one word and have each one begin with the title and name, where possible.

1) Come sta il sig. Segni?

_____

2) Come sta la sig.ᵃ S——?

_____

3) Sta benino il sig. Paglia, nɔ?

_____

4) Sta male il sig. Vegli?

_____

5) Sta male la sig.ᵃ Segni, nɔ?

_____

6) Non sta bɛne il sig. Vegli?

_____

7) Come sta il sig. ɛ——?

_____

8) Come sta la sig.ᵃ Segni?

_____

9) Non sta molto bɛne la sig.ᵃ S——?

_____

10) Sta così così il sig. ɛ——, nɔ?

_____

TEST B

(answers not recorded)

You will be asked ten questions about *yourself.* Answer each time by using a
verb form or verb phrase referring to yourself, together with the cues given
below.

Questions	Answers
1) Come sta?	1) (bɛne) _Sto bene_
2) È il sig. Segni?	2) (nɔ) _No, non è sono il SS_
3) Sôgna?	3) (nɔ) _no, non sogno_
4) C'è?	4) (sì) _Ci sono_
5) Le piace l'Italia?	5) (sì) _mi piace l'Italia_
6) Che cɔsa fa?	6) (niɛnte) _non faccio niente_
7) Non c'è mai?	7) (nɔ) _no, non è sono noi_
8) Chi chiama?	8) (Emilia) _chiama_
9) Non sta bɛne?	9) (sì) _Sto bene_
10) Non Le piace Emilio?	10) (nɔ) _no, non mi piace Emilio_

TEST C

(not recorded)

In the following blanks put in *la* or *il* where possible or required.

1) Come sta,_____ sig. Segni?

2) _____ sig.ᵃ Jones non sta molto bɛne.

3) Sôno _____ sig. Brown.

4) Le piace _____ sig.ⁿᵃ White?

5) _____ sig. Smith, che cɔsa fa Emilio?

6) – 7) _____ sig. Paglia chiama_____ sig.ᵃ Segni.

8) B. G. Come sta_____ sig.ⁿᵃ?

9) Non c'è male, g———, _____ sig. Vegli.

10) Bɛne, g———, e_____ sig. Vegli?

TEST D

(answers not recorded)

You will hear ten short utterances. For each utterance check *only one* of the four letters—a, b, c, d, according to which best approximates the thought behind the utterance. Do *not* expect literal translations. To test yourself cover the Italian words and just listen.

1) B. G.
   (a) Good afternoon.
   (b) How are you?
   (c) Thank you.
   (d) Are you ill?

2) B. S.
   (a) Good morning.
   (b) Hello!
   (c) Buenos Aires.
   (d) I'm well.

3) B. G.
   (a) Good evening.
   (b) Good night.
   (c) Good!
   (d) Hi!

4) B. S.
   (a) Good morning.
   (b) Thank you.
   (c) Good night.
   (d) Good!

5) E Lεi?
   (a) How about you?
   (b) And then?
   (c) Are you ill?
   (d) Is it a lei?

6) Le piace?
   (a) Does he like it?
   (b) Does she like it?
   (c) Do you like them?
   (d) Does he like her?

7) C'è.
   (a) He's around.
   (b) There he is!
   (c) It is.
   (d) It isn't.

8) Non c'è mai.
   (a) He's not there.
   (b) He's never in.
   (c) Not bad.
   (d) He's not ill.

9) Non c'è male.
   (a) He's not there.
   (b) He's never in.
   (c) Not bad.
   (d) He's not ill.

10) Ci sôno.
   (a) I'm here.
   (b) There I am!
   (c) Here he is!
   (d) There he is!

UNIT 17

1) Il sig. Segni sta bɛne.
2) La sig.ᵃ S—— non sta molto bɛne.
3) Sì, il sig. Paglia sta benino.
4) Nɔ, il sig. Vegli non sta male. (or) Nɔ, il sig. Vegli sta bɛne
5) Nɔ, la sig.ᵃ Segni non sta male.
6) Sì, il sig. Vegli sta bɛne.
7) Il sig. ɛ—— sta così così.
8) Non c'è male.
9) Nɔ, la sig.ᵃ S—— non sta molto bɛne.
10) Sì, il sig. ɛ—— sta così così.

1) Stɔ bɛne.
2) Nɔ, non sôno il sig. Segni.
3) Nɔ, non sôgno.
4) Sì, ci sôno.
5) Sì, mi piace l'Italia. (or) Sì, l'Italia mi piace.
6) Non faccio niɛnte.
7) Nɔ, non ci sôno mai.
8) Chiamo Emilia.
9) Sì, stɔ bɛne.
10) Nɔ, non mi piace Emilio. (or) Nɔ, Emilio non mi piace.

1) Come sta, sig. Segni?
2) La sig.ᵃ Jones non sta molto bɛne.
3) Sôno il sig. Brown.
4) Le piace la sig.ⁿᵃ White?
5) Sig. Smith, che cɔsa fa Emilio?
6)–7) Il sig. paglia chiama la sig.ᵃ Segni.
8) B. G. Come sta la sig.ⁿᵃ?
9) Non c'è male, g——, sig. Vegli.
10) Bɛne, g——, e il sig. Vegli?

1) a	3) d	5) a	7) a	9) c
2) b	4) c	6) b	8) b	10) a

UNIT 18

1. The following phrase should be familiar to you. Listen carefully and repeat.
   Che cɔs'è questo? (2)

*2. Translate the sentence.
   Che cɔs'è questo? (1)

*3. Try to remember the spelling of the Italian sentence (   ). Write the Italian sentence on the following line.

   _____

4. The sentence you should have written is: *Che cɔs'è questo?* Do not be alarmed if you misspelled any of the words. However, look at the correct spelling very carefully.

*5. Now how would you say in Italian, "Who is calling here?"

6. Repeat the Italian.
   Chi chiama qui? (2)

*7. Now try to write the Italian sentence on the following line, being careful of the spelling.

   _____

8. The sentence you should have written is *Chi chiama qui?* Again, do not be alarmed if you misspelled any word. However, look at the correct spelling very carefully.

9. In the two Italian questions you have just heard there are six instances of a sound-type that was first introduced in Unit 2, called the UNASPIRATED /K/. Repeat the sentences without putting any puff of air after this sound.
   (Che cɔs'è questo?)X   (Che cɔs'è questo?)X
   (Chi chiama qui?)X   (Chi chiama qui?)X

*10. Now look carefully at the way the /K/ is represented in these two sentences. You should notice three different spellings for this sound-type. What are they?

11. The letter *k* is not normally used in Italian writing and occurs mainly in foreign words like *Kɔdak* and *Pakistan*, for example.

12. Before the following semivowel /W/, sound-type /K/ is normally represented by the letter *q*. Repeat the following words, looking at the spelling.

    (questo)X (questo)X
    (qui)X   (qui)X

13. Three exceptions to the preceding are:
cuɔco	"cook"
cuɔio	"leather"
scuɔla	"school"

*14. Looking at the two model sentences of frame No. 9, tell before which letters the symbol *ch* occurs.

15. Repeat the following words while looking at the spelling.

    (che)X   (che)X
    (chi)X   (chi)X
    (chiama)X   (chiama)X

16. In other cases sound-type /k/ is normally represented by the letter *c*, as in the following word.

    (cɔsa)X (cɔsa)X

17. A general rule, then, for the spelling representations of the following sound-type /K/ in Italian would be:
    1) use *q* before the semivowel /W/;
    2) use *ch* before the letter *e* or *i* (conventional Italian spelling);
    3) Use *c* elsewhere.

*18. The following are words you have already had with sound-type /K/. Write the words in Italian repeating each one as you hear it and trying *not* to pronounce any strong puff of air.

    (   )X
    (   )X
    (   )X
    (   )X
    (   )X
    (   )X
    (   )X

```
                    (            )X
                    (            )X
                    (            )X
                    (            )X
                    (            )X
                    (            )X
                    (            )X
                    (            )X
                    (            )X
                    (            )X
                    (            )X
                    (            )X
                    (            )X
names:              (            )X
                    (            )X
                    (            )X
                    (            )X
                    (            )X
                    (            )X
                    (            )X
                    (            )X
                    (            )X
```

19. Check yourself. You should have written the following:
    chi, cane, come, chimɔno, consolato, chiamo, cɔno, cɔsa, così, chianti, conto, qui,
    fico, che, fuɔco, bɔsco, questo, cuɔco, cuɔio, scuɔla, Colomba, Bianca, Clɛo, Luca,
    Quinto, Cɔla, Nicɔla, Clɔe, Pasquale

    If you made any mistakes repeat the exercise until you are able to spell
    each word correctly.

*20. Now write the following ten Italian words, repeating each one as you hear
    it and try *not* to pronounce any strong puff of air.

```
        (        )X        "captain"
        (        )X        "kiosk, newstand"
        (        )X        "kilogram"
        (        )X        "cube"
        (        )X        "cover, lid (metal or stone)"
        (        )X        "daily newspaper"
        (        )X        "field"
        (        )X        "nail"
        (        )X        "excuse me" (said to one person formally)
        (        )X        "I opened"
```

21. Check yourself. You should have written the following: *capitano, chiɔsco, chilo, cubo, chiusino, quotidiano, campo, chiɔdo, scusi, schiusi*

    If you made any mistakes repeat the exercise until you are able to spell each word correctly.

                              * * * * *

*22. How do you say, "It's a sweater" in Italian?

23. The initial sound-type in the Italian word for "sweater" may be represented /G/.

*24. This sound-type also begins the following three given names that you have already had. As you hear each one, say it and then write it in the space provided.

    (   )X
    (   )X
    (   )X

25. You should have written: *Gosto, Guendalina, Guido.*

*26. So far we have seen that the sound-type /G/ is represented in ordinary Italian spelling by what letter?

27. However, like the sound-type discussed in the first twenty-one frames (/K/), whenever the following sound-type /G/ would occur before the letter *e* or the letter *i*, an *h* is found in the spelling.

28. Repeat the following words while looking at their spellings

    (ghetto)X   (ghetto)X   "ghetto"
    (spaghetti)X   (spaghetti)X   "spaghetti"
    (ghigno)X   (ghigno)X   "grin"
    (ghiottone)X   (ghiottone)X   "glutton"

29. A general rule for the spelling representations of the following sound-type /G/ in Italian is:

    1) use *gh* before the letter *e* or *i* (conventional Italian spelling);
    2) use *g* elsewhere.

*30. Here are three new Italian words. Repeat each one as you hear it and write it in the space provided.

(   )X   "gas"
(   )X   "owl"
(   )X   "glove"

31. Check yourself. You should have written the following: *gas, gufo, guanto.*

*32. Now write the following words in Italian, repeating each one as you hear it.

(   )X
(   )X
(   )X
(   )X
(   )X
(   )X
(   )X
(   )X
(   )X
(   )X
(   )X

33. Check yourself. You should have written the following: *golf, gas, ghetto, gufo, spaghetti, ghigno, guanto, ghiottone, Gosto, Guido, Guendalina.*

If you made any mistakes repeat the exercise until you are able to spell each word correctly.

34. So far you have had three kinds of INFORMATION QUESTIONS in Italian:

1) questions asking for identification of people
— *chi* questions;
2) questions asking for identification of things
— *che*
— *cɔsa* 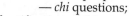 questions;
— *che cɔsa*
3) questions asking for manner
— *come* questions.

35. A fourth kind of information question is the one asking for location. The location interrogative is *dove* in Italian. Repeat.

    (dove)X   (dove)X   (dove)X

*36. How do you say, "Where?" in Italian?

37. When it immediately precedes the verb form *è*, the word *dove* loses its last vowel, and the combination is stressed on the ending and is written as follows:

    (dov'è)X   (dov'è)X   (dov'è)X

*38. Thus, how do you say, "Where is Amanda?" in Italian?

*39. How do you say, "Where is Bologna?" in Italian?

*40. How might you translate the following question into English?

    (Dov'è un cɔno?)X   (Dov'è un cɔno?)X

*41. How would you say, "Where can one find a captain?" in Italian?

42. Notice that regardless or whether one is talking about a person (e.g. *Amanda* or *un capitano*), place (e.g. *Bolôgna*) or thing (e.g. *un cɔno*) and regardless of whether it is pre-identified (e.g. *Amanda, Bolôgna*) or not pre-identified (e.g. *un cɔno, un capitano*), the Italian question begins the same way. Repeat the following questions:

    (Dov'è Amanda?)X
    (Dov'è Bolôgna?)X
    (Dov'è un cɔno?)X
    (Dov'è un capitano?)X

43. With pre-identified items such as those of the first two questions above one may answer by repeating the name followed by *è* + the location word or phrase, as follows:

    (Amanda è qui.)X   "Amanda is (over) here."
    (Bologna è qui.)X   "Bologna is (over) here."

*44. Study the following model.

    S: Dov'è Amanda?   "Where is Amanda?"
    R: Amanda è qui.   "Amanda is (over) here."
        or
    Amanda è lì.   "Amanda is (over) there."

You will now be asked questions beginning with *Dov'è*. Answer as in the model by repeating the name. Use *qui* for any name shown here and *lì* for names not shown. (*Colomba, Cleo, Luca, Cola, Pasquale, Gosto, Guendalina, Guido, Quinto*)

(1) Dov'è Cola?	(11) Dov'è Bianca?
(2) Dov'è Giunio?	(12) Dov'è Emilia?
(3) Dov'è Dina?	(13) Dov'è Quinto?
(4) Dov'è Gosto?	(14) Dov'è Sonia?
(5) Dov'è Colomba?	(15) Dov'è Nina?
(6) Dov'è Lavinia?	(16) Dov'è Cleo?
(7) Dov'è Guido?	(17) Dov'è Elio?
(8) Dov'è Luca?	(18) Dov'è Giulia?
(9) Dov'è Guendalina?	(19) Dov'è Emilio?
(10) Dov'è Giulio?	(20) Dov'è Pasquale?

45. The name need not be repeated in the answer, however, and one may say simply,

(è qui.)X

"He ⎫
"She ⎬ is (over) here."
"It ⎭

*46. You will now be asked questions as in frame No. 44. Answer without the name, again using *qui* for the names shown in frame No. 44 and *lì* for names not shown.

(1) Dov'è Dina?	(11) Dov'è Giunio?
(2) Dov'è Pasquale?	(12) Dov'è Emilia?
(3) Dov'è Guendalina?	(13) Dov'è Luca?
(4) Dov'è Cleo?	(14) Dov'è Cola?
(5) Dov'è Emilio?	(15) Dov'è Elio?
(6) Dov'è Guido?	(16) Dov'è Sonia?
(7) Dov'è Bianca?	(17) Dov'è Lavinia?
(8) Dov'è Nina?	(18) Dov'è Giulia?
(9) Dov'è Giulio?	(19) Dov'è Quinto?
(10) Dov'è Gosto?	(20) Dov'è Colomba?

47. In the case of non-pre-identified items such as those of the last two questions of frame No. 42, the normal answer is different. Repeat the following.

    (C'ɛ un cɔno qui.)X   "There is a cone (over) here."
                                         "A cone is (over) here."

    (C'ɛ un capitano qui.)X   "There is a captain (over) here."
                                         "A captain is (over) here."

48. This construction should not seem strange to you since it appeared before in frame No. 63 of Unit 13 and again in frames No. 47 and No. 48 of Unit 14. You may want to pause briefly to review the models given in those frames.

*49. Study the following model.

    S: Dov'è un cɔno?   "Where is a cone?"
    R: C'ɛ un cɔno qui.   "There is a cone (over) here."
       or
    C'ɛ un cɔno lì.   "There is a cone (over) there."

You will now be asked questions beginning with *Dov'è*. Answer as in the model by repeating the name. Use *qui* for any name shown here and *lì* for names not shown.
(*cane, chimono, cɔno, chianti, fico, cubo, quotidiano, chiɔdo, gɔlf, guanto*)

(1) Dov'è un cubo?	(11) Dov'è un chimono?
(2) Dov'è un ghetto?	(12) Dov'è un fico?
(3) Dov'è un cane?	(13) Dov'è un fuɔco?
(4) Dov'è un chiodo?	(14) Dov'è un cɔno?
(5) Dov'è un consolato?	(15) Dov'è un chianti?
(6) Dov'è un guanto?	(16) Dov'è un chiɔsco?
(7) Dov'è un chiusino?	(17) Dov'è un quotidiano?
(8) Dov'è un ghiottone?	(18) Dov'è un gufo?
(9) Dov'è un bɔsco?	(19) Dov'è un gɔlf?
(10) Dov'è un cuɔco?	(20) Dov'è un campo?

50. With non-pre-identified items, if one does *not* repeat the name of the item, *ce n'è uno* occurs instead of *c'è un* (+ name).

*51. You will now be asked questions as in Frame No. 49. Answer by using _ce n'è uno_ "there's one (over) here" for the names shown in frame No. 49; use _ce n'è uno lì_ "there's one (over) there" for names not shown.

(1) Dov'è un campo?	(11) Dov'è un chiusino?
(2) Dov'è un cuoco?	(12) Dov'è un chiosco?
(3) Dov'è un chimono?	(13) Dov'è un cane?
(4) Dov'è un cubo?	(14) Dov'è un fuoco?
(5) Dov'è un ghetto?	(15) Dov'è un ghiottone?
(6) Dov'è un fico?	(16) Dov'è un quotidiano?
(7) Dov'è un golf?	(17) Dov'è un chianti?
(8) Dov'è un bosco?	(18) Dov'è un chiodo?
(9) Dov'è un consolato?	(19) Dov'è un guanto?
(10) Dov'è un cono?	(20) Dov'è un gufo?

* * * * *

52. Listen carefully to the way the following English word is pronounced.

(stutter)   (stutter)   (stutter)

53. The pronunciation you just heard contains the TONGUE-FLAP introduced in Unit 15. If there were an English word spelled s-t-u-d-d-e-r it could be pronounced exactly the same as s-t-u-t-t-e-r, that is, with the same TONGUE-FLAP. Listen and repeat.

"stutter"   (3)

54. Some speakers of English pronounce words ending in -_er_ differently from what you have just heard. Listen and repeat, retaining the TONGUE-FLAP.

"stutter"   (3)

55. Now try shifting the stress to the last syllable. Repeat, retaining the TONGUE-FLAP.

56. Now try to say this same utterance so fast that it becomes one syllable. Remember to keep the TONGUE-FLAP.

/STRA/ (3)

57. The syllable you have just learned is heard in the Italian phrases for "on the left" and "on the right." For the time being we will abbreviate each phrase here as *a s*——— and *a d*——— respectively. Repeat.

(a s———)X (a s———)X (a s———)X
(a d———)X (a d———)X (a d———)X

* * * * *

*58. Using the following cues, ask a *Dov'è* question about the people or things mentioned. Your question will be confirmed on the tape.

(1) Sonia
(2) a dog
(3) a fig
(4) a consulate
(5) Egle
(6) a glutton
(7) a newsstand
(8) Pasquale
(9) Giunio
(10) a sweater
(11) Mr. Segni
(12) a nail
(13) a cone
(14) Miss Paglia
(15) Mrs. Vegli

Repeat this frame until you have mastered the drill.

*59. Study the following model.

S: Dov'è Luca?   "Where is Luca?"
R: è a s———.   "He is on the left."
    or
è a d———.   "He is on the right."

Give the appropriate answer to the question you hear according to whether the person's name is to the left or the right of the dividing line below. Your answer will be confirmed each time.

Giovanni	Silvio	Mr. Segni	Ugo	Beniamino	Miss Paglia
Tina	Magda	Quinto	Ɛlio	Augusta	Mrs. Vegli
Lidia	Fede		Nina	Bianca	
Ɛva	Lavinia		Antɔnio	Giulio	

Repeat this frame until you have mastered the drill.

(1) Dov'è Magda?   (11) Dov'è Giovanni?

(2) Dov'è Bianca?   (12) Dov'è Ɛva?

(3) Dov'è la sig.na   (13) Dov'è Ugo?
      Paglia?   (14) Dov'è Beniamino?

(4) Dov'è Nina?   (15) Dov'è Fede?

(5) Dov'è Tina?   (16) Dov'è Quinto?

(6) Dov'è il sig. Segni?   (17) Dov'è Silvio?

(7) Dov'è Augusta?   (18) Dov'è Giulio?

(8) Dov'è la sig.a Vegli?   (19) Dov'è Lavinia?

(9) Dov'è Ɛlio?   (20) Dov'è Antɔnio?

(10) Dov'è Lidia?

*60.   Study the following model.

     S: Dov'è un gɔlf?   "Where is a sweater?"

     R: C'è un gɔlf a s——.   "There is a sweater on the left."
        or
     C'è un gɔlf a d——.   "There is a sweater on the right."

Give the appropriate answer to the question you hear according to whether the item's name is to the left or the right of the dividing line below. Your answer will be confirmed each time.

nail	fire	kimono	kiosk
cube	woods	sweater	metal lid
cone	captain	glove	ghetto
chianti	field	owl	daily newspaper

Repeat this frame until you have mastered the drill.

(1) Dov'è un chiɔsco?   (9) Dov'è un chiusino?

(2) Dov'è un gufo?   (10) Dov'è un chianti?

(3) Dov'è un campo?   (11) Dov'è un guanto?

(4) Dov'è un cubo?   (12) Dov'è un quotidiano?

(5) Dov'è un chiɔdo?   (13) Dov'è un chimɔno?

(6) Dov'è un fuɔco?   (14) Dov'è un capitano?

(7) Dov'è un gɔlf?   (15) Dov'è un ghetto?

(8) Dov'è un bɔsco?   (16) Dov'è un cɔno?

• **End of Tape 5B** •

Tape 6A

*61. Study the following model.

    S: Dov'è un gɔlf?   "Where is a sweater?"

    R: Ce n'è uno a s——.   "There is one on the left."

        or

    Ce n'è uno a d——.   "There is one on the right."

Answer the questions you hear by using the items mentioned in frame No. 60.

(1) Dov'è un guanto?	(9) Dov'è un ghetto?
(2) Dov'è un chiɔsco?	(10) Dov'è un chiɔdo?
(3) Dov'è un bɔsco?	(11) Dov'è un chimɔno?
(4) Dov'è un chianti?	(12) Dov'è un gɔlf?
(5) Dov'è un fuɔco?	(13) Dov'è un quotidiano?
(6) Dov'è un capitano?	(14) Dov'è un cɔno?
(7) Dov'è un cubo?	(15) Dov'ɛ un chiusino?
(8) Dov'è un gufo?	(16) Dov'è un campo?

62. The following is a drill that uses sentences from frames No. 59 and No. 61. Reply accordingly. Your answer will be confirmed each time.

Giovanni	Silvio	Mr. Segni	Ugo	Beniamino	Miss Paglia
Tina	Magda	Quinto	Ɛlio	Augusta	Mrs. Vegli
Lidia	Fede		Nina	Bianca	
Ɛva	Lavinia		Antɔnio	Giulio	

nail	fire		kimono	kiosk
cube	woods		sweater	metal lid
cone	captain		glove	ghetto
chianti	field		owl	daily newspaper

Repeat this frame until you have mastered the drill.

(1) Dov'è un chimɔno?	(11) Dov'è Quinto?
(2) Dov'è un cɔno?	(12) Dov'è Ɛva?
(3) Dov'è la sig.a Vegli?	(13) Dov'è Nina?
(4) Dov'è un fuɔco?	(14) Dov'è il sig. Segni?
(5) Dov'è Antɔnio?	(15) Dov'è un chiɔsco?
(6) Dov'è un chianti?	(16) Dov'è Silvio?
(7) Dov'è un capitano?	(17) Dov'è un chiɔdo?
(8) Dov'è Lidia?	(18) Dov'è un quotidiano?
(9) Dov'è un guanto?	(19) Dov'è Beniamino?
(10) Dov'è Ugo?	(20) Dov'è la sig.na Paglia?

*63. Study the following model.

    S: C'è Tina?   "Is Tina there?"
    R: Sì, è lì a s——.   "Yes, she is there on the left."
        or
    Sì, è lì a d——.   "Yes, she is there on the right."
        or
    Nɔ, non c'è.   "No, she isn't (around)."

Using the items of frame No. 62, reply accordingly. Your answer will be confirmed each time.

(1) C'è Guendalina?	(9) C'è Luca?
(2) C'è il sig. Segni?	(10) C'è la sig.na Paglia?
(3) C'è Giunio?	(11) C'è Bianca?
(4) C'è Magda?	(12) C'è Ugo?
(5) C'è Gosto?	(13) C'è Ɛgle?
(6) C'è Antɔnio?	(14) C'è Nina?
(7) C'è la sig.a Paglia?	(15) C'è Beniamino?
(8) C'è Giovanni?	

*64. Study the following model.

    S: C'è un chiɔdo?   "Is there a nail around?"
    R: Sì ce n'è uno lì   "Yes. there is one there on the left."
    a s——.
        or
    Sì, ce n'è uno lì   "Yes, there is one there on the right."
    a d——.
        or
    "Nɔ."   "No."

Again using the items of frame No. 62, reply accordingly. Your answer will be confirmed each time.

(1) C'è un chiɔdo?	(9) C'è un fuɔco?
(2) C'è un bɔsco?	(10) C'è un fico?
(3) C'è un bastone?	(11) C'è un cane?
(4) C'è un capitano?	(12) C'è un chiɔsco?
(5) C'è un gas?	(13) C'è un voto?
(6) C'è un consolato?	(14) C'è un chimɔno?
(7) C'è un anglicano?	(15) C'è un tɔpo?
(8) C'è un quotidiano?	

*65. The following is a drill that uses sentences from frames No. 63 and No. 64.
Reply accordingly, using the items of frame No. 62. Your answer will be
confirmed each time. Repeat this frame until you have mastered the drill.

(1) C'è Nina?	(11) C'è un bastone?
(2) C'è un chiɔdo?	(12) C'è la sig.na Paglia?
(3) C'è Ugo?	(13) C'è Silvio?
(4) C'è un anglicano?	(14) C'è un fuɔco?
(5) C'è Giunio?	(15) C'è il sig. Segni?
(6) C'è Giovanni?	(16) C'è un gas?
(7) C'è un voto?	(17) C'è Guendalina?
(8) C'è Beniamino?	(18) C'è un chimɔno?
(9) C'è Gosto?	(19) C'è un cane?
(10) C'è un tɔpo?	(20) C'è un chiɔsco?

*66. Study the following model, imagining that you are looking at a picture of
several people.

S: Chi c'è qui?	"Who is here?"
R: C'è Amanda.	"There is Amanda."
S: Dov'è	"Where is Amanda?"
R: è a s——.	"She is on the left."
or	
è a d——.	"She is on the right."

Using the items of frame No. 62 plus the cues below, participate in the conversation illustrated in the model. A space is provided on the tape for each
response which will then be confirmed.

(1) Silvio	(11) Ɛva
(2) Mr. Segni	(12) Fede
(3) Tina	(13) Giovanni
(4) Ugo	(14) Giulio
(5) Mrs. Vegli	(15) Lavinia
(6) Antɔnio	(16) Lidia
(7) Augusta	(17) Magda
(8) Beniamino	(18) Nina
(9) Bianca	(19) Miss Paglia
(10) Ɛlio	(20) Quinto

*67. Study the following model, again imagining that you are looking at a picture.

S: Che cɔsa c'è qui?	"What have we here?"
R: C'è un chiɔdo.	"There's a nail."
S: Dov'è?	"Where is it?"
R: È a s——.	"It's on the left."
or	
È a d——.	"It's on the right."

Again using the items on frame No. 62, together with the cues below, participate in the conversation illustrated in the model. A space is provided on the tape for each response, which will then be confirmed.

(1) sweater	(9) fire
(2) woods	(10) ghetto
(3) captain	(11) glove
(4) chianti	(12) kimono
(5) cone	(13) kiosk
(6) cube	(14) metal lid
(7) daily newspaper	(15) nail
(8) field	(16) owl

*68. The following is a drill that uses sentences from frames No. 66 and No. 67. Reply accordingly using the items of frame No. 62, together with the cues below. A space is provided on the tape for each response, which will then be confirmed.

Questions	Cues
(1) Chi c'è qui? - Dov'è?	Antɔnio
(2) Chi c'è qui? - Dov'è?	Beniamino
(3) Che cɔsa c'è qui? - Dov'è?	nail
(4) Che cɔsa c'è qui? - Dov'è?	daily newspaper
(5) Chi c'è qui? - Dov'è?	Ɛlio
(6) Chi c'è qui? - Dov'è?	Fede
(7) Chi c'è qui? - Dov'è?	Giovanni
(8) Che cɔsa c'è qui? - Dov'è?	kimono
(9) Chi c'è qui? - Dov'è?	Lavinia
(10) Chi c'è qui? - Dov'è?	Magda
(11) Chi c'è qui? - Dov'è?	Nina
(12) Che cɔsa c'è qui? - Dov'è?	owl
(13) Chi c'è qui? - Dov'è?	Miss Paglia
(14) Chi c'è qui? - Dov'è?	Quinto
(15) Chi c'è qui? - Dov'è?	Silvio
(16) Chi c'è qui? - Dov'è?	Tina
(17) Chi c'è qui? - Dov'è?	Ugo
(18) Chi c'è qui? - Dov'è?	Mrs. Vegli
(19) Che cɔsa c'è qui? - Dov'è?	woods
(20) Che cɔsa c'è qui? - Dov'è?	metal lid

*69. Now still using sentences from frames No. 66 and No. 67, *you* are to initiate
the conversation and ask either *Chi c'è qui?* or *Che cosa c'è qui?* according to
whether the cue below is the name of a person or a thing, respectively.
When you are given the response, ask *Dov'è?* A space is provided on the
tape for your utterances, which will always be confirmed. The final
response will be in accordance with the items in frame No. 62.

Cues	Responses
(1) Giovanni	C'è Giovanni. - è a s——.
(2) Lidia	C'è Lidia. - è a s——.
(3) Tina	C'è Tina. - è a s——.
(4) a fire	C'è un fuoco. - è a s——.
(5) a newsstand	C'è un chiosco. - è a d——.
(6) a daily newspaper	C'è un quotidiano. - è a d——.
(7) a nail	C'è un chiodo. - è a s——.
(8) a field	C'è un campo. - è a s——.
(9) ɛva	C'è ɛva. - è a s——.
(10) an owl	C'è un gufo. - è a d——.
(11) a metal lid	C'è un chiusino. - è a d——.
(12) Ugo	C'è Ugo. - è a d——.
(13) a ghetto	C'è un ghetto. - è a d——.
(14) Fede	C'è Fede. - è a s——.
(15) a glove	C'è un guanto. - è a d——.
(16) ɛlio	C'è ɛlio. - è a d——.
(17) Bianca	C'è Bianca. - è a d——.
(18) a cone	C'è un cono. - è a s——.
(19) Nina	C'è Nina. - è a d——.
(20) Augusta	C'è Augusta. - è a d——.
(21) Mr. Segni	C'è il sig. Segni. - è a s——.
(22) a cube	C'è un cubo - è a s——.
(23) Mrs. Vegli	C'è la sig.[a] Vegli. - è a d——.
(24) a kiosk	C'è un chiosco. - è a d——.
(25) Miss Paglia	C'è la sig.[na] Paglia. - è a d——.

TEST A

(answers not recorded)

Write the words you hear as you think they are spelled in Italian. Each word contains either of the following sound-types——/K/ or /G/

1)_____
2)_____
3)_____
4)_____
5)_____
6)_____
7)_____
8)_____
9)_____
10)_____
11)_____
12)_____
13)_____
14)_____
15)_____
16)_____
17)_____
18)_____
19)_____
20)_____
21)_____
22)_____
23)_____
24)_____
25)_____

TEST B

(answers not recorded)

You will hear a statement that is partially garbled. For each statement *write* in the space provided a complete question that you might ask to find out about the unintelligible portion. Start each question with one of the following question words: *Chi ? - Che cosa? - Come? - Dove?*

Example:
S: Tina è (garbled).
R: Dov'è Tina?

1) _chi c'è lì a destra_

2) _____

3) _____

4) _____

5) _____

6) _____

7) _____

8) _____

9) _____

10) _____

11) _____

12) _____

13) _____

14) _____

15) _____

TEST C

(not recorded)

Translate the following thoughts into Italian as best you can by using *only* what has been presented so far.

1) What are you doing there on the right?

Che cosa fa lì a d.

2) What is this here on the left?

Che cos'è questo qui a S.

3) What is there here on the left?

Che cosa c'è qui a S.

4) Bologna is situated here.

Bologna è qui

5) A rat is over here.

C'è un topo qui

6) Is there one over there?

Ce n'è uno lì?

7) Isn't Mr. Jones in?

Non è il sig. Jones

8) What do we have here?

Che cosa c'è qui

9) He doesn't like it there on the right.

Non gli piace lì a d.

10) I don't feel well here.

Non sto bene qui.

11) I'm not doing anything over here.

Non faccio niente qui

12) Do you see a nail around there?

C'è un chiodo lì?

13) Excuse me, sir. Where can I find a newsstand?

Scusi, sig. Dove un chiosco

14) Excuse me. Do you know where Mr. Vegli is?

Scusi Dove'lsig Vegli

15) You can see her there on the left.

è lì a S.

16) Isn't she on the right?

   Non è a d.

17) Who is around here?

   Chi c'è qui

18) I don't know who she is. Do you?

   chi è?

19) Who is that? - That's Miss White.

20) No, that's not Miss White. *There's* Miss White!

   No, non è la sign.

TEST A ANSWERS

1) cheto
2) laghi
3) qualifichiamo
4) chiglia
5) banca
6) gaüdioso
7) squagliamo
8) achenio
9) qualcosa
10) schiuma
11) ghiaioso
12) chiesta
13) ancona
14) benedico
15) questione
16) guglie
17) chiusa
18) ghignate
19) anche
20) quaglia
21) ago
22) banchiglia
23) cut
24) vaghe
25) schema

TEST B ANSWERS

Statements	Answers
1) Il sig. (garbled) è lì a d——.	Chi c'è lì a d——?
2) C'è un (garbled) a s——.	Che cosa c'è a s——?
3) Lina sta (garbled).	Come sta Lina?
4) Colomba è a (garbled).	Dov'è Colomba?
5) Questo è un (garbled).	Che cos'è questo?
6) Lì c'è un (garbled).	Che cosa c'è lì?
7) (garbled) non sta bɛne.	Chi non sta bɛne?
8) Ɛva chiama la sig.na (garbled).	Chi chiama Ɛva?
9) Dina D—— è a (garbled).	Dov'è Dina D——?
10) Nina sta (garbled).	Come sta Nina?
11) Non c'è la sig. (garbled).	Chi non c'è?
12) Il sig. Paglia è a (garbled).	Dov'è il sig. Paglia?
13) Chiamo il sig. (garbled).	Chi chiama?
14) Sôgno (garbled).	Che cosa sôgna? (or)
	Chi sôgna?
15) Mi piace il sig. (garbled).	Chi Le piace?

TEST C   ANSWERS

1) Che cosa fa lì a d——?
2) Che cos'è questo qui a s——?
3) Che cosa c'è qui a s——?
4) Bolôgna è qui.
5) C'è un topo qui.
6) Ce n'è uno lì?
7) Non c'è il sig. Jones?
8) Che cosa c'è qui?
9) Non gli piace lì a d——.
10) Non sto bene qui.
11) Non faccio niente qui.
12) C'è un chiodo lì?
13) Scusi, sig. Dov'è un chiosco?
14) Scusi. Dov'è il sig. Vegli?
15) È lì a s——.
16) Non è a d——?
17) Chi c'è qui?
18) Chi è?
19) Chi è? - È la sig.na White.
20) No, non è la sig.na White. La sig.na White è lì.

UNIT 19

*1. How do you say, "Is (s)he in" in Italian?

*2. In answering the preceding question, how do you say, "Yes, (s)he is" in Italian?

*3. To what time do the two preceding Italian utterances seem to refer, to past time, present time or future time?

4. Now listen carefully to the following.
c'era (3)

5. What you just heard may sound something like the English word "Cheddar." Listen again and repeat.
c'era (3)

6. The utterance you have been hearing contains the TONGUE-FLAP found in "Betty" and "Eddie."
c'era (3)

7. Actually, this utterance is the counterpart of *c'è* that refers to past time.
c'era (3)

*8. Therefore, if *c'è?* is like the English "Is (s)he in?" how might the question (   ) be translated into English?
c'era ? (1)

*9. How do you say, "Is Tina around?" in Italian?

*10. Therefore, how do you say, "Was Tina around?" in Italian?

*11. In answering the preceding question, how do you say, "No, she wasn't" in Italian?

*12. Using the same (   ), how do you say, "Who was there?" in Italian?
c'era (1)

*13. In answering the preceding question, how do you say, " Luca was there" in Italian?

14. In Unit 15 (specifically, in frames No. 23 through No. 36) the TONGUE-FLAP was discussed as a sound-type frequently heard in COL-LOQUIAL American English.

*15. As was seen in Unit 15, the TONGUE-FLAP in COLLOQUIAL American English occurs in many words spelled with what letters?

16. So far in these units, the spelling of Italian words containing the TONGUE-FLAP has been purposely avoided because the TONGUE-FLAP is *never* represented by the letter *t* or *d* in Italian.

17. Repeat the following words and phrases that you have had, all of which contain the TONGUE-FLAP.

   (sig.)X
   (sig.^{a})X
   (sig.^{na})X
   (B. S.)X
   (Bianca B——)X
   (Ɛlio Ɛ——)X
   (Lavinia L——)X
   (Nina N——)X
   (Dina D——)X
   (Sɔnia S——)X

18. Repeat again the past counterpart of *c'è*.

   c'era   (3)

19. Now say it again, this time looking at the spelling and paying attention to the TOUNGUE-FLAP.

   (c'era)X   (c'era)X   (c'era)X

*20. In this utterance what letter do we see representing the TONGUE-FLAP in Italian?

*21. Because the TONGUE-FLAP is always represented in Italian by the letter r, it should not be difficult for you to do the following exercise. Write the following Italian utterances in their non-abbreviated form in the spaces provided.

   (sig.)X _____

   (sig.^{a})X_____

(sig.^{na})X_____

(B. S.)X_____

(Bianca B——)X_____

(Ɛlio Ɛ——)X_____

(Lavinia L——)X_____

(Nina N——)X_____

(Dina D——)X_____

(Sɔnia S——)X_____

22. In the preceding frame you should have written the following: *signore, signora, signorina, buɔna sera, Bianca Bɛri, Ɛlio Ɛri, Lavinia Lira, Nina Nɛra, Dina Dari, Sɔnia Sɛiri.*

* * * * *

23. Now listen to the future counterpart of c'è.
    ci sarà (3)

*24. Does this contain the TONGUE-FLAP, too?
    ci sarà (3)

25. Look at its spelling and repeat.
    (ci sarà)X   (ci sarà)X   (ci sarà)X

*26. If *C'è?* is like the English "Is (s)he in?" and *C'èra* is like the English "Was (s)he in?" how might the question *Ci Sarà* be translated into English?

*27. How do you say, "Will Gina be around?" in Italian?

*28. In answering the preceding question, how do you say, "No, she won't be" in Italian?

*29. Using the same *ci sarà*, how do you say, "Who will be there?" in Italian?

*30. In answering the preceding question, how do you say, "Nicɔla will be there" in Italian?

* 31. Translate the following, writing in the spaces provided.

"He will be } in.
               there." _____
               around."

"He is } in."
          there." _____
          around."

"He was } in."
            there." _____
            around."

32. You should have written:
    Ci sarà.
    C'è
    C'èra.

* * * * *

33. Notice that these three utterances may refer to the person addressed
    ("you") or to a third person ("he" or "she").

*34. In Unit 17 you learned how to say, "I am in" in Italian. What was it?

35. In order to say, "I was in" and "I will be in," change the *-a* of the ending on
    the appropriate word to *-o* and *-ɔ* respectively. Thus:

    C'èro   "I was in."
    Ci sarɔ.   "I will be in."

    When a word shows variations in form corresponding to a difference in the
    person being referred to, as in the two columns below, what is such a word
    called? (See Unit 17)

"I"		"you, he, she"
ci sarɔ	ci sara	(for future time)
ci sôno	c'è	(for present time)
c'ero	c'era	(for past time)

37. The differences shown between the forms on the left and those on the right
    are differences in the PERSON being referred to. Therefore, VERBS in
    Italian are said to show PERSON variations.

38. The examples you have just seen illustrate that Italian VERBS show another kind of difference—one that has to do with the time referred to. Therefore, VERBS in Italian are also said to show TENSE variations.

* * * * *

39. Here are three important time words, the words for "yesterday," "today," and "tomorrow." Repeat.

ieri (1)	"yesterday"
oggi (1)	"today"
domani (1)	"tomorrow"

*40. One of these three words contains the TONGUE-FLAP. Which is it?

    ieri (1)   oggi (1)   domani (1)
     a   b   c

*41. Write the Italian word for "yesterday" in the space below.

_____

42. You should have written ieri.

43. Here are the three words for "yesterday," "today" and "tomorrow" respectively.

    (ieri)X   (oggi)X   (domani)X

* * * * *

*44. In Unit 17 you learned the phrase for "Good Evening." It contains the TONGUE-FLAP. What was the phrase?

*45. If the word sera is the word for "evening" translate ieri sera into English.

*46. Referring to the evening hours, how would you translate "last night" into Italian?

*47. And "tomorrow night"?

48. For "tonight" or "this evening," Italians usually say:

    (stasera)X   (stasera)X   (stasera)X

* * * * *

49. This is the word for "morning," Make sure you pronounce the second consonant (/T/) strongly.

     (mattina)X   (mattina)X   (mattina)X

*50. How would you say, "yesterday morning" in Italian?

*51. What about, "tomorrow morning"?

52. For "this morning," Italians usually say:

     (stamattina)X   (stamattina)X   (stamattina)X

＊＊＊＊＊

53. Here is the word for "afternoon." It contains the TONGUE-FLAP.

     (pomeriggio)X   (pomeriggio)X   (pomeriggio)X

*54. How would you say, "yesterday afternoon" in Italian?

*55. What about, "tomorrow afternoon"?

56. For "this afternoon,"Italians say:

     (questo pomeriggio)X   (questo pomeriggio)X   (questo pomeriggio)X

＊＊＊＊＊

57. The following is an Italian word for "now." Notice how it sounds a little like the colloquial English "oughta."

     (ora)X   (ora)X   (ora)X

58. The following is the phrase for "two minutes ago." Repeat.

     (due minuti fa)X   (due minuti fa)X   (due minuti fa)X

＊＊＊＊＊

59. Here is a recapitulation of the time words and phrases introduced in this Unit so far.

(iɛri)X	(ɔggi)X	(domani)X
(iɛri mattina)X	(stamattina)X	(domani mattina)X
(iɛri pomeriggio)X	(questo pomeriggio)X	(domani pomeriggio)X
(iɛri sera)X	(stasera)X	(domani sera)X
	(ora)X	
	(due minuti fa)X	

60. Look at the following chart and repeat the names shown in each column. Notice that the first column names as well as the very last name all contain the tongue-flap. The pronunciation of the ending of the first three names might remind you of the colloquial English "oughta."

sometime yesterday	two minutes ago	now	sometime tomorrow
(Cɔra)X	(Amanda)X	(Ɛva)X	(Augusta)X
(Dɔra)X	(Bianca)X	(Lɛa)X	(Colomba)X
(Nɔra)X	(Donata)X	(Pia)X	(Guendalina)X
(Mara)X	(Adɔlfo)X	(Lɛo)X	(Antɔnio)X
(Sara)X	(Nicɔla)X	(Noè)X	(Beniamino)X
(Vɛra)X	(Silvio)X	(Ugo)X	(Oliviɛro)X

This chart will be used for the drills in frames No. 61 through No. 65 and No. 68 through No. 71.

• **End of Tape 6A** •

Tape 6B

*61. Observe the following model:

a $\begin{cases} \text{S: C'è Cɔra?} \\ \text{R: Nɔ, non c'è, ma} \\ \quad \text{c'èra iɛri.} \\ \quad \text{(or)} \end{cases}$ "Is Cora in?"
    "No, she's not in, but she
        was (in) yesterday."

b $\begin{cases} \text{S: C'è Amanda?} \\ \text{R: Nɔ, non c'è, ma} \\ \quad \text{c'èra due minuti fa.} \end{cases}$ "Is Amanda in?"
    "No, she's not in, but she
        was (in) two minutes ago."

The only new word in this drill is *ma*, the word for "but." Answer as in (a) or (b) according to whether the person's name is in the "yesterday" column or the "two minutes ago" column. Your answer will be confirmed each time Remember to pronounce the tongue-flap correctly. NOTE: the word *ma* is followed by a strongly-pronounced consonant.

Questions

(1) C'è Adɔlfo?	(6) C'è Sara?
(2) C'è Mara?	(7) C'è Nicɔla?
(3) C'è Bianca?	(8) C'è Silvio?
(4) C'è Donata?	(9) C'è Vɛra?
(5) C'è Dɔra?	(10) C'è Nɔra?

*62. Observe the following model:

 a. { S: C'è Ɛva?   "Is Eva in?"
   { R: Sì, c'è.   "Yes, she is.

 (or)

 b. { S: C'è Augusta?   "Is Augusta in?"
   { R: Nɔ, non c'è, ma ci   "No, she isn't, but she'll
       sarà domani.   be in tomorrow."

Answer as in (a) or (b) according to whether the person's name is in the "now" column or the "tomorrow" column. Your answer will be confirmed each time. Remember to pronounce the tongue-flap correctly! Note: the words sarà and sarɔ are each followed by a strongly-pronounced consonant:

Questions	
(1) C'è Antɔnio?	(6) C'è Lɛa?
(2) C'è Beniamino?	(7) C'è Guendalina?
(3) C'è Colomba?	(8) C'è Ugo?
(4) C'è Lɛo?	(9) C'è Oliviɛro?
(5) C'è Noè?	(10) C'è Pia?

*63. Observe the following model:

 a. { S: C'è Cɔra?
   { R: Nɔ, non c'è, ma c'èra iɛri.
    (or)

 b. { S: C'è Amanda?
   { R: Nɔ, non c'è, ma c'ɛra due minuti fa.
    (or)

 c. { S: C'è Ɛva?
   { R: Sì, c'è.
    (or)

 d. { S: C'è Augusta?
   { R: Nɔ, non c'è, ma ci sarà domani.

Answer as in (a), (b), (c), or (d) according to whether the person's name is in the "yesterday" column, the "two minutes ago" column, the "now" column or the "tomorrow" column. Your answer will be confirmed each time. Remember to pronounce the tongue-flap correctly.

Questions	
(1) C'è Dɔra?	(4) C'è Amanda?
(2) C'è Nicɔla?	(5) C'è Lɛa?
(3) C'è Sara?	(6) C'è Augusta?

Questions

(7) C'è Antɔnio?	(16) C'è Cɔra?
(8) C'è Adɔlfo?	(17) C'è Bianca?
(9) C'è Lɛo?	(18) C'è Pia?
(10) C'è Ɛva?	(19) C'è Guendalina?
(11) C'è Donata?	(20) C'è Beniamino?
(12) C'è Ugo?	(21) C'è Mara?
(13) C'è Noè?	(22) C'è Nɔra?
(14) C'è Vɛra?	(23) C'è Colomba?
(15) C'è Oliviɛro?	(24) C'è Silvio?

Repeat this frame as many times as are necessary to master the drill.

*64. Observe the following model:

a. { S: C'è Cɔra ɔggi?   "Is Cora in today?"
     { R: Nɔ, ɔggi non c'ɛ̀,   "No, she's not in today,
           ma c'èra iɛri.   but she was in yesterday."
                  (or)
b. { S: C'è Ɛva ɔggi?   "Is Eva in today?"
     { R: Sì, c'ɛ.   "Yes, she is."
                  (or)
c. { S: C'è Augusta ɔggi?   "Is Augusta in today?"
     { R: Nɔ, ɔggi non c'ɛ, ma   "No, she's not in today,
           ci sarà domani.   but she'll be in tomorrow."

As before, give the appropriate answer to the questions you hear. Your response will be confirmed each time. Remember to pronounce the tongue-flap correctly. Repeat this frame until you have mastered the drill.

Questions

(1) C'è Vɛra ɔggi?	(9) C'è Lɛa ɔggi?
(2) C'è Noè ɔggi?	(10) C'è Pia ɔggi?
(3) C'è Antɔnio ɔggi?	(11) C'è Mara ɔggi?
(4) C'è Colomba ɔggi?	(12) C'è Lɛo ɔggi?
(5) C'è Dɔra ɔggi?	(13) C'è Sara ɔggi?
(6) C'è Ugo ɔggi?	(14) C'è Beniamino ɔggi?
(7) C'è Guendalina ɔggi?	(15) C'è Oliviɛro ɔggi?
(8) C'è Nɔra ɔggi?	

*65. Observe the following model:

a. $\begin{cases} \text{S: C'è Eva?} \\ \text{R: Sì, c'è ora.} \end{cases}$ "Is Eva in?"
 "Yes, she's in now."

(or)

b. $\begin{cases} \text{S: C'è Cɔra?} \\ \text{R: Nɔ, non c'è ora.} \end{cases}$ "Is Cora in?"
 "No, she's not in now."

Answer as in (a) or (b) according to whether the person's name is in the "now" column or some other column. Your answer will be confirmed each time. Remember to pronounce the tongue-flap correctly.

Questions

(1) C'è Donata?	(9) C'è Guendalina?
(2) C'è Augusta?	(10) C'è Mara?
(3) C'è Ugo?	(11) C'è Antɔnio?
(4) C'è Cɔra?	(12) C'è Adɔlfo?
(5) C'è Lɛa?	(13) C'è Lɛo?
(6) C'è Amanda?	(14) C'è Silvio?
(7) C'è Eva?	(15) C'è Noè?
(8) C'è Pia?	

*66. This drill uses the following time phrases:

(1) iɛri mattina	(6) stasera
(2) iɛri pomeriggio	(7) domani mattina
(3) iɛri sera	(8) domani pomeriggio
(4) stamattina	(9) domani sera
(5) questo pomeriggio	

Model:

S: Iɛri mattina?   "Yesterday morning?"
R: Nɔ, iɛri   "No, yesterday afternoon."
  pomeriggio.

You will be asked a question as in the model. Reply by using the time phrase that refers to the *next* time period. If asked about the *last* time period (No. 9), reply with the *first* time period (No. 1). Your answer will be confirmed each time. Remember to pronounce the tongue-flap correctly.

Questions

(1) Iɛri mattina?	(4) Domani mattina?
(2) Questo pomeriggio?	(5) Domani sera?
(3) Iɛri pomeriggio?	(6) Stasera?

Questions

(7) Ieri sera?	(12) Domani mattina?
(8) Stamattina?	(13) Ieri sera?
(9) Domani pomeriggio?	(14) Questo pomeriggio?
(10) Ieri mattina?	(15) Domani sera?
(11) Stamattina?	

*67. You will now hear a question containing a verb or a time word or phrase. Reply, referring to yourself, by using the appropriate one of the following:

C'èro.   Ci sôno.   Ci sarò.

Your response will be confirmed each time. Remember to pronounce the tongue-flap correctly!

Repeat this frame until you have mastered the drill.

Questions

(1) C'è?	(11) Domani sera?
(2) Ieri?	(12) C'è?
(3) Due minuti fa?	(13) C'è oggi?
(4) C'è oggi?	(14) Ieri pomeriggio?
(5) Ieri sera?	(15) Ci sarà?
(6) Ci sarà domani?	(16) Ieri mattina?
(7) C'era?	(17) C'èra ieri sera?
(8) Domani pomeriggio?	(18) Domani?
(9) Ci sarà?	(19) C'era?
(10) C'era ieri?	(20) Domani mattina?

*68. Study the following model:

a. { S. Dov'è Eva?   "Where is Eva?"
   { R: È qui.   "She's here."
       (or)

b. { S: Dov'è Cora?   "Where is Cora?"
   { R: Non so dov'è.   "I don't know where she is."

The new phrase in this drill is *non so* "I don't know." Using the chart of frame No. 60, answer as in (a) or (b) according to whether the person's name is in the "now" column or another column. Your answer will be confirmed each time. Remember to pronounce the tongue-flap correctly! Note: the word *so* is followed by a strongly pronounced consonant.

Questions

(1) Dov'è Lɛo?	(6) Dov'è Pia?
(2) Dov'è Ugo?	(7) Dov'è Amanda?
(3) Dov'è Dɔra?	(8) Dov'è Augusta?
(4) Dov'è Donata?	(9) Dov'è Lɛa?
(5) Dov'è Antɔnio?	(10) Dov'è Nɔra?

*69. Study the following model:

a. { S: Ieri dov'era Cɔra?   "Where was Cora yesterday?"
     { R: Era qui.   "She was here."
          (or)
b. { S: Ieri dov'era Eva?   "Where was Eva yesterday?"
     { R: Non sɔ dov'era.   "I don't know where she was."

Again using the chart of frame No. 60, answer as in (a) or (b) according to whether the person's name is in the "yesterday" column or not. Your answer will be confirmed each time. Remember to pronounce the tongue-flap correctly.

Questions

(1) Ieri dov'era Mara?	(6) Ieri dov'era Nora?
(2) Ieri dov'era Adɔlfo?	(7) Ieri dov'era Vera?
(3) Ieri dov'era Lɛo?	(8) Ieri dov'era Bianca?
(4) Ieri dov'era Antɔnio?	(9) Ieri dov'era Lɛa?
(5) Ieri dov'era Cɔra?	(10) Ieri dov'era Beniamino?

*70. Study the following model:

a. { S: Domani dove sarà   "Where will Augusta be tomorrow?"
     {   Augusta?
     { R: Sarà qui.   "She will be here."
          (or)
b. { S: Domani dove sarà   "Where will Eva be tomorrow?"
     {   Eva?
     { R: Non sɔ dove sarà.   "I don't know where she will be."

Again using the chart of frame No. 60, answer as in (a) or (b) according to whether the person's name is in the "tomorrow" column or not. Your answer will be confirmed each time. Remember to pronounce the tongue-flap correctly.

Questions
---

(1) Domani dove sarà Sara?
(2) Domani dove sarà Nicɔla?
(3) Domani dove sarà Silvio?
(4) Domani dove sarà Ɛva?
(5) Domani dove sarà Noè?
(6) Domani dove sarà Colomba?
(7) Domani dove sarà Guendalina?
(8) Domani dove sarà Cɔra?
(9) Domani dove sarà Pia?
(10) Domani dove sarà Oliviɛro?

*71. The following is a combination of the drills of frames No. 68, No. 69, and No. 70. Reply accordingly. Your answer will be confirmed each time. Remember to pronounce the tongue-flap correctly.

Questions
---

(1) Dov'è Cɔra?
(2) Ieri dov'ɛra Amanda?
(3) Domani dove sarà Ɛva?
(4) Dov'è Augusta?
(5) Ieri dov'ɛra Dɔra?
(6) Domani dove sarà Bianca?
(7) Dov'è Noè?
(8) Ieri dov'ɛra Vɛra?
(9) Domani dove sarà Beniamino?
(10) Dov'è Silvio?
(11) Domani dove sarà Antɔnio?
(12) Dov'è Lɛo?

(13) Ieri dov'ɛra Ugo?
(14) Domani dove sarà Oliviɛro?
(15) Dov'è Lɛa?
(16) Ieri dov'ɛra Colomba?
(17) Domani dove sarà Nɔra?
(18) Dov'è Donata?
(19) Ieri dov'ɛra Pia?
(20) Domani dove sarà Guendalina?
(21) Dov'è Mara?
(22) Ieri dov'ɛra Adɔlfo?
(23) Ieri dov'ɛra Sara?
(24) Domani dove sarà Nicɔla?

TEST A

(answers not recorded)

You will hear twenty familiar Italian items all of which should be pronounced with the TONGUE-FLAP. *Some* will be pronounced incorrectly with the con sonant sound-type of the English word "era." Put a check in the appropriate column according to whether the item is pronounced with the TONGUE-FLAP or not.

	tongue-flap	other
1) signore		
2) signora		
3) signorina		
4) buɔna sera		
5) iɛri		
6) ora		
7) pomeriggio		
8) c'ɛra		
9) Dɔra		
10) Nɔra		
11) Mara		
12) Sara		
13) Vɛra		
14) Oliviɛro		
15) sera		
16) c'ɛra		
17) ci sarà		
18) c'ɛrɔ		
19) ci sarɔ̀		
20) stasera		
21) iɛri mattina		
22) iɛri pomeriggio		
23) iɛri sera		
24) domani pomeriggio		
25) domani sera		

TEST B

(answers not recorded)

You will hear four short dialogs in Italian, each followed by five English statements about the dialogs. After each statement write *true* or *false* basing your answer on the information given in the dialog. To test yourself cover the dialogs and try to give the required answers after only listening to the dialogs.

DIALOG I

A. B. G. Come sta?
B. Non stɔ molto bene ɔggi. C'è il sig. Vegli?
A. C'εra due minuti fa, ma ora non sɔ dov'è.

    statements
    1) It's evening. _____
    2) Mr. Vegli is one of the two speakers. _____ F _____
    3) One of the speakers is not feeling well. _____ F _____
    4) Mr. Vegli was around a short time ago. _____ T _____
    5) We don't know exactly where he is now. _____ T _____

DIALOG II

A. Scusi, signore. Dov'è un capitano?
B. Ce n'è uno lì a d——; Oliviεro Segni.
A. Grazie.

    statements
    1) The two speakers are women. _____ F _____
    2) Oliviero Segni is a captain. _____ T _____
    3) He is on the left. _____ F _____
    4) The first speaker is looking for someone. _____ T _____
    5) The second speaker is thanked for his information. _____ F _____

DIALOG III

A. C'è un vaso lì?
B. Nɔ, ma c'èra un vaso qui iεri.

    statements
    1) Someone is pointing to a vase. _____ F _____
    2) There is one near the first speaker. _____ F _____
    3) There is one near the second speaker. _____ F _____
    4) There was one near the second speaker yesterday. _____ T _____
    5) The second speaker doesn't see any vase. _____ T _____

DIALOG IV

A. Buɔna sera. Ci sarà domani mattina la signorina Lira?

B. Nɔ, domani mattina non ci sarà. Ci sarà domani pomeriggio.

statements

1) It's morning. _____ F _____

2) Miss Lira won't be in tomorrow morning. _____ T _____

3) She will be in today, but in the afternoon. _____ F _____

4) Miss Lira is one of the two speakers. _____ F _____

5) Miss Lira will not be in tomorrow afternoon. _____ F _____

(answers not recorded)

You will hear ten utterances. For each utterance check only *one* of the four letters—a, b, c, d—according to which best approximates the thought behind the utterance. Do *not* expect literal translations. To test your understanding of spoken Italian, cover the Italian statements and mark your answers after only hearing the Italian.

1) Non c'ɛra Vɛra.
    (a) Vera isn't well.
    (b) Vera isn't here.
   .(c) Vera wasn't here.
    (d) Vera won't be here.

2) Ci sarò domani pomeriggio.
  . (a) I'll be there tomorrow afternoon.
    (b) He'll be there tomorrow afternoon.
    (c) She'll be there this afternoon.
    (d) You were there yesterday afternoon.

3) C'ɛ un sasso qui a s——.
  . (a) There's a stone here on the left.
    (b) There's a bone here on the left.
    (c) A bone was here on the left.
    (d) A stone was here on the right.

4) Non ci sarà niɛnte.
    (a) No one is there.
    (b) Nothing is there.
  • (c) There won't be anything there.
    (d) Nothing will be possible.

5) C'ɛ̀ra ma non ɛra qui.
  .(a) It was around, but not here.
    (b) He was there but he isn't there now.
    (c) I was there but I wasn't over here.
    (d) She was in the area, over here.

6) Non sɔ dove sarà domani mattina.
    (a) I don't know where I'll be tomorrow morning.
  • (b) I can't imagine where he'll be tomorrow morning.
    (c) I don't have any idea where he'll be tomorrow night.
    (d) I don't know where he is this morning.

7) Iɛri *c'ɛra* Ɛlio Ɛri.
    (a) Elio and I were here yesterday.
    (b) Lest night Elio was around.
    (c) Elio Eri wasn't here yesterday.
    (d) Yesterday Elio Eri was present.

8) Ci sarà un anglicano domani.
    (a) They are having an Anglican come in tomorrow.
    (b) He's becoming an Anglican tomorrow.
    (c) The Anglican will be here in the morning.
    (d) I'll be with an Anglican tomorrow.

9) Iɛri dov'ɛra, sig. Jones?
    (a) Eddie is with Mr. Jones.
    (b) Eddie was with Mr. Jones.
    (c) Where was Mr. Jones yesterday?
    (d) Where were you yesterday, Mr. Jones?

10) C'è il signore ora, ma non c'èra due minute fa.
    (a) There's the lady, but she wasn't there two minutes ago.
    (b) The gentleman is there now, but he wasn't two minutes ago.
    (c) The man was there two minutes ago.
    (d) She wasn't there two minutes ago, but she's there now.

TEST D

(not recorded)

Translate the following thoughts into Italian as best you can by using *only* what has been presented so far.

1) Cora was here this morning, wasn't she?

   C'era Cora gui sta mattina, no

2) Two minutes ago I saw a nail over here, but now it's gone.

   Due minuto fa c'era un chiodo giù, ma ora non c'è

3) Do you see Amanda anywhere around there at this time?

   C'è Amanda lì ora?

4) I won't be coming in tomorrow. I don't feel too well.

   non ci sarò domani, Non sto molto bene

5) He has already left. Miss Vegli is in, though.

   Non c'è, ma c'è Sing.ra Vegli

6) He's not doing anything right now. How about you?

   non fa niente, E tu

7) Last night you would have found a glutton here.

   Ieri sera c'era un ghiottone giù.

8) Will he be around tonight?

   ci sarà stasera

9) I don't know where he has gone, but he'll be in this afternoon.

   Non c'è, ma ci sarà questo pom.

10) I don't have any idea where he will be tomorrow night. Do you?

   Non so dove ci sarà domani sera

TEST A ANSWERS

With a tongue-flap: 1, 2, 5, 10, 11, 13, 15, 16, 17, 20, 21, 22, 25

TEST B ANSWERS

DIALOG I
  statements: (1) false, (2) false, (3) true, (4) true, (5) true,

DIALOG II
  statements: (1) false, (2) true, (3) false, (4) true, (5) true,

DIALOG III
  statements: (1) false, (2) false, (3) false, (4) true, (5) true,

DIALOG IV
  statements: (1) false, (2) true, (3) false, (4) false, (5) false

TEST C ANSWERS

1) c	3) a	5) a	7) d	9) d
2) a	4) c	6) b	8) a	10) b

TEST D ANSWERS

1) C'èra Cɔra (qui) stamattina, nɔ?
2) Due minuti fa c'èra un chiɔdo qui, ma ora non c'è.
3) C'è Amanda lì ora?
4) Non ci sarɔ domani. Non stɔ molto bɛne.
5) Non c'è (ora), ma c'è la signorina Vegli.
6) Non fa niɛnte ora. E Lei?
7) Iɛri sera c'ɛra un ghiottone qui.
8) Ci sarà stasera?
9) Non sɔ dov'è, ma ci sarà questo pomeriggio.
10) Non sɔ dove sarà domani sera. E Lɛi?

UNIT 20

1. Here are several words and phrases you have already had. Repeat.

    (c'è)X
    (ce n'è uno)X
    (c'èra)X
    (ci sarà)X
    (piace)X
    (cece)X
    (cemento)X
    (cestino)X
    (Felice)X
    (Cice)X
    (Cecè)X

2. The preceding utterances have one sound-type in common. This sound-type will be represented here as /č/.

3. Notice that in the sample Italian utterances the sound-type /č/ is represented, as is normal in Italian, by the letter *c*.

4. This should not seem strange, since even in English the words "cello" and "cellist" which contain the same type of sound are spelled with a *c*.

5. Notice that in the Italian utterances of frame No. 1 the letter *c* always occurs before the letter *e* or *i* (conventional Italian spelling).

6. Thus, one should not confuse the conventional spelling representations for

    (spelling) $\left\{ \begin{array}{c} /\check{c}\varepsilon/ \text{ or } /\check{c}E/ \\ ce \end{array} \right.$ and $\left\{ \begin{array}{c} /K\varepsilon/ \text{ or } /KE/ \\ che \end{array} \right.$

    (spelling) $\left\{ \begin{array}{c} /\check{c}I/ \\ ci \end{array} \right.$ $\left\{ \begin{array}{c} /KI/ \\ chi \end{array} \right.$

7. But what is the situation before other vowel letters? We already saw in Unit 18 that the letter *c* before other vowel letters represents sound-type /K/, as, for example, in the words:

(cane)X (cɔsa)X (conto)X (cubo)X

8. Because of this, something else is used in normal Italian spelling before letters other than *e* and *i* to represent our new sound-type /č/. This "something else" is the symbol *ci*. Look at the following words and repeat them, remembering that the letter *i* represents no vowel sound here but is simply part of the symbol for /č/.

(ciancia)X	(ciɔcia)X	(Lucio)X	(ciuco)X
"groundless rumor"	"sandal"	name, cognate of "Lucius"	"donkey"

9. A general rule, then, for the spelling representations of sound-type /č/ in Italian is:

(1) use *c* before the letter *e* or *i* (conventional Italian spelling);
(2) use *ci* elsewhere.

10. Exceptions to the preceding rule do exist, but they are rare. In any case, within a word *never* pronounce a /Y/ or unstressed sound-type No. 3 (/I/) after sound-type /č/, regardless of the spelling. Here are several exceptions to the rule stated in frame No. 9. Repeat carefully!

(ciɛlo)X	/čèLO/	"sky"
(ciɛco)X	/čèKO/	"blind man"
(deficiɛnte)X	/DEFIčèNTE/	"deficient, deficient one"
(società) X	/SOčETÁ/	"society" "society"
(spɛcie) X	/SPÉCE/	"kind, sort"

11. Instead of sound-type /č/ between vowel sounds, some speakers, especially Tuscans, pronounce something slightly different. Listen carefully to the following words pronounced first as most Italians pronounce them and secondly as you might hear them from *some* Italians.

(piace)	(piace)
(cece)	(cece)
(Felice)	(Felice)
(Cice)	(Cice)

12. Remember that the first pronunciation is the one more commonly heard.

*13. You will now hear several Italian given names. Repeat each one as you hear it. Some of the names contain one sound-type (that is, /K/) and others contain another sound-type (that is /č/). On the line following each "X" write one of the following two symbols - /K/ or /č/ according to which sound-type the name contains.

(1) (	)X_____	
(2) (	)X_____	
(3) (	)X_____	
(4) (	)X_____	
(5) (	)X_____	FEMININE
(6) (	)X_____	
(7) (	)X_____	
(8) (	)X_____	
(9) (	)X_____	
(10) (	)X_____	
(11) (	)X_____	
(12) (	)X_____	
(13) (	)X_____	
(14) (	)X_____	
(15) (	)X_____	MASCULINE
(16) (	)X_____	
(17) (	)X_____	
(18) (	)X_____	
(19) (	)X_____	
(20) (	)X_____	

14. Check yourself. You should have written /K/ for Nos. 3, 7, 8, 10, 11, 15, 19; for all the rest you should have written /č/.

*15. Now you will hear the names again. This time repeat each one as you hear it and *write* the name in the parentheses.

16. Check yourself. You should have written:

Cecilia, Celɛste, Michɛla, Alice, Licia
Berenice, Lodovica, Chiara, Bice, Micaɛla

Michɛle, Cino, Lucio, Ciro, Lodovico
Cesco, Bonifacio, Luciano, Cherubino, Sancio.

If you made any mistakes repeat the exercise until you are able to spell each name correctly.

* * * * *

• **End of Tape 6B** •

```
 ○      ○
 Tape 7A
```

17. Repeat the following utterances. They should all be familiar to you.

(giôgo)X
(maggio)X
(giugno)X
(negligɛnte)X
(B. G.)X
(Giovanni)X
(Giovanna)X
(Gino)X
(Gina)X
(Edvige)X
(Giulio)X
(Giulia)X
(Giunio)X

18. The preceding utterances have one sound-type in common. This sound-type is represented here as /Ğ/.

19. Notice that in the sample Italian utterances this soundtype /ğ/ is represented, as is normal in Italian, sometimes by the letter *g* and sometimes by the symbol *gi*.

*20. The general rule for the two spelling representations of sound-type /Ğ/ in Italian parallels the rule given for the sound-type (/Č/) referred to in frame No. 9. What would it be for /Ğ/?

21. Exceptions to the preceding rule do exist but they are rare. In any case, within a word *never* pronounce a /Y/ or unstressed sound-type No. 3 (/I/) after sound-type /Ǧ/, regardless of the spelling. Here is one exception to the rule stated in frame No. 20. Repeat carefully.

    (igiɛne)X   /IGÉNE/   "hygiene"

*22. Here are two Italian given names. The first one is masculine and is also the word for "hyacinth." The second is feminine and is also the word for "joy." Write the two words in the spaces provided.

    (   )X
    (   )X

23. You should have written: *Giacinto* and *Giɔia.*

24. Paralleling what we saw for /Č/ in frame No. 11, instead of sound-type /Ǧ/ between vowel sounds, some speakers, especially Tuscans, pronounce something slightly different. Listen carefully to the following words pronounced first as most Italians pronounce them and secondly as you might hear them from some Italians.

    (negligɛnte)   (negligɛnte)
    (Edvige)   (Edvige)
    (igiɛne)   (igiɛne)

25. Remember that the first pronunciation is the one more commonly heard.

*26. You will now hear several Italian given names. Repeat each one as you hear it. Some of the names contain one sound-type (that is /Ǧ/) and others contain another sound-type (that is,/Ǧ/). On the line following each "X" write one of the following two symbols - /Ǧ/ or /Ǧ/ according to which sound-type the name contains.

    (1) (   )X_____
    (2) (   )X_____
    (3) (   )X_____
    (4) (   )X_____
    (5) (   )X_____   FEMININE
    (6) (   )X_____
    (7) (   )X_____
    (8) (   )X_____
    (9) (   )X_____

(10) (	)X_____		
(11) (	)X_____		
(12) (	)X_____		
(13) (	)X_____		
(14) (	)X_____		
(15) (	)X_____		MASCULINE
(16) (	)X_____		
(17) (	)X_____		
(18) (	)X_____		
(19) (	)X_____		
(20) (	)X_____		

27. Check yourself. You should have written /G/ for Nos. 3, 4, 7, 9, 10, 11, 14, 17, 20; for all the rest you should have written /Ǧ/.

*28. Now you will hear the names again. This time repeat each one as you hear it and *write* the name in the parentheses.

29. Check yourself. You should have written:

 Gilda, Gisɛlda, Ghita, ɔlga, Gigi
 Gɛgia, Glɔria, Pelagia, Godiva, Galatɛa

 Gaetano, Biagio, Vigilio, Gugliɛlmo, Lüigi
 Giuliano, Ughino, Giusto, Genɛsio, Guɛlfo

If you made any mistakes repeat the exercise until you are able to spell each name correctly.

* * * * *

30. The following chart shows some common Italian letter combinations that may be troublesome for speakers of English. Repeat the combinations shown on each row after the voice on the tape.

English word to remind you of the sound

sound type	e	ε	i	a	o	ɔ	u
/K/ chemistry	che	chε	chi	ca	co	cɔ	cu*
/G/ ghetto	ghe	ghε	ghi	ga	go	gɔ	gu
/č/ cello	ce	cε	ci	cia	cio	ciɔ	ciu
	(rarely,						
	cie - ciε)						
/ǧ/ gem	ge	gε	gi	gia	gio	giɔ	giu
	(rarely,						
	gie - giε)						

*But *qu* is the usual spelling for /KW/

* * * * *

31. Repeat the familiar name that follows. Remember to pronounce the TONGUE-FLAP correctly.

(Dina Dari)X   (Dina Dari)X   (Dina Dari)X

32. Now just pronounce the last part, as follows.
ari   (3)

33. Now change the last vowel to /E/.
are   (3)

34. Now change the *first* vowel to /E/.
/ÉRE/   (3)

35. Now change the first vowel to /I/.
ire   (3)

36. Now repeat the utterances of the last three frames.
/ÁRE/   /ÉRE/   /ÍRE/

37. Repeat them once more, this time looking at the spelling but remembering to pronounce the TONGUE-FLAP.

    (are)X (ere)X (ire)X

38. Now repeat the following word, which is the general word expressing the idea of "listening." It contains the TONGUE-FLAP.

    (ascoltare)X (ascoltare)x (ascoltare)X

*39. How do you say, "Do you like it?" in Italian?

*40. How might you express, "Does it appeal to you?" in Italian?

*41. How might you express, "Do you find it to your liking?" in Italian?

*42. How do you say, "Do you like Italy?" in Italian?

*43. How would you translate, *Le piace ascoltare?* into English?

*44. Answer the preceding question in Italian with the equivalent of, "I like to listen."

45. "I like to see" is expressed in Italian as follows:

    (Mi piace vedere.)X   (Mi piace vedere.)X   (Mi piace vedere.)X

46. "I like to understand" is expressed in Italian as follows:

    (Mi piace capire.)X   (Mi piace capire.)X   (Mi piace capire.)X

47. Now repeat.

    (Mi piace ascoltare.)X   (Mi piace vedere.)X   (Mi piace capire.)X

*48. How would you say, "Do you like to see?" in Italian?

*49. How would you say, "Do you like to understand" in Italian?

*50. How would you say, "Does he like to listen?" in Italian?

*51. How would you say, "No, but he likes to understand" in Italian?

52. You will notice that the word we have been using after *Le piace, mi piace, gli piace,* etc. expresses an idea that in English often comes out as "to......." or "........-ng," for example, "to listen" or "listening," "to see" or "seeing," "to understand" or "understanding."

53. Notice also that the word in Italian ends in *-re* or, more specifically, in *-are, -ere, -ire.*

    (ascoltare)X   (vedere)X   (capire)X

54. This word, traditionally called the INFINITIVE, is a verb form that occurs in many constructions in Italian.

55. Because Italian verbs show changes such as PERSON and TENSE variations, when speaking of the entire class of related verb forms it has been found convenient to use *one* verb form to refer to all. This form has traditionally been the INFINITIVE.

56. The INFINITIVE, therefore, is the dictionary form of a verb.

57. In these units whenever something like the INFINITIVE is used to refer to an entire family of related forms, it will be preceded by ╁ . Thus, *sognare* (an infinitive) means just the one word *sognare,* but ╁*sognare* refers to the entire family of verb forms meaning "dream," such as and including *sôgno* and *sôgna.*

58. Here are infinitives for the verbs you have already had in previous units.

(chiamare)X	(chiamare)X	"call"
(fare)X	(fare)X	"do, make"
(sognare)X	(sognare)X	"dream"
(stare)X	(stare)X	"be" (referring to health in sentences like: *Come sta?, Stɔ bɛne.*)
(ɛssere)X	(ɛssere)X	"be" (not to be confused with *stare*)
(piacere)X	(piacere)X	"be liked"
(sapere)X	(sapere)X	"know"

59. Sometimes a verb used to express a certain idea always occurs in conjunction with a particle. One such verb you have had is the one you used in utterances like: C'ɛ *Tina*, C'ɛra. *Ci sarɔ*. The infinitive of this verb is:

   (ɛsserci)X   (ɛsserci)X   "be around, be in, be there, be here"

60. The following are some new infinitives that you should learn.

-are

(andare)X	(andare)X	"go"
(cominciare)X	(cominciare)X	" begin, start "
(dare)X	(dare)X	"give"
(domandare)X	(domandare)X	"ask, ask for"
(fumare)X	(fumare)X	"smoke"
(imparare)X	(imparare)X	" learn"
(lavorare)X	(lavorare)X	"work"
(mangiare)X	(mangiare)X	"eat"
(studiare)X	(studiare)X	"study"
(spiegare)X	(spiegare)X	"explain"

-ere

(avere)X	(avere)X	"have"
(bere)X	(bere)X	"drink"

-ire

(dire)X	(dire)X	"say, tell"
(finire)X	(finire)X	"finish, end"
(sentire)X	(sentire)X	"hear"
(venire)X	(venire)X	"come"

* * * * *

*61. Now you will be asked the question: *Le piace* (+ infinitive)? Answer the question with: *Sì, mi piace* (+ infinitive), while looking at the following English translations as meaning cues. Your response will be confirmed each time.

Questions	Cues
(1) Le piace chiamare qui?	"calling here"
(2) Le piace sognare?	"dreaming"
(3) Le piace stare bɛne?	"being well"
(4) Le piace non fare niɛnte?	"not doing anything"
(5) Le piace ɛssere qui?	"being here"
(6) Le piace piacere?	"being liked"

Questions	Cues
(7) Le piace sapere dove sara?	"knowing where he'll be"
(8) Le piace ascoltare?	"listening"
(9) Le piace vedere Cecilia?	"seeing Cecilia"
(10) Le piace capire?	"understanding"

*62. You will now be asked the same questions as in frame No. 61. This time cover the English cues and test yourself on the meaning. As you give your response which will be confirmed, think of an English translation and then uncover the appropriate meaning cue. Repeat this frame until you are satisfied that you know the meaning of each utterance.

*63. Again you will be asked the question: *Le piace* (+ infinitive)? This time answer the question in the negative with: *No, non mi piace* (+ infinitive), while looking at the following English translations as meaning cues. Your response will be confirmed each time.

Questions	Cues
(1) Le piace andare lì?	"going there"
(2) Le piace cominciare qui?	"starting here"
(3) Le piace non dare niɛnte?	"not giving anything"
(4) Le piace non domandare niɛnte?	"not asking for anything"
(5) Le piace fumare?	"smoking"
(6) Le piace non imparare niɛnte?	"not learning anything"
(7) Le piace lavorare?	"working"
(8) Le piace mangiare male?	"eating poorly"
(9) Le piace studiare?	"studying"
(10) Le piace spiegare ?	"explaining"

*64. You will now be asked the same questions as in frame No. 63. This time cover the English cues and test yourself on the meaning. As you give your response, which will be confirmed, think of an English translation and then uncover the appropriate meaning cue. Repeat this frame until you are satisfied that you know the meaning of each utterance.

*65. Now you will be asked the questions *Mi piace* (+ infinitive)? – "Do I like......?" Answer the question with: *Sì, Le piace* (+ infinitive) – "Yes, you like......" while looking at the following English translations as meaning cues. Your response will be confirmed each time.

Questions	Cues
(1) Mi piace non avere niɛnte?	"not having anything"
(2) Mi piace bere?	"drinking"
(3) Mi piace non dire niɛnte?	"not saying anything"
(4) Mi piace finire qui?	"ending here"
(5) Mi piace non sentire niɛnte?	"not hearing anything"
(6) Mi piace venire qui ?	"coming here"

*66. You will now be asked the same questions as in frame No. 65. This time cover the English cues and test yourself on the meaning. As you give your response, which will be confirmed, think of an English translation and then uncover the appropriate meaning cue. Repeat this frame until you are satisfied that you know the meaning of each utterance.

*67. Study the following model.

    S: ɛ̀ lì Cecilia?   "Is Cecilia (over) there?"

    (cue)......"working"   "Yes, she likes to work there."

    R: Sɔ, le piace lavorare lì.   "Yes, she likes to work there."

        (or)

    Nɔ, non le place   "No, she doesn't like to

      lavorare lì.   work there. "

You will now be asked questions about different women, as in the model above. Reply as in the model, by using the cues below. Your response will be confirmed each time.

Questions	Cues
(1) ɛ̀ lì Cecilia?	Sì,........ *lavorare*
(2) ɛ̀ lì Celɛste?	Sì,........ *andare*
(3) ɛ̀ lì Michɛla?	Sì,........ *essere*
(4) ɛ̀ lì Alice?	Nɔ,....... *mangiare*
(5) ɛ̀ lì Licia?	Nɔ,....... *bere*
(6) ɛ̀ lì Gilda?	Sì,........ *studiare*
(7) ɛ̀ lì Gisɛlda?	Sì,........ "drinking"
(8) ɛ̀ lì Ghita?	Nɔ,....... "working"
(9) ɛ̀ lì Ɔlga?	Nɔ,....... "going"
(10) ɛ̀ lì Gigi?	Sì,........ "eating"
(11) ɛ̀ lì la signora Segni?	Nɔ,....... "being"
(12) ɛ̀ lì la signorina Paglia?	Nɔ,....... "studying"

*68. Study the following model.

> S: Cino? (or)   "Cino?" (or)
> Cino e Lucio?   "Cino and Lucio?"
> (cue)...... "working"   { he
> R: Sì, gli piace   "Yes, { they like(s) to work there."
>   lavorare lì.
>   (or)   { he doesn't
> Nɔ, non gli piace   "No, { they don't like to work there."
>   lavorare lì.

You will now be asked questions about a man or about two people as in the model above. Reply as in the model, by using the cues below. Your response will be confirmed each time.

Questions	Cues
(1) Cino?	Sì,........ "working"
(2) Michɛle?	Nɔ,........ "going"
(3) Lucio e Ciro?	Sì,........ "being"
(4) Lodovico?	Nɔ,........ "eating"
(5) Pelagia e Galatɛa?	Nɔ,........ "drinking"
(6) Gaetano?	Nɔ,........ "studying"
(7) Biagio e Egidio?	Sì,........ "drinking"
(8) Gugliɛlmo?	Nɔ,........ "being"
(9) Lüigi?	Sì,........ "eating"
(10) Ughino e Giusto?	Sì,........ "studying"
(11) Glɔria e Godiva?	Sì,........ "going"
(12) il sig. Segni?	Sì,........ "working"

*69. You have just learned from the previous drill that the "he like to......" and "they like to......" may be expressed in Italian by the same phrase. What is it?

*70. Study the following model.

> S: Vi piace lavorare?   "Do you like to work?"
>
> (cue)......Sì (or) Nɔ
> R: Sì, ci piace lavorare.   "Yes, we like to work."
>   (or)
> Nɔ, non ci piace lavorare.   "No, we don't like to work."

You will now be asked the question: *Vi piace* (+ infinitive)? used in addressing more than one person. Answer the question as in the model, by using the cues below. The English translations are provided simply to remind you of the meaning. Your response will be confirmed each time.

Questions	Cues
(1) Vi piace ascoltare?	Sì,........ "listening"
(2) Vi piace non vedere niεnte?	Sì,........ "seeing nothing"
(3) Vi piace capire?	Sì,........ "understanding"
(4) Vi piace mangiare qui?	Nɔ,....... "seating here"
(5) Vi piace bere qui?	Nɔ,....... "drinking here"
(6) Vi piace non fare niεnte?	Sì, ... "doing nothing"
(7) Vi piace cominciare qui?	Nɔ,....... "starting here"
(8) Vi piace finire qui?	Nɔ,....... "ending here"
(9) Vi piace chiamare?	Sì,........ "calling"
(10) Vi piace fumare qui?	Nɔ,....... "smoking here"

*71. If the *vi* in the preceding drill is a plural counterpart of *Le*, what is *ci* the plural counterpart of?

*72. You will now be asked the same questions as in frame No. 70. This time cover the English cues and test yourself on the meaning. As you give your response, which will be confirmed, think of an English translation and then uncover the appropriate meaning cue. Repeat this frame until you are satisfied that you know the meaning of each utterance.

*73. Study the following model.
    S: Che cɔsa (non) ci piace fare?   "What do(n't) we like to do?"
    (cue)......"work"
    R: (Non) vi piace lavorare.   "You (don't) like to work."

Reply as in the model by using the cues below. Your response will be confirmed each time.

Questions	Cues
(1) Che cɔsa ci piace fare?	"dream"
(2) Che cɔsa non ci piace fare?	"study"
(3) Che cɔsa non ci piace fare?	"explain"
(4) Che cɔsa non ci piace fare?	"go there"
(5) Che cɔsa ci piace fare?	"ask"
(6) Che cɔsa ci piace fare?	"not give anything"
(7) Che cɔsa ci piace fare?	"learn"
(8) Che cɔsa ci piace fare?	"not say anything"
(9) Che cɔsa non ci piace fare?	"work"
(10) Che cɔsa non ci piace fare?	"listen"

Repeat this frame until you are satisfied that you know the meaning of each utterance.

*74. Study the following models.

a.
S: Mi piace Cecilia.   "I like Cecilia."
(or) Cecilia mi piace.
R-S: Chi Le piace?   "Whom do you like?"
R: Mi piace Cecilia.   "I like Cecilia."
(or)

b.
S: Mi piace l'Italia.   "I like Italy."
(or) l'Italia mi piace.
R-S: Che cɔsa Le piace?   "What do you like?"
R: Mi piace l'Italia.   "I like Italy."
(or)

c.
S: Mi piace lavorare.   "I like to work."
R-S: Che cɔsa Le piace fare?   "What do you like to do?"
R: Mi piace lavorare.   "I like to work."

You will hear a statement about someone liking or not liking (a) a person, (b) a thing or a place, or (c) to do something. Ask the appropriate question as in the models. Your question will be confirmed each time, followed by the final response.

NOTE: If *le* is in the statement it is to be understood as referring to a third person, "she."

Statements

(1) Mi piace Berenice.	(16) Non gli piace Giacinto.
(2) Mi piace l'ɔlio.	(17) Gli piace bere.
(3) Non ci piace imparare.	(18) Giɔia ci piace.
(4) Non gli piace luglio.	(19) Non mi piace Cherubino.
(5) Gli piace Micaɛla.	(20) Mi piace mangiare.
(6) Gli piace Giulio.	(21) Mi piace capire.
(7) Non le piace cominciare qui.	(22) Non mi piace Sancio.
(8) Non ci piace Giunio.	(23) Chiara non ci piace.
(9) Ci piace la Campania.	(24) Ci piace la vigna.
(10) Giugno mi piace.	(25) Ci piace Bolôgna.
(11) Non mi piace studiare.	(26) Non gli piace Lavinia.
(12) Non gli piace venire qui.	(27) Non le piace Luciano.
(13) Ci piace ascoltare.	(28) Ci piace l'Italia.
(14) Ci piace finire qui.	(29) Non le piace Bice.
(15) Lodovica non mi piace.	(30) La camgpagna non mi piace.

TEST A

(answers not recorded)

You will hear words that have appeared in this unit. Write them on the appropriate line, being very careful of the spelling.

1) _Cece_

2) _Covca_

3) _Monghava_

4) _____

5) _____

6) _____

7) _____

8) _____

9) _____

10) _____

11) _____

12) _____

13) _____

14) _____

15) _____

16) _____

17) _____

18) _____

19) _____

20) _____

TEST B

(answers not recorded)

You will hear ten questions in Italian. For each question pick the best response
—a, b, c ,or d. (Cover the Italian questions; just listen.)

1) Non Le piace l'ɔlio?
   (a) Sì, non mi piace.
   (b) Sì, non Le piace.
   (c) Nɔ, mi piace.
   (d) Nɔ, non my piace.

2) B. G. Come sta, sig. Brown?
   (a) Il sig. Brown non sta molto
      bɛne.
   (b) Stɔ così così, g——.
   (c) Il sig. Brown non mi piace.
   (d) Sta male.

3) Dov'ɛra il signore due minuti fa?
   (a) Non sɔ dov'ɛra.
   (b) Èra il sig. Segni.
   (c) Due minuti fa c'ɛra il signore.
   (d) Il signore è qui a d——.

4) Chi vi piace ora?
   (a) Non mi piace l'Italia.
   (b) Le piace Genɛsio.
   (c) Ci piace Guɛlfo.
   (d) Ci piace cominciare qui.

5) Ci sarà domani?
   (a) Ci sarɔ ma non mi piace
      lavorare qui.
   (b) Sì, c'è.
   (c) Nɔ, non c'ɛra.
   (d) Nɔ, non c'è male.

6) Non Le piace lavorare lì?
   (a) Sì, mi piace ma non fa niɛnte.
   (b) Sì, mi piace. Non faccio niɛnte.
   (c) Nɔ, mi piace e non c'è niɛnte.
   (d) Nɔ, non Le piace e non ci sarɔ
      domani.

7) C'è an cestino lì a s——?
   (a) Sì, dov'è un cestino?
   (b) Sì, c'ɛra un cestino.
   (c) Sì, ma non ci sarà domani.
   (d) Sì, iɛri pomeriggio.

8) Chi chiama ora?
   (a) Chiamo Vigilio.
   (b) Sôgna.
   (c) Chiama qui a d——.
   (d) Gli piace chiamare.

9) Il signore sta bɛne ora, nɔ?
   (a) Sì, non sta bɛne ora.
   (b) Nɔ, non chiamo.
   (c) Nɔ, c'è un cemento qui.
   (d) Sì, ma non fa niɛnte.

10) Che cɔsa non mi piace fare?
   (a) Sì, mi piace bere qui.
   (b) Non mi piace spiegare.
   (c) Non gli piace domandare.
   (d) Non Le piace fumare.

TEST C

(answers not recorded)

You will hear ten utterances. For each utterance check *only one* of the four letters
—a, b, c, d, according to which best approximates the thought behind the utterance. Do *not* expect literal translations! (To test your understanding of spoken
Italian, cover the Italian).

1) C'è Cecè ora?
   (a) Is he there now?
   (b) It is. Is it Cora?
   (c) Is there a chick-pea now?
   (d) Is Cece there now?

2) Gioia non gli piace.
   (a) Gioia doesn't like him.
   (b) He doesn't like Gioia.
   (c) She doesn't like Gioia.
   (d) Gioia doesn't like them.

3) Le piace non sapere niente?
   (a) She doesn't like anything.
   (b) Do you like not knowing
       anything?
   (c) Does she like not drinking
       anything?
   (d) She doesn't like not knowing
       anything.

4) Che casa non Le piace spiegare?
   (a) What is it that you don't like to
       explain?
   (b) Whom don't you like to listen to?
   (c) What doesn't she want to say?
   (d) Who doesn't like to explain it?

5) Mi piace lavorare ma non mi piace
   lavorare lì.
   (a) I'm interested in working, but
       not there.
   (b) I like to work, but I want to
       work there.
   (c) I don't like to work here
       although I like working.
   (d) I'd like to work, but never
       over there.

6) Non so dove vi piace studiare.
   (a) I don't know if you like to
       study.
   (b) Not so! Where do you like to
       study?
   (c) I have no idea where you like to
       study.
   (d) You don't know where I like to
       study.

7) Ci piace piacere.
   (a) We enjoy being liked.
   (b) He likes us.
   (c) He is liked there.
   (d) We are liked here.

8) Domani pomeriggio ci sarà cice.
   (a) He'd like to be there in the
       afternoon.
   (b) You'll see a chick-pea tomorrow
       afternoon.
   (c) Tomorrow evening he'll be
       there as he is now.
   (d) Cice will be around tomorrow
       afternoon.

9) C'era, c'è e ci sarà.
   (a) He was there before, he is there
       now and he'll be there in the
       future.
   (b) Cece will be there as he was
       before.
   (c) Sarah was there with a chick-
       pea.
   (d) It was, it is and it will always be.

10) C'è un cede a s—— ora.
    (a) It's around on the left now.
    (b) Cecilia is on the left now.
    (c) On the left is a chick-pea.
    (d) Now there is Cece on the left.

• **End of Tape 7A** •

TEST D

(not recorded)

Translate the following thoughts into Italian by using *only* what has been presented so far.

1) I like to dream.

_____

2) I don't like being sick.

_____

3) Do you like calling Olga? (singular)

_____

4) Don't you like to listen? (singular)

_____

5) You like doing nothing, don't you? (singular)

_____

6) He likes being where he is now.

_____

7) She likes being liked.

_____

8) She doesn't like to see Cino.

_____

9) He doesn't like not knowing anything.

_____

10) She enjoys eating.

_____

11) Does she like to drink?

_____

12) We don't like not understanding anything.

_____

13) We don't like to work.

_____

14) We take pleasure out of coming here.

_____

15) You mean you don't like to study? (plural)

_____

16) What do you like to smoke? (plural)

_____

17) What don't you like to explain? (plural)

_____

18) Do you like to go there? (plural)

_____

19) They don't like to start over there.

_____

20) They like to ask.

_____

21) Do they like not having anything?

_____

22) Do they like not saying anything?

_____

23) He likes not giving anything.

_____

24) He doesn't like to give anything.

_____

25) He doesn't like to give nothing.

_____

TEST E

(not recorded)

Translate the following thoughts into Italian by using *only* what has been presented so far.

1) A donkey is on the right. Do you like it? (addressing one person)

_____

2) There's a blind man here on the left.

_____

3) What aren't you interested in doing, miss?

_____

4) Do you get any pleasure out of smoking? (addressing three people)

_____

5) We like her, but she's never around.

_____

6) Nothing suits them.

_____

7) Last night they saw him in the area, but today he's missing.

_____

8) There's one over there, but he doesn't care for it.

_____

9) I like Gloria, but I don't know where she is right now.

_____

10) They don't like to work, but they like the country.*

_____

*as opposed to "the city."

TEST A ANSWERS

1) cece	6) giugno	11) piacere	16) Guglielmo
2) ciocia	7) Ghita	12) giôgo	17) Giovanna
3) Chiara	8) ciancia	13) Sancio	18) deficiente
4) mangiare	9) Giacinto	14) cominciare	19) igiene
5) spiegare	10) Lucio	15) ciuco	20) Ughino

TEST B ANSWERS

1) d	3) a	5) a	7) c	9) d
2) b	4) c	6) b	8) a	10) d

TEST C ANSWERS

1) d	3) b	5) a	7) a	9) a
2) b	4) a	6) c	8) d	10) c

TEST D   ANSWERS

1) Mi piace sognare.
2) Non mi piace stare male.
3) Le piace chiamare Ɔlga?
4) Non Le piace ascoltare?
5) Le piace non fare niɛnte, nɔ?
6) Gli piace ɛssere dov'è ora.
    or
   Gli piace ɛssere lì.
7) Le piace piacere.
8) Non le piace vedere Cino.
9) Non gli piace non sapere
   niɛnte.
10) Le piace mangiare.
11) Le piace bere?

12) Non ci piace non capire niɛnte.
13) Non ci piace lavorare.
14) Ci piace venire qui.
15) Non vi piace studiare?
16) Che cɔsa vi piace fumare?
17) Che cɔsa non vi piace spiegare?
18) Vi piace andare lì?
19) Non gli piace cominciare lì.
20) Gli piace domandare.
21) Gli piace non avere niɛnte?
22) Gli piace non dire niɛnte?
23) Gli piace non dare niɛnte.
24) Non gli piace dare niɛnte.
25) Non gli piace non dare niɛnte.

TEST E   ANSWERS

1) C'è un ciuco a d——. Le piace?
2) C'è un ciɛco qui a s——.
3) Che cɔsa non Le piace fare, signorina?
4) Vi piace fumare?
5) Ci piace, ma non c'è mai.
6) Non gli piace niɛnte.
7) Iɛri sera c'èra, ma oggi non c'è.
8) Ce n'è uno lì, ma non gli piace.
9) Mi piace Glɔria, ma non sɔ dov'è ora.
10) Non gli piace lavorare, ma gli piace la campagna.

RECAPITULATION (Units 16–20)

Sound-Types

sound-types	written symbols	as in:	unit
/K/	q [before /W/] ch [before ε, e, i] c [elsewhere]	qui che, chi cane, cosa, cubo	18
/G/	gh [before ε, e, i] g [elsewhere]	ghetto, ghigno gas, golf, Guido	18
/R/	r	c'εro, ieri	19
/č/	c [before ε, e, i] ci [elsewhere]	c'εra, cece, Cice ciancia, ciocia, ciuco	20
/ğ/	g [before ε, e, i] gi [elsewhere]	Edvige, Gina Giacinto, Gioia, giugno	20

Greetings (Unit 17)

Buon giorno — used during the daylight hours (morning or afternoon) as a greeting or a leave-taking expression.

Buona sera — used during the evening or late afternoon hours as a greeting or a leave-taking expression.

Titles in Direct Address or Not (Unit 17)

direct address	other
signore "sir"	*il signore*
signora "madam"	*la signora*
signorina "miss"	*la signorina*
signor Segni "Mr. Segni"	*il signor Segni*
signora Segni "Mrs. Segni"	*la signora Segni*
signorina Segni "Miss Segni"	*la signorina Segni*

Person Differences (Unit 19)

Differences between forms like *sarò* and *sarà, ero* and *era.*

Tense Differences (Unit 19)

Differences between forms like *sarò* and *ero, è,* and *era.*

Verb (Units 17 and 19)

A class of forms most of which show variation for PERSON and TENSE. For example: *essere, sôno, ero, è, sarà.*

Finite Verb Form (Unit 17)

A verb form that shows limitations regarding the person being referred to. For example: *sôno, ero, è, sarà.*

Infinitive (Unit 20)

The dictionary form of a verb, used as the name of an entire family of related verb forms. For example, the INFINITIVE form *essere,* when written ┼*essere* refers to the entire family of verb forms meaning "to be," such as and including *sôno, ero, è,* and *sarà.*

"Liking to Do Something" (Unit 20)

My piace lavorare.	"I like to work."
Le piace lavorare.	"You [sg.] like to work." or "She likes to work."
Gli piace lavorare.	"He likes to work." or "They like to work."
Ci piace lavorare.	"We like to work."
Vi piace lavorare.	"You [pl.] like to work."
Non mi piace lavorare.	"I don't like to work."
Non Le piace lavorare.	"You [sg.] don't like to work."
Non le piace lavorare.	"She doesn't like to work."
Non gli piace lavorare.	"He doesn't like to work." or "They don't like to work."
Non ci piace lavorare.	"We don't like to work."
Non vi piace lavorare.	"You [pl.] don't like to work."

HEALTH SENTENCES (Unit 16)

Affirmative Statements	Verification Questions	Negative Statements	Yes-No Questions	Information Questions
Amanda sta bene. "Amanda is well."	*Amanda sta bene, nɔ?* "Amanda is well, isn't she?"	*Amanda non sta (molto) bene* "Amanda is not (very) well."	*(Non) sta bɛne Amanda?* "Is(n't) Amanda well?"	*Come sta Amanda?* "How is Amanda?"

LOCATION SENTENCES (Unit 18)

Affirmative Statements	Information Questions
C'è un cɔno qui. "There's one here." *Ce n'è uno qui.* "There's one here."	*Dov'è un cɔne?* "Where is a cone?"
Amanda è qui. "Amanda is here." *È qui.* "(S)he is here."	*Dov'è Amanda?* "Where is Amanda?"

Tape 7B

UNIT 21

*1. What did we call the consonant sound-type that occurs in the following?
   /èRI/ èRA/

*2. How is the tongue-flap represented in normal Italian spelling?

*3. Is the following statement true or false?
   "In American English the letter *r* normally does not stand for a tongue-flap, but often, between vowels; the tongue-flap is heard in words spelled with *t* or *d*."

4. The following English utterances may all be pronounced with a tongue-flap, and they usually are by many speakers of American English. Reading across each row, listen carefully to each item and imitate the pronunciation carefully, being sure to pronounce a tongue-flap in each one. The Italian sound-types indicated are only close approximations.

   NOTES:
   (a) Underlined letters are not to represent any sound for purposes of this drill.
   (b) "N.E." means that a New England type of pronunciation is called for.
   (c) For the third column pronounce the items of the second column with /E/ in place of /I/.
   (d) For the last column use final /U/ instead of the final vowel + /l/.

/A/ - /A/	/A/ - /I/	/A/ - /E/	/A/ - /O/	/A/ - /U/
(gotta)X	(Dotty)X		(lotto)X	(bottle)X
(lot o')X	(knotty)X		(motto)X	
N.E.	N.E.			N.E.
(ga<u>r</u>ter)X	(Ma<u>r</u>ty)X			(sta<u>r</u>tle)X

/ε/ - /A/	/ε/ - /I/	/ε/ - /E/	/ε/ - /O/	/ε/ - /U/
(Etta)X	(Betty)X		(ghetto)X	(settle)X
(Nedda)X	(Eddie)X			

/E/ - /A/	/E/ - /I/	/E/ - /E/	/E/ - /O/	/E/ - /U/
(Ada)X	(eighty)X		(Nato)X	(ladle)X
(waiter)X	(Sadie)X		(tomato)X	

/I/ - /A/	/I/ - /I/	/I/ - /E/	/I/ - /O/	/I/ - /U/
(Lita)X	(meaty)X		(Mito)X	(needle)X
(seater)X	(needy)X		(Seato)X	

/ɔ/ - /A/	/ɔ/ - /I/	/ɔ/ - /E/	/ɔ/ - /O/	/C/ - /U/
(oughta)X	(naughty)X		(auto)X	N.E.(model)X

/O/ - /A/	/O/ - /I/	/O/ - /E/	/O/ - /O/	/O/ - /U/
(quota)X	(Jody)X		(moto)X	(modal)X

/U/ - /A/	/U/ - /I/	/U/ - /E/	/U/ - /O/	/U/ - /U/
(barracuda)X	(booty)X		(Pluto)X	(noodle)X
(suitor)X	(duty)X			

5. The English utterances on the preceding page, when pronounced as they were with a tongue-flap, would probably be represented as follows by a native speaker of Italian; Reading across each row, look at the items and repeat after the voice on the tape, always bearing in mind that the letter *r* represents a tongue-flap.

/A/ - /A/	/A/ - /I/		/A/ - /O/	/A/ - /U/
(gara)X	(dari)X		(laro)X	(baru)X
(lara)X	(nari)X		(maro)X	(staru)X
(bara)X	(mari)X			

/ε/ - /A/	/ε/ - /I/		/ε/ - /O/	/E/ - /U/
(Era)X	(beri)X		(ghero)X	(seru)X
(nera)X	(eri)X			

/E/ - /A/	/E/ - /I/	/E/ - /O/	/E/ - /U/
(era)X	(eri)X	(nero)X	(leru)X
(uera)X	(seri)X	(mero)X	

/I/ - /A/	/I/ - /I/	/I/ - /O/	/I/ - /U/
(lira)X	(miri)X	(miro)X	(niru)X
(sira)X	(niri)X	(siro)X	

/ɔ/ - /A/	/ɔ/ - /I/	/ɔ/ - /O/	/ɔ/ - /U/
(ɔra)X	(nɔri)X	(ɔro)X	(mɔru)X

/O/ - /A/	/O/ - /I/	/O/ - /O/	/O/ - /U/
(quora)X	(giori)X	(moro)X	(moru)X

/U/ - /A/	/U/ - /I/	/U/ - /O/	/U/ - /U/
(ura)X	(buri) X	(pluro)x	(nuru)X
(sura)X	(duri)X		

6. The items of frame no. 5 were all pronounced with the stress on the first vowel. Repeat them, this time stressing the *last* vowel.

7. Once you can pronounce these items using a tongue-flap, you should not find it difficult to produce the tongue-flap in all of the following combinations. Reading across each row, look at the spelling and repeat carefully. The underlined vowel letter indicates the vowel that is to be stressed.

(ara)X	(ari)X	(are)x	(aro)X	(aru)X
(ara)X	(ari)X	(are)X	(aro)X	(aru)X
		(arɛ)X	(arɔ)X	

(ɛra)X	(ɛri)X	(ɛre)X	(ɛro)X	(ɛru)x

(era)X	(eri)X	(ere)X	(ero)X	(eru)X
(era)X	(eri)X	(ere)x	(ero)X	(eru)X
		(erɛ)X	(erɔ)X	

(i̱ra)X	(i̱ri)X	(i̱re)X	(i̱ro)X	(i̱ru)X
(ira̱)X	(iri̱)X	(ire̱)X	(iro̱)X	(iru̱)X
		(irɛ)X	(irɔ)X	

(ɔ̱ra)X	(ɔ̱ri)X	(ɔ̱re)X	(ɔ̱ro)X	(ɔ̱ru)X

(o̱ra)X	(o̱ri)X	(o̱re)X	(o̱ro)X	(o̱ru)X
(ora̱)X	(ori̱)X	(ore̱)X	(oro̱)X	(oru̱)X
		(orɛ)X	(orɔ)X	

(u̱ra)X	(u̱ri)X	(u̱re)X	(u̱ro)X	(u̱ru)X
(ura̱)X	(uri̱)X	(ure̱)X	(uro̱)X	(uru̱)X
		(urɛ)X	(urɔ)X	

8. Listen to the following Italian word.

   americano (2)

9. Notice how this word sounds a little like what a Southern American named Eddie Cano might say in introducing himself. Repeat.

   americano (2)

10. Actually, what has just been presented is the Italian word used to refer to an American man or boy. Repeat once more.

    americano (2)

11. Now repeat while looking at the actual spelling but remembering the pronunciation hint given in frame no. 9.

    (americano)X   (americano)X

* * * * *

12. Repeat the following utterances, stressing the last vowel each time.

    (ara̱)X (ari̱)X (are̱)X (arɛ̱)X (aro̱)X (arɔ̱)X (aru̱)X

13. Now try to pronounce these items while omitting the first syllable. You might try *thinking* of the initial /A/ but either *not pronouncing it* at all or pronouncing it so softly that only you can hear it.

    (ra) (ri) (re) (rɛ) (ro) (rɔ) (ru)

14. What you have been trying to pronounce is the tongue-flap that *begins* a
    syllable. Actually, what to an Italian sounds like a syllable-initial
    tongue-flap *can* be heard in American English. The utterances you just
    repeated in frame no. 13 are approximately represented in column A as
    English phrases, and in column B they are represented as Italian syllables.
    Repeat them again.

A (English)	B (Italian)		
at "Ah"	ra	(	)X
at "Ee"	ri	(	)X
at "A"	re	(	)X
at "Eh"	rɛ	(	)X
at "Oh"	ro	(	)X
at "Aw"	rɔ	(	)X
at "Oo"	ru	(	)X

15. Although the pronunciation of this consonant in syllable-initial position
    may vary among Italians, what you have just heard appears to be most
    common, that is, a single tongue-flap. Repeat the following, noticing how
    what you hear might be approximately represented in American English as
    "at Oma," but that the Italian ear hears the Italian name of the capital of
    Italy, *Roma*.

    Roma (2)

16. Now repeat the following given names that begin with the tongue-flap.

    (Rachɛle)X
    (Regina)X
    (Renata)X
    (Rina)X   } FEMININE
    (Rita)X
    (Rɔsa)X
    (Rosina)X

(Renato)X
(Rico)X
(Rinaldo)X   } MASCULINE
(Rodɔlfo)X
(Rolando)X
(Romɛo)X

* * * * *

17. Repeat the following utterance that contains two tongue-flaps.
    (arari̱)X   (arari̱)X   (arari̱)X

18. Now try omitting the middle vowel, reducing the utterance to two sylla-
    bles.
    (ar-ri̱)X   (ar-ri̱)X   (ar-ri̱)X

19. If you find it hard to make two successive tongue-flaps, practice by saying
    the utterance of frame no. 17 rapidly several times. Repeat.
    (arri̱)X   (arri̱)X   (arri̱)X   (arri̱)X   (arri̱)X

20. When two or more tongue-flaps occur successively as in *arri*, the result is
    referred to as a "trill."

*21. What do two or more successive tongue-flaps constitute?

22. The following is the word used to indicate that something or someone
    other than the speaker is arriving. Repeat.
    (arriva)X   (arriva)X   (arriva)X

*23. Does this word contain a single tongue-flap or a trill?

*24. How is the tongue-flap represented in Italian spelling?

*25. How is the trill represented between vowels within a word?

*26. Putting the name at the end of the question, *as is normal in Italian questions*,
    how would you ask, "Is Rachele arriving?" in Italian?

*27. How do you think you would say, "I'm arriving now" in Italian?

* * * * *

28. Listen carefully to the following question-answer pair:
    Chi è?   - *È Rɔsa.*

    "Who is ⎰ it?"
            ⎱ she?" - "It's Rosa?"

*29. Does the previous response contain a flap or a trill? Listen again and repeat.

  (È Rɔsa.)x (È Rɔsa.)X (È Rɔsa.)X

30. The previous frame illustrates that words that normally begin with a tongue-flap (such as *Rosa*) are pronounced with an initial trill after certain words, many of which are one-syllable words (such as: *è, c'è, chi, qui, lì, sì, nɔ*)

31. You may remember that after such words a following consonant is normally strongly pronounced. See RECAP. (1–10) 2.

32. Repeat the following.

Flap	Trill
(Rachɛle)X	(È Rachɛle.)X
(Regina)X	(È Regina.)X
(Renata)X	(È Renata.)X
(Rina)X	(È Rina.)X
(Rita)X	(È Rita.)X
(Rɔsa)X	(È Rɔsa.)X
(Rosina)X	(È Rosina.)X
(Renato)X	(È Renato.)X
(Rico)X	(È Rico.)X
(Rinaldo)X	(È Rinɔldo.)X
(Rodɔlfo)X	(È Rodɔlfo.)X
(Rolando)X	(È Rolando.)X
(Romɛo)X	(È Romɛo.)X

      * * * * *

33. Here is another one-syllable word after which a following consonant is normally strongly pronounced——*a*. Hence, after *a*, words that usually begin with a tongue-flap are normally pronounced with a trill. The word *a* followed by the name of a city or town indicates "movement to" or "location in or at."

  (a)X (a)X (a)X

34. Thus, the Italian equivalent of "to Riva" (a city in Northern Italy) sounds like *arriva*. Repeat.

  (a Riva)X (a Riva)X (a Riva)X

*35. How do you say "in Rome" in Italian?

*36. How do you say, "He's arriving in Rome" in Italian?

37. The word *ad* is frequently found instead of *a* whenever the following word begins with the vowel /A/.

*38. Therefore, how would you say "in Ancona" in Italian?

* * * * *

39. Not all one-syllable words are followed by a strongly pronounced consonant, however, and after the word *do*, for example, a tongue-flap (and *not* a trill) is normal. Repeat.

   (di Roma)X   (di Roma)X   (di Roma)X

40. When followed by the name of a city, the word *di* indicates origin. Hence, *di Roma* means "originating in Rome," "born in Rome."

*41. How do you say, "She's a native of Rome" in Italian?

*42. What is the Italian equivalent of, "I'm from Rio," meaning, "I was born and raised in Rio"?

* * * * *

43. So far you have heard the following verb forms used in referring to present time. For this reason such verb forms may be called PRESENT TENSE examples. Repeat.

referring to the speaker	referring to a thing or a person other than the speaker
(chiamo)X	(chiama)X
(sôgno)X	(sôgna)X
(faccio)X	(fa)X
(stɔ)X	(sta)X
(sôno)X	(è)X
(hi sôno)X	(c'è)X
(arrivo)X	(arriva)X

44. The PRESENT TENSE has various meanings, the most important of which is "something in progress or in existence at the time of utterance."

45. This "something" may be a *single, durative event*, as in:

(Chiama ora.)X	"(S)he is calling now."
(Sôgna ora.)X	"(S)he is dreaming now."
(Non fa niɛnte ora.)X	"(S)he is not doing anything now."
(Sta bɛne ora.)X	"(S)he is fine now."
(Ɛ̀ qui ora.)X	"(S)he is here now."
(C'ɛ̀ ora.)X	"(S)he is $\begin{cases} \text{in} \\ \text{around now.}" \end{cases}$

46. The events mentioned in the preceding frame are "durative" because the *beginning* and the *end* of each event are separated by a *duration of time*.

47. With certain other verbs, however, the *beginning* and the *end* of the event referred to are *not* separated, but simultaneous. Such verbs are said to refer to "punctual" rather than "durative" events.

48. Thus, an "arrival" is punctual, whereas events like "eating" and "sleeping" are durative.

49. When we say, "The train is arriving now," the "now" is not referring to an intermediate point between the beginning and the end of the arrival, since an arrival, by definition, is punctual and can have no intermediate point.

50. What we *are* referring to when we say, "The train is arriving now," however, is an intermediate point of the *events leading to the actual arrival*. Thus, the idea contained in the sentence is similar to the idea behind, "The train is about to arrive."

51. With such "punctual" verbs the "something" referred to in frame no. 44 is the *events leading to the punctual act*, as in:

(Arriva ora.)X	"It $\begin{cases} \\ \end{cases}$ "(S)he is arriving now."

*52. Does the verb "begin" express a durative or a punctual idea?

*53. What about the verb "work"?

*54. And the verb "write"?

*55. And the verb "leave"?

*56. And the verb "walk"?

57. The "something" referred to in frame no. 44 may also be a *series consisting of the repetition of an event,* as in:

(Chiama ogni sera.)X	"(S)he calls every evening."
(Sôgna spesso.)X	"(S)he dreams often."
(Che cɔsa fa?)X	"What (kind of work) does (s)he do?"
(Sta male ogni mattina.)X	"(S)he is sick every morning."
(È qui ogni pomeriggio.)X	"(S)he is here every afternoon."
(C'è spesso.)X	"(S)he is often around."
(Arriva spesso con Rɔsa.)X	"(S)he often arrives with Rosa."
(Sôgna molto.)X	"(S)he dreams a lot."

58. A fourth "something" referred to in frame no. 44 is a *plan or schedule* for *something* (most usually a punctual act) to happen in the future (especially in the immediate future). The emphasis is on the fact that it *is* planned or scheduled. For example:

(Arrivo domani sera.)X
{
"I am arriving tomorrow night."
"I arrive tomorrow night."
"I am going to arrive tomorrow night."
"I am planning on arriving tomorrow night."
"I am due to arrive tomorrow night."
"I am scheduled to arrive tomorrow night."
}

(Quando arriva Rico?)X   "When is Rico due to arrive?"

* * * * *

*59. You will now be given some English sentences. For each one put a check under the appropriate heading, according to the reference being made. Take a moment to study the four headings very carefully before beginning.

	no. 1 a single, durative event in progress	no. 2 the events leading to a punctual act	no. 3 a series consisting of the repetition of an event	no. 4 something planned or scheduled to happen in the future

1) He's going tomorrow.
2) The play is starting.
3) He always gives money.
4) They are already asking him.
5) He's smoking in the next room.
6) He's smoking a lot these days.
7) He learns very fast.
8) He's working at this very moment.
9) He's working hard nowadays.
10) He's working tomorrow.
11) We eat soon.
12) They never study.
13) He's still explaining it.
14) We have it now.
15) He's been drinking wine for years.
16) I'll tell him next week.
17) The party is ending now.
18) The party is ending soon.
19) I don't hear you.
20) The bus is coming.

*60. Study the following model. (a single, durative event in progress)
    S: Che cɔsa fa Rachɛle?   "What is Rachele doing? Is she
       Fuma?   smoking?"
    R: Sì, fuma.   "Yes, she's smoking."

You will be asked some questions. Answer according to the model, while looking at the following English translations as meaning cues. Your response will be confirmed each time.

Questions	Cues
(1) Che cɔsa fa Regina? Impara?	"learning"
(2) Che cɔsa fa Renata? Lavora?	"working"
(3) Che cɔsa fa Rina? Mangia?	"eating"
(4) Che cɔsa fa Renato? Studia?	"studying"
(5) Che cɔsa fa Rico? Spiɛga?	"explaining"
(6) Che cɔsa fa Rinaldo? Sôgna?	"dreaming"
(7) Che cɔsa fa Rita? Chiama?	"calling"
(8) Che cɔsa fa Rodɔlfo? Domanda?	"asking"
(9) Che cɔsa fa Rɔsa? Fuma?	"smoking"
(10) Che cɔsa fa Rolando? Ascolta?	"listening"

*61. Study the following model. (a single, durative event in progress)
    S: Che cɔsa fa Rachɛle?   "What is Rachele doing? Is
       Fuma?   she smoking?"
    R: Nɔ, non fuma.   "No, she's not smoking."

Answer according to the model, while looking at the following English translations as meaning cues. Your response will be confirmed each time.

Questions	Cues
(1) Che cɔsa fa Rosina? Domanda?	"asking"
(2) Che cɔsa fa Romɛo? Chiama?	"calling"
(3) Che cɔsa fa Rachɛle? Sôgna?	"dreaming"
(4) Che cɔsa fa Regina? Mangia?	"eating"
(5) Che cɔsa fa Rolando? Spiɛga?	"explaining"
(6) Che cɔsa fa Renata? Impara?	"learning"
(7) Che cɔsa fa Rɔsa? Fuma?	"smoking"
(8) Che cɔsa fa Rina? Studia?	"studying"
(9) Che cɔsa fa Rodɔlfo? Lavora?	"working"
(10) Che cɔsa fa Renato? Ascolta?	"listening"

*62. Study the following model. (a series consisting of the repetition of an
     event)
     S: Che cɔsa fa lì Rachɛle?   "What does Rachele do there?"
     R: Lavora lì.

Answer the questions, using the following English translations as meaning
cues. Your response will be confirmed each time.

Questions	Cues
(1) Che cɔsa fa lì Rita?	"works"
(2) Che cɔsa fa lì Rico?	"eats"
(3) Che cɔsa fa lì Rinaldo?	"studies"
(4) Che cɔsa fa lì Rosina?	"does nothing"

63. Study the following model. (a series)

    S: Chiama spesso?   "Does (s)he call often?"
    R: Sì, chiama ogni mattina. "Yes, (s)he calls every morning."

Answer the questions according to the model, using the following English
translations as meaning cues *for the end of the sentence*. Remember that two
unstressed vowels coming together normally form one syllable. (See Unit 13,
Frame 55). Your response will be confirmed each time.

Questions	Cues
(1) Sôgna spesso?	"every morning"
(2) Ɛ̂ spesso qui?	"every afternoon"
(3) Arriva spesso con Rɔsa?	"every evening"
(4) Lavora spesso qui?	"every afternoon"
(5) Mangia spesso qui?	"every night"
(6) Studia spesso?	"often"
(7) Domanda spesso?	"frequently"
(8) Chiama spesso qui?	"every morning"
(9) Fuma spesso?	"on frequent occasions"
(10) C'ɛ̀ spesso?	"every night"

*64. Study the following model. (a series)

     S: Chiama spesso qui?   "Does (s)he call here often?"
     R: Nɔ, non chiama mai qui.   "No, (s)he never calls here."

Answer the questions—the same questions as in frame 63—according to the
model, noticing that both *spesso* and *mai* immediately follow the verb. Your
response will be confirmed each time.

*65. Study the following model. (something planned or scheduled to happen in the future)

S: Quando arriva Renato?

"When is Renato ⎰ arriving?"
⎱ going to arrive?"
⎱ due to arrive?"

R: Arriva ɔggi.   "He's arriving today."

Answer the questions according to the model, using the following English translations as meaning cues. Your response will be confirmed each time.

Questions	Cues
(1) Quando arriva Renato?	"today"
(2) Quando comincia Romɛo?	"tomorrow"
(3) Quando lavora Rodɔlfo?	"this morning"
(4) Quando mangia Rachɛle?	"this afternoon"
(5) Quando studia Rina?	"tonight"
(6) Quando chiama Regina?	"tomorrow morning"
(7) Quando arriva Rɔsa?	"tomorrow afternoon"
(8) Quando comincia Rolando?	"tomorrow night"

*66. Study the following model.

S: Fuma Lɛi?   "Are you smoking?"
                                     (or) "Do you smoke?"
                                     (or) "Are you going to smoke?"

R: Sì, fumo.   "Yes, I.............."
   (or)
No, non fumo.   "No, I.............."

Answer the questions by changing the verb as in the model. Use the following cues to reply affirmatively or negatively. Your response will be confirmed each time. Notice that when referring to the person addressed, it is natural to add *Lɛi* to clarify who is meant. In most questions *Lɛi* appears at the end of the sentence.

Questions	Cues
(1) Impara Lɛi?	Sì
(2) Lavora Lɛi?	Nɔ
(3) Mangia Lɛi?	Sì
(4) Studia Lɛi?	Sì
(5) Spiɛga Lɛi?	Nɔ
(6) Sôgna Lɛi?	Nɔ
(7) Chiama Lɛi?	Nɔ
(8) Domanda Lɛi?	Sì
(9) Arriva Lɛi?	Nɔ
(10) C'è Lɛi?	Sì
(11) Non fa niɛnte Lɛi?	Nɔ
(12) Sta bɛne Lɛi?	Sì

*67. Study the following model.

  S: Dov'è Rachele?   "Where is Rachele?"
  R: Rachele è a Roma.   "Rachele is in Rome."

Answer the questions as in the model by using the following names of Italian cities. Remember to pronounce the consonant following *a* very strongly. Your response will be confirmed each time.

Questions	Cities
(1) Dov'è Regina?	Torino
(2) Dov'è Renata?	Genova
(3) Dov'è Rina?	Milano
(4) Dov'è Rita?	Udine
(5) Dov'è Rosa?	Bologna
(6) Dov'è Rosina?	Ancona
(7) Dov'è Renato?	Perugia
(8) Dov'è Rico?	Roma
(9) Dov'è Rodolfo?	Napoli
(10) Dov'è Rolando?	Bari
(11) Dov'è Romeo?	Cagliari

*68. Study the following model.

  S: Dove va Rachele?   "Where is Rachele going?"
  R: Rachele va a Roma.   "Rachele is going to Rome."

Answer the questions as in the model by using the city names or frame no. 67 in the order given. Remember to pronounce the consonant following the word *a* very strongly. In addition, notice that *va* in the question is followed by a strongly-pronounced consonant. Your response will be confirmed each time.

Questions
(1) Dove va Cora?
(2) Dove va Dora?
(3) Dove va Nora?
(4) Dove va Amanda?
(5) Dove va Bianca?
(6) Dove va Donata?
(7) Dove va Leo?
(8) Dove va Noè?
(9) Dove va Ugo?
(10) Dove va Mara?
(11) Dove va Vera?

*69. Study the following model.

      S. Dove va Lɛi?   "Where are you going?"
      R: Vado a Roma.   "I'm going to Rome."

Answer the questions as in the model by using the city names of frame no. 67 in the order given. Remember to pronounce the consonant following *a* very strongly. Your response will be confirmed each time.

*70. Study the following model.

      S: Quando arriva a Roma?   "When does (s)he arrive in Rome?"
      R: Arriva a Roma Domani.   "(S)he arrives in Rome tomorrow."

Answer the questions as in the model, using the following translations as meaning cues. Notice that the word *a* fuses with the last vowel of *arriva* but that the consonant following *a* is still pronounced very strongly. Your response will be confirmed each time.

Questions	Cues
(1) Quando arriva a Torino?	"today"
(2) Quando arriva a Gɛnova?	"this morning"
(3) Quando arriva a Milano?	"tomorrow morning"
(4) Quando arriva a Ụdine?	"this evening"
(5) Quando arriva a Bolôgna?	"today"
(6) Quando arriva ad Ancona?	"this afternoon"
(7) Quando arriva a Perugia?	"tomorrow evening"
(8) Quando arriva a Roma?	"tomorrow afternoon"
(9) Quando arriva a Nạpoli?	"tomorrow"
(10) Quando arriva a Bari?	"tomorrow night"
(11) Quando arriva a Cạgliari?	"tonight"

*71. Study the following model.

      S: Quando arriva Lɛi?   "When do you arrive?"
      R: Arrivo domani.   "I arrive tomorrow."

Answer the questions as in the model, using the translations of frame no. 70 as meaning cues. Your response will be confirmed each time.

*72. Study the following model.

      S: Di dov'è Rosina?   "Where is Rosina from?"
      R: Rosina è di Roma.   "Rosina is from Rome."

Answer the questions as in the model, using the following names of Italian cities. Your response will be confirmed each time.

Questions	Cities
(1) Di dov'è Tino?	Torino
(2) Di dov'è Gina?	Genova
(3) Di dov'è Mino?	Milano
(4) Di dov'è Ulisse?	Udine
(5) Di dov'è Bianca?	Bolôgna
(6) Di dov'è Agata?	Ancona
(7) Di dov'è Pina?	Perugia
(8) Di dov'è Rosina?	Roma
(9) Di dov'è Nini?	Napoli
(10) Di dov'è Bɔbi?	Bari
(11) Di dov'è Carolina?	Cagliari

*73. Study the following model.

S: È di Roma Lɛi?   "Are you from Rome?"
R: Nɔ, non sôno di Roma.   "No, I'm not from Rome."

Answer the questions as in the model. Your response will be confirmed each time.

Questions
(1) È di Ancona Lɛi?
(2) È di Bari Lɛi?
(3) È di Bolôgna Lɛi?
(4) È di Cagliari Lɛi?
(5) È di Genova Lɛi?
(6) È di Milano Lɛi?
(7) È di Napoli Lɛi?
(8) È di Perugia Lɛi?
(9) È di Roma Lɛi?
(10) È di Torino Lɛi?
(11) È di Udine Lɛi?

(answers not recorded)

You will hear fifteen Italian words which should all be pronounced with an initial tongue-flap. *Some* will be pronounced incorrectly with the consonant sound-type of the English word "ray." Put a check in the appropriate column according to whether the word is pronounced with the tongue-flap or not.

	Tongue-Flap	**Other**
1) Roma		
2) riso		
3) rado		
4) regno		
5) rɛndo		
6) rɔsa		
7) ruba		
8) riva		
9) risata		
10) romano		
11) rudimento		
12) radio		
13) regime		
14) rimasto		
15) risɔlto		

TEST B

(answers not recorded)

You will hear a short narrative and three short dialogs in Italian, each followed
by five English statements about them. Put a check in the appropriate column
according to whether each statement is *true* or *false*. (To test yourself cover the
Italian.)

I   Rodolfo Bondi è di Perugia ma lavora a Torino. Va spesso a Perugia. Lì c'è
una signorina, Mara De Angelis. Mara gli piace molto. Quando Rodolfo
va a Perugia, è con Mara ogni sera.

(1) Mr. Bondi never goes to Perugia now.
(2) Mara is in Perugia.
(3) Mara and Rodolfo are often together in Perugia.
(4) Rodolfo does not like Mara.
(5) Mr. Bondi is from Torino.

	True	False
1)		
2)		
3)		
4)		
5)		

II   —B. G. signorina. Come sta?
—Così così, g—— E Lɛi?
—Non c'è male, g——. Scusi, Le piace lavorare qui?
—Sì, mi piace molto.

(1) It is evening.
(2) The dialog takes place in or near a work area.
(3) One of the speakers claims to be very sick.
(4) It is clear that both speakers work.
(5) The lady claims to like her work a lot.

	True	False
1)		
2)		
3)		
4)		
5)		

III   —B. G. Rina. Quando arriva il sig. Spina?
       —Arriva domani mattina. Ora è a Bari.
       —È di Bari il sig. Spina?
       —Nɔ, è di Nąpoli, ma Bari gli piace molto.

       (1) Mr. Spina is in Bari.
       (2) Mr. Spina is from Bari.
       (3) Mr. Spina is due to arrive in the morning.
       (4) It is obvious that Mr. Spina likes Naples very much.
       (5) Someone is due to arrive tomorrow.

	True	False
1)		
2)		
3)		
4)		
5)		

IV   —Non imparo niɛnte.
       —Non impara niɛnte? Non studia?
       —Sì, lavoro molto. Studio ogni mattina e ogni sera, e
       mi piace studiare ma.....

       (1) One of the speakers does a lot of studying.
       (2) One of the speakers claims that he likes to study.
       (3) One of the speakers claims that he isn't learning anything.
       (4) One of the speakers claims that he is going to study tomorrow
           morning.
       (5) One of the speakers claims that he works a lot.

	True	False
1)		
2)		
3)		
4)		
5)		

*23. Translate the following thoughts into Italian. You will hear the Italian version after a pause following the English sentence.

"What is he carrying?"
"He's taking a child there."
"He's going to bring a cook tomorrow."
"What is she wearing?"
"I don't know what she's wearing."
"He's bringing an egg."
"I'm going to take the oil there this afternoon."
"I often take a dog along."
"He's carrying a basket."
"Who is wearing a glove?"
"I'm going to bring Amanda."
"Is he bringing a vase?"
"He's going to bring a blind man."
"He's not bringing a donkey."
"Are you wearing a glove?"
"Are you taking a captain there?"
"I'm not planning on bringing Mr. Vegli here."

24. Here is a special form of the verb ‡portare used in a formal situation to request that someone bring something.

(porti)X   (porti)X   (porti)X

25. "Bring me" said to one person in a somewhat formal situation is expressed as:

(mi porti)X   (mi porti)X   (mi porti)X

26. Here are some phrases using mi porti that you might use in talking to a waiter in a restaurant situation. Listen and repeat each one.

(Mi porti un arrosto.)XX	"Bring me a roast."
(Mi porti un gelato.)XX	"Bring me an ice cream."
(Mi porti un caffè.)XX	"Bring me a coffee."
(Mi porti an uovo sodo.)XX	"Bring me a hard-boiled egg."
(Mi porti un tovagliolo.)XX	"Bring me a napkin."

*27. Now you will be asked the question Che desidera? "What do you wish?" Answer each time by using the following sentences in the order given. Your response will be confirmed each time.

(1) Mi pɔrti un arrɔsto.
(2) ....gelato.
(3) ....caffè.
(4) ....uɔvo sɔdo.
(5) ....tovagliɔlo.

*28. You will now be asked the same question. Answer as in frame no. 27. Do so, however, by translating the following sentences. Your response will be confirmed each time.

   (1) "Bring me a roast."
   (2) "Bring me an ice cream."
   (3) "Bring me a coffee."
   (4) "Bring me a hard-boiled egg."
   (5) "Bring me a napkin."

If you did not feel comfortable with this last frame, repeat frames no. 27 and no. 28 until you know the five utterances well. When you feel you have mastered them, continue with frame no. 29.

* * * * *

29. The five new words we have been using are words that can refer to countable items, that is, we can talk about one roast, two roasts, etc. or one ice cream, two ice creams, etc. Therefore, *arrɔsto, gelato, caffè, uɔvo sɔdo* and *tovagliɔlo* as used in frames no. 27 and no. 28 are COUNT WORDS.

30. Sometimes, however, some words are commonly used to refer not to countable items, but to a quantity or a mass of something. Such words may be called MASS WORDS.

31. *Acqua,* the word for "water" is a MASS WORD.

32. Some words may be used as either COUNT or MASS WORDS. For instance, *caffè* may be used as a COUNT WORD to refer either to a "cup of coffee" or to a "kind of coffee," but it may also be used as a MASS WORD to refer to a "quantity of coffee."

33. When an Italian word is preceded by *un,* it is being used as a COUNT WORD.

If you did not feel comfortable with this last frame, repeat frames no. 42 and no. 43 until you know the utterances well. When you feel you have mastered them, continue with frame no. 44.

* * * * *

44. So far you have learned a number of words occurring after *un* and others that occur after *una* (or *un'*). Such words *name* things like: *arrosto, capitano, insalata.* Such words are called NOUNS.

*45. What do we call words that name things and which occur after *un* or *una* (or *un'*)?

46. Because many nouns are used after un or una (or *un'*) it is convenient to call *un, una* and *un'* NOUN MARKERS.

*47. What may things that mark nouns be called?

48. *Un, una* and *un'* are not the only NOUN MARKERS. They are special kinds of NOUN MARKERS. A noun marked by any one of them is a COUNT WORD thought of as a singular unit. In fact, therefore, in addition to being NOUN MARKERS, *un, una* and *un'* may also be called UNIT MARKERS.

*49. What may NOUN MARKERS that mark units be called?

*50. We have already learned an Italian phrase used to mark MASS WORDS. What was it?

*51. Is *un pɔ' di* a NOUN MARKER?

*52. Is *un pɔ' di* a UNIT MARKER?

* * * * *

53. We have already seen that some words occur after *un* whereas others occur after *una* (or *un'*). This distinction is important, for *un* cannot be used in place of *una* and *una* cannot be used in place of *un*.

54. We could talk, therefore, of two classes of words—those used after *un* and those used after *una* (or *un'*).

55. These two classes might even be labeled respectively, "*un* words" and "*una* words."

56. Let us take a few moments to study the class of "*un* words" and how it differs from the class of "una words."

57. The following are "un words" you should already be familiar with:

aceto	chiɔso	gas	ɔsso
americano	chiɔsco	gelato	ospedale
anglicano	ciɛco	ghetto	pane
animale	ciɛlo	ghigno	poɛta
arrɔsto	ciuco	ghiottone	pomeriggio
bambino	cognome	giacinto	ponte
bastone	colombo	giôgo	pôsto
bébé	cɔno	globo	quotidiano
bɔsco	consolato	gɔlf	sasso
caffè	conto	guanto	signore
campo	cubo	gufo	sofà
cane	cuɔco	italiano	tĕmpio
capitano	cuɔio	jo-jo	tɔpo
cece	dɛnte	lombo	tovagliɔlo
cemento	düɛllo	lupo	uɔmo
cestino	elefante	mese	uɔvo
chianti	elemento	monumento	vaso
chilo	fico	naso	velo
chimɔno	film	nome	vino
chiɔdo	fuɔco	ɔlio	voto

58. Here is another "*un* word," the word for "boss." Repeat.

(capo)X (capo)x

59. You have had more "*un* words" than "*una* words" so far. The following should be familiar to you. They are "*una* words."

aranciata	haïtiana
birra	igiɛne
bistecca	insalata
campagna	mattina
casa	mela
cassa	pera
ciancia	persona
ciɔcia	pɛsca
cɔsa	pesca
colomba	scuɔla
giɔia	sera

signora	spεcie
signorina	vigna
società	vôga

60. If we carefully examine the two groups of words, we notice the following:
    Of the "*un* words,"

    a) most (though not all) end in -*o*
    b) most (though not all*) of those that refer to people or other animate beings refer to males only.

    Of the "*una* words,"

    a) most (though not all) end in -*a*
    b) most (though not all**) of those that refer to people or other animate beings refer to females only.

    *Capo refers to a boss, whether male or female.
    **Persona refers to a person, whether male or female.

61. The observations just made are very useful and it is because of the (b) observations that the two word-classes have traditionally been called MASCULINE and FEMININE respectively.

62. The term GENDER is used to refer to this MASCULINE-FEMININE distinction.

63. Thus, the word *chianti* is said to belong to the MASCULINE GENDER simply because it belongs to the "*un*" class and not because there is anything masculine about it.

64. Remember that despite the usefulness of these observations, it is *neither* the ending of a word nor the meaning of a word that makes it MASCULINE or FEMININE.

*65. If a word ends in -*a* does that make it FEMININE?

*66. If a word refers to a male being does that make it MASCULINE?

*67. If a word is used after *un* but not after *una*, of what gender is the word?

*68. If a word is used after *una* but not after *un*, of what gender is the word?

*69. Therefore, would you say that the following statement is true?

"The gender of many words may be definitely determined by their UNIT MARKER."

70. Other kinds of MARKERS or other gender-determining clues will be studied in later units. By the way, of all the new Italian words in frame no. 36 only *acqua* is FEMININE.

* * * * *

71. In Italian it is important to know whether a word is classfiable as MASCULINE or FEMININE.

*72. Therefore, is the concept of GENDER important in Italian?

73. Nouns in Italian are just *one* category of words that have something to do with gender. Other gender-related categories will be learned soon enough.

74. Because Italian has many words that have something to do with gender it is useful to refer to such words by one term. The term we have invented for this use in this course is the term GENDERABLE (literally, "given to gender").

*75. What do we call words that have something to do with gender in Italian?

*76. Are nouns GENDERABLES?

*77. Are nouns the only GENDERABLES in Italian?

* * * * *

78. In Italian many GENDERABLES are classifiable as exclusively MASCULINE or exclusively FEMININE. For example, arrosto is MASCULINE but *bistecca* is FEMININE; *capo* is MASCULINE but *persona* is FEMININE.

79. However, most GENDERABLES that may be used to refer to animate beings have both MASCULINE and FEMININE forms. When referring directly to an animate being, the MASCULINE form is used to refer to the male being and the FEMININE form is used to refer to the female being.

80. One such GENDERABLE you have had consists of the MASCULINE *colombo* "male pigeon or dove" and the FEMININE *colomba* "female pigeon or dove."

81. Because these two forms, are related, the GENDERABLE in this case is said to be made up of *more than one form.*

82. In such cases to refer to the family of related forms, the MASCULINE SINGULAR form is normally used. Thus, +*colombo* refers not to just the single form *colombo* but to the family of GENDERABLE forms meaning "pigeon or dove," singular and plural.

83. The dictionary form of a GENDERABLE is its SINGULAR form (if it has one) and then its MASCULINE form (if it has one).

*84. What is the dictionary form of the Italian word for "pigeon or dove"?

85. Most GENDERABLES with both MASCULINE and FEMININE forms end in -*o* for the MASCULINE and -*a* for the FEMININE.

*86. Thus, change the following MASCULINE items to the FEMININE.

un americano   –   _____

un anglicano   –   _____

un bambino   –   _____

un cieco   –   _____

un colombo   –   _____

un cuoco   –   _____

un haïtiano   –   _____

un italiano   –   _____

un lupo   –   _____

87. For some, however, you must change the MASCULINE vowel ending to
    -*essa* to derive the FEMININE form.

*88. The following are three such MASCULINE items. Change them to the
    FEMININE.

    un capitano   –   _____

    un elefante   –   _____

    un poɛta   –   _____

89. Sometimes the FEMININE counterpart of a MASCULINE form is some-
    what different. Repeat the following:

Masculine	Feminine
(cane)X	(cagna)X
(gnɔmo)X	(gnɔmide)X
(signore)X	(signora)X
	(signorina)X

90. Sometimes the FEMININE counterpart is entirely different. Repeat the fol-
    lowing:

    (un uɔmo)X "a man"   (una dɔnna)X "a woman"

91. In some cases the same form is used for both the MASCULINE and the
    FEMININE. Repeat the following, but notice the different UNIT MARKER
    used to mark gender.

Masculine		Feminine
(un insegnante)X	"a teacher"	(un'insegnante)X
(un pilɔta)X	"a pilot"	(una pilɔta)X

92. Many GENDERABLES that have the same form for both the MASCULINE
    and the FEMININE end in -*e*, like *insegnante*. Many others end in -*ista* and
    are cognates of English words in "-ist." Repeat the following, always pay-
    ing attention to the UNIT MARKER.

Masculine	Feminine
(un artista)X	(un'artista)X
(un capitalista)X	(una capitalista)X
(un comunista)X	(una comunista)X
(un dentista)X	(una dentista)X
(un linguista)X	(una linguista)X
(un turista)X	(una turista)X

*93. What are the English cognates of the preceding six words?

94. In any case, whether a GENDERABLE that may be used to refer to animate beings is *only* MASCULINE, *only* FEMININE, or *both* MASCULINE and FEMININE can only be learned through observation. There is no way to predict this.

* * * * *

95. You have already learned that before FEMININE words beginning with a vowel sound the UNIT MARKER is *un'*.

*96. Does the MASCULINE form of the UNIT MARKER show any distinction between words beginning with a vowel sound and other words?

97. However, the MASCULINE form of the UNIT MARKER does have a variant, namely *uno*. This variant is used (among other places) before words beginning with *gn-* or *s* + consonant letter. Repeat the following:

    (uno gnɔmo)X   "a gnome"
    (uno sbaglio)X   "a mistake"
    (uno studɛnte)X   "a student"

98. The FEMININE counterpart of *studɛnte* is *studentessa*. Repeat.

    (studentessa)X (studentessa)X

In the following drills answer according to the models while looking at the English translations given as meaning cues. Your response will be confirmed each time.

*99. (things)

      S: Che cɔs'è questo?   "What's this?"

          un
      R: è uno
            una   ....   It's a............"
            un'

    Cues

    "thing"
    "basket"
    "box"
    "cane
    "fire
    "mistake
    "napkin"
    "sandal"
    "sofa"
    "sweater"
    "course"

*100. (places or buildings)

> S: Che cos'è questo? "What's this?"
>
> R: è un / uno / una / un' .... "It's a ...."

(1) "place"
(2) "consulate"
(3) "field"
(4) "ghetto"
(5) "hospital"
(6) "house"
(7) "school"
(8) "temple"
(9) "vineyard"

*101. (things to eat or drink)

> S: Che desidera? "What would you like?"
> R: Mi porti.............. "Bring me ...."

(1) "an apple"
(2) "a beer"
(3) "a loaf of bread"
(4) "a coffee"
(5) "an egg"
(6) "a fig"
(7) "an ice cream"
(8) "an orange"
(9) "a peach"
(10) "a pear"
(11) "a roast"
(12) "a salad"
(13) "a steak"
(14) "a (glass of) tea"

*102. (COUNT versus MASS WORDS)

> S: Che desidera? "What would you like?"
> R: Vorrei.......... "I'd like ...."

NOTE: Some words like *cemento* are more often used as MASS WORDS, although they may be used as COUNT WORDS (e.g. un cemento), especially when one goes on to describe or qualify the kind intended. Although no such qualification appears in any of the responses required here, one would normally occur in non-classroom situations. Such words are included in this drill only in order to review more fully the distinction between COUNT and MASS WORDS.

(1) "a beer"
(2) "a little beer"
(3) "a loaf of bread"
(4) "a little bread"
(5) "a kind of butter"
(6) "a little butter"
(7) "a (kind of) cement"
(8) "a little cement"
(9) "a (kind of) cheese"
(10) "some cheese"

(11) "a (kind of) Chianti"
(12) "a little Chianti"
(13) "a coffee"
(14) "some coffee"
(15) "a gas"
(16) "a little gas"
(17) "a few hors d'oeuvres"
(18) "an ice cream"
(19) "some ice cream"
(20) "a kind of leather"

(21) "a little leather"
(22) "an oil"
(23) "a little oil"
(24) "a kind of pepper"
(25) "some pepper"
(26) "a kind of salt"
(27) "a little salt"
(28) "a tea"
(29) "some tea"
(30) "a little wine"

*103. (animate beings)

S: Che cosa c'è lì?   "What is over there?"

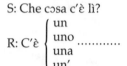

R: C'è { un
          uno ....   "There's a............"
          una
          un'

(1) "male American"
(2) "female American"
(3) "animal"
(4) "male artist"
(5) "female artist"
(6) "blind male"
(7) "blind female"
(8) "male Capitalist"
(9) "female Capitalist"
(10) "male captain"
(11) "female captain"
(12) "male child"
(13) "female child"
(14) "male Communist"
(15) "female Communist"
(16) "male cook"
(17) "female cook"
(18) "male dentist"
(19) "female dentist"
(20) "male dog"
(21) "female dog"
(22) "male elephant"
(23) "female elephant"
(24) "gentleman"
(25) "married woman"

(26) "unmarried woman"
(27) "male gnome"
(28) "female gnome"
(29) "male Haitian"
(30) "female Haitian"
(31) "male Italian"
(32) "female Italian"
(33) "male linguist"
(34) "female linguist"
(35) "man"
(36) "woman"
(37) "person"
(38) "male pigeon"
(39) "female pigeon"
(40) "male pilot"
(41) "male poet"
(42) "female poet"
(43) "male student"
(44) "female student"
(45) "male teacher"
(46) "female teacher"
(47) "male tourist"
(48) "female tourist"
(49) "male wolf"
(50) "female wolf"

*104. Study the following model:
    S: Dov'è una birra?   "Where is a beer?"
    R: Ce n'è una lì a s——.   "There's one there on the left."
         (or)
    Ce n'è una lì a d——.   "There's one there on the right."

Give the appropriate answer to the question you hear according to whether the item's name is to the left or the right of the dividing line below. Your answer will be confirmed each time.

roast	apple	coffee	pear
mistake	glove	tea	sweater
napkin	(female) dentist	hard-boiled egg	(male) dentist
orangeade	(male) cook	beer	(female) cook
sandal	(female) student	nail	(male) student

    (1) Dov'è un caffè?   (11) .... un tovagliolo?
    (2) .... un chiodo?   (12) .... un dentista?
    (3) .... una studentessa?   (13) .... uno sbaglio?
    (4) .... una dentista?   (14) .... un golf?
    (5) .... un uovo sodo?   (15) .... un'aranciata?
    (6) .... un arrosto?   (16) .... una cuoca?
    (7) .... una mela?   (17) .... un guanto?
    (8) .... una pera?   (18) .... un cuoco?
    (9) .... una ciocia?   (19) .... un tè?
   (10) .... uno studente?   (20) .... una birra?

*105. Study the following model.
    S: Dov'è una birra?   "Where is a beer?"
    R: Non so, ma ce n'era una   "I don't know, but there was
       lì due minuti fa.   one there two minutes ago."

Answer the questions you hear in accordance with the model. You will need to use *uno* or *una*. Your answer will be confirmed each time.

    (1) Dovè un'insalata?   (7) .... un uovo sodo?
    (2) .... un tè?   (8) .... un'aranciata?
    (3) .... un tovagliolo?   (9) .... un cane?
    (4) .... una bistecca?   (10) .... una pera?
    (5) .... un gelato?   (11) .... una birra?
    (6) .... una mela?

*106. Study the following model.

> S: Dov'è un pɔ' di birra?   "Where is a little beer?"
>
> R: Ce n'è un pɔ' $\begin{cases} \text{lì} \\ \text{qui.} \end{cases}$ "There is a little $\begin{cases} \text{over there."} \\ \text{here."} \end{cases}$

Using the cues given, reply as in the model. The question may be asked in the PRESENT TENSE or the PAST TENSE. Your response will be confirmed each time.

Questions	Cues
(1) Dov'è un po; d'acqua?	lì
(2) ....εra un pɔ' d'insalata?	qui
(3) ....è un pɔ' di tè?	qui
(4) ....sale?	lì
(5) ....εra un pɔ' di pepe?	qui
(6) ....formaggio?	lì
(7) ....caffè?	qui
(8) ....è un pɔ' di burro?	qui
(9) ....d'antipasto?	lì
(10) ....εra un pɔ' di birra?	qui

*107. Study the following model.

> S: C'è un animale lì?   "Is there an animal there?"
>
> R: Sì, ce *n'è* uno lì.   "Yes, there's one there."
>
>   (or)
>
> Nɔ, non *c'è* un animale lì.   "No, there *is'nt* an animal there."

Using the cues given, reply as in the model. Notice that in the negative you are to repeat the name mentioned in the question. Your response will be confirmed each time.

Questions	Cues
(1) C'è un capitalista lì?	Sì
(2) ......una capitalista lì?	Sì
(3) ......uno sbaglio lì?	Nɔ
(4) ......uno studεnte lì?	Nɔ
(5) ......una dɔnna lì?	Sì
(6) ......un uɔmo lì?	Nɔ
(7) ......un poεta lì?	Nɔ
(8) ......un elefante lì?	Sì
(9) ......un capitano lì?	Sì
(10) ......un linguista lì?	Nɔ
(11) ......un americano lì?	Sì
(12) ......un'italiana lì?	Sì
(13) ......un animale lì?	Nɔ

• **End of Tape 8A**•

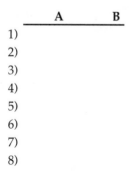

TEST A

(answers not recorded)

In this unit you were introduced to some new utterances containing the tongue-flap before a consonant. You will now hear these utterances sometimes pronounced accurately with a tongue-flap and other times pronounced with an American accent and no tongue-flap. Put a check in column A if the item is pronounced correctly; put a check in column B if it is pronounced incorrectly.

	A	B		A	B
1) artista			10) formaggio		
2) Virginia			11) persona		
3) per favore			12) per favore		
4) artista			13) per piacere		
5) mi porti			14) arrivederLa		
6) per piacere			15) formaggio		
7) arrivederci			16) arrivederLa		
8) mi porti			17) Virginia		
9) persona			18) arrivederci		

TEST B

(answers not recorded)

You will hear a number of utterances as in frame no. 7. Put a check under A for the equivalent of "Mr. So-and-So" and under B for the equivalent of "Mrs. So-and-So."

	A	B
1)		
2)		
3)		
4)		
5)		
6)		
7)		
8)		

TEST C

(answers not recorded)

Put a check in the appropriate column according to whether the GENDERABLE you hear would be marked by *un, uno, una or un'*.

	un	uno	una	un'
1) americano				
2) birra				
3) pôsto				
4) mela				
5) gnɔmo				
6) cɔsa				
7) capitano				
8) cane				
9) uɔmo				
10) aranciata				
11) pilɔta				
12) aceto				
13) insalata				
14) bistecca				
15) arrɔsto				
16) signora				
17) sale				
18) vigna				
19) pera				
20) tè				
21) sbaglio				
22) studentessa				
23) gɔlf				
24) lupo				
25) elefante				

(continued)

	un	uno	una	un'
26) poɛta				
27) cagna				
28) dɔnna				
29) chianti				
30) acqua				
31) mattina				
32) studɛnte				
33) vôga				
34) persona				
35) ospedale				
36) uɔvo				
37) italiana				
38) pane				
39) pepe				
40) caffè				
41) haïtiano				
42) haïtiana				
43) gnɔmide				
44) anglicana				
45) italiano				
46) cuɔca				
47) dɛnte				
48) gas				
49) spɛcie				
50) igiɛne				

TEST D

(answers not recorded)

You will hear eight short dialogs or narratives in Italian, each followed by four English statements about them. Write whether each statement is *true* or *false*.

I —Buɔn giorno, signore. Desịdera?
—Non sɔ, the cɔsa c'è?
—Tè, caffè, vino, birra.
—Vorrɛi mangiare ora, non bere.
—Scusi, c'è arrɔsto, insalata, formaggio.
—Mi pɔrti un'insalata, un po' di formaggio, pane e vino.

    (1) It's late in the evening. _____
    (2) The waitress suggests something to eat first. _____
    (3) They don't serve food. _____
    (4) The man orders a light meal._____

II —Buɔna sera, signore. Che desidera?
—Vorrɛi un pɔ' d'antipasto; una bistecca e un'insalata
—Che desịdera bere, signore?
—Mi pɔrti an po' di chianti, per piacere.

    (1) Someone is asking for something to eat. _____
    (2) Someone is ordering some tea. _____
    (3) More than one steak is being ordered. _____
    (4) The first thing ordered is something to drink._____

III —Mi pɔrti un pɔ' di formaggio e un gelato, per favore.
—Desịdera un caffè?
—Sì, g——.

    (1) A heavy meal is being ordered. _____
    (2) Bread is one of the things ordered. _____
    (3) A salad is mentioned. _____
    (4) Ice cream is mentioned._____

IV —Scusi, vorrɛi un tovagliɔlo, per favore.
   —Non ce n'è uno lì?
   —È un tovagliɔlo questo?
   —Scusi, ma ce n'ɛra uno lì due minuti fa.

    (1) Someone is missing something._____
    (2) Someone is apparently mistaken._____
    (3) Someone is asking for a napkin._____
    (4) A time is mentioned._____

V —Le piace bere tè?
   —Nɔ, non mi piace bere tè, mi piace bere caffè.
   —Desịdera un pɔ' di caffè ora?
   —Nɔ, ora nɔ, g——.

    (1) Coffee and tea are being discussed._____
    (2) Someone is drinking coffee now._____
    (3) Someone likes to drink coffee._____
    (4) Someone would like to drink some coffee now._____

VI —Ora Robɛrto mangia un pɔ' d'arrɔsto e un'insalata, e Bɛrta mangia un
   uɔvo sɔdo. Bɛrta non mangia mai molto. Non le piace mangiare molto.

    (1) The man eats more than the woman._____
    (2) She is eating a salad._____
    (3) She likes to eat a lot._____
    (4) He is eating a steak._____

VII —Lɛi mangia spesso qui?
   —Sì, ogni sera. Non mi piace mangiare a casa.
   —Che cɔs'è questo, per favore?
   —È un'insalata con formaggio.
   —Che cɔsa mangia Lɛi?
   —Stasera vorrɛi una bistecca e un pɔ' d'insalata.

    (1) Two friends are having dinner at home._____
    (2) Both like to eat at home._____
    (3) One of the two definitely orders some cheese._____
    (4) One of the two is already eating a steak and a salad._____

VIII —Buona sera, signora.
      —Buona sera, signor Riva. Dove va?
      —Vado a Roma, e Lɛi?
      —Vado a Bari. Lɛi è di Roma, Signor Riva?
      —Nɔ, sôno di Milano, ma vado spesso a Roma.
      —Le piace Roma?
      —Sì, ma piace molto. Vorrɛi lavorare lì.
          (1) The man is from Milan._____
          (2) They are going to the same city._____
          (3) One is definitely from Rome and goes there often._____
          (4) One definitely works in Rome._____

TEST E

(not recorded)

Translate the following thoughts into Italian by using *only* what has been presented so far.

1) Could I have a napkin, please?

_____

2) Thank you; goodbye, sir.

_____

3) What will you have? A little wine, a beer?

_____

4) What do you have?—(answer) There's some bread, some butter and an egg.

_____

5) I'm thinking of eating there tomorrow night.

_____

6) Where is the coffee that was here two minutes ago?

_____

7) Carlo is going to start tomorrow afternoon.

_____

8) When you want a cup of coffee, where do you go?

_____

9) Would you like to have a few hors d'oeuvres?

_____

10) He's never found eating here. He dislikes it.

_____

11) You can never find any water here.

_____

12) No, it's not a dentist. It's Rodolfo Binaldi, a teacher from Turin.

_____

13) Is he bringing a linguist?

_____

14) There's a student over there. He's from Naples.

_____

15) Are you taking a dog to Genoa?

_____

TEST A   ANSWERS

	A	B
1)		X
2)		X
3)	X	
4)	X	
5)	X	
6)	X	
7)	X	
8)		X
9)		X
10)		X
11)	X	
12)		X
13)		X
14)		X
15)	X	
16)	X	
17)	X	
18)		X

TEST B   ANSWERS

	A	B
1)		X
2)	X	
3)	X	
4)	X	
5)		X
6)		X
7)	X	
8)		X

TEST C   ANSWERS

	un	uno	una	un'
1)	X			
2)			X	
3)	X			
4)			X	
5)		X		
6)			X	
7)	X			
8)	X			
9)	X			
10)				X
11)	X		X	
12)	X			
13)				X
14)			X	
15)	X			
16)			X	
17)	X			
18)			X	
19)			X	
20)	X			
21)		X		
22)			X	
23)	X			
24)	X			
25)	X			
26)	X			
27)			X	
28)			X	
29)	X			

	un	uno	una	un'
30)				X
31)			X	
32)		X		
33)			X	
34)			X	
35)	X			
36)	X			
37)				X
38)	X			
39)	X			
40)	X			
41)	X			
42)				X
43)			X	
44)				X
45)	X			
46)			X	
47)	X			
48)	X			
49)			X	
50)				X

TEST D   ANSWERS

I	II	III	IV
1) false	1) true	1) false	1) true
2) false	2) false	2) false	2) true
3) false	3) false	3) false	3) true
4) true	4) false	4) true	4) true

V	VI	VII	VIII
1) true	1) true	1) false	1) true
2) false	2) false	2) false	23 false
3) true	3) false	3) false	3) false
4) false	4) false	4) false	4) false

TEST E   ANSWERS

(The following is only one of the possible versions.)

1) Mi porti un tovagliolo, per favore.
2) G——, arrivederLa, signore.
3) Che desidera? Un po' di vino, una birra?
4) Che cosa c'è? - C'è un po' di pane, un po' di burro e un uovo.
5) Mangio lì domani sera.
6) C'era un caffè qui due minuti fa. Dov'è ora?
7) Carlo comincia domani pomeriggio.
8) Quando desidera un caffè, dove va?
9) Desidera un po' d'antipasto?
10) Non mangia mai qui. Non gli piace.
11) Non c'è mai acqua qui.
12) No, non è un dentista. È Rodolfo Binaldi, un insegnante di Torino.
13) Porta un linguista?
14) C'è uno studente lì. È di Napoli.
15) Porta un cane a Genova Lei?

UNIT 23

1-4. Of all the Italian words you have learned so far, would you say that:

(a) most have their stress on the *last* vowel sound,
(b) most have their stress on the *next-to-the-last* vowel sound, or
(c) most have their stress *someplace else?*

5. Most Italian words end in a vowel and for most Italian words stress does fall on the sound represented by the *next-to-the-last vowel letter.* Here are some examples with the stressed vowel represented by the underlined letter.

(Amanda)X
(haïtiana)X
(negligente)X
(Sara)X
(Beniamino)X
(persona)X
(tovagliolo)X
(capitalista)X

6. In those words *that end in a stressed vowel,* the stress is shown on the written word by an accent mark, usually written as in the following words:

Cecè	(or)	Cecɛ'	(	)X
Noè	(or)	Noɛ'	(	)X
sarɔ̀	(or)	sarɔ'	(	)X
sarà	(or)	sara'	(	)X
sofà	(or)	sofa'	(	)X
così così	(or)	cosi' cosi'	(	)X
società	(or)	societa'	(	)X
caffè	(or)	caffɛ'	(	)X

*7. Therefore, are the following two words the same?

(Sara) - (sarà)
  a   b

8. No mark is normally written to indicate stress in other cases, even when a word ends in a *stressed vowel followed by a consonant,* as in the following four names of foreign cities. The stressed vowel is here indicated by the underlined letter.

(Bagdad)X
(Beirut)X
(Cabul)X   "Kabul"
(Saigɔn)X

9. Even with shortened forms of longer words, whenever the shortened form ends in a *stressed vowel followed by a consonant* no special mark is normally written. Thus, the form *signor* appears without any special mark for its stress that falls on /O/ as in the longer form *signore*.

10. Because of what has been stated in frames no. 5 through 9 there is no way for you to predict where the stress falls on (a) any word that ends in a conso-nant and (b) any word that ends in an unaccented vowel letter and that has more than two vowel letters in it. For example, notice where the stress falls in the following cases in which it is represented by the underlined letter.

(a) (Porto Said)X   "Port Said" (but) (Bagdad)X
(b) (Italia)X (but) (Natalia)X [femine given name]

11. In these units you are helped in the normally unpredictable cases if you learn the following.
    General Rule
        When *no* accent mark appears on the end of a written word, the stressed vowel is represented by:

(a) the *last vowel letter* in all words ending in a consonant.
        examples: (signor)X (Bagdad)X (Beirut)X
                        (Cabul)X   (Saigɔn)X
(b) the *third* (when there is one) *vowel letter from the end* in words ending in *-ia, -ie, -ii, -io, -ua, -ue, -ui, -uo.*
        examples: (Italia)X   (Licia)X (Perugia)X
                        (spεcie)X (ɔlio)X   (Lucio)X
                        (pomeriggio)X (acqua)X
(c) the *next-to-the-last vowel letter* in all other cases.
        examples: (italiano)X (insegnante)X
    Exceptions
        Exceptions to the above are marked in these units by either:

(a) a dot beneath the vowel letter representing a stressed vowel.
        examples: (Agata)X (glandola)X (glutine)X
                        (Udine)X (Napoli)X (Cagliari)X
                        (desidera)X (Porto Said)X (Natalia)X
                        (costui)X "that man" (Cesare)X "Caesar"
                        (giovane)X "young"

or (b) the special type ɛ and ɔ.

    examples: (ɛssere)X (ɛsserci)X

                 (Amɛrica)X "America" (Gɛnova)X

                 (ɔrdine)X "order" masculine

*12. Applying everything that has been said about stress in these eleven frames, in the pauses provided on tape read the following names of cities with the appropriate stress. Your response will be confirmed after each pause.

(1) *Addis Abɛba* "Addis Ababa"

(2) *Alcalà*

(3) *Algɛri* "Algiers"

(4) *Amman*

(5) *Ankara*

(6) *Bagdad*

(7) *Baltimora* "Baltimore"

(8) *Bangkɔk*

(9) *Beirut*

(10) *Berlino* "Berlin"

(11) *Bogotà*

(12) *Bɔston*

(13) *Bucarɛst* "Bucharest"

(14) *Budapest*

(15) *Buɛnos Aires*

(16) *Cabul* "Kabul"

(17) *Caracas*

(18) *Cagliari* (It.)

(19) *Catania* (It.)

(20) *Città del Guatemala* "Guatemala City"

(21) *Colonia* "Cologne"

(22) *Copenaghen* "Copenhagen"

(23) *Cɔrdova*

(24) *Damasco* "Damascus"

(25) *Filadɛlfia* "Philadelphia"

(26) *Helsinki*

(27) *Kartum* "Khartoum"

(28) *Lagos*

(29) *Las Vɛgas*

(30) *L'Avana* "Havana"

(31) *Lisbona* "Lisbon"

(32) *Los Angeles*

(33) *Managua*

(34) *Miami*

(35) *Mɔnaco di Baviɛra* "Munich"

(36) *Mosca* "Moscow"

(37) *Nuɔva Dɛlhi* "New Delhi"

(38) *Padova* "Padua" (It.)

(39) *Palɛrmo* (It.)

(40) *Pechino* "Peking"

(41) *Rabat*

(42) *Saigɔn*

(43) *Santiago*

(44) *Siviglia* "Seville"

(45) *Sɔfia*

(46) *Tangeri* "Tangiers"

(47) *Tokio* "Tokyo"

(48) *Toronto*

(49) *Tunisi* "Tunis"

(50) *Varsavia* "Warsaw"

*13. There are many place names that end in -*ia* in Italian. Most are stressed like *Italia,* that is, on the vowel represented by the third vowel letter from the end. Read the following in the pauses provided on tape. Your response will be confirmed each time.

(1) *Abissinia* (country)
(2) *Aquitania* (region)
(3) *Arabia Saudita* (country)
(4) *Asia* (continent)
(5) *California* (state)
(6) *Cambɔgia* (country)
(7) *Castiglia* (region)
(8) *Colombia* (country)
(9) *Estɔnia* (republic)
(10) *Etiɔpia* (country)
(11) *Finlandia* (country)
(12) *Germania* (country)
(13) *Giordania* (country)
(14) *India* (country)
(15) *Ischia* (It. island)
(16) *Iugoslavia* (country)
(17) *Libɛria* (country)
(18) *Libia* (country)

(19) *Liguria* (It. region)
(20) *Macedɔnia* (region)
(21) *Malɛsia* (country)
(22) *Manciuria* (territory)
(23) *Mauritania* (country)
(24) *Moravia* (region)
(25) *Nigɛria* (country)
(26) *Norvɛgia* (country)
(27) *Patagɔnia* (region)
(28) *Pɛrsia* (country)
(29) *Polɔnia* (country)
(30) *Russia* (country)
(31) *Sibɛria* (region)
(32) *Sicilia* (It. island)
(33) *Siria* (country)
(34) *Tasmania* (island)
(35) *Thailandia* (country)

*14. Relatively few place names end in -*ia* in Italian. The following are twelve
that you should learn. Read them in the pauses provided on tape. Your
response will be confirmed each time.

    (1) *Albania*
    (2) *Algeria*
    (3) *Andalusia*
    (4) *Barberia*
    (5) *Bulgaria*
    (6) *Lombardia* (It. region)
    (7) *Nicosia*
    (8) *Normandia*
    (9) *Pavia* (It. city)
    (10) *Tunisia*
    (11) *Turchia*
    (12) *Ungheria*

*15. What do you think the preceding twelve place names are in English?

16. Here are two other place names in -*ia*. Notice how they contrast with place
names in -*ia*. Repeat.

    (Bahia)X   "Baia"   [in Brazil] - (Baia)X   [city near Naples]
    (Romania)X   "Romania" - (Romania)X   [the neo-Latin world]

* * * * *

17. Some words written with only *two vowel letters* deserve special comment.
We have already seen that whenever the two vowel letters represent *two
vowel sound-types* the absence or presence of the accent mark tells us where
the stress falls. Thus:

    (Sara)X   but   (sarà)X
    (Lia)X   but   (Noè)X

18. On the other hand, *two vowel letters* next to each other may represent a *semivowel followed by a vowel sound-type*. In such cases the absence or the presence of the accent mark tells us whether two vowel sound-types are involved or whether a *semivowel plus vowel sound-type* is involved. Thus:

    (Pia)X but (più)X "more"

19. Notice that the following words need no accent mark, since the combination *qu* normally represents /KW/. A translation of either one is "here."

    (qui)X (qua)X

20. If you check back to Unit 9, frame no. 49, you will be reminded that the letter *i* in word-final position after a vowel letter may normally stand for either /Y/ or /I/, indifferently. Thus:

    mai may be either (/MAY/)X or (/MAI/)X

21. Furthermore, *two vowel letters* next to each other may represent *only one vowel sound-type*. Such cases involve *ci-* or *gi-*. The absence or presence of the accent mark tells us whether two vowel sound-types are involved or whether only one is involved. Thus:

    (Cia)X [feminine given name] but (ciɔ)X "this thing; that thing"
    (Gia)X [feminine given name] but (già)X "already"

*22. Read the following Italian words in the spaces provided on tape. Your response will be confirmed each time. NOTE: For those followed by the number (2) give two pronunciations, first as a one-syllable word and then as a two-syllable word.

(1) *bue*	(7) *già*	(13) *mia*	(19) *qua*
(2) *ciɔ*	(8) *giù*	(14) *noi* (2)	(20) *qui*
(3) *cui* (2)	(9) *io*	(15) *piè*	(21) *sɛi* (2)
(4) *dio*	(10) *lɛi* (2)	(16) *pio*	(22) *sii* (2)
(5) *due*	(11) *lui* (2)	(17) *pɔi* (2)	(23) *stai* (2)
(6) *fui*(2)	(12) *mai* (2)	(18) *puɔ*	(24) *voi* (2)

* * * * *

23. In addition to what has been said so far, the accent mark in Italian has another function, that is, to show a difference between certain words written with *only one vowel letter* and other words spelled the same but having different meanings.

24. One such pair of contrasting words is the following, which you have already had.

   (è)X   as in *è qui.*
   (e)X   as in: *E Lei?*

25. The following words (which you have already had) are written with an accent mark to differentiate them from other words (which you have not yet had) spelled the same but having different meanings. Remember these words.

   (dà)X   as in: *glielo dà.*
   (lì)X   [the opposite of *qui*]
   (sì)X   [the opposite of *no*]
   (tè)X   "tea"

                              * * * * *

26. In frame no. 3 you were told that the term STRESS primarily means relative loudness. However, you *may* have noticed another feature that is often involved in stress in Italian.

27. Listen to the following contrastive pair very carefully.

   (Sara) - (sarà)
   (Sara) - (sarà)

*28. Is the stressed vowel of *Sara* the same length as the last vowel? Listen.

   (Sara)

*29. Is the stressed vowel of *Sara* longer or shorter than the last vowel? Listen again.

   (Sara)

*30. Is the stressed vowel of *Sara* longer or shorter than the stressed vowel of *sarà*? Listen carefully.

   (Sara) - (sarà)
   (Sara) - (sarà)

31. What we have been trying to illustrate in these last five frames is the following principle: Generally speaking, stressed vowels in Italian tend to be *longer* than unstressed vowels. This is especially true of stressed vowels within a word, as in *Sara.*

   Further will be said about this principle in a later unit.

*32. Is it a fair statement to say that stress in Italian implies greater *loudness* and usually (though not necessarily) greater *length?*

33. Repeat the following words while keeping the stress principle in mind.
(signore)X
(italiano)X
(Italia)X
(Roma)X
(bambina)X
(tovagliɔlo)X

* * * * *

34. The following are the Italian names of the days of the week, beginning with the equivalent of "Monday." This sequence is the normal one Italians use in naming the days of the week, the first day being the equivalent of "Monday." Pay close attention to stress and notice that the Italian names of the days of the week are not normally capitalized.

(lunedì)X	(lunedì)X
(martedì)X	(martedì)X
(mercoledì)X	(mercoledì)X
(giovedì)X	(giovedì)X
(vernerdì)X	(vernerdì)X
(sạbato)X	(sạbato)X
(domẹnica)X	(domẹnica)X

35. Learn the following:

(dopodomani)X	(dopodomani)X	"the day after tomorrow"
(avantiɛri)X	(avantiɛri)X	"the day before yesterday"

*36. Imagine that today is Wednesday. Answer the following questions. Your responses will be confirmed on the tape.

Che giorno è ɔggi? – ɔggi ....
 "What day is today?"
Che giorno ɛra iɛri? – _____
Che giorno sarà domani? – _____
Che giorno ɛra avantiɛri? – _____
Che giorno sarà dopodomani? – _____

*37. Imagine that today is Sunday. Answer the questions you will hear. Your response will be confirmed each time. Repeat this drill until you have mastered it.

    (1) Che giorno è ɔggi?
    (2) Che giorno sarà domani?
    (3) Che giorno sarà dopodomani?
    (4) Che giorno ɛra iɛri?
    (5) Che giorno ɛra avantiɛri?

*38. Continue as in the two preceding frames, this time imagining that today is Friday.

    (1) Che giorno ɛra avantiɛri?
    (2) Che giorno sarà dopodomani?
    (3) Che giorno è ɔggi?
    (4) Che giorno ɛra iɛri?
    (5) Che giorno sarà domani?

39. The verb ǂpensare "to think" used before *di* + INFINITIVE has the force of "planning to do something," "planning on doing something," "thinking of doing something," etc.

*40. Study the following model and in accordance with it answer the questions you will hear. The place expressions together with the appropriate day of the week to be used are translated for you. Your response will be confirmed each time.

    S: Quando pɛnsa di andare a New Yɔrk Lɛi?
      "When do you plan to go to New York?"
    R: Vado a New Yɔrk lunedì.
      "I'm going to New York (on) Monday."

Questions	Response Cues
(1) Quando pɛnsa di andare a scuola Lɛi?	to school (on) Monday
(2) ....a casa Lɛi?	home (on) Tuesday
(3) ....a cena fuɔri Lɛi?	dine out (on) Wednesday
(4) ....in città Lɛi?	to the city (on) Thursday
(5) ....in campagna Lɛi?	to the country (on) Friday
(6) ....in montagna Lɛi?	to the mountains (on) Saturday

Questions	Response Cues
(7) ....in chiɛsa Lɛi?	to church (on) Sunday
(8) ....in classe Lɛi?	to class (on) Monday
(9) ....in ufficio Lɛi?	to the office (on) Tuesday
(10) ....in ospedale Lɛi?	to the hospital (on) Wednesday
(11) ....in banca Lɛi?	to the bank (on) Thursday
(12) ....a Boston Lɛi?	to Boston (on) Friday

Repeat this drill until you have mastered it.

41. In Unit 21 you learned that "movement to" or "location in or at" was normally expressed by *a* or *ad* before names of cities or towns. In the preceding "movement to" drill you had place expressions sometimes preceded by *a* and sometimes preceded by *in*. Thus:

  (a scuɔla)X
  (a casa)X
  (a cena fuɔri)X
but:
  (in città)X
  (in campagna)X
  (in montagna)x
  (in chiɛsa)X
  (in classe)X
  (in ufficio)X
  (in ospedale)X
  (in banca)X

42. Whether referring to "movement to" or "location in or at" these above-mentioned places, the expressions given are the normal ones used. Thus, for example, *a scuɔla* may be translated as "to school," "in school," or "at school."

43. When, as in drill no. 40, one is referring to such places not so much as buildings or specific locales, but rather with emphasis on the *activities normally associated with these places,* there is no way to predict whether Italians use *a* or *in*. Each place expression must be learned through observation.

*44. Study the following model and in accordance with it answer the questions you will hear. Use as response cues the phrases given in frame no. 40. Your response will be confirmed each time.

    S: Dove sarà lunedì Lei?   "Where will you be (on) Monday?"

    R: Sarò a New York lunedì.   "I'll be in New York (on) Monday."

    (1) Dove sarà lunedì Lei?
    (2) ....martedì Lei?
    (3) ....mercoledì Lei?
    (4) ....giovedì Lei?
    (5) ....venerdì Lei?
    (6) ....sabato Lei?
    (7) ....domenica Lei?
    (8) ....lunedì Lei?
    (9) ....martedì Lei?
    (10) ....mercoledì Lei?
    (11) ....giovedì Lei?
    (12) ....venerdì Lei?

* * * * *

45. In drill no. 40 the place expression of the question was repeated in the response. Although this is proper, Italians frequently avoid repeating the place expression. When this happens however, A PLACE REPLACER must appear next to the verb.

46. The normal unemphatic PLACE REPLACER in Italian is *ci*. It appears immediately before FINITE VERB forms. (See Unit 17, frame no. 9.)

*47. In accordance with the following model, answer the questions you will hear by using the cues given. Your response will be confirmed each time.

    S: Quando pensa di andare a   "When do you plan to go
       New York Lei?   to New York?"
    R: Ci vado lunedì.   "I'm going (there) (on) Monday."

Questions	Cues
(1) Quando pensa di andare a cena fuori Lei?	Wednesday
(2) ....in montagna Lei?	Saturday
(3) ....a scuola Lei?	Monday
(4) ....in campagna Lei?	Friday
(5) ....in chiesa Lei?	Sunday
(6) ....in città Lei?	Thursday
(7) ....in classe Lei?	Monday
(8) ....in ospedale Lei?	Wednesday
(9) ....a casa Lei?	Tuesday
(10) ....a Boston Lei?	Friday
(11) ....in ufficio Lei?	Tuesday
(12) ....in banca Lei?	Thursday

48. When a verb appears in an infinitive construction, it is common to find *ci* attached to the infinitive minus its final *-e*. Thus. *Penso di andarci.*

*49. In accordance with the following model, answer the questions you will hear by using the cues given. Your response will be confirmed each time.

S: Quando pensa di andare a New York Lei?
R: Penso di andarci lunedì.   "I plan to go (there) (on) Monday."

Questions	Cues
(1) Quando pensa di andare in chiesa Lei?	Sunday
(2) ....a casa Lei?	Tuesday
(3) ....in campagna Lei?	Friday
(4) ....a scuola Lei?	Monday
(5) ....in città Lei?	Thursday
(6) ....in montagna Lei?	Saturday
(7) ....a cena fuori Lei?	Wednesday
(8)...............................in classe Lei?	Monday
(9) ....in ufficio Lei?	Tuesday
(10) ....in banca Lei?	Thursday
(11) ....in ospedale Lei?	Wednesday
(12) ....a Boston Lei?	day

50. The PLACE REPLACER *ci* seems to be freely used with *movement verbs* like †*andare,* †*arrivare,* †*portare,* "bring, carry."

51. This *ci* is also used with other kinds of verbs; however, sometimes special meanings are involved which may not be readily clear to beginning students. Because of this, use this PLACE REPLACER only with *movement verbs* until you are sure of its other uses.

* * * * *

52. In order to express the idea of "on Sundays," "on Mondays," etc., Italian uses *la* before *domęnica* and *il* before the other names of the days of the week.

*53. Study the following model and in accordance with it answer the questions you will hear by using the cues given. Your response will be confirmed each time.

S: Che cɔsa fa la domenica Lɛi? "What do you do on Sundays?"
R: Vado in chiɛsa la domenica. "I go to church on Sundays."

Questions	Cues
(1) Che cɔsa fa il lunedì Lɛi?	I work on Mondays.
(2) ....il martedì Lɛi?	I study on Tuesdays.
(3) ....il mercoledì Lɛi?	I don't do anything on Wednesdays.
(4) ....il giovedì Lɛi?	I do my shopping (*faccio le spese*) on Thursdays.
(5) ....il venerdì Lɛi?	I do my grocery shopping (*faccio la spensa*) on Fridays.
(6) ....il sąbato Lɛi?	I stay (*stɔ*) home on Saturdays.
(7) ....la domęnica Lɛi?	I sleep (*dɔrmo*) on Sundays.
(8) ....il lunedì Lɛi?	I play tennis (*giɔco a*) on Wednesdays.
(9) ....il martedì Lɛi?	I go shopping on Tuesdays.
(10) ....il mercoledì Lɛi?	I go grocery shopping on (*tɛnnis*) on Mondays.

Repeat this drill until you have mastered it.

*54. Now study the following. You will be asked questions as in Model (a) or model (b). Reply accordingly. Your response will be confirmed each time.

(a)
- S: Va a New York lunedì? — "Are you going to New York (on) Monday?"
- R: Sì, penso di andarci lunedì. — "Yes, I plan to go (there) (on) Monday."

(b)
- S: Va a New York il lunedì? — "Do you go to New York (on) Mondays?"
- R: Sì, ci vado ogni lunedì. — "Yes, I go (there) every Monday."

 (1) Va a scuola lunedì?
 (2) Va a scuola il lunedì?
 (3) Va in officio martedì?
 (4) Va in campagna il venerdì?
 (5) Va a Boston il venerdì?
 (6) Va in banca giovedì?
 (7) Va a casa il martedì?
 (8) Va in montagna il sabato?
 (9) Va in chiesa domenica?
 (10) Va a cena fuori il mercoledì?

• **End of Tape 8B** •

```
 ⊙      ⊙
 Tape 9A
```

*55. Complete the following statement:

"In order to express 'movement to' or 'location in or at' before names of cities or towns, Italian normally uses_____or_____."

56. The above holds true for many islands, too, especially the smaller ones. Thus:

(a Corfù)X
(ad Elba)X
(ad Ischia)X
(a Cuba)X
(a Malta)X
(a Taiti)X
(ad Haiti)X

57. Before *Corsica, Sardegna, Sicilia* and most other geographical place names these same concepts are normally expressed by *in*.

*58. Thus, translate the following into Italian.

    (a) "I'm going to Italy." _____

    (b) "Are you going to Sicily?" _____

    (c) "It's in Virginia." _____

59. With place names that are grammatically masculine, it is, as a rule, preferable to use *nel* (before a consonant) or *nell'* (elsewhere) instead of *in*.

*60. Thus, translate the following into Italian. The place names in these sentences are all masculine.

    (a) "(S)he's going to Chile." (use: *Cile*) _____

    (b) "I'm going to Mississippi."_____

    (c) "Are you going to the Veneto region?"(use: *Veneto*) _____

    _____

    (d) "It's in the Middle East." (use: *Medio Oriente*) _____

    _____

61. However, even with masculine names the use of *in* is becoming more and more frequent and acceptable, especially with *masculine names of countries* and *masculine names* of states in the U.S.A.

62. Thus, you may hear

    either (in Vietnam)X   or   (nel Vietnam)X
          (in Maryland)X   or   (nel Maryland)X

*63. Are the place names *Vietnam* and *Maryland* masculine or feminine?

64. The gender of geographical place names may sometimes present a problem to you. However, the following are, as a rule, feminine:

    a) names of cities and towns
    b) names of islands
    c) the following eight states in the U.S.A.—
        (Alasca)X (Arizona)X (California)X (Florida)X
        (Georgia)X (Lüisiana)X (Pensilvania)X (Virginia)X

*65. What is the gender of the following names of islands?
    (Corsica)X   (Sardegna)X
    (Cuba)X   (Sicilia)X

66. The following are, as a rule, masculine:

   a) names of oceans, seas, rivers and lakes
   b) names of most states in the U.S.A.

*67. What is the gender of the following:

   large bodies of water

   (Atlạntico)X
   (Pacịfico)X
   (Mediterrạneo)X

   Italian rivers

   (Arno)X
   (Ɔglio)X
   (Piave)X
   (Pɔ)X
   (Tɛvere)X   "Tiber"

   Italian lake

   (Garda)X

68. Most other geographical place names are feminine if they end in -*a* and masculine if they end in something else. The following are five masculine exceptions to this rule:

   (Canadà)X   (Ghana)X   (Guatemala)X   (Nicaragua)X   (Venezuɛla)X

*69. What would you say is the gender of the following names of continents? Put "m" for masculine and "f" for feminine after each name below.

   (1) _____   Amɛrica_____
   (2) _____   Asia_____
   (3) _____   Eurɔpa_____

*70. Do the same for the following names of countries:

   (1) _____   Afganistan_____
   (2) _____   Argentina_____
   (3) _____   Canadà_____
   (4) _____   Cile_____
   (5) _____   Cina_____
   (6) _____   Danimarca_____
   (7) _____   Germania_____
   (8) _____   Giappone_____
   (9) _____   Guatemala_____

(10) _____	Iraq_____
(11) _____	Italia_____
(12) _____	Libano_____
(13) _____	Marocco_____
(14) _____	Portogallo_____
(15) _____	Spagna_____
(16) _____	Sudan_____
(17) _____	Vietnam_____

*71. Do the same for the following names of islands.

(1) _____	Corsica_____
(2) _____	Cuba_____
(3) _____	Sardegna_____
(4) _____	Sicilia_____
(5) _____	Haiti_____

*72. Do the same for the following names of states in the U.S.A.

(1) _____	Alabama_____
(2) _____	Alasca_____
(3) _____	California_____
(4) _____	Colorado_____
(5) _____	Florida_____
(6) _____	Kansas_____
(7) _____	Kentucky_____
(8) _____	Lüisiana_____
(9) _____	Maryland_____
(10) _____	Massachusetts_____
(11) _____	Mississippi_____
(12) _____	Nevada_____
(13) _____	Nord Dakota_____
(14) _____	Ohio_____
(15) _____	Pensilvania_____
(16) _____	Virginia_____

*73. Do the same for the following names of Italian regions.

    (1) _____Liguria_____
    (2) _____Lombardia_____
    (3) _____Piemonte_____
    (4) _____Toscana_____
    (5) _____Veneto_____

*74. Do the same for the following place names.

    (1)_____Nord_____   "North"
    (2)_____Sud_____   "South"
    (3)_____Est_____   "East"
    (4)_____Ovest_____   "West"
    (5)_____Medio Oriente_____

*75. Return to the place names of frames no. 67 through no. 74 and express "movement to" or "location in or at" by putting *a, in, nel* or *nell'* before each one in accordance with the rules stated in frames no. 55, no. 57, and no. 59.

76. In response to the preceding frame you should have put:
    for frame no. 69: *in*
    for frame no. 70: *in* for all the feminine ones; *nell'* for no. 1 and no. 10; *nel*
            for all the others
    for frame no. 71: *a* for no. 2 and no. 5; *in* for the others
    for frame no. 72: *in* for all the feminine ones, *nell'* for no. 1 and no. 14; *nel*
            for all the others
    for frame no. 73: *in* for no. 1, 2, 4; *nel* for no. 3 and no. 5
    for frame no. 74: *nell'* for no. 3 and no. 4; *nel* for the others

*77. What do you think the English equivalents of the place names listed in frames no. 69 through no. 72 are?

TEST A

(answers not recorded)

Listed below are some of the place names used in this unit. Each will be pronounced either with its correct STRESS or with an incorrect STRESS. Put a check in column A if the word is pronounced correctly with its proper STRESS. Otherwise, put a check in column B.

	A (correct)	B (incorrect)
1) Italia		
2) Perugia		
3) Ụdine		
4) Beiru		
5) Nạpoli		
6) Pɔrto Sạid		
7) Cạgliari		
8) Saigɔn		
9) Gɛnova		
10) Alcalà		
11) Catania		
12) Copenạghen		
13) Bagdad		
14) Pạdova		
15) Tạngeri		
16) Etiɔpia		
17) Cabul		
18) Bulgarịa		
19) Normandia		
20) Baia		
21) Bogotà		
22) Flɔrida		
23) Asia		
24) Pavịa		
25) Algerịa		

(answers not recorded)

You will now hear some Italian words that are written with two vowel letters. Some require a written accent mark on them; others do not. Write the words correctly below as you hear them, including any accent marks that are required.

1) _____

2) _____

3) _____

4) _____

5) _____

6) _____

7) _____

8) _____

9) _____

10) _____

11) _____

12) _____

13) _____

14) _____

15) _____

16) _____

17) _____

18) _____

19) _____

20) _____

TEST C

(answers not recorded)

You will hear some statements. Check whether they would be true or false if today were Monday.

	True	False
1)		
2)		
3)		
4)		
5)		
6)		
7)		
8)		
9)		
10)		

TEST D

(answers not recorded)

The following is a drill designed to test your control of *a, in, nel* and *nell'* before geographical place names. You will be asked a question about the location of a particular city. The city names used will be those listed in frame no. 12 of this unit. Incomplete answers to the questions are listed below with a blank for you to fill in the appropriate item (*a, in, nel* or *nell'*) in accordance with the rules stated in frames nos. 55, 57 and 59.

Questions	Answers
1) Dov'è Addis Abeba?	Addis Abeba è_____Etiopia.
2) ....Alcalà?	Alcalà è_____ Spagna.
3) ....Algeri?	Algeri è_____Algeria.
4) ....Amman?	Amman è_____Giordania.
5) ....Ankara?	Ankara è_____Turchia.
6) ....Bagdad?	Bagdad è_____Iraq.
7) ....Baltimora?	Baltimora è_____Maryland.
8) ....Bangkok?	Bangkok è_____Thailandia.
9) ....Beirut?	Beirut è_____Libano.
10) ....Berlino?	Berlino è_____ Germania.
11) ....Bogotà?	Bogotà è_____ Colombia.
12) ....Boston?	Boston è_____Massachusetts.
13) ....Bucarest?	Bucarest è_____Romania.
14) ....Budapest?	Budapest è_____ Ungheria.
15) ....Buenos Aires?	Buenos Aires è_____ Argentina.
16) ....Cabul?	Cabul è_____Afganistan.
17) ....Caracas?	Caracas è_____Venezuela.
18) ....Cagliari?	Cagliari è_____ Sardegna.
19) ....Catania?	Catania è_____ Sicilia.
20) ....Città del Guatemala?	Città del Guatemala e
21) ....Colonia?	_____Guatemala.
22) ....Copenaghen?	Colonia è_____Germania.
	Copenaghen è_____ Danimarca.

Questions	Answers
23) ....Cordova?	Cordova è_____Spagna.
24) ....Damasco?	Damasco è_____Siria.
25) ....Filadelfia?	Filadelfia è_____Pensilvania.
26) ....Helsinki?	Helsinki è_____Finlandia.
27) ....Kartum?	Kartum è_____Sudan.
28) ....Lagos?	Lagos è_____Nigeria.
29) ....Las Vegas?	Las Vegas è_____Nevada.
30) ....L'Avana?	L'Avana è_____Cuba.
31) ....Lisbona?	Lisbona è_____Portogallo.
32) ....Los Angeles?	Los Angeles è_____California.
33) ....Managua?	Managua è_____Nicaragua.
34) ....Miami?	Miami è_____Florida.
35) ....Monaco di Baviera?	Monaco di Baviera è_____Germania.
36) ....Mosca?	Mosca è_____Russia.
37) ....Nuova Delhi?	Nuova Delhi è_____India.
38) ....Padova?	Padova è_____Veneto.
39) ....Palermo?	Palermo è_____Sicilia.
40) ....Pechino?	Pechino è_____Cina.
41) ....Rabat?	Rabat è_____Marocco.
42) ....Saigon?	Saigon è_____Vietnam.
43) ....Santiago?	Santiago è_____Cile.
44) ....Siviglia?	Siviglia è_____Spagna.
45) ....Sofia?	Sofia è_____Bulgaria.
46) ....Tangeri?	Tangeri è_____Marocco.
47) ....Tokio?	Tokio è_____Giappone.
48) ....Toronto?	Toronto è_____Canadà.
49) ....Tunisi?	Tunisi è_____Tunisia.
50) ....Varsavia?	Varsavia è_____Polonia.

TEST E

(not recorded)

Translate the following thoughts into Italian by using *only* what has been presented so far.

1) When do you think you'll be going to New York?

_____

2) Do you go to church on Sundays?

_____

3) When do you do your grocery shopping, on Saturdays?

_____

4) I'm thinking of going shopping in Washington tomorrow.

_____

5) Don't you ever stay home?

_____

6) I'm playing tennis the day after tomorrow.

_____

7) What day will you be arriving in Malta?

_____

8) Mr. Jones is scheduled to go to the hospital on Wednesday.

_____

9) Wasn't there some salt there the day before yesterday?

_____

10) Will you be in the office tomorrow afternoon?

_____

11) I go to school every day but I don't like it.

_____

12) Are you dining out with Virginia tonight?

_____

13) When are you going to go to the bank?

_____

14) In the mountains I sleep a lot.

_____

15) I don't work in Virginia and I don't work in Maryland. I work in Washington.

_____

16) Are you dreaming of Naples? Do you like the Campania region?

_____

17) Milan is in the Lombardy region, isn't it?

_____

18) I thought it was in the Piedmont region. (HINT: Put this idea into Italian in the form of a question.)

_____

19) I'm scheduled to go to Guatemala, but not to Guatemala City.

_____

20) I'm going to Genoa on Thursday but I don't go every Thursday.

_____

TEST A   ANSWERS

	A	B	Correct Stress
1)		X	/ITALÍA/
2)		X	/PERUǦÍA/
3)	X		
4)	X		
5)	X		
6)		X	/PɔRTOSAÍD/
7)		X	/KAĽÁRI/
8)		X	/SÁYGON/
9)	X		
10)		X	/ÁLKALA/
11)	X		
12)		X	/KÓPENAGEN/
13)		X	/BÁGDAD/
14)		X	/PADÓVA/
15)	X		
16)	X		
17)	X		
18)		X	/BULGÁRYA/
19)	X		
20)		X	/BAÍA/
21)	X		
22)		X	/FLORÍDA/
23)	X		

	A	B	Correct Stress
24)		X	/PÁVIA/
25)		X	/ALǦÉRYA/

TEST B ANSWERS

1) mai	5) qui	9) pio	13) qua	17) stai
2) mia	6) ciò	10) piè	14) fui	18) giù
3) poi	7) dio	11) Gia	15) già	19) io
4) può	8) sii	12) bue	16) voi	20) più

TEST C ANSWERS

	True	False
1) Domani sarà mercoledì.		X
2) Avantieri era sabato.	X	
3) Ieri era venerdì.		X
4) Oggi è lunedì.	X	
5) Dopodomani sarà mercoledì.	X	
6) Avantieri era domenica.		X
7) Ieri era domenica.	X	
8) Oggi è giovedì.		X
9) Domani sarà martedì.	X	
10) Dopodomani sarà lunedì.		X

TEST D ANSWERS

1) in	11) in	21) in	31) nel	41) nel
2) in	12) nel	22) in	32) in	42) nel
3) in	13) in	23) in	33) nel	43) nel
4) in	14) in	24) in	34) in	44) in
5) in	15) in	25) in	35) in	45) in
6) nell'	16) nell'	26) in	36) in	46) nel
7) nel	17) nel	27) nel	37) in	47) nel
8) in	18) in	28) in	38) nel	48) nel
9) nel	19) in	29) nel	39) in	49) in
10) in	20) nel	30) a	40) in	50) in

TEST E ANSWERS

1) Quando pensa di andare a New York Lei?
2) Va in chiesa la domenica Lei?
3) Quando fa la spesa Lei, il sabato?
4) Penso di fare le spese a Washington domani.
5) Non sta mai a casa Lei?
6) Gioco a tennis dopodomani.
7) Che giorno arriva a Malta Lei?
8) Il signor Jones va in ospedale mercoledì.
9) Non c'era un po' di sale qui avantieri?
10) Sarà in ufficio domani pomeriggio Lei?
11) Vado a scuola ogni giorno ma non mi piace.
12) Va a cena fuori con Virginia stasera Lei?
13) Quando va in banca Lei?
14) In montagna dormo molto.
15) Non lavoro in Virginia e non lavoro nel Maryland. Lavoro a Washington.
16) Sôgna Napoli Lei? Le piace la Campania?
17) Milano è Lombardia, no?
18) Non è nel Piemonte?
19) Vado nel Guatemala, ma non a Città del Guatemala.
20) Vado a Genova giovedì ma non ci vado ogni giovedì.

UNIT 24

*1. In Unit 17 you learned the word for "Thanks," or "Thank you." What was it?

2. In Unit 18 you learned the phrases for "on the left" and "on the right." What were they?

3. Those utterances each contained a consonant followed by a tongue-flap. Listen again and repeat.

(g——)X   (a s——)X   (a d——)X

*4. You have already learned that the tongue-flap in Italian is represented by what letter?

*5. How, then, would you spell the phrases for "on the left" and "on the right" in Italian?

6. Because, as we saw it Unit 15, the tongue-flap is heard between vowels in many words in "colloquial" American English, it is sometimes helpful in pronouncing it after a consonant in Italian to think of a soft, quick vowel right before it. Thus, for a *sinistra* you might want to think of (*a si-ni-st(a)ra*), and for a *destra* you might want to think of (*a dɛ-st(a)ra*).

7. Remembering this principle, try pronouncing the following words, all of which contain *consonant + tongue-flap*.

(pronto)X	"ready; hello [said on the phone]"	(Pronto)X
(prego)X	[used in many cases to express such varied ideas as: go ahead or the answer to *g*—— "Thank you"	(Prego)X
(sɛmpre)X	"always"	(sɛmpre)X
(tre)X	"three"	(tre)X
(segretario)X	"(male) secretary"	(segretario)X
(segretaria)X	"(female) secretary"	(segretaria)X
(Centralino)X	"telephone exchange"	
(Centralino)X		
	[normally used in calling the telephone operator]	

(aprile)X	"April"	(aprile)X
(novεmbre)X	"November"	(novεmbre)X
(dicεmbre)X	"December"	(dicεmbre)X
(Africa)X	"Africa"	(Africa)X
(Australia)X	"Australia"	(Australia)X
(Brasile)X	"Brazil"	(Brasile)X
(Francia)X	"France"	(Francia)X
(Grεcia)X	"Greece"	(Grεcia)X
(Brasilia)X	"Brasilia"	(Brasilia)X
(Francofɔrte)X	"Frankfurt"	(Francofɔrte)X
(Londra)X	"London"	(Londra)X
(Alfrεdo)X	[masculine given name]	(Alfrεdo)X
(Andrεa)X	[masculine given name, cognate of Andrew]	(Andrεa)X
(Cristina)X	[feminine given name]	(Cristina)X
(Grisεlda)X	[feminine given name]	(Grisεlda)X

* * * * *

8. The infinitive was introduced in Unit 20. So far we have used it as a secondary verb form following a finite verb (defined in Unit 17).
   For example:

   My piace *studiare*.   "I like to study."
        (infinitive)
   Pεnso di *andare* a New York   "I'm planning on going
   domani. (infinitive)   to New York tomorrow."

*9. Notice that in the second example above, a word is used as a connector between the finite verb and the infinitive. What is the word?

10. A connector like *di* ocurring in such constructions usually depends on the preceding verb. Thus, ┼*pensare* requires *di* before a following infinitive in order to express the idea of "planning to do something."

11. In most cases, however, no connector is needed between a finite verb and an infinitive.

12. Four verbs that commonly occur in such constructions without any connector are:
    ┼*desiderare*, ┼*volere*, ┼*potere*, and ┼*dovere*. Except for ┼*desiderare* these are irregular verbs with forms that cannot be predicted.

13. Study and learn the following:

(Desidera)X + INFINITIVE?	– (Sì, desidero)X + INFINITIVE.
"Do you wish to ....?"	"yes, I wish to ...."
(Vuɔle)X + INFINITIVE?	– (Sì, vɔglio)X + INFINITIVE.
"Do you want to ....?"	"Yes, I want to ....."
"Would you like to .....?"	
(Puɔ̀)X + INFINITIVE?	– (Sì, pɔsso)X + INFINITIVE.
"Can you .....?"	"Yes, I can ....."
"Are you able to ....?"	"Yes, I am able to....."
(Dĕve)X + INFINITIVE?	– (Sì, dĕvo)X + INFINITIVE.
"Must you .....?"	or
"Do you have to ....?"	(Sì, dĕbbo)X + INFINITIVE.
	"Yes, I must ....."
	"Yes, I have to ....."

14. Of the different forms given in the preceding frame, *vuɔle* is often shortened to *vuɔl* before an infinitive, and a consonant following *puɔ̀* is usually strongly pronounced.

*15. How would you say, "Do you wish to call now?" in Italian?

*16. How would you say, "Does he want to listen?" in Italian?

*17. How about, "I want to understand?"

*18. And, "She can't understand?"

*19. Translate, "I'm not able to drink wine."

*20. Translate, "Do I have to go now?"

*21. Translate, "Would you like to know where he is?"

*22. Translate, "You have to work, don't you?"

*23. Translate, "I don't wish to eat now."

24. The verb forms given in frame no. 13 are all PRESENT TENSE verb forms of high frequency. Make sure you learn them.

* * * * *

25. In order to refer to present time ideas such as those referred to by the verb forms of frame no. 13, but with the idea of *reserve* or *deference*, Italian uses another tense. Study and learn the following:

(Desidererĕbbe)X + INFINITIVE? – (Sì, desidererɛi)X + INFINITIVE.
"Would you wish to ....?"   "Yes, I'd like to...."
"Would you want to .....?"
"Would you like to ....?"

(Vorrĕbbe)X + INFINITIVE? – (Sì, vorrɛi)X + INFINITIVE.
"Would you like to ....?"   "Yes, I'd like to........."
                                      Vorrɛi is heard more often than
                                      desidererɛi.

(Potrĕbbe)X + INFINITIVE?   (Sì, potrɛi)X + INFINITIVE.
"Could you..........?"   "Yes, I could ...."

(Dovrĕbbe)X + INFINITIVE?   (Sì, dovrɛi)X + INFINITIVE.
"Should you ....?"

                                    "Yes, I should ...."

26. Because the eight verb forms given in the preceding frame all *share the same time reference* and *differ only in the person referred to* they may be considered as belonging to one TENSE.

27. Because /Rɛ/ or /RE/ is the characteristic sound combination found in all the verb forms of this tense, we shall refer to this tense as the "RE" TENSE.

28. The name "RE" TENSE may also be helpful in reminding us that *one* of the uses of this tense, at least, is to express a present idea with *REserve* or *defeREnce.*

*29. Translate, "Do you wish to begin now?"

*30. Translate, "Would you wish to begin now?"

*31. Translate, "I want to come."

*32. Translate, "I'd like to come."

*33. Translate, "Can he work tomorrow?"

*34. Translate, "Could he work tomorrow?"

*35. Translate, "She has to ask."

*36. Translate, "She should ask."

*37. Translate, "I shouldn't do anything now."

*38. Translate, "Wouldn't you like to learn?"

*39. Translate, "Could I smoke here?"

* * * * *

40. A verb form that can be considered as belonging to another tense is one used to *request* that someone do something.

41. You have already had some examples of REQUEST FORMS. For example:
    scusi   "excuse (me)" from the verb †scusare
    porti   "bring" from the verb †portare

42. These two forms are used in *formal* situations when addressing *one* person.

43. A special plural form used in highly formal situations when one wishes to be very polite, simply adds -*no*. Thus:
    (Scusino)X
    (portino)X

44. REQUEST FORMS may indicate requests with implications ranging from a mild suggestion, invitation or wish to a direct command. The tone of voice used often indicates which meaning is implied.

45. Formal REQUEST FORMS of regular -*are* verbs always end in -*i* (for the singular) and -*ino* (for the highly formal plural). Thus:

    (arrivi)X   (arrivino)X
    (ascolti)X   (ascoltino)X
    (chiami)X   (chiamino)X
    (cominci)X   (comincino)X
    (domandi)X   (domandino)X
    (fumi)X   (fumino)X
    (giochi)X   (giochino)X
    (impari)X   (imparino)X
    (lavori)X   (lavorino)X
    (mangi)X   (mangino)X

(pɛnsi)X	(pɛnsino)X
(sôgni)X	(sôgnino)X
(spiɛghi)X	(spiɛghino)X
(studi)X	(studino)X

*46. Here are two more.

(aspɛtti)X	(aspɛttino)X	"wait, wait for"
(insegni)X	(insɛgnino)X	"teach"
(parli)X	(parlino)X	"speak, talk"

*47. What are the infinitives of the three preceding verbs?

* * * * *

48. Observe the following:

(Imparo l'italiano.)X	"I'm learning Italian."
(Ascolto l'iltaliano.)X	"I'm listening to Italian."
(Sôgno l'italiano.)X	"I'm dreaming about Italian."
(Spiɛgo l'italiano.)X	"I'm explaining Italian."
(Mi piace l'italiano.)X	"I like Italian."

49. In most cases the Italian language is referred to as *l'italiano*.

50. Normally, however, no *l'* is present after *in* and *d'* (standing for *di*). Repeat:

(in italiano)X	"in Italian"
(uno studɛnte d'italiano)X	"a student of Italian"
(uno indegnante d'italiano) X	"a teacher of Italian"

51. In some cases *l'* is often omitted after a few verbs like ┼*parlare* and ┼*studiare*, especially when *italiano* immediately follows these verbs. However, students are never wrong if they use *l'* even in such cases.

52. What has just been explained for *italiano* also applies to *inglese* "English."

*53. Translate the following, applying the principles just explained. Write out your translation next to the English sentences.

(1) He speaks English. _____

(2) He's speaking in English. _____

(3) He never speaks Italian. _____

(4) He has to speak Italian well. _____

(NOTE: Put *bene* immediately after the second verb.)

(5) I'm studying Italian. _____

(6) Do you teach English? _____

(7) It's an Italian teacher, not an Italian student. _____

The tape will give you the correct translations.

* * * * *

Drills - frames no. 54–59: Reply in accordance with each model. Your answer will be confirmed each time. Repeat these drills until you have mastered them.

*54. S: Desidero studiare.　　　　　　"I wish to stady."
　　　R: Che cɔsa desidera fare?　　　"What do you wish to do?"

(1) Desidero ascoltare.　　　　(6) Vɔglio studiare.
(2) Vɔglio chiamare.　　　　　(7) Dĕvo aspettare.
(3) Pɔsso cominciare.　　　　　(8) Desidero mangiare.
(4) Dĕvo giocare.　　　　　　(9) Pɔsse fumare.
(5) Dĕbbo lavorare.　　　　　(10) Dĕbbo parlare.

*55. S: Desidererɛi studiare.　　　　"I'd like to study."
　　　R: Che cɔsa desidererĕbbe　　"What would you like to do?"
　　　　　fare?

(1) Desidererɛi imparare.　　　(5) Vorrɛi sognare.
(2) Vorrɛi domandare.　　　　(6) Dovrɛi finire.
(3) Dovrɛi pensare.　　　　　(7) Potrɛi venire.
(4) Potrɛi spiegare.　　　　　(8) Desidererɛi bere.

*56. S: Desidera studiare?
    R: Sì, desidero studiare.

(1) Desidera ascoltare?
(2) Vuol chiamare?
(3) Può cominciare?
(4) Děve giocare?
(5) Děve lavorare?

"Do you wish to study?"
"Yes, I wish to study."

(6) Vuole studiare?
(7) Děve aspettare?
(8) Desidera mangiare?
(9) Può fumare?
(10) Děve parlare?

*57. S: Desidererěbbe studiare?
    R: No, non desidererei studiare.

(1) Desidererěbbe imparare?
(2) Vorrěbbe domandare?
(3) Dovrěbbe pensare?
(4) Potrěbbe spiegare?

"Would you like to study?"
"No, I wouldn't like to study."

(5) Vorrěbbe sognare?
(6) Dovrěbbe finire?
(7) Potrěbbe venire?
(8) Desidererěbbe bere?

*58. S: Desidera studiare?
    R: Sì, desidero studiare ma
       non desiderererei studiare
       qui.

(1) Desidera ascoltare?
(2) Vuol chiamare?
(3) Può cominciare?
(4) Děve giocare?
(5) Děve lavorare?

"Do you wish to study?"
"Yes, I wish to study but
I wouldn't want to study
here."

(6) Vuole studiare?
(7) Děve aspettare?
(8) Desidera mangiare?
(9) Può fumare?
(10) Děve parlare?

*59. S: Desidero studiare.
    R: Studi!

(1) Desidero ascoltare.
(2) Voglio chiamare.
(3) Posso cominciare?
(4) Děvo giocare.
(5) Děbbo lavorare.
(6) Voglio studiare.
(7) Děvo aspettare.

"I wish to study."
"Study!"

(8) Desidero mangiare.
(9) Posso fumare?
(10) Děbbo parlare.
(11) Vorrei pensare.
(12) Potrei domandare?
(13) Dovrei spiegare.

60. Here are some genderables that can be useful in answering the phone. Memorize them.

MASCULINE

"moment"	(ɫmomento)X	(ɫmomento)X
"number"	(ɫnumero)X	(ɫnumero)X
"telephone"	(ɫtelɛfono)X	(ɫtelɛfono)X

FEMININE

"American Embassy"	(ɫA. A.)X	(ɫA. A.)X
"guard"	(ɫguardia)X	(ɫguardia)X

61. Here are some verbs and verb phrases that can be useful in answering the phone. Memorize them.

"to make a mistake"	(ɫsbagliare)X	(ɫsbagliare)X
"You must have dialed the wrong number."	(Avrà sbagliato numero)X	(Avrà sbagliato numero)X
"Who shall I say is calling (her)?"	(Chi la desidera?)X	(Chi la desidera?)X
"Who shall I say is calling (him)?"	(Chi lo desidera?)X	(Chi lo desidera?)X
"I'm sorry."	(Mi dispiace.)X	(Mi dispiace.)X
"This is the office...."	(Qui è l'ufficio)X	(Qui è l'ufficio)X
"to stay, remain"	(ɫrestare)X	(ɫrestare)X
"stay on the line"	(Rɛsti in linea.)X	(Rɛsti in linea.)X
"Speaking [= I am the one]"	(Sôno io.)X	(Sôno io.)X
"I'll see if (s)he is in."	(Vedo se c'è.)X	(Vedo se c'è.)X

62. Here are some other utterances that can be useful in answering the phone. Memorize them.

"slowly"	(adagio)X	(adagio)X
"on the phone"	(al telɛfono)X	(al telɛfono)X
"Mr. White's"	(del signor White)X	(del signor White)X
"Mrs. Smith's"	(della signora Smith)X	(della signora Smith)X
"Dr. Russo"	(il dottor Russo)X	(il dottor Russo)X
"the guard at the American Embassy"	(la guardia all' A.A.)X	(la guardia all'A.A.)X

Repeat this frame and the two previous ones several times until you feel you have mastered both the pronunciation and the meaning of the utterances given.

63. You will now hear a series of six short diologs useful as opening telephone
    conversations. Repeat each line, limiting as closely as possible. You should
    review this section several times until you feel you have *memorized* each dia-
    log. NOTE: "A" stands for "American and "I" stands for "Italian."

    I
      A: Pronto?
       I: Desịdero parlare con il signor White, per piacere.
      A: Sôno io.

    II
      A: Pronto?
       I: Chi parla?
      A: L'ufficio della signora Smith.
       I: C'è la signora, per favore?

    III
      A: Pronto…
       I: Parlo con la signorina Jones?
      A: Nɔ, sôno la segretaria. Vuɔl parlare con la signorina?
       I: Sì, per favore.

    IV
      A: Pronto. Qui è l'ufficio del signor White.
       I: Con chi parlo?
      A: Con la segretaria del signor White.
       I: Potrɛi parlare con il signor White, per favore?

    V
      A: Pronto. A.A.
       I: Chi è al telɛfono?
      A: Parla la guardia all'A.A. Con chi desidera parlare?
       I: Vorrɛi parlare con il signor White, per favore.
      A: Rɛsti in lịnea, per favore.

    VI
      A: Pronto?
       I: Parla la signora Marchegiano?
      A: Scusi, non parlo molto bene l'italiano. Parli adagio, per favore.
       I: Potrɛi parlare con la signora Marchegiano, per favore?
      A: Mi dispiace. Avrà sbagliato nụmero.

64. Here are two short exchanges that might be used to continue some of the
    previous conversations. Again, repeat each line, imitating very closely.
    Review this frame several times until you have memorized the two
    exchanges.

I A: Chi lo desidera?
   I: Il dottor Russo.
   A: Aspɛtti un momento, per favore.

II A: Chi la desidera?
   I: Il dottor Russo.
   A: Aspɛtti un momento, per favore. Vedo se c'ɛ.

• End of Tape 9A •

TEST A

(answers not recorded)

You will hear several Italian utterances which should all be pronounced with *consonant + tongue-flap*. This consonant combination will sometimes be pronounced incorrectly. Put a check in the appropriate column according to whether you hear a correct pronunciation or not.

	Correct	Incorrect
1) a destra		
2) Africa		
3) Alfredo		
4) Andrea		
5) april		
6) a sinistra		
7) Australia		
8) Brasile		
9) Brasilia		
10) Centralino		
11) Cristina		
12) dicembre		
13) Francia		
14) Francoforte		
15) g—— "Thank you"		
16) Greci		
17) Griselda		
18) Londra		
19) novembre		
20) prego		
21) pronto		
22) segretaria		
23) segretario		
24) sempre		
25) tre		

TEST B

(answers not recorded)

You will hear ten utterances. For each utterance check *only one* of the four letters… a, b, c, d, according to which best approximates the thought behind the utterance. Do *not* expect literal translation.

1) Pronto? Chi parla?

    (a) Hello? Who is it?
    (b) Who shall I say is calling?
    (c) Ready? Who is leaving?
    (d) Hello? How are you?

2) Dĕvo andare in Australia dopodomani.

    (a) I'll be arriving in Australia tomorrow.
    (b) I have to go to Australia in two days.
    (c) He has to leave for Australia day after tomorrow.
    (d) She must go to Australia tomorrow.

3) Scusi, ma vado a Francofɔrte ɔggi.

    (a) I'm sorry. I leave for France today.
    (b) Excuse me, but I'm going to Frankfurt today.
    (c) Pardon me, but I have to go to Frankfurt today.
    (d) I know. I want to go to France.

4) Sì, vado in Italia e dovrɛi imparare bɛne l'italiano.

    (a) Yes, I'm scheduled to go to Italy and I should learn Italian well.
    (b) Yes, I'm going to Italy and I'm learning Italian well.
    (c) Yes, I'll be going to Italy and I have to learn Italian.
    (d) Yes, by learning Italian I can go to Italy.

5) Vorrɛi mangiare. Che c'ɛ̀?

    (a) I want to eat chick-peas.
    (b) I'd like to eat. What would *you* like?
    (c) I feel like eating. What have you got?
    (d) *I* wish to eat. Who else?

6) Parli adagio, per favore. Vɔglio capire.

    (a) Would you speak slowly, please? I want to understand.
    (b) Could you speak slowly, please? I have to understand.
    (c) Speak slowly, please. I can't understand.
    (d) Speak faster, please, so that he won't understand.

7) Chiami il dottor Russo domani mattina.

    (a) Tomorrow I want you to call Dr. Russo.
    (b) Call Dr. Russo this morning.
    (c) Can you call Dr. Russo now?
    (d) Tomorrow morning call Dr. Russo.

8) Chi vuɔl parlare con la segretaria del signor White?

    (a) Can I talk to Mr. White?
    (b) Can I talk to Mr. White's secretary.
    (c) Who is talking with Miss White's secretary?
    (d) Who would like to talk to Mr. White's secretary?

9) Potrɛi lavorare domani pomeriggio ma non pɔsso venire dopodomani.

    (a) I could work tomorrow afternoon but I can't come in the next day.
    (b) I could work tomorrow morning but I can't work in the afternoon.
    (c) I should work tomorrow but in the afternoon I can't come in.
    (d) I'd like to work tomorrow afternoon but not the day after tomorrow.

10) Pronto? è qui l'ufficio della signorina Jones?

    (a) Hello? Is this Mr. Jones's office?
    (b) Hello? Do I have Miss Jones's office?
    (c) Hello? Is Miss Jones in the office?
    (d) Hello? Is this the office of Mrs. Jones?

TEST C

(answers not recorded)

You will hear twenty-four English sentences containing the verb "work." For each English sentence you hear, write in the appropriate space the form of ~~desiderare~~, ~~volere~~, ~~potere~~, or ~~dovere~~ that best conveys the thought expressed in the English.

1) He can work. _____

2) Do you want to work? _____

3) Can you work? _____

4) Could you work? _____

5) Do you wish to work? _____

6) Must you work? _____

7) Are you able to work? _____

8) Does he want to work? _____

9) I shouldn't work. _____

10) I wish to work. _____

11) Could she work? _____

12) I don't want to work. _____

13) Should he work? _____

14) She would like to work. (use: ~~volere~~) _____

15) Don't you have to work? _____

16) I'd like to work. (use: ~~volere~~) _____

17) I must work. (two ways) _____

18) Should you work? _____

19) He doesn't want to work. _____

20) I can work. _____

21) I have to work. (two ways) _____

22) Would you wish to work? _____

23) I could work. _____

24) I am not able to work. _____

TEST D

(answers not recorded)

You will hear two dialogs and one narrative in Italian, each followed by ten English statements about them. Put a check in the appropriate column according to whether each statement is definitely *true* or *false*.

I   —Buon giorno. Sôno Cesare Prato. Vorrei parlare con il signor Rossi, per favore.
     —Il signor Rossi non c'è oggi. Potrĕbbe ritornare domani?
     —Domani non posso, potrei ritornare lunedì pomeriggio.
      Ci sarà il signor Rossi?
     —Ora non so. Chiami lunedì mattina, per favore.
     —G——. Buon giorno.

   (1) Someone is asking to see Mr. Rossi.
   (2) Mr. Rossi doesn't want to see anyone.
   (3) Mr. Prato is asked to come back next week.
   (4) Tomorrow the office is closed.
   (5) Tomorrow is Monday.
   (6) Mr. Rossi will definitely be in on Monday.
   (7) Mr. Prato is willing to come back Monday afternoon.
   (8) The appointment is made for Monday.
   (9) Mr. Prato is asked to phone before coming in Monday afternoon.
   (10) Mr. Prato goes away angry, without saying good-bye.

	True	False
1)		
2)		
3)		
4)		
5)		
6)		
7)		
8)		
9)		
10)		

II
—Signora Gabrini, che cɔsa fa qui?
—Dĕvo andare in banca con Andrɛa; e Lɛi, lavora qui?
—Nɔ, nɔ, aspɛtto una persona do Londra, an insegnante d'inglese.
—Ma non c'è il signor White?
—C'ɛra il signor White, ma ora è nel Portogallo e pɛnsa di ritornare in dicɛmbre.
—Che cɔsa fa nel Portogallo il signor White?
—Insegna inglese in una scuɔla a Lisbona.

(1) Two people are talking in the office where they work.
(2) The lady is meeting someone for lunch.
(3) The gentleman is waiting for someone from London.
(4) The English teacher is a Londoner.
(5) At the present time Mr. White is not teaching here.
(6) Mr. White is touring Europe.
(7) He plans to come back before the end of the year.
(8) Mr. White is vacationing in Portugal.
(9) There is mention of a school in Lisbon where English is taught.
(10) Mr. White teaches there.

	True	False
1)		
2)		
3)		
4)		
5)		
6)		
7)		
8)		
9)		
10)		

III   La signorina Virginia Brosio è una studentessa d'inglese. Studia molto e
      parla già benino. In novembre vorrĕbbe andare a San Francisco dove
      dovrĕbbe lavorare in una banca. Ora Virginia vorrĕbbe stare a casa, ma
      non puɔ, dĕve andare sempre fuɔri. Ɔggi, giovedì, dĕve fare le spese in
      città. Domani pomeriggio dĕve andare all'A.A. Domani sera dovrĕbbe
      vedere un film in inglese.

      (1) Miss Brosio is a student from England.
      (2) She seems to be a very serious student.
      (3) Miss Brosio is planning a trip to the United States.
      (4) She doesn't speak a word of English.
      (5) Virginia is definitely going to work in San Francisco.
      (6) She doesn't like to stay home.
      (7) Virginia has to be out of the house a lot although she would
          rather stay home.
      (8) She has to buy several things.
      (9) She has to go to the American Embassy on Sunday.
     (10) The day after tomorrow she is going to the movies.

	True	False
1)		
2)		
3)		
4)		
5)		
6)		
7)		
8)		
9)		
10)		

TEST E

(not recorded)

Translate the following thoughts into Italian by using *only* what has been presented so far.

1) I'd like to go out to eat tonight but I have no idea of where I could get some good food.

2) Excuse me. Ask over there on the right, please. (said in a highly formal situation addressing more than one person)

3) Andrew would like to go to Brazil but he doesn't like Brasilia. He wants to go to Rio.

4) When will you be arriving in Greece, Saturday morning?

5) You can speak English when you are in London and in Australia, but in Italy you should speak Italian.

6) (addressing one person) Study a lot at home. In class you have to listen, understand, and do a lot of talking.

7) (addressing one person) I don't want to explain anything in English. Listen carefully. You *can* understand.

8) (addressing one person) Excuse me. I have to wait here. Is it all right if I smoke?

9) I should be in tomorrow. Could you call tomorrow morning?

10) Mr. White isn't in. Would you wish to see [= speak with] Mr. White's secretary?

11) (addressing two people) Wait here, please. I'll see if he's in.

12) (on the phone) Is it possible for you to come over now? There's an Italian teacher here and she speaks English very well.

13) (on the phone) Hello. Who's this, please?

_____

14) (on the phone) Dr. Russo? May I ask who's calling, please?

_____

15) (on the phone) I'm sorry. You must have the wrong number.

_____

16) (on the phone) Is this Mrs. Marchegiano? Is Cristina in?

_____

17) (on the phone) This is the American Embassy guard speaking. May I help you?

_____

18) (on the phone) I wish to speak with the guard, please. Isn't he $\begin{cases} \text{around?} \\ \text{there?} \end{cases}$

_____

19) (on the phone) Is my presence required this afternoon? $\big\}$
             Do you want me to come in this afternoon?

I'd like to stay home. I'm not feeling very well.

_____

20) (on the phone) Am I supposed to come in this afternoon?
       Won't Marla be in?

_____

TEST A   ANSWERS

	Correct	Incorrect
1)	X	
2)		X
3)	X	
4)	X	
5)		X
6)		X
7)	X	
8)	X	
9)		X
10)		X
11)		X
12)		X
13)	X	
14)	X	
15)	X	
16)		X
17)	X	
18)		X
19)	X	
20)	X	
21)		X
22)		X
23)	X	
24)	X	
25)	X	

TEST B   ANSWERS

1) a	3) b	5) c	7) d	9) a
2) b	4) a	6) a	8) d	10) b

TEST C   ANSWERS

1) Può lavorare.
2) Vuol(e) lavorare (Lεi)?
3) Può lavorare (Lεi)?
4) Potrěbbe lavorare (Lεi)?
5) Desịdera lavorare (Lεi)?
6) Děve lavorare (Lεi)?
7) Può lavorare (Lεi)?
8) Vuol(e) lavorare?
9) Non dovrεi lavorare.
10) Desịdero lavorare.
11) Potrěbbe lavorare?

12) Non vɔglio lavorare.
13) Dovrĕbbe lavorare?
14) Vorrĕbbe lavorare.
15) Non dĕve lavorare (Lɛi)?
16) Vorrɛi lavorare.
17) Dĕvo lavorare. Dĕbbo lavorare.
18) Dovrĕbbe lavorare (Lɛi)?
19) Non vuɔl(e) lavorare.
20) Pɔsso lavorare.
21) Dĕvo lavorare. (or) Dĕbbo lavorare.
22) Desidererebbe lavorare (Lɛi)?
23) Potrɛi lavorare.
24) Non pɔsso lavorare.

TEST D   ANSWERS

I		II		III	
1) true		1) false		1) false	
2) false		2) false		2) true	
3) false		3) true		3) true	
4) false		4) true		4) false	
5) false		5) true		5) false	
6) false		6) false		6) false	
7) true		7) true		7) true	
8) false		8) false		8) true	
9) true		9) true		9) false	
10) false		10) true		10) false	

TEST E   ANSWERS

1) Vorrɛi andare a cena fuɔri stasera ma non sɔ dove potrɛi mangiare bɛne.
2) Scusino. Domandino lì a dɛstra, per favore.
3) Andrɛa vorrĕbbe andare nel Brasile ma non gli piace Brasilia. Vuɔl(e) andare a Rio.
4) Quando arriva in Grɛcia Lɛi, sabato mattina?
5) Lɛi puɔ parlare inglese quando è a Londra e in Australia, ma in Italia dovrĕbbe parlare italiano.
6) Studi molto a casa. In classe dĕve ascoltare, capire e parlare molto.
7) Non vɔglio spiegare niɛnte in inglese. Ascolti bɛne. Lɛi Puɔ capire.
8) Scusi. Dĕvo } aspettare qui. Pɔsso fumare?
  Dĕbbo
9) Dovrɛi ɛsserci domani. Potrĕbbe chiamare domani mattina?
10) Il signor White non c'è. Desidererĕbbe parlare con la segretaria del signor White?
11) Aspɛttino qui, per favore. Vedo se c'è.
12) Puɔ venire ora? C'è un insegnante d'italiano qui e parla molto bɛne l'inglese.

13) Pronto. Chi parla, per favore? (or) Pronto. Con chi parlo, per favore? (or) Pronto. Chi è al telɛfono, per favore?

14) Il dottor Russo? Chi lo desidera, per favore?

15) Mi dispiace. Avrà sbagliato numero.

16) Parla la signora Marchegiano? C'ɛ Cristina?

17) Parla la guardia all'A.A. Che desidera?

18) Desidero parlare con la guardia, per favore. Non c'ɛ?

19) Dĕvo venire questo pomeriggio? Vorrɛi stare a casa. Non stɔ molto bɛne.

20) Dĕvo venire questo pomeriggio? Non ci sarà Marta?

UNIT 25

1. Here is the word for "pope." Listen carefully.

   (papa) (papa)

*2. Does the stress on this word fall on the first /PA/ or the second /PA/ of the word? Listen again.

3. So far you have heard the word pronounced with both vowels having the same (or almost the same) length. Listen again and repeat.

   (papa)X (papa)X

4. However, you learned in Unit 23 that Italian stressed vowels (especially within a word) tend to be *longer* than unstressed vowels. Thus, a more common pronunciation you may hear will have the first /A/ longer than the second. Listen and repeat.

   (papa)X (papa)X

5. Notice that as we go from the *first vowel* to the *following consonant* there is no break or pause. We may even say that there is SMOOTH TRANSITION as we go from the vowel to the consonant.

   (papa)X (papa)X

6. In Italian SMOOTH TRANSITION between a vowel and a following consonant is an important feature to remember because without it one can change the sound of what the Italian listener hears and even change the meaning of what he hears.

7. The opposite of SMOOTH TRANSITION involves a slight break or pause before the consonant. In this case the consonant is pronounced somewhat more strongly than it otherwise would. Listen to the following and repeat. You will hear four utterances of a word that has nothing to do with "pope". Notice that the first two times the word is pronounced with a short stressed vowel and the last two times with a long stressed vowel.

   pappa (2) (pronounced with a short stressed vowel)
   pappa (2) (pronounced with a long stressed vowel)

8. What you have just been pronouncing is the word for "pap," a special kind of baby food.

*9. In frame no. 7 was the length of the stressed vowel an important feature of this word?

*10. In frame no. 7 was the absence of SMOOTH TRANSITION an important feature of this word?

11. For the sake of convenience we will call a consonant that follows a vowel in SMOOTH TRANSITION a SLACK consonant; a strongly pronounced consonant following a slight break or pause we will call a TENSE consonant.

*12. Is the second /P/ in the Italian word for "pope" SLACK or TENSE?

*13. Is the second /P/ in the Italian word for "pap" SLACK or TENSE?

* * * * *

*14. Although we have learned that length of a stressed vowel preceding a consonant is *not* the distinguishing feature of a word (see frames no. 3 and no. 7), we did learn something about the stressed vowel of the Italian word for "pope" in frame no. 4. Was it that the stressed vowel is usually longer or shorter than the unstressed vowel?

15. The same is *not* true in the Italian word for "pap," that is, the stressed vowel is not usually pronounced longer than the unstressed vowel. Listen carefully and repeat.

    pappa (2)   (pronounced with a short stressed vowel)

16. These comments about the length of stressed vowels in Italian lead us to the following generalization:
    In Italian, stressed vowels preceding SLACK consonants are usually *longer* than stressed vowels preceding TENSE consonants.

17. Now listen and repeat the words "pope" and "pap," keeping in mind the principle of vowel length.

    papa   *pappa*
    "pope"   "pap"

* * * * *

*18. Write the Italian word for "pope."

19. So far we have not told you how the Italian word for "pap" is spelled. Here it is.

    pappa

20. Italian writing usually represents a TENSE consonant following a vowel within a word by *two like consonant letters.*

21. One important exception to this rule is the combination /KW/ which, if TENSE within a word is represented as -*qqu*- only in the word *soqquadro* "confusion, disorder" and related words. Otherwise, it is represented as -*cqu*- as in *acqua*.

* * * * *

22. So far you have learned that a strongly pronounced consonant following a slight break or pause is called a TENSE consonant. However, this is not the only kind of consonant that an Italian recognizes as being TENSE.

23. If instead of the break or pause coming *before* the consonant, it comes *during the production* of the consonant, an Italian hears no difference in meaning and again recognizes a TENSE consonant.

24. In the case of *pappa*, then, this quick break or pause may come after the two lips have come together for the TENSE /P/. Listen to the two pronunciations of *pappa* both with a TENSE /P/. In the first case the break or pause comes *before* the /P/ and in the second case it comes *during the production* of the /P/.

    (pappa) (pappa)

25. Perhaps the second kind of TENSE consonant is more common than the first. In any case, regardless of which of these ways you choose to pronounce a TENSE consonant, you will never change the meaning of the word. On the other hand, the difference between TENSE and SLACK consonants should always be kept clearly in mind.

* * * * *

26. Here are some words illustrating the contrast between SLACK consonants and TENSE consonants. This list reviews all of the important Italian consonants that present this kind of distinction.

SLACK		TENSE	
/P/ (cɔpia)x	"copy"	(cɔppia)X	"couple"
/B/ (libra)X	"Libra"	(libbra)X	"pound"
/T/ (fato)X	"fate"	(fatto)X	"fact"
/D/ (cade)X	"(s)he falls"	(cadde)X	"(s)he fell"
/K/ (baco)X	"worm"	(Bacco)X	"Bacchus"
/G/ (fuga)X	"flight [= escape]"	(fugga)X	"flee"
/F/ (bufalo)X	"buffalo"	(Buffalo)X	"Buffalo" [city]

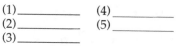

/V/ (piɔve)X	"it rains"	(piɔvve)X	"it rained"
/S/ (casa)X	"house"	(cassa)X	"case, box"
/Č/ (Lucio)X	"Lucius"	(luccio)X	"pike"
/Ǧ/ (agio)X	"ease"	(aggio)X	"premium"
/M/ (camino)X	"chimney"	(cammino)X	"way"
/N/ (pena)X	"penalty"	(penna)X	"pen"
/L/ (pala)X	"shovel"	(palla)X	"ball"
/R/ (caro)X	"dear, expensive"	(carro)X	"wagon, cart"

*27. Now let's try a test. You will hear five of the Italian words of frame no. 26. Write "S" or "T" according to whether you hear a SLACK or a TENSE consonant.

(1)_____   (4)_____
(2)_____   (5)_____
(3)_____

28. In the preceding frame you should have written........
(1) *agio* (2) *bacco* (3) *bufalo* (4) *cade* (5) *camino*

*29. If you missed any of the five, return to frame no. 27 and listen again. Here are five more. Continue as in frame no. 27.

(1)_____   (4)_____
(2)_____   (5)_____
(3)_____

30. In the preceding frame you should have written........
(1) *caro* (2) *cassa* (3) *cɔpia* (4) *fatto* (5) *fugga*

*31. If you missed any of these five, return to frame no. 29 and listen again. Here are five more. Continue as before.

(1)_____   (4)_____
(2)_____   (5)_____
(3)_____

32. In the preceding frame you should have written........ If you missed any of the five, return to frame no. 31 and listen again.
(1) *libra* (2) *Lucio* (3) *palla* (4) *penna* (5) *piɔvve*

* * * * *

33. In Italian the SLACK-TENSE distinction is important only *immediately after a vowel* and especially next to a stressed syllable.

34. In general, this distinction is important only *between vowels*.

35. In other positions within a word most consonants occur only SLACK. However, in the case of the first seven consonants listed in frame no. 26 the SLACK-TENSE distinctions is also important before /L/ or /R/.

36. Here are some examples of these seven consonants both SLACK and TENSE before /L/ or /R/.

/P/ (replica)X	"reply; replica"	(applica)X	"(s)he applies [something]"
/B/ (libro)X	"book"	(febbraio)X	"February"
/T/ (atrïo)X	"entrance hall"	(quattro)X	"four"
/D/ (quadro)X	"painting"	(raddrizza)X	"(s)he straightens"
/K/ (acredine)X	"bitterness"	(accredita)X	"(s)he (ac)credits"
/G/ (agrario)X	"agrarian"	(aggravio)X	"load, burden"
/F/ (africano)X	"Africano"	(affresco)X	"fresco"

* * * * *

37. So far we have been examining the SLACK-TENSE contrast within isolated words. However, it is important to know that this contrast may also exist within breath groups as one goes from one word to the next.

38. We have already been trying to prepare you for this by telling you that after
certain words a following consonant was to be pronounced very strongly. (See RECAPITULATION of Units 1–10.)

39. Although it would be impractical here to try to teach all those words after which a following consonant is to be stongly pronounced, we *can* give a few guidelines that may help.

40. Remember, however, that these are simply guidelines to follow and that not *all* Italians conform to these guidelines 100 percent.

41. Rule no. 1: Of all the consonants listed in frame no. 26 all may occur TENSE in word-initial position except /S/ followed by a consonant. Thus: (a Sara) pronounced as if written: (assara)X but (a Stella)X

42. Rule no. 2: Except for /S/ followed by a consonant, a word-initial consonant is TENSE after a *stressed vowel.*
    Thus: (Sarà lì.) pronounced as if written: (Sarallì.)X
      (Ci sarò domani.) pronounced as if written:
              (Cisaroddomani.)X

43. Rule no. 3: Except for /S/ followed by a consonant, a word-initial consonant is TENSE after *most one-vowel words that end in a vowel.*

Thus:	pronounced as if written
(È Luca.)	(Elluca.)X
(C'è Bianca)	(Cɛbbianca.)X
(Chi c'è?)	(Chiccè?)X
(È qui Pia?)	(Ecquippia?)X
(È lì Tina?)	(Ɛllittina?)X
(Sì, c'è.)	(Siccè.)X
(No, non c'è.)	(Nɔnnoncè.)X
(Che cos'è?)	(Checcɔsè?)X
(Non fa niente.)	(Nɔnfanniɛnte.)X
(Sta bene.)	(Stabbɛne.)X
(Stɔ male.)	(Stɔmmale.)X
(E lei?)	(Ellɛi?)X
(Ma sì.)	(Massì.)X
(Non sɔ dov'è.)	(Nonsɔddovè.)X
(Vado a Roma.)	(Vadoarroma.)X
(Va lì.)	(Vallì.)X
(Che può fare?)	(Cheppuɔffare?)X

44. One-vowel words that constitute exceptions to rule no. 3 are:
    a) the word *di*
      Thus: (di Roma)X   - SLACK /R/
    b) noun markers
      Thus: (la vigna)X   - SLACK /V/
    c) pre-verbal object replacers such as *ci, mi,* etc.
      Thus: (ci vado)X - SLACK /V/
        (mi piace)X - SLACK /P/

45. Rule no. 4: Except for /S/ followed by a consonant, a word-initial consonant is TENSE after *qualche* and a few other words of more than one vowel.
    Thus: (qualche giorno) "a few days [= one or more days]"
      pronounced as if written: (qualcheggiorno)X

*59. Don't let the following words fool you. Apply the same rule as before and write the plural form after the word *due.*

(1) *una mano*	"a hand"	due_____
(2) *un programma*	"a program"	due_____
(3) *una guardia*		due_____
(4) *una persona*		due_____
(5) *un francese*	"a Frenchman"	due_____
(6) *una francese*	"a Frenchwoman"	due_____
(7) *un inglese*	"an Englishman"	due_____
(8) *un'inglese*	"an Englishwoman"	due_____

60. You should have written words ending in -*e* for Nos. 3 and 4. For the others you should have written words ending in -*i.*

61. Looking now at the words of frame no. 59, repeat them after the voice on the tape.

62. Genderables with singular endings other than unstressed -*o*, -*a*, or -*e* normally show no change in the plural.

63. Thus, repeat the following:

(un sofà)X		(due sofà)X
(un caffè)X		(due caffè)X
(una città)X		(due città)X
(un'università)X	"a university"	(due università)X
(una virtù)X	"a virtue"	(due virtù)X
(un bar)X	"a bar"	(due bar)X
(un film)X		(due film)X
(uno sport)X	"a sport"	(due sport)X
(una crisi)X	"a crisis"	(due crisi)X
(una gru)X	"a crane"	(due gru)X

64. Frames no. 55 and no. 62 give you the general plural formation of Italian genderables. Any genderable whose plural is not in accordance with these rules is exceptional and must be learned as an exception.

65. Here are a few such exceptions you should learn.

(un cinema)X	"a movie-theater"	(due cinema)X
(un portacenere)X	"an ashtray"	(due portacenere)X
(un vaglia)X	"a money order"	(due vaglia)X
(una radio)X	"a radio"	(due radio)X

(un'ala)X	"a wing"	(due ali)X
(un'arma)X	"a weapon"	(due armi)X
(un bue)X	"an ox"	(due buɔi)X
(un dio)X	"a god"	(due dɛi)X
(un uɔmo)X	"a man"	(due uɔmini)X
(un uɔvo)X	"an egg"	(due uɔva)X

* * * * *

66. When genderables that have both a "masculine plural" and a "feminine plural" form are used to refer to people or animals, the "feminine plural" form is only used to refer to two or more females.
    Thus: *americane* "Americans" (all female)

67. On the other hand, the so-called "masculine plural" form referring to people or animals refers either to two or more males or to two or more people or animals at least one of which is male. Thus: *americani* "Americans" (*not* all female)

68. In this connection, *i signori White* is the normal way of referring to "Mr. and Mrs. White."

69. Notice from the preceding example that last names do not change for the plural in Italian.

* * * * *

70. Here are some words and phrases that could be useful in receiving messages on the phone. Memorize them.

Generable	(Masculine / Feminine)	
"busy"	(-ǀoccupato)X	(-ǀoccupato)X

Verbs		
"to call back, to call again"	(-ǀrichiamare)X	(-ǀrichiamare)X
"to call you back, to call you again"	(-ǀrichiamarLa)X	(-ǀrichiamarLa)X
"to return [= to go back, to come back"	(-ǀritornare)X (-ǀtornare)X	(-ǀritornare)X (-ǀtornare)X
"to telephone"	(-ǀtelefonare)X	(-ǀtelefonare)X
"to call back, to call again"	(-ǀritelefonare)X	(-ǀritelefonare)X

71. Here are some verb forms and verb phrases that could be useful in receiving messages on the phone. Memorize them.

"tell him that..."	(gli dica che...)X	(gli dica che...)X
"tell her that..."	(le dica che...)X	(le dica che...)X
"tell him to phone me"	(gli dica di telefonarmi)X	(gli dica di telefonarmi)X
"tell her to phone me"	(le dica di telefonarmi)X	(le dica di telefonarmi)X
"it doesn't matter, that's all right"	(non impɔrta)X	(non impɔrta)X
"I'll call back"	(richiamerɔ)X	(richiamerɔ)X
"would you like to leave a message?" (literally: "Do I have to relay something?")	(dĕvo riferire qualcɔsa?)X	(dĕvo riferire qualcɔsa?)X
"I'll relay the message"	(riferirɔ)	(riferirɔ)
"if you wish"	(se vuɔle)X	(se vuɔle)X
"O.K., all right, it's all right"	(va bɛne)X	(va bɛne)X

72. Here are some other utterances that could be useful in receiving messages on the phone. Memorize them.

"X days from now"	(fra X giorni)X	(fra X giorni)X
"shortly [= a little while from now]"	(fra pɔco)X	(fra pɔco)X
"out of town"	(fuɔri città)X	(fuɔri città)X
"in the afternoon"	(nel pomeriggio)X	(nel pomeriggio)X
"for a few days"	(per qualche giorno)X	(per qualche giorno) X
"later"	(più tardi)X	(più tardi)X
"only"	(soltanto)X	(soltanto)X

Repeat this frame and the two previous ones several times until you feel you have mastered both the pronunciation and the meaning of the utterances given.

73. You will now hear a series of seven short dialogs that could be used to
continue the telephone conversations of Unit 24. Repeat each line, imitating
as closely as possible. You should review this section several times until you
feel you have memorized each dialog. NOTE: "A" stands for "American"
and "I" stands for "Italian."

   I. A: Mi dispiace. Il signor White è occupato ora. Può ritelefonare più tardi?
       I: Va bɛne, g——.
      A: Prɛgo. Buɔn giɔrno.

  II. A: Mi dispiace. La signora è occupata ora. Può richiamare più tardi?
       I: ɔh, non pɔsso. Le dica che ha telefonato il dottor Paglia.
      A: Va bɛne, dottor Paglia. Riferirɔ.

III. A: Mi dispiace. La signorina non è in ufficio e non sɔ quando ritorna.
       I: Va bɛne, g——. Richiamerɔ domani.
      A: Prɛgo. Buɔna sera.
       I: Buɔna sera.

 IV. A: Mi dispiace. Il signor White ora non è in ufficio. Dovrěbbe tornare fra
         pɔco.
       I: Per piacere, gli dica di telefonarmi quando ritorna.
      A: Va bɛne. Riferirɔ.

  V. A: Mi dispiace. Il signor White non è in ufficio. Ritorna nel pomeriggio.
         Se vuɔle, il signor White può richiamarLa quando ritorna.
       I: ɔh, bɛne.

 VI. A: Mi dispiace. La signora è fuɔri città. Ritorna fra tre giorni. Děvo
         riferire qualcɔsa?
       I: Nɔ, g——.
      A: Prɛgo.

VII. A: Mi dispiace. Il signor White è fuɔri città per qualche giorno. Torna in
         ufficio lunedì. Děvo riferire qualcɔsa?
       I: Non impɔrta, g——. Gli dica soltanto che ha telefonato il signor Vegli.
      A: Va bɛne, signor Vegli. Riferirɔ.

3) When Stella comes in, tell her that she has to work this afternoon.

_____

4) I don't want three coffees; I'd like two coffees and one tea, please.

_____

5) I don't see two men over there. I only see a man and a woman.

_____

6) Lucio has to see four films every month, not every two months.

_____

7) It's expensive, but he likes it and Vanda gives it to him.*
   *This expression was introduced in Unit 15.

_____

8) He shows up with a radio, two paintings, three books, four balls and a shovel.

_____

9) Mara wants three eggs and two cups of coffee every morning.

_____

10) Is there a university in Perugia? Yes, there is one and I like it a lot.

_____

11) Would you like two kilograms of cheese? - No, I want two pounds of cheese.

_____

12) You don't have to come back tomorrow. Just call tomorrow morning.
    (addressing one person)

_____

13) She never falls in the office. She always falls when she's home.

_____

14) (on the phone) I'm sorry. Miss White is busy now. Do you mind calling back
    later?

_____

15) (on the phone) All right, Dr. Russo. I'll tell them.

_____

16) (on the phone) Tell him to phone me tomorrow morning when he gets in.

_____

17) (on the phone) I can call back if you'd like, but I'd rather wait.

_____

18) (on the phone) That doesn't matter. I'll call back in two days.

_____

19) (on the phone) I'd like to call you again in three days. Is that alright?

_____

20) (on the phone) Tell her that John Bradley called and that I'll be in Rome only for a few days.

(not recorded)

Write two short narratives, one using only the items listed in G_1 and another using only the items listed in G_2.

G_1

America	Washington	Antonio	scapolo
di	è	ora	Milano
Spada	a	un	è
insegnante	e	una	in
insegna	in	giovane	italiano
scuola	è	e	

G_2

martedì	posso	ufficio	non
e	è	giovedì	è
Rodolfo	in	è	telefonare
città	e	dovrei	dovrèbbe
due	dĕvo	ma	giorni
aspettare	non	ritornare	fuori

TEST A   ANSWERS

1) papa
2) cade
3) bacco
4) casa
5) copia
6) cammino
7) fatto
8) raddrizza
9) pappa
10) accredita
11) bufalo
12) carro
13) aggio
14) cadde
15) coppia
16) baco
17) Lucio
18) libra
19) penna
20) pena
21) fato
22) febbraio
23) fugga

24) acredine
25) camino
26) agrario
27) libbra
28) quadro
29) quattro
30) fuga
31) aggravio
32) pala
33) palla
34) affresco
35) piovve
36) cassa
37) atrïo
38) piove
39) libro
40) applica
41) caro
42) luccio
43) agio
44) replica
45) Buffalo
46) africano

TEST B ANSWERS

I. (three instances)
   A: Mi dispiace. Il signor White è occupato ora.
   Può ritelefonare più tardi?
     I: Va bene, g——.
   A: Prego. Buon giorno.

II. (five instances)
   A: Mi dispiace. La signora è occupata ora. Può richiamare piu tardi?
     I: Oh, non posso. Le dica che ha telefonato il dottor Paglia.
   A: Va bene, dottor Paglia. Riferirò.

III. (four instances)
   A. Mi dispiace. La signorina non è in ufficio e non so quando ritorna.
     I: Va bene, g——. Richiamerò domani.
   A: Prego. Buona sera.
     I: Buona sera.

IV. (two instances)
   A: Mi dispiace. Il signor White ora non è in ufficio. Dovrèbbe tornare fra
       poco.
     I: Per piacere, gli dica di telefonarmi quando ritorna.
   A: Va bene. Rifertrò.

V. (three instances)
   A: Mi dispiace. Il signor White non è in ufficio. Ritorna nel pomeriggio.
       Se vuole, il signor White può richiamarLa quando ritorna.
     I: Oh, bene.

VI. (four instances)
   A: Mi dispiace. La signora è fuori città. Ritorna fra tre giorni. Dèvo riferire
       qualcosa?
     I: No, g——.
   A: Prego.

VII. (four instances)

A: Mi dispiace. Il signor White è fuori città per qualche giorno. Torna in ufficio lunedì. Dĕvo riferire qualcosa?

I: Non importa, g——. Gli dica soltanto che ha telefonato il signor Vegli.

A: Va bene, signor Vegli. Riferirò.

TEST C ANSWERS

1) Chi c'è?
2) Che cos'è?
3) È lì.
4) Non c'è niente.
5) È a casa.
6) Dov'è Cecè?
7) È qui Cloe?
8) È una cassa.
9) E Lei, non ci va?
10) Ma sì, se vuole.

TEST D ANSWERS

1) una signora	11) una penna	21) un poeta
2) due uova	12) due giorni	22) una persona
3) uno scapolo	13) una signorina	23) due turisti
4) due libri	14) due studentesse	24) un'ala
5) due pomeriggi	15) due guardie	25) un telefono
6) una mano	16) un uomo	26) un insegnante -
7) un quadro	17) un'arma	un'insegnante
8) due italiane	18) uno studente	27) una città -
9) un programma	19) due americane	due città
10) due studenti	20) un'italiana	28) un portacenere -
		due portacenere
		29) un inglese -
		un'inglese
		30) un vaglia -
		due vaglia

TEST E ANSWERS

1) una città	due città	19) due sofà	un sofà
2) un dio	due dei	20) un vaglia	due vaglia
3) due crisi	una crisi	21) due chiese	una chiesa
4) due coppie	una coppia	22) due africane	un'africana
5) un caffè	due caffè	23) un dentista	due dentisti
6) due programmi	un programma	24) una copia	due copie
7) due università	un'università	25) due capitalisti	un capitalista
8) due libbre	una libbra	26) due poeti	un poeta
9) un film	due film	27) un'arma	due armi
10) una francese	due francesi	28) un bufalo	due bufali
11) due cinema	un cinema	29) due scapoli	uno scapolo
12) due libri	un libro	30) un uomo	due uomini
13) uno sport	due sport	31) un camino	due camini
14) due studenti	uno studente	32) una turista	due turiste
15) due virtù	una virtù	33) due ali	un'ala
16) una palla	due palle	34) due pale	una pala
17) una radio	due radio	35) una mano	due mani
18) due italiane	un'italiana	36) un papa	due papi

TEST F ANSWERS

1) Non vado mai fuori quando piove.
2) Sarò a Roma fra qualche giorno. Ci sarà Lei?
3) Quando Stella arriva le dica che deve lavorare questo pomeriggio.
4) Non voglio tre caffè; vorrei due caffè e un tè, per favore.
5) Non vedo due uomini lì. Vedo soltanto un uomo e una donna.
6) Lucio deve vedere quattro film ogni mese, non ogni due mesi.
7) È caro, ma gli piace e Vanda glielo dà.
8) Arriva con una radio, due quadri, tre libri, quattro palle e una pala.
9) Mara vuole tre uova e due caffè ogni mattina.
10) C'è un'università a Perugia? - Sì, ce n'è una e mi piace molto.

11) Vuɔle } due chili di formaggio? - Nɔ, vɔglio due libbre
    Vorrĕbbe }   di formaggio.

12) Non dĕve ritornare domani. Chiami domani mattina.
13) Non cade mai in ufficio. Cade sɛmpre quando è a casa.
14) Mi dispiace. La signorina White è occupata ora. Puɔ richiamare più tardi?
15) Va bɛne, dottor Russo. Riferirɔ.
16) Gli dica di telefonarmi domani mattina quando arriva.
17) Pɔsso richiamare se vuɔle, ma vorrɛi aspettare.
18) Non impɔrta. Richiamerɔ fra due giorni.
19) Vorrei richiamarLa fra tre giorni. Va bɛne?
20) Le dica che ha telefonato John Bradley e che sarɔ a Roma soltanto per
    qualche giorno.

TEST G   ANSWERS

G₁
    Antɔnio Spada è un insegnante di Milano. È giovane e scạpolo. Ora è in
    Amɛrica e insegna italiano in una scuɔla a Washington.

G₂
    È martedì e Rodɔlfo non è in ufficio. È fuɔri città e dovrĕbbe ritornare
    giovedì. Dovrɛi telefonare ma non pɔsso. Dĕvo aspettare due giorni.

RECAPITULATION (Units 21–25)

The Tongue Flap in Different Postions

between vowels.	ora	di Roma	(Unit 21)
syllable-initial:	Roma		(Unit 21)
before a consonant:	giorno		(Unit 22)
after a consonant	prego		(Unit 24)

The Trill (Unit 21)

Two or more successive tongue-flaps constitute a TRILL, as in:
arriva
È Rɔsa (pronounced as if written: *errɔsa*)

Stress and Vowel Length (Unit 23)

STRESS in Italian refers to greater *loudness* and usually (though not necessarily) greater *length* of vowels.

Stressed vowels are usually pronounced longer when they occur *within* words as opposed to at the *end* of words. For example, the first vowel in *Sara* is usually pronounced longer than the last vowel in *sarà*, and either of these is usually pronounced longer than the unstressed vowel in either word.

In addition, stressed vowels preceding SLACK consonants are usually *longer* than stressed vowels preceding TENSE consonants. Thus, the first vowel in *papa* is usually pronounced longer than the stressed vowel in *pappa*. (Unit 25)

Word Stress and the Accent Mark (Unit 23)

For words that end in a stressed vowel, the stress is shown on the written word by an accent mark, usually written as in the followings words: *sofà* or *sofa'*.

General Stress Rule for Other Cases: When *no* accent mark appears on the end of a written word, the stressed vowel is represented by:

a) the *last vowel letter* in all words ending in a consonant.

E.g., Cabul

b) the *third* (when there is one) *vowel letter from the end* in words ending in -ia, -ie, -ii, -io, -ua, -ue, -ui, -uo.

E.g., Italia, Lucio

c) the *next-to-the last vowel letter* in all other cases.

E.g., italiano

Exceptions to the above are marked in these units by either:
a) a dot beneath the vowel letter representing a stressed vowel (e.g., *Agata*, *Natalia*) or
b) the special type *ɛ* and *ɔ* (e.g., *ɛssere*, *ɔrdine*).

Accent Mark not Indicating Stress (Unit 23)

The ACCENT MARK is also used:
a) to indicate that two vowel letters at the end of a word do *not* represent a stressed vowel followed by a vowel or a semivowel (e.g., *più*, *già*) and
b) to show a difference between certain words written with *only one vowel letter* and other words spelled the same but having different meanings (e.g., *è* as in *è qui*, but *e* as in e *Lei*).

Smooth Transition (Unit 25)

SMOOTH TRANSITION is what occurs in the pronunciation of an Italian vowel followed by a consonant with *no* break or pause between the two sounds, as in the word papa or the phrase di Pia.

Slack Consonant (Unit 25)

A consonant with *no* break or pause either *before it* or *during its production* is a SLACK CONSONANT, as, for example, the second consonant in either papa or di Pia.

Tense Consonant (Unit 25)

A consonant with a slight break or pause either right *before it* or *during its production* is a TENSE CONSONANT, as, for example, the second consonant in either pappa or a Pia (read as if written: *appia*). Italian writing usually represents a TENSE CONSONANT following a vowel within a word by *two like consonant letters*.

Importance of Slack-Tense Distinction (Unit 25)

The Italian SLACK-TENSE distinction is important only *immediately after a vowel* and especially next to a stressed syllable. Although, generally speaking, this distinction is important only *between vowels*, it is also important before /L/ or /R/. Compare: *replica* and *applica*, *atrio*, and *quattro*.

Word-Initial Tense Consonants in Breath Groups (Unit 25)

a) Most Italian consonants may occur TENSE in word-initial position except /S/ followed by a consonant.

Thus: *a Pia* (pronounced as if written: *appia*)

    a Sara (pronounced as if written: *assara*)

but: *a Stella*

b) Except for /S/ followed by a consonant, a word-initial consonant is TENSE after a *stressed vowel*.

Thus: *Ci sarò domani.* (pronounced as if written: *cisarɔddomani*)

c) Except for /S/ followed by a consonant, a word-initial consonant is TENSE after *most one-vowel words that end in a vowel.*

Thus: *È lì.* (pronounced as if written: *ɛllì*)

    Sta bɛne. (pronounced as if written: *stabbɛne*)

Exceptions to this rule are:

    (1) the word *di*

        Thus: *di Roma*   (SLACK /R/)

    (2) noun markers

        Thus: *la vigna*   (SLACK /V/)

    (3) pre-verbal object replacers such as *ci, mi,* etc.

        Thus: *ci vado*   (SLACK /V/)

           mi piace   (SLACK /P/)

d) Except for /S/ followed by a consonant, a word-initial consonant is TENSE after *qualche* and a few other words of more than one vowel.

Thus: *qualche giorno* (pronounced as if written: *qualcheggiorno*)

e) The word for "god," *dio* usually begins with a TENSE consonant after any vowel.

Thus: *Ama Dio.* (pronounced as if written: *amaddio*)

Count Words and Mass Words (Unit 22)

Words that can refer to countable items are COUNT WORDS; words that refer to a quantity or a mass of something are MASS WORDS. *Uɔvo* is a COUNT WORD; *acqua* is a MASS WORD.

Nouns (Unit 22)

NOUNS are words used to name things like: *arrɔsto, capitano, insalata.*

Noun Markers (Unit 22)

NOUN MARKERS are words or phrases that occur before (i.e., that *mark*) nouns. For example, the following underlined items are NOUN MARKERS.

un arrɔsto
uno sbaglio
una persona
*un'*insalata
un pɔ' di birra
il signore
la signora

Unit (Noun) Markers (Unit 22)

Noun markers that mark singular units are called UNIT NOUN MARKERS or, simply, UNIT MARKERS. For example, the first four underlined items under NOUN MARKERS above are UNIT MARKERS. NOTE: the masculine form *uno* occurs before *s* + consonant letter, *gn*, and a few other places; the feminine form *un'* occurs before vowels

Gender: "Masculine" and "Feminine" (Unit 22)

The term GENDER is used to refer to the following MASCULINE-FEMININE distinction.

The terms MASCULINE and FEMININE are used to classify a large number of words into two categories:
  a) those words are MASCULINE which may occur after un (or uno). They are called MASCULINE since most words that are used to refer clearly to male beings may be preceded by *un* (or *uno*).
  b) those words are FEMININE which may occur after *una* (or *un'*). They are called FEMININE since *most* words that are used to refer clearly to female beings may be preceded by *una* (or *un'*).

Thus:
MASCULINE	FEMININE
americano	*signora*
sofa	*specie*
capo	*persona*

Genderables (Unit 22)

Words (including nouns) that have something to do with gender are called GENDERABLES (literally, "given to gender").

Exclusively Masculine	Exclusively Feminine	Masculine/ Feminine
┼arrɔsto	┼bistecca	┼colombo
┼capo	┼persona	┼poɛta
		┼cane
		┼insegnante
		┼artista

Gender of Geographical Place Names (Unit 23)

As a Rule Feminine	As a Rule Masculine
1) names of cities and towns	1) names of oceans, seas, rivers and lakes
2) names of islands	2) names of most states in the U.S.A.
3) the following eight states in the U.S.A.	

Alasca
Arizona
California
Florida
Georgia
Lüisiana
Pensilvania
Virginia

Most other geographical place names are feminine if they end in *-a* and masculine if they end in something else. Five masculine exceptions to this rule are: *Canadà, Ghana, Guatemala, Nicaragua, Venezuela.*

Number: "Singular and Plural" (Unit 25)

The term NUMBER is used to refer to the following SINGULAR-PLURAL distinction.

As applied to genderables, the terms SINGULAR and PLURAL are used to classify forms into two categories:

    a) those forms are SINGULAR which may occur after a SINGULAR MARKER like *ɬuno*.

    b) those forms are PLURAL which may occur after a PLURAL MARKER like *due*.

From Singular to Plural (Genderable Rules) (Unit 25)

For similar genderables ending in unstressed -o, unstressed -a or unstressed -e
A FEMININE SINGULAR form ending in unstressed *-a* changes to unstressed *-e* in the PLURALS all others change to unstressed *-i* in the PLURAL.

singular	plural
un libro	due libri
una mano	due mani
un poeta	due poeti
un(a) francese	due francesi
una studentessa	due studentesse

For Other Genderables

Other genderables normally show no change in the PLURAL.

Singular	Plural
un sofà	due sofà
un bar	due bar
una crisi	due crisi

Masculine Plural for a Mixed Group (Unit 25)

The "MASCULINE PLURAL" form of a genderable referring to people or animals refers either to two or more males or to two or more people or animals at least one of which is male.

Thus: *americani* (*not* all female)
but: *americane* (all female)

Days of the Week (Unit 23)

lunedì	"Monday"
martedì	"Tuesday"
mercoledì	"Wednesday"
giovedì	"Thursday"
venerdì	"Friday"
sabato	"Saturday"
domenica	"Sunday"

"On Sundays," "On Mondays," etc. (Unit 23)

In order to express the idea of "on Sundays," "on Mondays," etc., Italian uses *la* before *domenica* and *il* before the other names of the days of the week.

L'Italiano versus Italiano (Unit 24)

In most cases the Italian language is referred to as *l'italiano*. Normally, however, no *l'* is present after *in* or *d'* (standing for *di*) and in some cases it is often omitted after a few verbs like *⁺parlare* and *⁺studiare*.

Thus: *Mi piace l'italiano.*
In italiano.
Un insegnante d'italiano.
Parla italiano.   (also: *Parla l'italiano.*)
The same holds true for *l'inglese* versus *inglese*.

Infinitive Constructions (Units 23 and 24)

Desidero studiare.	"I wish to study."
Voglio studiare.	"I want to study."
Posso studiare.	"I can study."
Dĕvo studiare.	"I have to study."
Mi piace studiare.	"I like to study."
Penso di studiare.	"I plan on studying."

Meaning of Present Tense (Unit 21)

The most important meaning of the PRESENT TENSE is "something in progress or in existence at the time of utterance." This "something" may be:

a) *a single, durative event*
   Chiama ora.   "(S)he is calling now."

b) *the events leading to a punctual act*
   Arriva ora.   "(S)he is arriving now."

c) *a series consisting of the repeition of an event*
   Chiama ogni sera.   "(S)he calls every evening."

d) *a plan or schedule for something to happen in the future*

Chiama domani.
- "(S)he is going to call tomorrow."
- "(S)he is (planning on) calling tomorrow."
- "(S)he is due to call tomorrow."

"RE" Tense (Unit 24)

The "RE" TENSE is the tense that has /RE/ or /RE/ in all its verb endings and *one* of whose meanings is to express a present idea with *reserve* or *deference*.

E.g., *Desidererei lavorare.*
      Vorrĕbbe venire?
      Potrĕbbe cominciare?
      Dovrei domandare.

Formal Request Forms of Regular -are Verbs (Unit 24)

FORMAL REQUEST FORMS of regular *-are* verbs always end in *-i* (for the singular) and *-ino* (for the highly formal plural).
Thus:

Lei	Loro
arrivi	*arrivino*
aspetti	*aspettino*
scusi	*scusino*

Place of Origin: di + (Name of City or Town) (Unit 21)

È di Roma. "(S)he is from Rome." ("(S)he was born and
raised in Rome.")

Movement To or Location In or At (Units 21 and 23)

a) a(d)+ (name of city or town)

a Riva	"to Riva"	-	"in Riva"
a Roma	"to Rome"	-	"in Rome"
ad Ancona	"to Ancona"	-	"in Ancona"

b) *a(d)* is also used for many islands, especially the smaller ones.

a Corfù
ad Êlba
a Cuba
ad Haiti

c) Before *Corsica, Sardegna, Sicilia* and most other geographical place names,
these same concepts are normally expressed by *in*.

in Corsica
in Italia
in Virginia

NOTE: Although with names of countries and states that are grammatically
masculine, it is, as a rule, preferable to use *nel* (before a consonant) or
nell' (elsewhere) instead of *in*, the use of *in* even in these cases is becoming more and more frequent and acceptable. Thus, you may hear either
in Vietnam or *nel Vietnam, in Maryland* or *nel Maryland*.

d) When referring to other places not so much as buildings or specific
locales, but rather with emphasis on the *activities normally associated with
these places,* there is no way to predict whether to use *a* or *in*.

Thus: *a scuola*	*in città*
a casa	*in campagna*
a cena	*in montagna*
	in chiesa
	in classe
	in ufficio
	in ospedale
	in banca

The Place Replacer: ci (Unit 23)

To refer to a place previously mentioned, *especially with movement verbs*, ci is used either before a finite verb or attached to an infinitive minus its final -*e*.

Quando va a New York? { Cì vado lunedì.
{ Penso di andarci lunedì.

Answering the Phone (Units 24 and 25)

Utterances useful in answering the phone are found in the final frames of Units 24 and 25.

UNIT 26

1. In Unit 13 the Italian sound-type /š/ was introduced.

2. This sound-type is practically identical to one heard in the following English words:

(sure)X	(mission)X	(nation)X
(machine)X	(special)X	(she)X
(anxious)X	(conscience)X	(fascistic)X

3. As you can see from these six examples, the spelling representation of this type of sound in English is varied.

4. As a general rule, in Italian the spelling representation of /š/ is:
   sc before the letter *e* or *i* (conventional Italian spelling) and *sci* elsewhere.

5. Thus:

(scemo)X	"stupid; fool."
(scɛna)X	"scene"
(sci)X	"ski"
(scià)X	"Shah"
(sciɔpero)X	"strike"
(sciupare)X	"to waste, spoil"
(ambasciata)X	"embassy"

6. One way to remember the spelling *sc* is to keep the English word "fascistic" in mind.

7. Exceptions to the rule stated in frame no. 4 do exist, but they are rare.

8. Notice, however, that in examples like the above, you should *never* pronounce a /Y/ after sound-type /š/, regardless of the spelling. Repeat the following:

(cosciɛnte)X	/KOŠÉNTE/	"conscious, aware"
(scientifico)X	/ŠENTÍFIKO/	"scientific"

9. Note that an unstressed /I/ before a vowel occurs after /š/ in a few words, such as:

(sciɛnte)X	"knowing"
(sciare)X	"to ski"
(sciovia)X	"ski-lift"

10. In Unit 25 you were introduced to the SLACK-TENSE consonant distinction that is very important in Italian. The sound-type /š/ presents *no* such contrast since it is *always tense* between vowels in words like:

> (pasce)X   "it grazes"
> (lascia)X   "it leaves [something]"
> (finisce)X   "it ends"
> (capisce)X   "it understands"

11. If a slack sound similar to /š/ *is* heard it will more than likely be what was pointed out in frame no. 11 of Unit 20, that is, a sound-type made by some speakers, especially Tuscans *instead of sound-type /č/ between vowel sounds.* Thus, the word *pace* "peace" may be pronounced (   ) by some speakers but either pronunciation will be different from that of *pasce* "it grazes."

*12. Now you will hear all the Italian words with /š/ that you have heard in this unit. Without looking back, try to write them correctly on the lines below.

> (1) _____   (9) _____
> (2) _____   (10) _____
> (3) _____   (11) _____
> (4) _____   (12) _____
> (5) _____   (13) _____
> (6) _____   (14) _____
> (7) _____   (15) _____
> (8) _____   (16) _____

13. Check your spelling. You should have written:

> (1) capisce   (9) scià
> (2) cosciɛnte   (10) scïare
> (3) finisce   (11) scïɛnte
> (4) lascia   (12) scientifico
> (5) pasce   (13) sciɔpero
> (6) scemo   (14) scïovia
> (7) scɛna   (15) sciupare
> (8) sci   (16) ambasciata

14. If you missed the letter *i* after *sc* in numbers (2) and (12) don't feel too bad since these two words are exceptions to the rule of frame no. 4. You should, however, have put the special marks involved in numbers no. 9, 10, 11, 12 and 14.

* * * * *

*15. In Unit 20 you were introduced to the dictionary form of a verb and were told its traditional name. What was it?

16. Three kinds of Italian infinitives were presented in Unit 20—those ending in -*are*, those ending in -*ere* and those ending in -*ire*.

17. These three groupings are important because they help us to talk about large classes of verbs that have features like one of the following three verbs:

(┼ascoltare)X   (┼vedere)X   (┼capire)X

18. In the discussion that follows, whatever is said about any one verb usually applies to its COMPOUND, that is, the same verb preceded by a prefix (like *ri-*). Thus, what will be said about ┼*vedere* also applies to ┼*rivedere* "see again."

19. No discussion of VERB CLASSES is complete, however, without some mention of SYNCOPATED INFINITIVES.

20. A SYNCOPATED INFINITIVE is one that has become shortened from an earlier, archaic form which can be useful in remembering some of the other forms of a given verb.

21. The only SYNCOPATED INFINITIVES in Italian are the following together with their COMPOUNDS:

(bere)X	"to drink,"	from an earlier, archaic (bevere)X
(dire)X	"to say, tell,"	from an earlier, archaic (dicere)X
(fare)X	"to do, make,"	from an earlier, archaic (facere)X
(porre)X	"to place,"	from an earlier, archaic (ponere)X
(trarre)X	"to draw,"	[=bring forth]," from an earlier, archaic (traere)X

and verbs ending in:
(-durre)X, like (produrre)X "to produce," from an earlier, archaic (producere)X

22. Of the SYNCOPATED INFINITIVES, the first three are commonly used verbs, whereas the others are important for their use in COMPOUNDS like the following:

(†apporre)X "to affix"	(†attrarre)X "to attract"	(†addurre)X "to adduce, allege"
(†comporre)X "to compose"	(†contrarre)X "to contract"	(†condurre)X "to conduct, conduce"
(†contrapporre)X "to set against, oppose"	(†detrarre)X "to detract, deduct"	(†dedurre)X "to deduct, deduce"
(†deporre)X "to depose"	(†distrarre)X "to distract"	(†indurre)X "to induce"
(†disporre)X "to dispose"	(†protrarre)X "to protract"	(†introdurre)X "to introduce [= lead or bring in]"
(†esporre)X "to expose"	(†ritrarre)X "to retract"	(†produrre)X "to produce"
(†imporre)X "to impose"	(†sottrarre)X "to subtract"	(†ridurre)X "to reduce"
(†interporre)X "to interpose"		(†sedurre)X "to seduce"X
(†opporre)X "to oppose"		(†tradurre)X "to translate"
(†posporre)X "to postpone"		
(†predisporre)X "to predispose"		
(†preporre)X "to place before"		
(†proporre)X "to propose"		
(†supporre)X "to suppose"		

*23. In the case of SYNCOPATED INFINITIVES, the VERB CLASS is determined by the earlier, archaic form. Thus, if CLASS I stands for -*are* verbs, CLASS II stands for -*ere* verbs and CLASS III stands for -*ire* verbs, what class do the SYNCOPATED INFINITIVES belong to?

* * * * *

*24. In Unit 17 you learned something about IRREGULAR verb forms. Would you say that verb forms that follow a "regular" pattern are REGULAR or IRREGULAR?

25. Most Italian verb forms are predictable because they follow a regular pattern.

26. Most Italian verb forms are REGULAR because they are patterned after the forms of model verbs like the three given in frame no. 17:

(+ascoltare)X   (+vedere)X   (+capire)X

27. We have already seen that REGULAR CLASS I verbs have forms like the following in the PRESENT TENSE.

INFINITIVE	(to indicate the person speaking)	(to indicate another)
(ascoltare)X	(ascolto)X	(ascolta)X
(chiamare)X	(chiamo)X	(chiama)X
"to call"		
(sognare)X	(sôgno)X	(sôgna)X
"to dream"		

*28. What seems to be the vowel that signals the person speaking in these examples?

*29. How do you say, "I am fine" in Italian?

*30. Does the verb form just used end in /O/ or /ɔ/?

31. The ending of *stɔ* (/ɔ/) is normal since /O/ is *not* normally found at the end of a one-syllable word or a word ending in a stressed vowel.

*32. What seems to be the vowel that signals a person other than the person speaking?

*33. How, then, would you express the following ideas in Italian, referring to yourself?

"I'm arriving."   -_____

"I'm starting."   -_____

"I'm smoking."   -_____

"I'm learning."   -_____

"I'm working."   -_____

*34. Now by using only one word for each of the following, how would you
     ask, referring to the person you are addressing:
       "Are you on the way?"   - _____
       "Are you beginning?"   - _____
       "Are you having a smoke?"   - _____
       "Are you acquiring knowledge?" - _____
       "Are you on the job?"   - _____

*35. Translate the following ideas into Italian, referring to a third person every
     time.
       "He is on the way."   - _____
       "Anna starts today."   - _____
       "He doesn't smoke."   - _____
       "Carlo never learns."   - _____
       "She is working."   - _____

*36. Translate the following, referring to a thing.
       "It is on the way."   - _____
       "It's starting."   - _____

*37. Is there any difference in Italian between the verb form used to refer to a
     third person and the verb form used to refer to a thing?

*38. Is there any difference in Italian between the verb form used to refer to a
     person you are addressing and the verb form used to refer to a third
     person?

*39. Because of the preceding observations, we could label the form used to
     refer to a person addressed or a third person or thing the OTHER FORM.
     We prefer instead to label it the LEI FORM.

*40. What is the PRESENT TENSE LEI FORM of the verb ɟmangiare?

*41. Give the PRESENT TENSE LEI FORM of the following verbs:
       ɟstudiare   "to study"   - _____
       ɟspiegare   "to explain"   - _____
       ɟdomandare   "to ask [for]"   - _____
       ɟportare   "to bring, take"   - _____
       ɟpensare   "to think"   - _____
       ɟgiocare   "to play [a game]"   - _____
       ɟaspettare   "to wait"   - _____
       ɟparlare   "to speak, talk"   - _____
       ɟsbagliare   "to make a mistake"   - _____

†amare	"to love"	- _____
†richiamare	"to call back"	- _____
†ritornare	"to return [some- where]"	- _____
†importare	"to matter"	- _____
†scusare	"to excuse"	- _____
†scïare	"to ski"	- _____
†sciupare	"to waste, spoil"	- _____
†lasciare	"to leave [some- thing]"	- _____
†stare	"to stay, be"	- _____
†dare	"to give"	- _____

42. Most CLASS I verbs follow the -o/-a pattern with forms derivable from the INFINITIVE.

*43. Thus, if †prenotare (un pôsto, un tavolo, un libro...) has the force of "to reserve (a seat, a table, a book...)," translate the following ideas into Italian, using a stressed /ɔ/in the verb form.

"I'm reserving a book."   - _____

"Carlo is not reserving a book." - _____

"Are you reserving a seat?"   - _____

"I always reserve a table there." - _____

*44. Study the following model.

S: Gisca qui lunedì?   "Are you playing here Monday?"
R: Sì, giɔco qui lunedì.   "Yes, I'm playing here Monday."

You will hear affirmative questions refering to yourself. Answer each one in the affirmative as in the model. Your response will be confirmed each time.

(1) Taglia soltanto questo?
(2) Stadia a Roma?
(3) Parla bɛne?
(4) Insegna qui?
(5) Pɛnsa di ritornare fra qualche mese?
(6) Chiama la signorina Rossi?
(7) Comincia fra due giorni?
(8) Fuma molto?
(9) Arriva giovedì?

(10) Pɔrta una cassa?
(11) Ritorna spesso in Italia?
(12) Lavora anche il sạbato?
(13) Raddrizza anche questo?
(14) Prenɔta due pôsti?
(15) Giɔca qui lunedì?

*45. Study the following model.

S: Non ascolta niɛnte?   "Don't you listen to anything?"
R: Nɔ, non ascolto niɛnte.   "No, I don't listen to anything."

You will now hear negative questions referring to yourself. Answer in the
negative as in the model. Your response will be confirmed each time.

(1) Non impara molto?
(2) Non aspɛtta fuɔri?
(3) Non mangia a casa?
(4) Non scia mai?
(5) Non dà niɛnte?
(6) Non spiɛga questo?
(7) Non sôgna mai in classe?
(8) Non lascia niɛnte in ufficio?
(9) Non ama fare la spesa?
(10) Non sta bɛne?
(11) Non domanda mai niɛnte?

* * * * *

*46. One CLASS I verb with forms that are not derivable from the INFINITIVE
and which therefore is classified as an IRREGULAR verb is the verb
†andare which you should remember. Give the two PRESENT TENSE
forms of this verb that you have had.

(to refer to the speaker)   (LEI FORM)

_____   _____

47. One peculiarity of several CLASS I verbs that cannot be predicted is that
    some with INFINITIVES of more than three syllables have their stress in the
    PRESENT TENSE SINGULAR forms on the *third vowel from the end* rather
    than on the second vowel from the end. Such are the following. Repeat.

INFINITIVE	(to refer to the speaker)	(LEI FORM)
(abitare)X "to live [= reside]"	(abito)X	(abita)X
(desiderare)X "to wish, want"	(desidero)X	(desidera)X
(applicare)X "to apply [something]"	(applico)X	(applica)X
(accreditare)X "to credit, accredit"	(accredito)X	(accredita)X
(telefonare)X "to phone"	(telɛfono)X	(telɛfona)X
(ritelefonare)X	(ritelɛfono)X	(ritelɛfona)X

48. Like the preceding are the following which you should learn.

INFINITIVE	(to refer to the speaker)	(LEI FORM)
(accelerare)X "to accelerate"X	(accɛlero)X	(accɛlera)X
(agevolare)X "to facilitate"	(agevolvo)X	(agevola)X
(considerare)X "to consider"	(considero)X	(considera)X
(manipolare)X "to manipulate"	(manipolo)X	(manipola)X
(partecipare)X "to participate"	(partɛcipo)X	(partɛcipa)X

49. It is interesting to note that *most* of the verb forms mentioned in frames no.
    47 and no. 48 have English cognates whose primary stress falls on the
    syllable that corresponds to the stressed syllable in the related Italian word.
    Compare, for example:

    (abita)X   and the English (inhabit)X
    (desidera)X   and the English (desire)X
    (applica)X   and the English (applicator)X
    (accredita)X   and the English (accredit)X
    (accelera)X   and the English (accelerate)X
    (considera)X   and the English (consider)X
    (partecipa)X   and the English (participate)X
    (manipola)X   and the English (manipulate)X

*50. Study the following model.

    S: Applica spesso questo?   "Do you apply this often?"
    R: Nɔ, non applico spesso   "No, I don't apply this often."
       questo.

    You will hear questions referring to yourself. Answer in the negative as in
    the model. Your response will be confirmed each time.

    (1) Abita sempre in montagna?
    (2) Considera soltanto questo?
    (3) Telefona nel pomeriggio?
    (4) Desidera mangiare?
    (5) Partecipa anche domani?
    (6) Accredita an artista?
    (7) Ritelefona dopodomani?
    (8) Applica spesso questo?

                              * * * * *

51. Regular CLASS II verbs have forms like the following in the PRESENT
    TENSE.

INFINITIVE	(to refer to the speaker)	(LEI FORM)
(vedere)X "to see"	(vedo)X	(vede)X
(cadere)X "to fall"	(cado)X	(cade)X
the SYNCOPATED		
(bere)X "to drink"	(bevo)X	(beve)X

*52. What seems to be the vowel that signals the person speaking in these examples?

*53. Does the same vowel signal the person speaking both for CLASS I verbs and CLASS II verbs?

*54. What seems to be the vowel that signals a person or thing other than the person speaking?

*55. Does the PRESENT TENSE LEI FORM of CLASS II verbs end in the same vowel as the PRESENT TENSE LEI FORM of CLASS I verbs?

*56. Study the following model.

     S: Cade spesso?   "Do you fall often?"
     R: Sì, cado spesso.   "Yes, I fall often."

You will hear questions referring to yourself. Answer in the affirmative as in the model. Your response will be confirmed each time.

     (1) Vede il signor Piave ogni mese?
     (2) Beve molto?
     (3) Cade sempre in ufficio?
     (4) Vede spesso Agata?
     (5) Beve birra?
     (6) Cade spesso?

57. *Many* CLASS II VERBS contain irregularities or peculiarities that should be noted.

58. One such peculiarity is that some INFINITIVES are stressed on the second vowel from the end (like *vedere*) and others are stressed on the third vowel from the end (like *piɔvere* "to rain"). There is no easy way to predict the stress on a CLASS II INFINITIVE. However, *most* CLASS II INFINITIVES are stressed like *piɔvere*, that is, on the third vowel from the end.

59. Another peculiarity of CLASS II verbs pertains to those with INFINITIVES in *-cere, -scere* or *-gere*. For the majority of such verbs the written forms used in the PRESENT TENSE to indicate the person speaking *look* regular but reflect important sound changes, as illustrated here:

INFINITIVE	(to refer to the speaker)	(LEI FORM)
the SYNCOPATED		
(dire)X	(dico)X	(dice)X
"to say, tell"		
SYNCOPATED verbs in		
(-durre)X	(-duco)X	(-duce)X
(pascere)X	(pasco)X	(pasce)X
"to graze"		
(leggere)X	(leggo)X	(legge)X
"to ready"		

60. Here are two new CLASS II verbs. Repeat them and learn them.

(vincere)X	"to win"	(vincere)X
(conoscere)X	"to be acquainted with"	(conoscere)X

*61. By using only one word for each of the ideas underlined, translate them into Italian.

"*Are you winning?*" - _____

"*Are you acquainted with Marlo?*" - _____

"*Are you producing?*" - _____

"*Are you translating?*" - _____

*62. Using complete sentences, answer the preceding questions in the affirmative in Italian.

Sì, _____

Sì, _____

Sì, _____

Sì, _____

63. Unlike CLASS I, CLASS II contains many highly irregular verbs. Learn the following PRESENT TENSE forms, most of which should already be familiar to you.

INFINITIVE	(to refer to the speaker)	(LEI FORM)
(avere)X	(ho)X	(ha)X
"to have"		

(piacere)X "to be liked"	(piaccio)X	(piace)X
(sapere)X "to know [something]"	(sɔ)X	(sa)X
(dovere)X "to have to, must"	(dĕvo)X or (dĕbbo)X	(dĕve)X
(potere)X "to be able to, can"	(pɔsso)X	(puɔ̀)X
(volere)X "to want"	(vɔglio)X	(vuɔle)X
(ɛssere)X "to be"	(sôno)X	(è)X
the SYNCOPATED (fare)X "to do, make"	(faccio)X	(fa)X
the SYNCOPATED (porre)X "to place"	(pongo)X	(pone)X
the SYNCOPATED (trarre)X "to draw [=bring forth]"	(traggo)X	(trae)X

*64. Translate the following into Italian.

"I don't have anything."   -_____

"Is she liked?"   -_____

"I don't know if I'm liked."   -_____

"He doesn't know what I have."   -_____

"Do you have to work
  tomorrow?"   -_____

"I don't want to work but
  I have to."   -_____

"I would like to come on
  Saturday but I can't."   -_____

"He wants to be liked but he
  never does anything."   -_____

"I never do the shopping.
  I don't like to."   -_____

"I attract but I don't distract."   -_____

"I'm *here*. What do I have to do?" -_____

*65. Here is a well-known Italian proverb. Try to translate it into English.
   L'uɔmo propone e Dio dispone.

66. Repeat this proverb and try to learn it.
   (   )X (   )X

*67. Study the following model.
   S: Piace molto?   "Are you well-liked?"
   R: Sì, piaccio molto.   "Yes, I'm well-liked."

You will hear questions referring to yourself. Answer in the affirmative as in the model. Your response will be confirmed each time.
   (1) È in classe lunedì?
   (2) Sa anche questo?
   (3) Ha soltanto an programma?
   (4) Puɔ lavorare domani?
   (5) Dĕve studiare stasera?
   (6) Vuɔl lavorare?
   (7) Vuɔle soltanto una penna?
   (8) Piace molto?

*68. Study the following model.
   S: Non propane questo?   "Don't you propose this?"
   R: Nɔ, non propongo questo.   "No, I don't propose this."

You will hear questions referring to yourself. Answer in the negative as in the model. Your response will be confirmed each time.
   (1) Non fa le spese nel pomeriggio?
   (2) Non dice mai niɛnte?
   (3) Non sottrae mai niɛnte?
   (4) Non produce soltanto formaggio?
   (5) Non propone questo?

* * * * *

69. Regular CLASS III verbs have forms like the following in the PRESENT
    TENSE.

INFINITIVE	(to refer to the speaker)	(LEI FORM)
(capire)X "to understand"	(capisco)X	(capisce)X
(finire)X "to end, finish"	(finisco)X	(finisce)X
(riferire)X "to refer, relay, report"	(riferisco)X	(riferisce)X

*70. Notice that instead of just a vowel signaling the person speaking in these
     examples, a two-syllable ending is used. What is it?

*71. And what two-syllable ending here signals a person or thing other than the
     person speaking?

*72. ‡preferire "to prefer" is a regular CLASS III verb. It often occurs followed
     by an INFINITIVE. How would you express the following ideas in Italian
     using this verb?

   "Do you prefer to stay here?"   -_____

   "Wouldn't you rather wait over there?" -_____

   "I'd rather stay home tomorrow."   -_____

*73. Study the following model.

   S: Riferisce a Wạshington Lɛi?   "Do you report [=submit reports] to
                                          Washington?"
   R: Sì, riferisco a Wạshington.   "Yes, I report to Washington."

   You will hear questions referring to yourself. Answer in the affirmative as in
   the model. Your response will be confirmed each time.

   (1) Finisce ɔggi?
   (2) Capisce bɛne?
   (3) Preferisce partire domani?
   (4) Riferisce a Washington?

                              * * * * *

74. Most CLASS III verbs have forms like +capire. However, a *small* group of CLASS III verbs (about twenty) have forms like the following in the PRESENT TENSE.

INFINITIVE	(to refer to the speaker)	(LEI FORM)
(sentire)X "to hear"	(sɛnto)X	(sɛnte)X
(dormire)X "to sleep"	(dɔrmo)X	(dɔrme)X
(aprire)X "to open"	(apro)X	(apre)X
(partire)X "to leave" [as when going on a trip]	(parto)X	(parte)X

*75. Notice that these verbs do *not* have forms that end in /ÍSKO/ - /ÍŠE/. Which of the following forms are REGULAR, that is, which are like the majority of verbs in CLASS III?

(sɛnto)   (capisco)   (riferisce)   (dɔrme)
  a   b   c   d

76. Several CLASS III verbs contain some irregular verb forms, that is, forms that cannot be predicted. Learn the following PRESENT TENSE forms.

INFINITIVE	(to refer to the speaker)	(LEI FORM)
(fuggire)X "to run away, flee"	(fuggo)X	(fugge)X
(venire)X "to come"	(vɛngo)X	(viɛne)X
(salire)X "to go up"	(salgo)X	(sale)X
(uscire)X "to go out"	(ɛsco)X	(ɛsce)X

*77. Translate the following into Italian.

"It's going to open this afternoon." -_____

"It leaves tomorrow morning." -_____

"I'm not running away." -_____

"When is Miss White coming?" -_____

"I'm not coming tomorrow." -_____

"I'm leaving [= going out] now." -_____

"I'm leaving [= going on a trip] now." -_____

"I'm going upstairs now."   -_____

"He's not going out; he's going up." -_____

"Would you rather go out tomorrow
    night?"   -_____

*78. Study the following model.
    S: Parte fra pɔco?   "Are you leaving soon?"
    R: Sì, parto fra pɔco.   "Yes, I'm leaving soon."

You will hear questions referring to yourself. Answer in the affirmative as in
the model. Your response will be confirmed each time.

    (1) Sɛnte bɛne al telɛfono?
    (2) Sale con la signora?
    (3) Fugge in montagna?
    (4) Viɛne domani?
    (5) Apre anche questo?
    (6) Ɛsce stasera?
    (7) Dɔrme spesso fuɔri città?
    (8) Parte fra pɔco?

                    * * * * *

*79. Repeat the following verb forms. What is the meaning of the ending -o or
    isco?

    (ascolto)X   (vedo)X   (capisco)X

*80. Thus, comparing the following English translations with the above, —"I
    listen," "I see," and "I understand" what does the English word "I" corre-
    spond to in the Italian words?

*81. Translate the following into Italian:
    "I study."   -_____

    "I drink."   -_____

    "I'm finishing."   -_____

82. As we see from the preceding examples, the idea of the person speaking,
    expressed in English by the word "I" is not expressed in Italian by any
    word separate from the verb form.

83. However, Italian does have a special word used to indicate the person speaking whenever no verb form is present. The word is *io*, uncapitalized within a sentence. Repeat the following examples.

(Io.)X	"I."
(Io nɔ)X (Non, io.)X }	"Not I."
(Anche io.)X (Anch'io.)X }	"I, too."
(Neanche io.)X (Neanch'io.)X }	"Me, neither."
(Soltanto io.)X	"Only I."
(E io?)X (Ed io?)X }	"And I?"

84. Of the preceding examples of words used before *io*, *anche* and *neanche* usually appear as *anch'* and *neanch'* respectively before any vowel, and *e* frequently appears as *ed* before a vowel (especially if the vowel is /E/ or /ɛ/.

85. The word *io* may be used together with verb forms like *studio, bevo, finisco*, but when so used it usually adds emphasis to the idea of "I" and contrasts or comparisons like the following are often involved.

Mario non studia, ma io studio.
   "Mario doesn't study, but *I* study."
Maria lavora, ma to studio.
   "Maria *works*, but I study."
Carlo studia e anch'io sudio.
   "Carlo studies and *I* study, too."

* * * * *

86. Similarly, the idea of the person addressed, expressed in English by the word "you" is not normally expressed in Italian by any word separate from the verb form in examples like:

"you study"	-	(studia)X
"you drink"	-	(beve)X
"you finish"	-	(finisce)X

*87. However, Italian does have a special word used to indicate the person being addressed whenever no verb form is present. The word is *Lei*, preferably capitalized. Translate the following into Italian.

"Not you." -_____

"You, too." -_____

"Only you." -_____

"And you?" -_____

88. The word *Lei* may be used together with verb forms like *studia, beve, finisce,* and it usually is in opening questions like:

(Studia Lɛi?)X   "Do you study?"

89. In addition, *Lei* may be used with a verb form to add emphasis to the idea of "you," to clarify who is meant, or simply because a contrast or comparison like the following is involved.

Io lavoro ma Lɛi studia.
    "I work but *you study."*
Io studio. Studia anche Lɛi?
    "I study. Do *you study, too?"*

* * * * *

90. The idea of a third person expressed in English by the word "she" or "he" is not normally expressed in Italian by any word separate from the verb form in examples like:

"(s)he studies"   -   (studia)X
"(s)he drinks"   -   (beve)X
"(s)he finishes"   -   (finisce)X

*91. However, Italian does have special words used to indicate a third person whenever no verb form is present. The usual words are lɛi (uncapitalized) for "she" and *lui* (uncapitalized) for *he.* Translate the following into Italian.

"Not she." -_____

"He, too." -_____

"Only her." -_____

"And him?" -_____

"He and she." -_____

92. Either of these two words may be used together with verb forms like *studia, beve, finisce,* but when so used they usually (a) add emphasis to the idea of "she" or "he," (b) clarify who is meant, or (c) involve contrasts or comparisons like the following:

Lui lavora ma lɛi studia.
"*He works* but *she studies.*"
Lui studia. Studia anche lɛi?
"*He* studies. Does *she* study, too?"

* * * * *

93. As we saw in frame no. 36, the idea of "it" is not normally expressed in Italian by any word separate from the verb form in examples like:

"It is on the way."   -   (Arriva.)X
"It is starting."   -   (Comincia.)X

*94. Thus, translate the following into Italian.

"It is falling."   -_____

"It is grazing."   -_____

"It is liked."   -_____

"It is ending."   -_____

"It is leaving (on a trip)."   -_____

"It is going up."   -_____

* * * * *

*95. What name have we decided to give to verb forms like the preceding that may refer to a person or thing other than the person speaking?

96. The verb form used to indicate the person speaking we will henceforth call the IO FORM.

* * * * *

*97. Study the following model.

S: Soltanto Lɛi?   "Only you?"
R: Sì, soltanto io.   "Yes, only me."

You will hear verb-less questions as in the model. Reply accordingly, always agreeing with the question. Your response will be confirmed each time. NOTE: The questions are shown here in the text purposely so that you can distinguish between *Lɛi* "you" and *lɛi* "she."

(1) Lui e lɛi?
(2) Anche lɛi?
(3) Io e lui?
(4) Soltanto io?

(5) Anche io?
(6) Anche Lεi?
(7) Soltanto Lεi?
(8) Non io?
(9) Non lεi?
(10) Neanch'io?
(11) Neanche Lεi?
(12) Neanche lεi?
(13) Neanche lui?

*98. Study the following model.

    S: Chi? Io?   "Who? Me?"
    R: Sì, Lεi.   "Yes, you."

(instructions as for the preceding drill)

(1) Chi? Lui?
(2) Chi? Io?
(3) Chi? Lεi? (referring to you)
(4) Chi? Lui e io?
(5) Chi? Io e Lεi?
(6) Chi? Io e lεi?

*99. Study the following model.

    S: Io giɔco ɔggi. E Lεi?   "I'm playing today. How about you?
    (domani)
    R: Io giɔco domani.   "I'm playing tomorrow."

You will hear statements followed by short tag questions as in the model.
Give a complete answer each time by using the cue given. Your response will
be confirmed each time. NOTE: In this drill, questions with /LƐY/ are
always to be interpreted as referring to you; questions referring to a third
person female are always to be answered with *lei* "she," and questions referring to a third person male are always to be answered with *lui*.

Questions	Cues
(1) Io taglio soltanto questo, e Lεi?	anch'io
(2) Lui studia in Francia, e Vanda?	in Germania
(3) Lεi parla con il dottor Rossi, e io?	la signora
(4) Lui insegna qui, e Stella?	a Napoli
(5) Cia pεnsa di ritornare fra qualche mese, e Lεi?	fra pɔco

Questions	Cues
(6) Lui chiama la signorina Russo, e Lɛi?	la guardia
(7) Io comincio ora, e Lɛi?	più tardi
(8) Lui fuma molto, e Lɛi?	non
(9) Andrɛa arriva venerdì, e Lɛi?	domɛnica
(10) Lui pɔrta un pɔ' di vino, e Lɛi?	un pɔ' di birra
(11) Io ritorno spesso in Italia, e Lɛi?	non......mai
(12) Albɛrto lavora anche il sabato, e Lɛi?	soltanto quattro giorni
(13) Lui raddrizza soltanto questo, e Lɛi?	anche questo
(14) Grisɛlda prenɔta una cɔpia di un libro d'italiano, e Lɛi?	due cɔpie
(15) Lui non ascolta mai, e Lɛi?	sɛmpre
(16) Io imparo molto, e Bɛrta?	non
(17) La signora aspɛtta qui, ma lui?	fuɔri
(18) Io mangio una bistecca, e Lɛi?	un pɔ' d'arrɔsto
(19) Io scio soltanto in dicɛmbre, e Lɛi?	anche in novɛmbre
(20) Lɛi spiɛga ciɔ ad Andrɛa, e io?	ad Alfrɛdo
(21) Io non sôgno mai, e Lɛi?	spesso
(22) Il dottor Stella dà sɛmpre nome e cognome, e la signora?	anche
(23) Io non lascio mai niɛnte in ufficio, e Lɛi?	sɛmpre qualcɔsa
(24) Lui non ama fare la spesa, e Carla?	neanche lɛi
(25) Io stɔ molto bɛne ɔggi, e Lɛi?	anch'io
(26) Tina domanda sɛmpre, e lui?	non......mai
(27) Io non sbaglio mai, e Lɛi?	neanch'io
(28) Io non sciupo mai niɛnte, e Lɛi?	neanch'io
(29) Lui non scusa mai la segretaria, e Lɛi?	sɛmpre
(30) Lui applica spesso questo, e Lɛi?	non......mai
(31) Io abito sɛmpre in montagna, e Lɛi?	anch'io

Questions	Cues
(32) Lui considera soltanto questo, e Carmela?	anche lei
(33) Mina telefona spesso nel pomeriggio. e Lei?	non......mai
(34) Io partecipo sempre, e lui?	non......mai
(35) Lui accredita soltanto un artista, e Virginia?	due artisti
(36) Io vado a Torino sabato, e lui?	anche lui
(37) Lucio cade spesso, e Cristina?	non......mai
(38) Gia vede il signor Segni ogni mese, e Cesare?	giorno
(39) Io non bevo acqua, e Lei?	non caffè
(40) Lui legge in italiano, e Lei?	in inglese
(41) Io non vinco mai, e Giovanni?	neanche
(42) Bianca conosce la signora Scirri, ma Lei no?	anch'io
(43) Io devo ritornare domani, e Lei?	fra quattro giorni
(44) Lui può lavorare soltanto oggi, e Lei?	oggi e anche domani
(45) Lui vuole una penna, e Lei?	due penne
(46) Marta piace molto, e Lei?	non
(47) Mario ha una casa in compagna, e Lei?	anch'io
(48) Io sono di Perugia, e Nina?	anche
(49) Rosa sa già qualcosa, e Lei?	non......niente
(50) Io non dico mai niente, e lui?	neanche
(51) Rachele fa le spese il lunedi, e Lei?	il sabato
(52) Lui propone Ancona, e Lei?	Udine
(53) Io produco questo in un giorno, e Luca?	due giorni
(54) Lui non sottrae bene, e Lei?	neanch'io

Questions	Cues
(55) Io finisco ɔggi, e Lui?	domani
(56) Lɛi riferisce a Napoli, e io?	a Roma
(57) Lɛi capisce bɛne, e lui?	non......molto bɛne
(58) Io preferisco vino, e Renato?	birra
(59) Io non sɛnto bɛne, e Lɛi?	neanch'io
(60) Lui sale ora, e Lɛi?	fra due minuti
(61) Alfrɛdo parte stamattina, e Lɛi?	nel pomeriggio
(62) Io fuggo in Africa, e Gina?	in Australia
(63) Lui non viɛne domani, e Lɛi?	non.......giovedì
(64) Lui ɛsce ogni sera, e Lɛi?	soltanto la domenica
(65) Lui non dɔrme sɛmpre qui, e Lɛi?	non......mai

• **End of Tape 10A** •

Tape 10B

*100. Study the following model.

S: Dĕve studiare Lɛi? "Do you have to study?"
R: Nɔ, studio soltanto "No, I only study because I
   perchè mi piace studiare. like to study."

This drill introduces a new word, *perchè*. Answer as in the model, using *mi piace, le piace, gli piace* or *Le piace* as appropriate. Your response will be confirmed each time.

(1) Dĕve lavorare Lɛi?
(2) Dĕve giocare Bianca?
(3) Dĕve aspettare Ugo?
(4) Dĕvo parlare io?
(5) Dĕve fare la spesa Lɛi?
(6) Dĕve leggere Lɛi?
(7) Dĕve sciare Augusta?
(8) Dĕve uscire Lɛi?
(9) Dĕve vincere Lɛi?
(10) Dĕve richiamare sɛmpre Adɔlfo?
(11) Dĕve venire Lɛi?

(12) Dĕve stare qui io?
(13) Dĕve ritornare Lɛi?
(14) Dĕve bere Lɛi?
(15) Dĕve telefonare Nino?
(16) Dĕve piacere Lɛi?
(17) Dĕve dormire qui Lɛi?
(18) Dĕve partecipare Ɛva?
(19) Dĕve andarci spesso Lɛi?
(20) Dĕve studiare Lɛi?

*101. Study the following model.

S: Perchè lavora Lɛi?   "Why do you work?"
R: Perchè mi piace   "Because I like to work."
     lavorare.

This drill shows how *perchè* has the force of both "why" and "because."
Answer accordingly. Your response will be confirmed each time.

(1) Perchè fuma Lɛi?
(2) Perchè fa la spesa Biance?
(3) Perchè insegna qui Ugo?
(4) Perchè non ascolta Lɛi?
(5) Perchè non mangia Lɛi?
(6) Perchè domando sɛmpre io?
(7) Perchè abita in città Adɔlfo?
(8) Perchè va spesso a Milano Lɛi?
(9) Perchè bevo acqua io?
(10) Perchè lɛgge molto Lɛi?
(11) Perchè ha due case Augusta?
(12) Perchè non viɛne Lɛi?
(13) Perchè ɛsce ogni sera Nino?
(14) Perchè non dɔrme qui Ɛva?
(15) Perchè lavora Lɛi?

TEST A

(answers not recorded)

You will hear words that have all occurred so far and which contain the consonant of *sci* (/š/) or the consonant of *ci* (/č/). Write each word in the appropriate column according to whether the word contains /š/ or /č/.

	/š/	/č/
1)	_____	_____
2)	_____	_____
3)	_____	_____
4)	_____	_____
5)	_____	_____
6)	_____	_____
7)	_____	_____
8)	_____	_____
9)	_____	_____
10)	_____	_____
11)	_____	_____
12)	_____	_____
13)	_____	_____
14)	_____	_____
15)	_____	_____
16)	_____	_____
17)	_____	_____
18)	_____	_____
19)	_____	_____
20)	_____	_____
21)	_____	_____
22)	_____	_____
23)	_____	_____
24)	_____	_____
25)	_____	_____
26)	_____	_____
27)	_____	_____
28)	_____	_____
29)	_____	_____
30)	_____	_____
31)	_____	_____
32)	_____	_____
33)	_____	_____
34)	_____	_____
35)	_____	_____
36)	_____	_____

TEST B

(answers not recorded)

You will hear some COMPOUND SYNCOPATED INFINITIVES. Give their English cognates.

1)_____

2)_____

3)_____

4)_____

5)_____

6)_____

7)_____

8)_____

9)_____

10)_____

11)_____

12)_____

13)_____

14)_____

15)_____

16)_____

17)_____

18)_____

19)_____

20)_____

21)_____

22)_____

23)_____

24)_____

TEST C

(answers not recorded)

You will hear sentences from Drill no. 99. As you hear them, write the INFINI-TIVE of the finite verb form contained in each sentence.

1)_____

2)_____

3)_____

4)_____

5)_____

6)_____

7)_____

8)_____

9)_____

10)_____

11)_____

12)_____

13)_____

14)_____

15)_____

16)_____

17)_____

18)_____

19)_____

20)_____

21)_____

22)_____

23)_____

24)_____

25)_____

TEST D

(answers not recorded)

You will hear a verb form that may be (a) the INFINITIVE or (b) the LEI FORM. For each verb form you hear write the appropriate PRESENT TENSE IO FORM.

1) _____	24) _____
2) _____	25) _____
3) _____	26) _____
4) _____	27) _____
5) _____	28) _____
6) _____	29) _____
7) _____	30) _____
8) _____	31) _____
9) _____	32) _____
10) _____	33) _____
11) _____	34) _____
12) _____	35) _____
13) _____	36) _____
14) _____	37) _____
15) _____	38) _____
16) _____	39) _____
17) _____	40) _____
18) _____	41) _____
19) _____	42) _____
20) _____	43) _____
21) _____	44) _____
22) _____	45) _____
23) _____	

TEST E

(answers not recorded)

You will hear a narrative in Italian followed by twenty English statements. Put a check in the appropriate column according to whether each statement is definitely *true* or *false*. (The narrative and statements are given in the Answer section.)

	True	False
1)		
2)		
3)		
4)		
5)		
6)		
7)		
8)		
9)		
10)		
11)		
12)		
13)		
14)		
15)		
16)		
17)		
18)		
19)		
20)		

TEST F

(not recorded)

Translate the following thoughts into Italian by using *only* what has been presented so far.

1) Are you leaving anything behind in the office?

_____

2) He understands a lot but he never says anything.

_____

3) What would you like to drink, a little wine? - Why not?

_____

4) I'm sorry, but it's very distracting.

_____

5) I'd like to reserve a table, please.

_____

6) Is there a seat over there?

_____

7) When do you see Renata?

_____

8) When you play, do you win all the time?

_____

9) He has a house in the country, but he never goes there.

_____

10) *He* reports to Rome, but *I* report to Milan.

_____

11) I have to study so I'm staying in tonight.

_____

12) I should go up now, but I'd rather wait.

_____

13) He sleeps while she works.

_____

14) *He's* not reading anything and *I'm* not reading either.

_____

15) Do you get a lot of rain there?

_____

16) I was born and raised in New York, but I live in Washington.

17) You have a house in the city, don't you?

_____

18) *He* hears without listening; *I* listen but I don't hear a thing.

_____

19) *She's* the only one who knows where he is. *I* don't.

_____

20) Man proposes and God disposes.

_____

TEST A   ANSWERS

1) pasce
2) pace
3) giacinto
4) scià
5) cieco
6) sciopero
7) sci
8) deficiente
9) cosciente
10) sciupare
11) Lucio
12) ambasciata
13) cielo
14) scientifico
15) cena
16) scemo
17) ciocia
18) capisce

19) ciancia
20) scïare
21) preferisce
22) società
23) ci
24) finisce
25) ciuco
26) uscire
27) Licia
28) scïovia
29) scena
30) specie
31) piaccio
32) lascia
33) ufficio
34) dicembre
35) scïente
36) Grecia

TEST B   ANSWERS

Infinitives	Cognates
1) attrarre	attract
2) comporre	compose
3) condurre	conduct (or) conduce
4) contrarre	contract
5) dedurre	deduct (or) deduce
6) deporre	depose
7) detrarre	detract
8) disporre	dispose
9) distrarre	distract
10) esporre	expose
11) imporre	impose
12) indurre	induce (or) induct
13) interporre	interpose
14) introdurre	introduce
15) opporre	oppose
16) posporre	postpone
17) predisporre	predispose
18) produrre	produce
19) proporre	propose
20) protrarre	protract
21) ridurre	reduce
22) sedurre	seduce
23) sottrarre	subtract
24) supporre	suppose

TEST C   ANSWERS

Sentences	Infinitives
1) Io taglio soltanto questo.	tagliare
2) Lɛi capisce bɛne.	capire
3) Lɛi riferisce a Napoḷi.	riferire
4) Lui vuɔle una penna.	volere
5) Lui studia in francia.	studiare
6) Io finisco ɔggi.	finire
7) Io abitọ sɛmpre in montagna.	abitare
8) Lui non sottrae bɛne.	sottrarre
9) Io preferisco vino.	preferire
10) Lui puɔ̀ lavorare soltanto ɔggi.	potere
11) Io vado a Torino sabạto.	andare
12) Io produco questo in un giorno.	produrre
13) Io non sɛnto bɛne.	sentire
14) Lui non dɔrme sɛmpre qui.	dormire
15) Gia vede il signor Segni ogni mese.	vedere
16) Lui propone Ancona.	proporre
17) Lui sale ora.	salire
18) Lui ɛsce ogni sera.	uscire
19) Io non bevo acqua.	bere
20) Io non vinco mai.	vịncere
21) Rachɛle fa le spese il lunedi.	fare
22) Io non dico mai niɛnte.	dire
23) Io fuggo in Afrịca.	fuggire
24) Lui non viɛne domani.	venire
25) Io dĕvo ritornare domani.	dovere
26) Mario ha una casa in campagna.	avere
27) Io sôno di Perugia.	ɛssere
28) Rɔsa sa già qualcɔsa.	sapere

TEST D   ANSWERS

Infinitive or lei Form	Present io Form	Infinitive or lei Form	Present io Form
1) tagliare	taglio	23) fa	faccio
2) sapere	sɔ	24) pɛnsa	pɛnso
3) propone	propongo	25) potere	pɔsso
4) pɔrta	pɔrto	26) finire	finisco
5) vince	vinco	27) giocare	giɔco
6) sentire	sɛnto	28) tradurre	traduco
7) impara	imparo	29) apre	apro
8) posporre	pospongo	30) dare	dɔ
9) spiɛga	spiɛgo	31) contrarre	contraggo
10) sta	stɔ	32) stare	stɔ
11) prenotare	prenɔto	33) ascoltare	ascolto
12) applicare	ạpplico	34) agevolare	agevolo
13) abitare	ạbito	35) accredita	accrɛdito
14) manịpola	manịpolo	36) partɛcipa	partɛcipo
15) lɛgge	lɛggo	37) conosce	conosco
16) vedere	vedo	38) vuɔle	vɔglio
17) piace	piaccio	39) bere	bevo
18) dice	dico	40) viɛne	vɛngo
19) è	sôno	41) capisce	capisco
20) uscire	ɛsco	42) dovere	dĕvo
21) sale	salgo	43) insegna	insegno
22) avere	hɔ	44) dormire	dɔrmo
		45) lavora	lavoro

TEST E   ANSWERS

Carlo Scirri non dĕve lavorare ɔggi e neanche domani perchè c'è uno sciɔpero di due giorni. Non gli piace stare a casa e vorrĕbbe fare qualcɔsa. Pɛnsa di andare in montagna e a cena fuɔri e vorrĕbbe andarci con Carmɛla. Chiama Carmɛla e le domanda che cɔsa vuɔle fare. Lɛi gli dice che non puɔ fare niɛnte perchè sta molto male e non puɔ uscire. Più tardi il signor Scirri chiama la signorina De Filippo in ambasciata. La guardia gli dice di ritelefonare dopodomani perchè la signorina è fuɔri città e dovrĕbbe ritornare fra due giorni. Ma fra due giorni anche il signor Scirri dĕve ritornare in ufficio. Ɔggi non puɔ fare molto. Potrĕbbe andare in banca ma preferisce non andarci ɔggi. Non impɔrta! Sta a casa e lɛgge un libro!

(1) Mr. Scirri has two days off from work.	true
(2) Offices are closed because it is a national holiday.	false
(3) The strike will go on indefinitely.	false
(4) Mr. Scirri is planning to stay home and do some work around the house.	false
(5) He decides against going to the bank today.	true
(6) He'd like to take a short trip to the mountains.	true
(7) Mr. Scurri tries to find out if Carmela is doing anything.	true
(8) He goes to see Carmela.	false
(9) Carmela will gladly go along with his plans for the day.	false
(10) She is not feeling well and has to stay in.	true
(11) Mr. Scirri telephones another female friend who works at the embassy.	true
(12) The friend does not work there anymore.	false
(13) The secretary answers the phone.	false

(14) Miss De Filippo will be back in two weeks.	false
(15) She is out of the office momentarily.	false
(16) She is going to return the call as soon as she comes back.	false
(17) Mr. Scirri is asked to call again in two days.	true
(18) Mr. Scirri is due back to work in two days.	true
(19) Mr. Scirri has a very busy day today.	false
(20) He decides to go to the bank.	false

TEST F ANSWERS

1) Lascia qualcosa in ufficio Lei?
2) Capisce molto ma non dice mai niente.
3) Che cosa vuol bere Lei, un po' di vino? - Perchè no?
4) Mi dispiace, ma distrae molto.
5) Vorrei prenotare un tavolo, per favore.
6) C'è un pôsto lì?
7) Quando vede Renata Lei?
8) Quando gioca Lei, vince sempre?
9) Lui ha una casa in campagna ma non ci va mai.
10) Lui riferisce a Roma ma io riferisco a Milano.
11) Non esco stasera perchè devo studiare.
12) Dovrei salire ora ma preferisco aspettare.
13) Lui dorme e lei lavora.
14) Lui non legge niente e neanch'io leggo.
15) Piove molto lì?
16) Io sôno di New York ma abito a Washington.
17) Ha una casa in città, no?
18) Lui sente ma non ascolta; io ascolto ma non sento niente.
19) Soltanto lei sa dov'è. { Non io
                            { Io no.
20) L'uomo propone e Dio dispone.

UNIT 27

1. Pronounce the following two English words.

    (bets)X   (Betsy)X

2. The sound-combination represented by *ts* is heard in many English words. Sometimes it occurs *at the end of a word* (as in "bets") and sometimes it occurs *within a word* (as in "Betsy").

3. It is *not* normal to find this sound-combination at the *beginning of a word* in English.

4. Italian has something that sounds very similar to the English sound-combination. Try pronouncing the two English words of frame no. 1 by making the sound-combination TENSE, that is, repeat carefully:

    (   )X (   )X

5. What you just heard was the way an Italian might pronounce the two English words of frame no. 1. Listen again and repeat.

    (   )X (   )X

6. This sound-combination in Italian should be treated as a unit, always strongly pronounced (TENSE). We will represent it here as /T͡S/.

7. In Italian /T͡S/ may occur at the beginning of a word and this is sometimes difficult for English speakers to pronounce. Say (   )X and then while only *thinking* the first syllable, try saying:

    /BéS͡TI/

8. In word-initial position, then, *think* of an unpronounced vowel before pronouncing syllables like:

    (/T͡SI/)X   (/T͡SA/)X   (/T͡SU/)X
    (/T͡SE/)X   (/T͡Sɛ/)X   (/T͡SO/)X   (/T͡Sɔ/)X

* * * * *

9. Now pronounce the following two English words.

    (suds)X   (sudsy)X

10. The sound-combination represented by *ds* is heard in many English words. Sometimes it occurs *at the end of a word* (as in "suds") and sometimes it occurs *within a word* (as in "sudsy").

11. It is *not* normal to find this sound-combination at the *beginning of a word* in English.

12. Italian has something that sounds very similar to the English sound-combination. Try pronouncing the two English words of frame no. 9 by making the sound-combination in question TENSE, that is, repeat carefully:

    (   )X (   )X

13. What you just heard was the way an Italian might pronounce the two English words of frame no. 9. Listen again and repeat.

    (   )X (   )X

14. This sound-combination in Italian should be treated as a unit, always strongly pronounced (TENSE). We will represent it here as /D͡S/.

15. In Italian /D͡S/ may occur at the beginning of a word and this is sometimes difficult for English speakers to pronounce. Say (   )X and then while only *thinking* the first syllable, try saying: /SÁD͡SI/

16. In word-initial position, then, think of an unpronounced vowel before pronouncing syllables like:

    (/D͡SI/)X (/D͡SA/)X (/D͡SU/)X
    (/D͡SE/)X (/D͡Sɛ/)X (/D͡SO/)X (/D͡Sɔ/)X

* * * * *

17. In Italian, as contrasted with English, no word is normally spelled with *ts* or *ds*.

18. In Italian there is no difference in the spelling representations of the following two sound-types—/T͡S/ and /D͡S/. Some words are spelled with a single *z* while other words use two *z's*.

19. The general rule for whether a word is written with one *z* or two *z's* is the following: Two *z's* are normally used *only* between vowel letters, but *not* before the semivowel /Y/. In the latter as in other cases, only one *z* is normal.

20. Thus, repeat the following words, carefully pronouncing one sound-type (that is, /T͡S/) for the left-hand column and the other sound-type—/D͡S/ for the right-hand column. Notice that these units use ż or żż for the words in the second column, although conventional Italian spelling has no such cut (') above any z.

/T͡S/		/D͡S/	
(razza)X	"race [= breed, lineage]"	(rażża)X	"skate" [type of fish]
(Lazio)X	"Latium" [Italian region]	(ażiɛnda)X	"business firm"
(zio)X	"uncle"	(żɛro)X	"zero"
(stanza)X	"room"	(prานżo)X	"dinner [= most important meal of the day]"
(Firɛnze)X	"Florence"		
(indirizzo)X	"address"		

*21. You have already had /T͡S/ in the following two Italian words. Write them correctly.
    raddrizza *grazie*
    "(s)he straightens" "thanks"

*22. Does the spelling of the two words in the preceding frame follow the general rule mentioned in frame no. 19?

*23. Here are two new words. Notice their spelling. Which one is an exception to the general rule of frame no. 19?
    (nazista)X   (razzista)X
    "nazi"   "racist"

*24. Here are two more new words. Notice their spelling. Which one is an exception to the general rule of frame no. 19?
    (ażalɛa)X   (ażżardo)X
    "azalea"   "hazard, risk"

*25. Are both of the following sound-types—/T͡S/ and /D͡S/ represented in conventional Italian spelling by the same letter or letters?

*26. Would it be easy, therefore, for you to know whether an unfamiliar Italian word spelled with z is to be pronounced /T͡S/ or /D͡S/?

27. The situation in Italian is complicated by the fact that there are many words spelled with z that are pronounced one way (that is, with /T͡S/) by some Italians and another way (that is, with /D͡S/) by other Italians.

28. Because it is very difficult to give any simple rule concerning /T͡S/ and /D͡S/ in Italian, what will be depicted in these units will be the most usual dictionary pronunciation, that is, the one based on Tuscan. /T͡S/ will be represented as z or zz and /D͡S/ will be represented as ż or żż.

29. It must be emphasized, however, that acceptable differences from the pronunciation depicted here are to be expected from native speakers of Italian.

30. One such noteworthy exception is found in the many Italian speakers who pronounce /D͡S/ (never /T͡S/) at the beginning of words spelled with initial z. Here are some words spelled with initial z. Repeat each word, first according to the Tuscan pronunciation depicted, then with initial /D͡S/. Before pronouncing these words, review frames no. 8 and no. 16.

	/T͡S/	/D͡S/
	(Tuscan pronunciation)	
zappa	( )X	( )X
"hoe"		
zia	( )X	( )X
"aunt"		
zitto	( )X	( )X
"quiet, silent"		
zɔppo		
"lame"		
zucchero	( )X	( )X
"sugar"		
zuppa	( )X	( )X
"soup"		

	/D͡S/	/D͡S/
	(Tuscan pronunciation)	
żɛbra	( )X	( )X
"zebra"		

žɛlo   (   )X   (   )X
　　"zeal"
žero   (   )X   (   )X
žinco   (   )X   (   )X
　　"zinc"
žɔna   (   )X   (   )X
　　"zone"
žɔo   (   )X   (   )X
　　"zoo"

31. Notice that the last six words given above are all cognates of English words spelled with initial *z*. This fact may help to remind you of which words should (according to dictionaries) be pronounced with initial /D͡S/.

* * * * *

*32. Do all consonant sound-types in Italian show the SLACK-TENSE distinction mentioned in Unit 25?

33. You have now had five Italian sound-types that you should *always* treat as TENSE. They are: /Ň/, /Ľ/, /š/ /T͡S/ and /D͡S/. Repeat the following words, pronouncing these five sound-types very strongly.

(bagno)X	/BAŇO/	"bathroom"
(aglio)X	/ÁĽO/	"garlic"
(fascio)X	/FÁŠO/	"bundle"
(Venɛzia)X	/VENÉT͡SYA/	"Venice"
(ažiendale)X	/AD͡SYENDÁLE/	"of the business"

* * * * *

34. In Unit 13 you were told of a regional pronunciation (mainly Central and Southern Italian) that has /T͡S/ instead of /S/ after some consonants. Thus, the following three words might be heard with /T͡S/ in them. Repeat them here as we advised in Unit 13, that is, with /S/.

(sɛnso)X	/SÉNSO/	"sense"
(salsa)X	/SÁLSA/	"sauce"
(discorso)X	/DISKÓRSO/	"speech"

* * * * *

*35. Now here is a review of all the Italian words that have appeared so far in this unit. As you hear each word, repeat it and write it below. Be careful. Not all these words have z or ż in them. (See Answer section for correct spelling.)

(1) _____   (19) _____

(2) _____   (20) _____

(3) _____   (21) _____

(4) _____   (22) _____

(5) _____   (23) _____

(6) _____   (24) _____

(7) _____   (25) _____

(8) _____   (26) _____

(9) _____   (27) _____

(10) _____   (28) _____

(11) _____   (29) _____

(12) _____   (30) _____

(13) _____   (31) _____

(14) _____   (32) _____

(15) _____   (33) _____

(16) _____   (34) _____

(17) _____   (35) _____

(18) _____

* * * * *

36. /T͡S/ appears in the frequently used word-ending (or suffix) -*zione*. This suffix corresponds to the English "-tion" or "-ction" and sometimes even "-ption."

37. Repeat the following words with this suffix. These words are related to the SYNCOPATED INFINITIVES listed in Unit 26, frame no. 22.

(posizione)X	(trazione)X	(adduzione)X
(composizione)X	(attrazione)X	(conduzione)X
(deposizione)X	(contrazione)X	(deduzione)X
(disposizione)X	(detrazione)X	(induzione)X
(esposizione)X	(distrazione)X	(introduzione)X
(imposizione)X	(protrazione)X	(produzione)X
(opposizione)X	(ritrazione)X	(riduzione)X
(posposizione)X	(sottrazione)X	(seduzione)X
(predisposizione)X		(traduzione)X
(preposizione)X		
(proposizione)X		
(supposizione)X		

*38. Translate the worus listed in frame no. 37, almost all of which have English cognates in "-tion" or "-ction."

39. Here are some more words in *-zione*. These are related to the verbs *ꝺdire* (those on the left) and *ꝺfare* (those on the right).

(dizione)X	(fazione)X
(benedizione)X	(soddisfazione)X
(contraddizione)X	
(maledizione)X	
(predizione)X	

*40. Translate the words listed in the preceding frame. Don't worry if you don't get the last one.

41. Here are some more words in *-zione*. These are related to verbs you have already had.

    (1) (abitazione)X
    (2) (accelerazione)X
    (3) (agevolazione)X
    (4) (applicazione)X
    (5) (aspettazione)X
    (6) (considerazione)X
    (7) (esportazione)X
    (8) (importazione)X
    (9) (manipolazione)X
    (10) (partecipazione)X
    (11) (prenotazione)x
    (12) (spiegazione)x
    (13) (volizione)x

*42. Try to give the infinitives of the verbs referred to in the preceding frame.

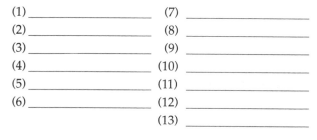

(1) _____   (7) _____
(2) _____   (8) _____
(3) _____   (9) _____
(4) _____   (10) _____
(5) _____   (11) _____
(6) _____   (12) _____
                        (13) _____

*43. What are the English cognates of all the words listed in frame no. 41 except *agevolazione* and *prenotazione?*

*44. Here is a long list of words in *-zione.* As you hear each one, repeat it and immediately try to give its English cognate before you hear it on the tape.

cognates in "-tion"

(addizione)X	
(alimentazione)X	"feeding, state or manner of being nourished"
(ambizione)X	
(assimilazione)X	
(attenzione)X	
(autorizzazione)X	
(aviazione)X	"Air Force"
(circolazione)X	
(circonvallazione)X	"circumferential road"
(coalizione)X	
(collaborazione)X	
(concentrazione)X	
(condizione)X	
(congratulazione)X	
(consolazione)X	
(contestazione)X	"protest"
(continuazione)X	
(coronazione)X	
(costituzione)X	
(dilazione)X	"extension" [of time]
(direzione)X	"management"
(emozione)X	
(esagerazione)X	
(giustificazione)X	
(indicazione)X	
(inflazione)X	
(informazione)X	
(integrazione)X	
(intenzione)X	
(investigazione)X	

49. Notice how the Italian stress on the singular verb forms parallels the
    English stress on most of the corresponding cognates.

Italian	English
(abita)X	(inhabit)X
(accelera)X	(accelerate)X
(applica)X	(applicator)X
(assimila)X	(assimilate)X
(collabora)X	(collaborate)X
(congratula)X	(congratulate)X
(considera)X	(consider)X
(esagera)X	(exaggerate)X
(indica)X	(indicate)X
(integra)X	(integrate)X
(investiga)X	(investigate)X
(irrita)X	(irritate)X
(limita)X	(limit)X
(litiga)X	(litigate)X
(manipola)X	(manipulate)X
(partecipa)X	(participate)X
(preoccupa)X	(preoccupy)X

• **End of Tape 10B** •

```
 ⊙        ⊙
 Tape 11A
```

*50. Now you will hear -*zione* words from frame no. 48 again. As you hear each
     one, repeat it and immediately see if you can give its English cognate
     before you hear it on the tape. (See answer section for Italian words.)

*51. You will now hear English words from frame no. 49. As you hear each one
     give the PRESENT TENSE LEI FORM of the corresponding Italian cognate
     without reading it from frame no. 49. Your response will be confirmed each
     time.

*52. Study the following model.

S: Vorrei domandare una raccomandazione.
  "I'd like to ask for a recommendation."
R: Domandi una raccomandazione!
  "Ask for a recommendation!"

You will hear a statement as in the model. Reply as in the model by using the appropriate REQUEST FORM. Your response will be confirmed each time.

(1) Vorrei portare una soluzione.
(2) ....spiegare una situazione.
(3) ....ascoltare una trascrizione.
(4) ....domandare una promozione.
(5) ....cominciare una trasformazione.
(6) ....ritornare con una condizione.
(7) ....domandare una raccomandazione.

*53. Study the following model.

S: Dĕvo tradurre?   "Do I have to translate?"
R: Sì, vorrei una traduzione,   "Yes, I'd like a translation, please."
  per favore.

Answer the questions you will hear as in the model, by using the appropriate -*zione* word. Your response will be confirmed each time.

(1) Dĕvo deporre?
(2) ....sottrarre?
(3) ....investigare?
(4) ....prenotare?
(5) ....tradurre?

*54. Study the following model.

S: Vorrei una traduzione,   "I'd like a translation, please."
  per favore.
R: Bene; dĕvo tradurre ora?   "Fine! Do I have to translate now?"

This is the opposite of the previous drill. Use the appropriate infinitive in your response which will be confirmed each time.

(1) Vorrei una deposizione, per favore.
(2) ....una sottrazione, per favore.
(3) ....un'investigazione, per favore.
(4) ....una prenotazione, per favore.
(5) ....una traduzione, per favore.

*55. Study the following model.

> S: Quando propongo che cɔsa   "When I propose something, what
>   faccio?   am I doing?"
> R: Fa una proposizione.   "You're making a proposition."

Answer the questions you will hear as in the model, by using the appropriate -zione word. Your response will be confirmed each time.

(1) Quando deduco che cɔsa faccio?
(2) ....compongo che cɔsa faccio?
(3) ....impongo che cɔsa faccio?
(4) ....espongo che cɔsa faccio?
(5) ....esagero che cɔsa faccio?
(6) ....propongo che cɔsa faccio?

*56. Study the following model.

> S: Quando autoriżża che cɔsa dà?   "When you authorize, what are
>   you giving?"
> R: Dɔ un'autorizzazione.   "I'm giving an authorization."

Answer the questions you will hear as in the model, by using the appropriate -zione word. Your response will be confirmed each time.

(1) Quando indica che cɔsa dà?
(2) ....informa che cɔsa dà?
(3) ....ispira che cɔsa dà?
(4) ....raccomanda che cɔsa dà?
(5) ....agevola che cɔsa dà?
(6) ....benedice che cɔsa dà?
(7) ....autoriżża che cɔsa dà?

*57. Translate the following into Italian.

(1) "a consulate"   -_____
(2) "one loaf of bread"   -_____
(3) "an Italian" (male)   -_____
(4) "one man"   -_____

*58. Now translate the following into Italian.

    (1) "a gnome"   - _____

    (2) "one mistake"   - _____

    (3) "a student" (male) - _____

    (4) "a strike"   - _____

*59. In Unit 22 you were told that the MASCULINE UNIT MARKER *uno* (and not *un*) occurs (among other places) before words that begin with *gn*. Where else?

60. Another place where *uno* (and not *un*) is found is before MASCULINE words beginning with the letter *z* (whether the *z* represents /T͡S/ or /D͡S/).

61. The following are words from frame no. 35 that begin with the letter *z*. They are all MASCULINE. Repeat each one used here with its correct UNIT MARKER.

(uno zio)X	(uno żɛlo)X
(uno zɔppo)X	(uno żero)X
(uno zucchero)X	(uno żinco)X
	(uno żɔo)X

*62. How do you say, "He's an uncle" in Italian?

*63. Without using the word *uɔmo*, how do you say, "He's a lame man" in Italian?

*64. How do you say, "It's a zero" in Italian?

*65. How do you say, "There's a zoo there" in Italian?

*66. How do you say, "She's an aunt" in Italian?

*67. How do you say, "one (kind of) sugar" in Italian?

*68. Without using the words *dɔnna* or *persona,* translate "She's a lame person" in Italian.

*69. In addition to the preceding cases, *uno* (and not *un*) occurs before the relatively few words beginning with *pn-, ps-,* and *x-* (representing /KS/), and before any other consonant group not normally found at the beginning of an Italian word.

70. Thus:

(uno pneumạtico)X	"a pneumatic tire"
(uno psichiatra)X	"a (male) psychiatrist"
(uno xilɔgrafo)X	"a xylographer"
(uno bdellịo)X	[name of a resin]

*71. If *psicologo* and *xilofono* are the Italian words for "psychologist" and "xylo-
phone," respectively, how would you translate the following sentences into
Italian?
"It's a psychologist."   -_____
"It's a xylophone."   -_____

*72. Translate the following into Italian.
(1) "one bathroom"   -_____
(2) "one risk"   -_____
(3) "one (male) student"   -_____
(4) "one ski"   -_____
(5) "one gnome"   -_____
(6) "one uncle"   -_____
(7) "one race"
   [= breed, lineage]"   -_____
(8) "one business firm"   -_____

*73. Is the Italian word for "one" different from the UNIT MARKER?

*74. Does the form of the Italian word for "one" depend on the word following
it?

*75. Give the plural of the following items:

bagno   _____ ⎫
ażżardo   _____ ⎪
studente   _____ ⎬ MASCULINE
sci   _____ ⎪
gnomo   _____ ⎪
zio   _____ ⎭

razza   _____ ⎫ FEMININE
ażienda   _____ ⎭

76. Now repeat the following.
(due bagni)X   (tre bagni)X   (quattro bagni)X
(due studenti)X   (tre studenti)X   (quattro studenti)X
(due ażiende)X   (tre ażiende)X   (quattro ażiende)X

*77. Judging from the preceding frame, would you say that the form of the Italian
word for "two," "three," or "four" depends on the word that follows?

78. As a matter of fact, although the Italian word for "one" has various forms, most of the other cardinal numerals in Italian are INVARIABLE (that is, have only one form).

79. Repeat the following familiar numerals as in counting. Notice that the MASCULINE form *uno* is used in counting.

(żero)X (uno)X (due)X (tre)X (quattro)X

80. Now repeat the following numerals:

(cinque)X	"5"	(cinque)X
(sɛi)X	"6"	(sɛi)X
(sɛtte)X	"7"	(sɛtte)X
(ɔtto)X	"8"	(ɔtto)X
(nɔve)X	"9"	(nɔve)X
(diɛci)X	"10"	(diɛci)x

81. In arithmetic, Italians often use the word *più* for adding and the word *meno* for subtracting. These words are actually cognates of the English "plus" and "minus" respectively.

82. Look at the following and repeat:

(0 più 0 fa 0.)X
(1 più 1 fa 2.)X
(2 + 2 = 4)X
(3 + 3 = 6)X
(4 + 4 = 8)X
(5 + 5 = 10)X

83. Look at the following and repeat:

(1 meno 1 fa 0.)X
(3 meno 2 fa l.)X
(5 - 3 = 2)X
(7 - 4 =3)
(9 - 5 = 4)X

84. Here are the cardinal numerals from eleven through twenty. Repeat.

(ųndici)X	"11"	(ųndici)X
(dǫdici)X	"12"	(dǫdici)X
(trẹdici)X	"13"	(trẹdici)X
(quattôrdici)X	"14"	(quattôrdici)X
(quịndici)X	"15"	(quịndici)X
(sẹdici)X	"16"	(sẹdici)X
(diciassɛtte)X	"17"	(diciassɛtte)X
(diciɔtto)X	"18"	(diciɔtto)X

32)_____

33)_____

34)_____

35)_____

TEST B

(answers not recorded)

You will hear words in *-zione*. As you hear each one, write the INFINITIVE that corresponds to it.

1)_____

2)_____

3)_____

4)_____

5)_____

6)_____

7)_____

8)_____

9)_____

10)_____

11)_____

12)_____

13)_____

14)_____

15)_____

16)_____

17)_____

18)_____

19)_____

20)_____

TEST C

(answers not recorded)

You will hear some INFINITIVES. As you hear each one, write its PRESENT
TENSE LEI FORM.

1)_____

2)_____

3)_____

4)_____

5)_____

6)_____

7)_____

8)_____

9)_____

10)_____

11)_____

12)_____

13)_____

14)_____

15)_____

16)_____

17)_____

18)_____

19)_____

20)_____

TEST D

(not recorded)

For each of the LEI FORMS of TEST C write the word in *-zione* that corresponds
to it.

1)_____

2)_____

3)_____

4)_____

5)_____

6)_____

7)_____

8)_____

9)_____

10)_____

11)_____

12)_____

13)_____

14)_____

15)_____

16)_____

17)_____

18)_____

19)_____

20)_____

TEST E

(answers not recorded)

You will hear a GENDERABLE that you have had. Write the word as you hear
it and put before it *un, uno, un', una* or *due,* whichever is appropriate.

1)_____

2)_____

3)_____   _____(two ways)

4)_____

5)_____

6)_____

7)_____

8)_____

9)_____

10)_____

11)_____

12)_____   _____(two ways)

13)_____

14)_____   _____(two ways)

15)_____

16)_____

17)_____

18)_____

19)_____

20)_____

21)_____   _____(two ways)

22)_____

23)_____

24)_____

25)_____

26)_____

27)_____

28)_____

29)_____

30)_____

31)_____
32)_____
33)_____
34)_____
35)_____
36)_____
37)_____   _____(two ways)

TEST F

(answers not recorded)

You will hear some *Quanto fa....?* questions. For each one write a number indicating the answer on the lines below.

1)_____   12)_____
2)_____   13)_____
3)_____   14)_____
4)_____   15)_____
5)_____   16)_____
6)_____   17)_____
7)_____   18)_____
8)_____   19)_____
9)_____   20)_____
10)_____   21)_____
11)_____

TEST G

(not recorded)

Translate the following thoughts into Italian by using *only* what has been presented so far.

1) I only have one uncle. How about you?

_____

2) Dr. Rossi works only fifteen days per month.

_____

3) She should have a solution for this.

_____

4) I could consider a coalition.

5) Tell her that I have only two rooms.

6) It's not a six; it's a zero.

7) Isn't there a reservation for Mr. Brown?

8) It's a way of giving nourishment.

9) Yes, it is both a nation and a city.

10) You won't find ⎱ corruption here.
    We don't have ⎰

11) What is it, doctor? An infection?

12) Congratulations! Two promotions! – Would you like a justification for two promotions?

13) Was there a strike in Rome the day before yesterday?

14) You must have dialed the wrong number; this is 3564890.

15) No, it's not a promotion. It's only a recommendation.

16) Does Rome have only one circumferential road?

17) We don't like it because it is an imposition.

18) Do you know a psychiatrist in Florence?

19) I can't come this morning. I have to listen to a speech.

20) Can you do a translation for tomorrow, please?

21) He has two places of residence, one in Rome and one in the north.

_____

22) Seven from twenty is thirteen, right?

_____

23) There will be a demonstration today. There was one yesterday, you know.

_____

24) Must I subtract? Why?

_____

25) I have to study sixteen lessons and I only have six days.

_____

26) He should explain this, but he doesn't like to give explanations.

_____

27) She is always on the phone. It's too much! (literally: "It's an exaggeration!")

_____

28) You'll find a bathroom on the left, and there's one on the right, too.

_____

29) He has two uncles. One owns a business firm for imports and exports.

_____

30) Isn't it a contradiction? I thought he was young. (HINT: Put this idea into Italian in the form of a question.)

_____

31) You are not ready, Mr. Jones, Why don't you ask for an extension?

_____

32) It's an investigation. Will there be a protest now?

_____

33) There is always some kind of interruption. I can never work well here.

_____

34) How come you never want to participate?

_____

35) Tell him that I need { an extension of four days.
                          { a four-day extension.

_____

36) I'm not exaggerating! He works hard every day and on Saturdays he goes to school where he studies English.

_____

37) I won't be in tomorrow. I suggest you call back in a few days.

_____

38) There is always a crisis here. Who can give an authorization?

___

39) But why does he do this? Doesn't he ever justify anything?

___

40) There will be a review tomorrow. Study well! (said in a highly formal situation addressing more than one person.)

___

FRAME ANSWERS

FRAME 35.

agilo	grazie	salsa	zio
ażalea	indirizzo	sɛnso	żinco
aziɛnda	Lazio	stanza	zitto
ażviendale	nazista	Venɛzia	żɔna
ażżardo	pranżo	zappa	żɔo
bagno	raddrizza	żebra	zoppo
discorso	razza	żelo	zucchero
fascio	rażża	żero	zuppa
Firɛnze	razzista	zia	

FRAME 50.

abitazione	litigazione
collaborazione	irritazione
esagerazione	considerazione
giustificazione	assimilazione
indicazione	accelerazione
limitazione	integrazione
manipolazione	congratulazione
partecipazione	applicazione
ratificazione	investigazione
preoccupazione	

FRAME 89.
(1) Quindici meno sɛtte fa ɔtto.
(2) Diciassɛtte più tre fa venti.
(3) Diciannɔve meno cinque fa quattôrdici.
(4) Diciassɛtte meno diciassɛtte fa żero.
(5) Ɔtto più ųndici fa diciannɔve.
(6) Diciassɛtte meno quindici fa due.
(7) Sɛdici meno trɛdici fa tre.
(8) Ɔtto più nɔve fa diciassɛtte.
(9) Dɔdici meno ɔtto fa quattro.
(10) Nɔve più sɛtte fa sedici.

TEST A ANSWERS

1) bagno	11) zappa	21) ażiendale	31) ražża
2) raddrizza	12) pranżo	22) zɔppo	32) zio
3) Venɛzia	13) ażalɛa	23) discorso	33) fascio
4) żɛlo	14) zucchẹro	24) żɔna	34) żinco
5) żɔo	15) nazista	25) grazie	35) indirizzo
6) zuppa	16) żɛro	26) razza	
7) stanza	17) sɛnso	27) zitto	
8) razzista	18) ażiɛnda	28) Firɛnze	
9) aglio	19) zia	29) salsa	
10) ażżardo	20) Lazio	30) żɛbra	

TEST B ANSWERS

1) posizione	porre
2) fazione	fare
3) abitazione	abitare
4) volizione	volere
5) ratificazione	ratificare
6) preoccupazione	preoccupare
7) raccomandazione	raccomandare
8) traduzione	tradurre
9) proposizione	proporre
10) autorizżazione	autorizżare
11) trazione	trarre
12) dizione	dire
13) produzione	produrre
14) supposizione	supporre
15) agevolazione	agevolare
16) prenotazione	prenotare
17) spiegazione	spiegare
18) distrazione	distrarre
19) limitazione	limitare
20) contraddizione	contraddire

TEST C   ANSWERS

1) benedire	benedice	11) partecipare	partecipa
2) aspettare	aspetta	12) irritare	irrita
3) fare	fa	13) limitare	limita
4) applicare	applica	14) ridurre	riduce
5) volere	vuole	15) abitare	abita
6) comporre	compone	16) indicare	indica
7) preoccupare	preoccupa	17) agevolare	agevola
8) tradurre	traduce	18) posporre	pospone
9) considerare	considera	19) sottrarre	sottrae
10) attrarre	attrae	20) sedurre	seduce

TEST D   ANSWERS

1) benedizione	11) partecipazione
2) aspettazione	12) irritazione
3) fazione	13) limitazione
4) applicazione	14) riduzione
5) volizione	15) abitazione
6) composizione	16) indicazione
7) preoccupazione	17) agevolazione
8) traduzione	18) posposizione
9) considerazione	19) sottrazione
10) attrazione	20) seduzione

TEST E   ANSWERS

1) pôsto	un pôsto	20) bagno	un bagno
2) ambasciate	due ambasciate	21) razzista	un razzista
3) sci	uno sci - due sci		una razzista
4) scɛna	una scɛna	22) scïovịe	due scïovịe
5) tavolọ	un tạvolo	23) fascio	un fascio
6) razze	due razze	24) zụcchero	uno zụcchero
7) zio	uno zio	25) scemo	uno scemo
8) stanza	una stanza	26) aglio	un aglio
9) ażienda	un'ażienda	27) żɔne	due żɔne
10) żɛro	uno żɛro	28) sɛnso	un sɛnso
11) pranżo	un pranżo	29) xilɔfono	uno xilɔfono
12) scià	uno scià - due scià	30) salse	due salse
13) stazioni	due stazioni	31) corso	un corso
14) nazista	un nazista –	32) posizione	una posizione
	una nazista	33) agevolazione	un'agevolazione
15) ażalɛa	un'ażalɛa	34) lezione	una lezione
16) ażżardo	un ażżardo	35) sbaglio	uno sbaglio
17) zappa	una zappa	36) telɛfono	un telɛfono
18) sciɔpero	uno sciɔpero	37) psichiatra	uno psichiatra-
19) zia	una zia		una psichiatra

TEST F   ANSWERS

1) Quanto fa 0 + 10?	10	12) ....16 - 16?	0
2) ....1 + 4?	5	13) ....2 + 18?	20
3) ....11 - 3?	8	14) ....8 + 7?	15
4) ....20 - 6?	14	15) ....17 - 16?	1
5) ....19 + 1?	20	16) ....6 + 7?	13
6) ....2 + 14?	16	17) ....15 - 13?	2
7) ....5 + 13?	18	18) ....12 - 1?	11
8) ....7 + 12?	19	19) ....1 + 2?	3
9) ....8 + 9?	17	20) ....4 + 5?	9
10) ....15 - 3?	12	21) ....20 - 16?	4
11) ....17 - 3?	14		

TEST G   ANSWERS

1) Hɔ soltanto uno zio. E Lɛi?
2) Il dottor Rossi lavora soltanto quindici giorni ogni mese.
3) Dovrĕbbe avere una soluzione per questo.
4) Potrɛi considerare una coalizione.
5) Le dica che hɔ soltanto due stanze.
6) Non ɛ un sɛi; è uno żero.
7) Non c'ɛ una prenotazione per il signor Brown?
8) È un'alimentazione.
9) Sì, è una nazione e anche una città.
10) Non c'è corruzione qui.
11) Che cɔs'è, dottore? Un'infezione?
12) Congratulazioni! Due promozioni! - Vorrĕbbe una giustificazione per due promozioni?
13) C'ɛra uno sciɔpero a Roma avantiɛri?
14) Avrà sbagliato numero; questo è 3-5-6-4-8-9-0
15) Nɔ, non è una promozione. È soltanto una raccomandazione.
16) Roma ha soltanto una circonvallazione?
17) Non ci piace perchè è un'imposizione.
18) Conosce uno psichiatra a Firɛnze?
19) Non pɔsso venire stamattina. Dĕvo ascoltare un discorso.
20) Puɔ fare una traduzione per domani, per favore?
21) Ha due abitazioni, una a Roma e una nel Nɔrd.
22) Venti meno sɛtte fa trɛdici, nɔ?
23) Ci sarà una manifestazione ɔggi. Ce n'ɛra una iɛri, sa
24) Dĕvo sottrarre? Perchè?
25) Dĕvo studiare sɛdici lezioni e hɔ soltanto sɛi giorni.
26) Dovrĕbbe spiegare questo, ma non gli piace dare spiegazioni.
27) È sɛmpre al telɛfono. È un'esagerazione!
28) C'è un bagno a sinistra, e ce n'è uno anche a dɛstra.
29) Ha due zii. Uno ha un'ażienda per importazioni ed esportazioni.

30) Non è una contraddizione? Non è giovane?
33) Lei non è pronto, signor Jones. Perchè non domanda una dilazione?
32) È un'investigazione. Ci sarà una contestazione ora?

33) C'è sempre qualche un'} interruzione. Non posso mai lavorare bene qui.
34) Perchè non vuole mai partecipare?
35) Gli dica che dĕvo avere una dilazione di quattro giorni.
36) Non esagero! Lavora molto ogni giorno e il sabato va a scuola dove studia
    inglese.
37) Non ci sarò domani. Richiami fra quache giorno. (or)
    Non ci sarò domani. Vuol richiamare fra qualche giorno? (or)
    Non ci sarò domani. Può richiamare fra qualche giorno?
38) C'è sempre una crisi qui. Chi può dare un'autorizzazione?
39) Ma perchè fa questo? Non giustifica mai niente?
40) Ci sarà una ripetizione domani. Studino bene!

UNIT 28

1.-2. If *pa* constitutes one SYLLABLE, how many SYLLABLES does the word *papa* constitute?

*3. How many SYLLABLES does the name *Amanda* have?

 4. If we divide the name *Amanda* into syllables we can show this by writing *A-man-da* with a SYLLABLE BREAK before *man* and another before *da*.

 5. In spoken Italian every syllable contains one VOWEL with or without one or more CONSONANTS or SEMIVOWELS.

*6. How many syllables, therefore, does each of the following words constitute?

    a   sɔ   sta   più   puɔ

 7. The act of dividing a word or phrase into syllables is called SYLLABICA-TION.

 8. In spoken Italian, syllables are separated in such a way that a SYLLABIC BREAK occurs *before* one of the following:

    a) a vowel that is preceded by another vowel
    b) a semivowel that is between vowels
    c) a single consonant sound-type (but see Unit 25, frame no. 24)
    d) the last consonant of a group
           or
    the entire group when it is represented by

$$\left.\begin{array}{c} p \\ b \\ t \\ d \\ c \\ g \\ f \\ v \end{array}\right\} \; + \; \left\{\begin{array}{c} l \\ r \end{array}\right.$$

*9. Thus, rewrite the following items in syllables to reflect the above rules.

    a) *zio*   - _____
    b) *l'Aia*
        "the Hague"   - _____

    c) *italiano*   -_____

       ogni   -_____

    d) *salsa*   -_____

      questo   -_____

      żebra   -_____

10. In Unit 25, frame no. 16 you learned that in Italian, stressed vowels preceding SLACK consonants are usually *longer* than stressed vowels preceding TENSE consonants.

*11. Thus, the stressed vowel in which of the following three words is longest?

    (pa̱pa)X   (pa̱ppa)X   (o̱gni)X
      a   b   c

12. Keeping the above in mind as a category in itself, one may add that in general, stressed vowels that *end syllables* are longer than those that do not end syllables.

*13. Thus, of the examples listed in frame no. 9, the stressed vowel of *ogni* is relatively short (see frame no. 11) like the stressed vowel of which two other words in the same list?

14. Italian SYLLABICATION is important in speech because a wrong SYLLABIC BREAK is often disturbing to the ear.

15. Since most Italian words end in a vowel, Italians prefer to end syllables in vowels whenever possible.

16. Thus, in the following breath groups, the consonant of the first word is pronounced in the same syllable as the *following vowel.*

                       with syllabic breaks.
    (in inglese)X   i-nin-gle-se
    (un'ażienda)X   u-na-żien-da

17. Repeat the following, keeping the SYLLABICATION rules in mind.
    (in italiano)X   (un insegnante)X

                      * * * * *

18. Italian SYLLABICATION is important in writing or printing since one needs to know what Italians do when they reach the end of a line on which there is only enough room for part of a word.

19. In writing and printing,the SYLLABICATION rule given in frame no. 8 is generally followed. However, there are four important exceptions.

20. One exception is that combinations of vowel letters (a, e, ε, i, o, ɔ, u) are generally not separated.

*21. Thus, does the SYLLABICATION shown in frame no. 9 for *zio* and *l'Aia* apply to writing or printing?

*22. In writing,when you have reached the end of a line should you ever separate the vowel letters in either of these two words — *zio, l'Aia?*

23. Another exception is that TENSE consonants represented by a symbol containing two like consonant letters or by -*cq*- show a SYLLABIC BREAK between the two consonant letters involved.

*24. Thus, rewrite the following words, showing the SYLLABIC BREAK that would occur in the written or printed form.

razza	- _____
zuppa	- _____
acqua	- _____
vacche	
"cows"	- _____

25. Still another exception is that *s* before a consonant is normally not separated from the consonant it precedes.

*26. Thus, does the SYLLABICATION shown in frame no. 9 for *questo* apply to writing or printing?

*27. Rewrite the word *questo*, showing the SYLLABIC BREAK that would occur in the written or printed form.

_____

28. Finally, some writers separate a PREFIX from the rest of the written word.

29. Thus, despite all that was said before, they would divide the following two words as:

   dis-po-si-zio-ne (PREFIX: *dis-*)
   in-a̬-bi-le "incapable" (PREFIX: *in-*)

30. In addition to these guidelines, students should know that some writers or printers dislike having the last word of a line end in an apostrophe. Because of this, you may find the full, unapostrophized word at the end of a line. For example:

.... una
artista...

31. However, not everybody conforms to the above, and apostrophes at the
end of a line are currently not uncommon. Thus,
.... un'
artista...

* * * * *

32. In Unit 26, verb forms like the following were given:

(ascolto)X	(ascolta)X
(desidero)X	(desidera)X
(vedo)X	(vede)X
(dico)X	(dice)X
(capisco)X	(capisce)X
(sɛnto)X	(sɛnte)X

*33. The forms in the left-hand column above were called IO FORMS. What do
we call the forms in the right-hand column?

34. Besides these two forms, Italian verbs show variations for other persons or
things.

35. One of these variations is the one used to refer to the person speaking *plus*
one or more people.

36. For the PRESENT TENSE this verb form always ends in *-iamo*. Thus:
(ascoltiamo)X
(desideriamo)X
(vediamo)X
(diciamo)X
(capiamo)X
(sentiamo)X

*37. If the English word "I" may be said to correspond to the verb-ending *-o* or
ɔ, what may the English word "we" be said to correspond to in the six
examples listed in frame no. 36?

*38. Translate the following into Italian.
a) We are listening.   -_____
b) We see.   -_____
c) We understand.   -_____

* * * * *

39. In the formation of this verb form, as in the formation of some other verb forms, you will have to remember the *i* RULE. Here it is.
"Two *i's* together are not normally found in the spelling of Italian words unless the first one stands for a stressed /I/."

40. Thus, the formations below yield the forms on the right.

(verb stem)		(verb ending)	(pronounced)	
mangi-	+	-iamo	= (mangiamo)X	/MANǦAMO/
studi-	+	-iamo	= (studiamo)X	/STUDYÁMO/
scï-	+	-iamo	= (scïamo)X	/ŠIÁMO/

*41. Translate the following into Italian.
   a) We begin.   - _____
   b) We are leaving a little sauce *there*. - _____
   c) We err [= make mistakes]. [Use +sbagliare.]

42. The *i* RULE of frame no. 39 also applies to the formation of PLURAL GEN-DERABLES.

43. Thus, the formations below yield the forms on the right.

(singular)	(singular stem)		(plural ending)		
(bacio)X	baci-	+	-i		= (baci)X "kisses"
(studio)X	studi-	+	-i		= (studi)X "studies; studios"
spεcie)X	spεci-	+	-i		(spεci)X "kinds"
BUT:					
(zio)X	zi-	+	-i		=(zii)X
	(with stressed /I/)				(pronounced:/T͡SÍI/)

*44. Give the plural of the following words.
   a) (atrïo)X -   - _____   "entrance halls"
   b) (aggravio)X -   - _____   "loads, burdens"

*45. Study the following model.
   S: Io dɔ un bacio.   "I give one kiss."
   R: Io dɔ due baci.   "I give two kisses."

As in the model, apply the verb form you hear to yourself, but change the GENDERABLE to the plural preceded by *due*. Your response will be confirmed each time.

(1) Io hɔ uno studio.	(6) Io faccio uno sbaglio.
(2) Io pɔrto an formaggio.	(7) Io desidero un ufficio.
(3) Io hɔ uno zio.	(8) Io hɔ an atrïo.
(4) Io vorrɛi un pomeriggio.	(9) Io produco un ɔlio.
(5) Io conosco una spɛcie.	(10) Io vedo un luccio.

46. The verb-ending *-iamo* is used to convey the idea of "we" for all PRESENT TENSE verbs, even though the *-i-* of *iamo* is not always needed to reflect the pronunciation. For example, the verb ⊥*sognare* /SOŇÁRE/ has *sogniamo* /SOŇÁMO/ even though the *-i-* here could have been omitted and the word would still be /SOŇÁMO/.

47. Sometimes in the formation of this verb form, as in the formation of some other verb forms, the spelling shows something that at first may seem peculiar but which is required in order to reflect the fact that a sound-type that occurs in the INFINITIVE is kept in the new verb form.

48. This happens in the case of verbs with infinitives in *-care* or *-gare*. With such verbs the letter is written after the *c* or *g* whenever these letters precede *e* or *i*.

49. Thus, ⊥*giocare* /ǦOKÁRE/ has *giochiamo* /ǦOKYÁMO/.

*50. What would the verbs ⊥*applicare* and ⊥*spiegare* be in this form?

51. The insertion of the letter *h* in verb forms like the above parallels what happens in the formation of certain PLURAL GENDERABLES.

52. For example, singular genderables ending in *-ca* or *-ga* generally insert *h* before the final *-e* or *-i* of the plural.

53. Thus, the formations below yield the forms on the right.

(singular)	(singular stem)		(plural ending)	
(pɛsca)X	pɛsc-	+	-e	= (pɛsche)X
				(pronounced: /PÉSKE/)
(vacca)X	vacc-	+	-e	= (vacche)X
(vôga)X	vôg-	+	-e	= (vôghe)X
				(pronounced: /VÔǴE/

*54. The following genderable ⊥*collega* "colleague" may refer to either a male or a female being and is therefore either MASCULINE or FEMININE. Write both the MASCULINE PLURAL and the FEMININE PLURAL forms below.

(masculine)_____(feminine)_____

55. The genderable ✝bɛlga "Belgian" is an exception in the masculine plural but *not* in the feminine plural.

*56. The masculine plural of this word is *bɛlgi*. What is the feminine plural?

57. The letter *h* is also used in the plural of most genderables that in the singular end in *-co*, provided the *-co* immediately follows the stressed syllable.

58. Thus, the formations below yield the forms on the right.

(singular)	(singular stem)		(plural ending)		(pronounced)
(fico)X	fic-	+	-i	=(fichi)X	/FÍKI/
(spɔrco)X "dirty"	spɔrc-	+	-i	=(spɔrchi)X	/SPƆ́RKI/

*59. Give the plural of the following two words.

    a) (baco)X   -_____

    b) (fuɔco)X   -_____

60. The following four masculine forms are exceptions to the statement of frame no. 57. Learn them.

		(plural)
(amico)X	"friend"	(amici)X
(grɛco)X	"Greek"	(grɛci)X
(nemico)X	"enemy"	(nemici)X
(pɔrco)X	"pig"	(pɔrci)X

*61. However, give the plural of the feminine forms below.

    a) (amica)X   -_____

    b) (grɛca)X   -_____

    c) (nɛmica)X   -_____

*62. Study the following model.

    S: C'è una pasta?   "Is there a peach?"

    R: Ci sôno due pɛsche.   "There are two peaches."

You will hear a *c'è* question involving a genderable in *-co, -ca,* or *-ga.* Reply by using *ci sôno* (which is the plural of *c'è*) + *due* + the appropriate plural genderable. In written Italian the plural genderables used here will always have the letter *h*, except for the masculine plurals *bɛlgi, amici, grɛci, nemici, pɔrci.*

    (1) C'è un alfresco?   (6) C'è un bɛlga?

    (2) C'è un'amica?   (7) C'è una bistecca?

    (3) C'è un amico?   (8) C'è un bɔsco?

    (4) C'è un baco?   (9) C'è un chiɔsco?

    (5) C'è una bɛlga?   (10) C'è una ciɛca?

(11) C'è un cieco?   (19) C'è un fuɔco?
(12) C'è una collega?   (20) C'è una greca?
(13) C'è un collega?   (21) C'è un greco?
(14) C'è una cuɔca?   (22) C'è una pesca?
(15) C'è un cuɔco?   (23) C'è un pɔrco?
(16) C'è una domenica?   (24) C'è una replica?
(17) C'è un fico?   (25) C'è una vacca?
(18) C'è una fuga?   (26) C'è una vôga?

63. Note that if a singular genderable ending in -*co* does not have the -*co* immediately following the stressed syllable the corresponding plural usually ends in -*ci*. Thus,

		(plural)
(medico)X	"doctor; medical"	(medici)X
(simpatico)X	"nice, pleasant"	(simpatici)X

*64. What is the plural of the following items?

    a) (diplomatico)X   "diplomat; diplomatic" -_____
    b) (fantastico)X   "fantastic"   -_____
    c) (magnifico)X   "magnificent"   -_____
    d) (politico)X   "politician; political"   -_____

*65. What is the plural of the following feminine forms?

    a) (diplomatica)X   -_____
    b) (fantastica)X   -_____
    c) (magnifica)X   -_____
    d) (medica)X   -_____
    e) (politica)X   -_____
    f) (simpatica)X   -_____

*66. Study the following model.

    S: Uno è medico?   "One is medical?"
    R: Nɔ, due sôno medici.   "No, two are medical."

You will hear a question involving a genderable in -*co* or -*ca*. Reply as in the model by using the appropriate plural genderable. The genderables used here end in -*ci* in the masculine and -*che* in the feminine.

(1) Uno è diplomatico?   (7) Una è simpatica?
(2) Uno è fantastico?   (8) Uno è simpatico?
(3) Una è politica?   (9) Una è medica?
(4) Uno è medico?   (10) Uno è politico?
(5) Una è dipolomatica?   (11) Uno è magnifico?
(6) Una è fantastica?   (12) Una è magnifica?

• **End of Tape 11A** •

67. The plural of singular genderables ending in -*go* is for some words -*ghi*, for others -*gi* and for still others either -*ghi* or -*gi* indifferently.

68. It is very difficult to give simple guidelines in this regard other than to state that in most cases the plural of such words is in -*ghi* and that the plural of words in -*ɔlogo* or -*ɔfago* that refer to people is generally in -*gi*.

69. Thus:

		(plural)
(giôgo)X	"yoke"	(giôghi)X
(dïalogo)X	"dialogue"	(dïaloghi)X
(lago)X	"lake"	(laghi)X
(luɔgo)X	"place"	(luɔghi)X

BUT:

(astrɔlogo)X	"astrologist"	(astrɔlogi)X
(antropɔfago)X	"cannibal"	(antropɔfagi)X

*70. Give the plural of the following masculine items.
   a) (antropɔlogo)X   "anthropologist"   -_____
   b) (archeɔlogo)X   "archeologist"   -_____
   c) (filɔlogo)X   "philologist"   -_____
   d) (geɔlogo)X   "geologist"   -_____
   e) (teɔlogo)X   "theologian"   -_____

*71. Study the following model.
   S: C'è anche un lago?   "Is there a lake, too?"
   R: Non uno, ci sôno due laghi.   "Not one; there are two lakes."

You will hear a question involving a genderable in -*go*. Reply as in the model by using the appropriate plural genderable which sometimes ends in -*ghi* and sometimes ends in -*gi*.

   (1) C'è anche an antropɔfago?   (7) ....un geɔlogo?
   (2) ....un antropɔlogo? (8) ....un giôgo?
   (3) ....un archeɔlogo?   (9) ....un lago?
   (4) ....un astrɔlogo?   (10) ....un luɔgo?
   (5) ....un dïalogo?   (11) ....un teɔlogo?
   (6) ....un filɔlogo?

* * * * *

87. In the previous frame you should have written.
    a) Lavorano.
    b) Vanno lì.
    c) Stanno bɛne.
    d) Parlano italiano. (or) Parlano l'italiano.
    e) Bevono.
    f) Vɔgliono mangiare.
    g) Non pɔssono studiare qui.
    h) Che cɔsa dicono?
    i) Finiscono ɔggi?
    j) Che cɔsa fanno?
    k) Ɛscono ora.
    l) Vɛngono?
    m) My piacciono.

88. The exceptions to the rule of frame no. 85 are:

    ꝉɛssere - (sôno)X
    ꝉesserci - (ci sôno)X

*89. How do you say, "They are at home" in Italian?"

*90. How do you say, "I am at home" in Italian?"

91. ꝉɛssere is the only basic verb for which the IO FORM is identical to the form used to refer to "they."

* * * * *

92. You have now had five different PRESENT TENSE forms used to refer to different persons or things. For example:

    ascolto   ascoltiamo
                   ascoltate
    ascolta   ascoltano

93. As we may see from the preceding examples, the idea of different persons or things, expressed in English by words like "I," "you," "it," "he," "she," "we," and "they" is found in the endings of verbs in Italian.

*94. However, we saw in Unit 26 how Italians does have special words for "I," "you" (referring to one person), "he" and "she" when no verb form is used. What are these four words?

95. Similarly, special words for "we," "you" (referring to one person *plus* one or more people) and "they" (for people) are, respectively,

    (nɔi)X   (voi)X   (loro)X

*96. We saw in Unit 26 that the idea of "it" is not normally expressed in Italian by any word separate from the verb form in cases like the following. Translate.

    a) It is arriving.   -_____

    b) It is over there.   -_____

*97. Similarly, the idea of "they" referring to things is normally expressed in Italian by the ending of the verb. Translate.

    They are arriving.   -_____
    (talking about luggage)

*98. Translate the following into Italian. The word "work" is emphasized.

    Does he *work*?   -_____

*99. Now translate the sentence below that emphasizes the word "he."

    "Does *he* work?"   -_____

100. In Unit 26 you learned how *io, Lɛi, lui* and *lɛi* can be used for certain kinds of emphasis.

101. Similarly, *noi, voi* and *loro* are used for emphasis in cases like the following. Translate.

    a) *We* are eating, but *they* are drinking. -_____

    b) *Are* you going up now? [said to a group of people]

                                  -_____

102. The words *io, Lɛi, lui, lɛi, noi, voi,* and *loro* will be referred to in these units as BASIC IDENTIFIERS.

                         * * * * *

*103. What did we call verb forms like *ascolto, vedo, capisco*?

*104. What did we call verb forms like *ascolta, vede, capisce*?

105. Verb forms in *-mo* used to refer to the person speaking plus one or more people we will call NOI FORMS.

106. Verb forms in *-te* used to refer to the person being addressed *plus* one or more people other than the person speaking we will call VOI FORMS.

107. Verb forms used to refer to anything else in the plural we will call LORO FORMS.

                         * * * * *

*108. Study the following model.
    S: Soltanto noi?   "Only us?"
    R: Sì, soltanto voi.   "Yes, only you."

You will hear verb-less questions as in the model. Reply accordingly, always agreeing with the question. Your response will be confirmed each time. NOTE: *Noi due* is to be interpreted here as including you, whereas *noi* alone is to be interpreted as excluding you. The questions are shown here in the text purposely so that you can distinguish between Lɛi "you" and *lei* "she."

(1) Per noi?	(9) Soltanto noi?
(2) Anche voi?	(10) Anche loro?
(3) Con loro?	(11) Per voi?
(4) Io?	(12) Lui e lɛi? [combine]
(5) Sɛmpre Lɛi?	(13) Lui e Lɛi? [combine]
(6) Non lui?	(14) Io e lui? [combine]
(7) Neanche lɛi?	(15) Io e Lɛi? [combine]
(8) Soltanto noi due?	(16) Io e lɛi? [combine]

*109. Study the following model.

    S: Chi? Voi?   "Who? You?"
    R: Sì, noi.   "Yes, us."

(instructions as for the preceding drill)

    (1) Chi? Voi?
    (2) Chi? Io?
    (3) Chi? Lui?
    (4) Chi? Noi due?
    (5) Chi? Noi?
    (6) Chi? Lɛi? [referring to you]
    (7) Chi? Lɛi? [referring to a third person]
    (8) Chi? Loro?
    (9) Chi? Lui ed io? [combine]
    (10) Chi? Lui e Lɛi? [combine]
    (11) Chi? Io e lɛi? [combine]
    (12) Chi? Lui e lɛi? [combine]
    (13) Chi? Io e Lɛi? [combine]

*110. The following drills are designed to practice the different PRESENT TENSE verb forms of some useful verbs. Answer in accordance with the model. Your response will be confirmed each time. NOTE: In these drills questions with /LɛY/ are always to be interpreted as referring to you; questions referring to a third person female are always to be answered with *lei* "she," and questions referring to a third person male are always to be answered with *lui*; questions with *noi due* are to be interpreted as including you, but questions with *noi* alone are to be interpreted as excluding you.

a) Model

    S: Io ascolto, e lui?   *"I* listen. What about *him?"*

    R: Anche lui ascolta.   *"He* listens, too."

(1) E Lɛi?	(6) E loro?
(2) E Vanda?	(7) E Lucio?
(3) E noi due?	(8) E io?
(4) E noi?	(9) E lui?
(5) E voi?	

b) Model

    S: Noi desideriamo   *"We* wish to eat. What
       mangiare, e voi?   about you?"

    R: Anche noi desideriamo   *"We* wish to eat, too."
       mangiare.

(1) E Vanda?	(6) E noi due?
(2) E noi?	(7) E voi?
(3) E loro?	(8) E Lucio?
(4) Ed io?	(9) E lui?
(5) E Lɛi?	

c) Model

    S: Io non vedo bɛne, e Lɛi?   *"I* don't see well. What about *you?"*
    R: Neanch'io vedo bɛne.   *"I* don't see well, either."

(1) E noi?	(6) E loro?
(2) E io?	(7) E Lɛi?
(3) E noi due?	(8) E lui?
(4) E Mario?	(9) E voi?
(5) Ed Anna?	

d) Model

    S: Lui non dice molto,   *"He* doesn't say much.
       e Maria?   What about Maria?"

    R: Neanche lɛi dice molto.   *"She* doesn't say much, either."

(1) Ed io?
(2) Ed Alfredo?
(3) E loro?
(4) E lui?
(5) E vol?

(6) E noi?
(7) E noi due?
(8) E Maria?
(9) E Lei?

e) Model

S: Voi capite, e noi?
R: Anche voi capite

"You understand. What about *us?"*
"You understand, too."

(1) E Andrea?
(2) E lui?
(3) E noi?
(4) E Cristina?
(5) E Lei?

(6) E io?
(7) E loro?
(8) E voi?
(9) E noi due?

f) Model

S: Loro non sentono bene,
    e noi due?
R: Neanche noi due
    sentiamo bene.

"They don't hear well."
What about the two of *us?"*
"The two of *us* don't
    hear well, either."

(1) E lui?
(2) E Griselda?
(3) Ed io?
(4) E voi?
(5) E noi due?

(6) E il signor White?
(7) E noi?
(8) E Lei?
(9) E loro?

g) Model

S: Gina mangia molto, e lui?
R: Lui non mangia molto.

"Gina eats a lot. What about *him?"*
"He doesn't eat a lot."

(NOTE: Do not stress *non.*)

(1) E Cia?
(2) E voi?
(3) E Cesare?
(4) E Lei?
(5) E loro?

(6) E lui?
(7) E io?
(8) E noi due?
(9) E noi?

h) Model

    S: Lɛi studia italiano, e io?   *"You* study Italian. What about *me?"*
    R: Lɛi non studia italiano.   *"You* don't study Italian."

(NOTE: Do not stress *non.*)

(1) E voi?	(6) E noi?
(2) E Lɛi?	(7) Ed Albɛrto
(3) E lui?	(8) E loro?
(4) E noi due?	(9) Ed io?
(5) E Gia?	

i) Model

    S: Voi scïate bɛne, e loro?   *"You* ski well. What about *them?"*
    R: Loro non sciano bɛne.   *"They* don't ski well."

(NOTE: Do not stress *non.*)

(1) E Lɛi?	(6) E voi?
(2) E noi due?	(7) E lui?
(3) E loro?	(8) E Bɛrta?
(4) E noi?	(9) E Armando?
(5) E io?	

j) Model

    S: Noi abbiamo una casa, e voi?   *"We* have a house. What about *you?"*
    R: Anche noi abbiamo una casa.   *"We* have a house, too."

(1) E Lɛi?	(6) E lui?
(2) Ed Arturo?	(7) E noi?
(3) E noi due?	(8) E voi?
(4) E Carla?	(9) Ed io?
(5) E loro?	

k) Model

    S: Voi dovete studiare, e noi?   *"You* have to study. What about *us?"*
    R: Voi non dovete studiare.   *"You* don't have to study."

(NOTE: Do not stress *non.*)

*111. Study the following model.

    S: Uscite stasera?   "Are you going out tonight?"
    R: Nɔ, non usciamo   "No, we are not going out
       stasera, e voi?   tonight. How about you?"
       Uscite stasera?   "Are you going out tonight?"

You will hear questions referring to *yourself*, the *speaker*, or *two or more people*. (NOTE: A NOI FORM question does *not* include you!) Answer the questions in the negative and follow up with a question as in the model. In this drill the two verb forms in your response should be one of the following combinations:

negative	question
NOI FORM	VOI FORM
IO FORM	LEI FORM
VOI FORM	NOI FORM
LEI FORM	IO FORM
LORO FORM	NOI FORM

Your response will be confirmed each time.

(1) Finite domani?
(2) Andiamo a Napoli?
(3) Ci vanno domenica?
(4) Conosce Bari Lei?
(5) Lavoro domani?
(6) Partite sabato?
(7) Salite ora?
(8) Dɔrme bɛne?
(9) Abitate in campagna?
(10) Ritornano dopodomani?
(11) Prenɔta un tavolo?
(12) Arrivate con la segretaria?
(13) Vincete sɛmpre?
(14) Pɔrta vino?
(15) Giocate ogni giorno?
(16) Dicono molto?
(17) Imparate molto?
(18) Telɛfona nel pomeriggio?
(19) Dĕvo andarci?

(20) Insegnate qui?
(21) Leggete in classe?
(22) Vuɔle tradurre?
(23) Lasciate una giustificazione?
(24) Possiamo salire?
(25) Parlate francese?
(26) Capiscono?
(27) Finiamo ɔggi?
(28) State sɛmpre bɛne?
(29) Traducete spesso?
(30) Sanno molto?
(31) Spiegate ogni lezione?
(32) Aspɛtta qui?
(33) Imponete una condizione?
(34) Viɛne domani?
(35) Sôno giovane?
(36) Sôno giovani?
(37) Siamo giovani?

TEST A

(not recorded)

The following are some of the new items introduced in this unit. Rewrite them with hyphens indicating the SYLLABIC BREAKS and put the number of syllables each item has. NOTE: These items would have the same SYLLABIC BREAKS shown in writing that they have in speech.

	rewritten	no. of syllables
1) abile	_____	_____
2) belga	_____	_____
3) magnifico	_____	_____
4) medico	_____	_____
5) simpatico	_____	_____
6) antropɔfago	_____	_____
7) antropɔlogo	_____	_____
8) bacio	_____	_____
9) filɔlogo	_____	_____
10) lago	_____	_____
11) luɔgo	_____	_____
12) studio	_____	_____
13) specie	_____	_____
14) studiamo	_____	_____
15) diciamo	_____	_____
16) ponete	_____	_____
17) parlano	_____	_____
18) scïamo	_____	_____
19) mangiamo	_____	_____
20) siĕte	_____	

TEST B

(not recorded)

Following the SYLLABICATION guidelines given in this unit, rewrite the eight items listed below with hyphens indicating the SYLLABIC BREAKS that occur in speech (column A) and in writing (column B).

	A	B
1) zia	_____	_____
2) l'Aia	_____	_____
3) razza 2 ways	_____	_____
	_____	
4) zuppa 2 ways	_____	_____
	_____	
5) acqua 2 ways	_____	_____
	_____	
6) vacche 2 ways	_____	_____
	_____	
7) questo	_____	_____
8) inabile	_____ 2 ways	_____
		_____

TEST C

(not recorded)

Rewrite the following utterances with hyphens indicating the SYLLABIC BREAKS that would normally occur in speech.

1) Un'insegnante d'italiano viene domani.

_____

2) In inglese, per favore.

_____

3) Una stanza per un giorno.

_____

4) Ad Ancona ci sôno Cecè ed Agata.

_____

5) Io non esco con Andrea

_____

TEST D

(answers not recorded)

You will hear a question in the PRESENT TENSE. Answer it in the affirmative
by using a complete sentence. Do *not* use BASIC IDENTIFIERS in your answers.
Questions with /LƐY/ are to be interpreted as referring to yous questions with
noi due are to be interpreted as including you, but NOI FORM questions without *noi due* are to be interpreted as excluding you.

1) Quando venite, più tardi? _____

2) Sôno di Milano loro? _____

3) Cominciamo domani noi due? _____

4) Finisce stasera Lɛi? _____

5) Andate fuɔri domęnica? _____

6) Hanno una casa in campagna loro? _____

7) Parla francese Emilio? _____

8) Preferite partire fra due giorni? _____

9) Dobbiamo aspettare qui? _____

10) Impara molto Marịa? _____

11) State bɛne? _____

12) Abbiamo soltanto uno studɛnte? _____

13) Capite ogni lezione? _____

14) Ci sôno Carlo e Cristina? _____

15) Richiamate più tardi? _____

16) Telɛfona domani Nino? _____

17) Vɔgliono una raccomandazione? _____

18) Pɔsso ritornare dopodomani? _____

19) Espɔrtano anche ɔlio? _____

20) Litigate per un pôsto? _____

21) Va in banca Lɛi? _____

22) Giochiamo a tɛnnis domani? _____

23) Giustificate solotanto uno sbaglio? _____

24) Produce anche vino Lɛi? _____

25) Fate le spese in città? _____

26) Pɛnsano di ascoltare una trascrizione
    di questo? _____

27) Scia bɛne Lɛi? _____

28) Bevete un'aranciata? _____

TEST F

(not recorded)

Translate the following thoughts into Italian by using *only* what has been presented so far. Unless the abbreviation "pl" (meaning "plural") follows the word "you," said word is to be interpreted as singular.

1) They are never in on Saturdays, but I am.

_____

2) We must consider this now.

_____

3) The two of you are working tomorrow, aren't you?

_____

4) They always drink wine, never beer

_____

5) We're planning to leave on Friday.

_____

6) Would you like two peaches and two figs?

_____

7) He's not only a friend; he's a colleague.

_____

8) We won't be in tomorrow. Will you?

_____

9) They have three kinds of cows.

_____

10) What are you (pl.) going to introduce now?

_____

11) Are they nice people?

_____

12) *We* are Americans; *they* are Greek.

_____

13) Do you (pl.) understand when we talk?

_____

14) They are diplomats but they are not politicians.

_____

15) Do you know one dialog? *I* know two dialogs.

_____

16) When are you (pl.) going to Greece? *I'm* going in a few days.

_____

17) We have two days. We have to study a lot tonight and tomorrow night.

_____

18) They are always making mistakes. We never make mistakes.

_____

19) Are you anthropologists? I thought you were doctors?
[HINT: Put this idea into Italian in the form of a questions

_____

20) We don't say much, but we understand a lot.

_____

21) Can we come back Tuesday? We want to come when *he's* not in.

_____

22) They speak Italian very well but they don't say a great deal.

_____

23) We don't know where *he* is, but we know where *she* is!

_____

24) What are you (pl.) doing tomorrow? Are you going to stay home?

_____

25) We never translate. Do they (translate)?

_____

TEST G

(not recorded)

Translate the following thoughts into Italian using the verb *┼piacere* "to be liked."

Impersonally liked or not liked

1) Am I liked?   -_____

2) Are you well-liked?   -_____

3) Mario isn't popular.   -_____

4) Maria is liked a lot.   -_____

5) We aren't popular.   -_____

6) Are you (pl.) liked?   -_____

7) They don't appeal to anyone.   -_____

8) Do people like me?   -_____

9) People don't like us.   -_____

10) People like you (pl.).   -_____

11) Don't people like you?   -_____

12) People like Maria but they
    don't like Mario.   -_____

13) People don't like them.   -_____

Personally liked or not liked (notice that the liker or non-liker is always an unemphatic "I," "you," "he," "she," "we," or "they.")

14) I like to work.   -_____

15) Don't you like to eat?   -_____

16) Does he like to drink?   -_____

17) Does she like to speak Italian?   -_____

18) We like to translate.   -_____

19) Do you (pl.) like making mistakes?   -_____

20) They don't like to listen.   -_____

21)   I like it.
      It appeals to me.   }   -_____
      It is liked by me.

22)   I like them.
      They appeal to me.   }   -_____
      They are liked by me.

23)   We like Italy.
      Italy appeals to us.   }   -_____
      Italy is liked by us.

24)   Do you (pl.) like Rome?
      Does Rome appeal to you?   }   -_____
      Is Rome liked by you?

25)   They don't like it.
      It doesn't appeal to them.   }   -_____
      It isn't liked by them.

26)   She doesn't like Naples.
      Naples doesn't appeal to her. }   -_____
      Naples isn't liked by her.

27)   He likes me.
      I appeal to him.   }   -_____
      I am liked by him.

TEST A ANSWERS

1) ạ-bi-le   3
2) bɛl-ga   2
3) ma-gnị-fi-co   4
4) mɛ-di co   3
5) sim-pạ-ti-co   4
6) an-tro-pɔ-fa-go 5
7) an-tro-pɔ-lo-go   5
8) ba-cio   2
9) fi-lɔ-lo-go   4
10) la-go 2

11) luɔ-go   2
12) stu-dio   2
13) spɛ-cie   2
14) stu-dia-mo   3
15) di-cia-mo   3
16) po-ne-te   3
17) pạr-la-no   3
18) scï-a-mo   3
19) man-gia-mo   3
20) siĕ-te   2

TEST B ANSWERS

A (speech)	B (writing)
1) zi-a	zia
2) l'A-ia	l'Aia
3) ⎰ ra-zza ⎱ raz-za	raz-za
4) ⎰ zu-ppa ⎱ zup-pa	zup-pa
5) ⎰ a-cqua ⎱ ac-qua	ac-qua
6) ⎰ va-cche ⎱ vac-che	vac-che
7) ques-to	que-sto
8) i-nạ-bi-le	⎰ in-ạ-bi-le ⎱ i-nạ-bi-le

TEST C ANSWERS

1) U-n'in-se-gnan-te-d'i-ta-lia-no-viɛ-ne-do-ma-ni.
2) I-nin-gle-se-per-fa-vo-re.
3) U-na-stan-za-pe-run-gior-no.
4) A-dAn-co-na-ci-sô-no-Ce-cè-e dẠ-ga-ta.
5) I-o-no-nɛs-co-co-nAn-drɛ-a.

TEST D   ANSWERS

1) Sì, veniamo più tardi.
2) Sì, sôno di Milano.
3) Sì, cominciamo domani.
4) Sì, finisco stasera.
5) Sì, andiamo fuori domẹnica.
6) Sì, hanno una casa in campagna.
7) Sì, parla francese.
8) Sì, preferiamo partire fra due giorni.
9) Sì, dovete aspettare qui.
10) Sì, impara molto.
11) Sì, stiamo bɛne.
12) Sì, avete soltanto uno studɛnte.
13) Sì, capiamo ogni lezione.
14) Sì, ci sôno.
15) Sì, richiamiamo più tardi.
16) Sì, telɛfona domani.
17) Sì, vɔgliono una raccomandazione.
18) Sì, puɔ̀ ritornare dopodomani.
19) Sì, espɔrtano anche ɔlio.
20) Sì, litighiamo per un pôsto.
21) Sì, vado in banca.
22) Sì, giocate a tɛnnis domani.
23) Sì, giustifichiamo soltanto uno sbaglio.
24) Sì, produco anche vino.
25) Sì, facciamo le spese in città.
26) Sì, pɛnsano di ascoltare una trascrizione di questo.
27) Sì, scio bɛne
28) Sì, beviamo un'aranciata.
29) Sì, mangiamo soltanto un uɔvo sɔdo e un'insalata.
30) Sì, conosce il signor Vegli.
31) Sì, propongono un'investigazione.
32) Sì, ci siamo venerdì.

TEST E ANSWERS

Question	Answer	Question	Answer
1) Bɔsco?	Nɔ, bɔschi.	29) Fuɔchi?	.......fuɔco.
2) Pɛsca?	.......pɛsche.	30) Nemica?	.......nemiche.
3) Atrïo?	.......atri.	31) Pɔrco?	.......pɔrci.
4) Laghi?	.......lago	32) Mɛdico?	.......mɛdici.
5) Vôga?	.......vôghe.	33) Luccio?	.......lucci.
6) Studi?	.......studio.	34) Spɔrco?	.......spɔrchi.
7) Dïaloghi?	.......dïalogo.	35) Simpatico?	.......simpatici.
8) Vacche?	.......vacca.	36) Simpatica?	.......simpatiche.
9) Aggravio?	.......aggravi.	37) Baci?	.......bacio
10) Luɔghi?	.......luɔgo.	38) Spɛcie?	.......spɛci.
11) Collɛghi?	.......collɛga.	39) Magnifico?	.......magnifici.
12) Dio?	.......dɛi.	40) Diplomatiche?	.......diplomatica.
13) Astrɔlogo?	.......astrɔlogi.	41) Antropɔfago?	.......antropɔfagi.
14) Bɛlgi?	.......bɛlga.	42) Zia?	.......zie.
15) Pomeriggi?	.......pomeriggio.	43) Politica?	.......politiche.
16) Collɛghe?	.......collɛga.	44) Cuɔco?	.......cuɔchi.
17) Filɔlogo?	.......filɔlogi.	45) Ciɛchi?	.......ciɛco.
18) Fico?	.......fichi.	46) Geɔlogo?	.......geɔlogi.
19) Amico?	.......amici.	47) Amica?	.......amiche.
20) Bɛlghe?	.......bɛlga.	48) Bistecche?	.......bistecca.
21) Sbagli?	.......sbaglio.	49) Grɛco?	.......grɛci.
22) Affreschi?	.......affresco.	50) Antropɔlogi?	.......antropɔlogo.
23) Giôgo?	.......giôghi.	51) Zio?	.......zii.
24) Formaggio?	.......formaggi.	52) Ciuchi?	.......ciuco.
25) Banca?	.......banche.	53) Cuɔca?	Nɔ, cuɔche.
26) Rɛplica?	.......rɛpliche.	54) Fantastico?	.......fantastici.
27) Ufficio?	Nɔ, uffici.	55) Archeɔlogo?	.......archeɔlogi.
28) Bachi?	.......baco.		

1) (Loro) non ci sôno mai il sabato ma io $\left\{\begin{array}{l}\text{sì} \\ \text{ci sôno.}\end{array}\right.$

2) Dobbiamo considerare questo ora.

3) Voi due lavorate domani, nɔ?

4) Bevono sɛmpre vino, mai birra.

5) Pensiamo di partire venerdì.

6) Vuɔle due pɛsche e due fichi?

7) Non è soltanto un amico; è un collɛga.

8) (Noi) non ci siamo domani. $\left\{\begin{array}{l}\text{E Lɛi?} \\ \text{Lɛi ci sarà.}\end{array}\right.$

9) Hanno tre spɛci di vacche.

10) Che cɔsa introducete ora?

11) Sôno simpatici?

12) Noi siamo americani; loro sôno grɛci!

13) Capite quando parliamo?

14) Sôno diplomatici ma non sôno poliţici.

15) Sa un dïạlogo (Lɛi)? Io sɔ due dïạloghi.

16) Quando andate in Grɛcia? Io ci vado fra qualche giorno.

17) Abbiamo due giorni. Dobbiamo studiare molto stasera e domani sera.

18) (Loro) fanno sɛmpre sbagli. Noi non facciamo mai sbagli.

   (or)

   (Loro) sbagliano sɛmpre. Noi non sbagliamo mai.

19) Siĕte antropɔlogi? Non siĕte $\left\{\begin{array}{l}\text{dottori?} \\ \text{mɛdici?}\end{array}\right.$

20) Non diciamo molto ma capiamo molto.

21) Possiamo (ri)tornare martedì? Vogliamo venire quando lui non c'è.

22) Pạrlano molto bɛne l'italiano ma non dịcono molto.

   (or)

   Pạrlano (l')italiano molto bɛne ma non dịcono molto.

23) Non sappiamo dov'è lui, ma sappiamo dov'è lɛi!

24) Che cɔsa fate domani? State a casa?

25) (Noi) non traduciamo mai. $\left\{\begin{array}{l}\text{E loro?} \\ \text{Tradụcono loro?}\end{array}\right.$

TEST G   ANSWERS

1) Piaccio?
2) Piace Lɛi?
3) Mario non piace.
4) Maria piace molto.
5) Non piacciamo.
6) Piacete?
7) Non piacciono.
8) Piaccio?
9) Non piacciamo.
10) Piacete.
11) Non piace Lɛi?
12) Maria piace ma Mario non piace.
13) Non piacciono.
14) Mi piace lavorare.
15) Non Le piace mangiare?
16) Gli piace bere?
17) Le piace parlare (l')italiano?
18) Ci piace tradurre.
19) Vi piace fare sbagli? (or)
    Vi piace sbagliare?
20) Non gli piace ascoltare.
21) Mi piace.
22) Mi piacciono.
23) Ci piace l'Italia.
24) Vi piace Roma?
25) Non gli piace.
26) Non le piace Napoli.
27) Gli piaccio.

UNIT 29

1. So far you have seen several instances of words written with an apostrophe. For example:

   (un'italiana)X
   (l'ufficio)X
   (c'è)X
   (ce n'è uno)X
   (che cɔs'è)X
   (dov'è)X
   (anch'io)X

2. The apostrophe in the above cases indicates that the final vowel of a word has been dropped. For example, *una* has become *un'* in *un'italiana.*

3. The dropping of the *final vowel* of a word immediately before a vowel or a semivowel of another word is very common in certain breath groups and is referred to as ELISION.

4. ELISION is normally represented in writing by an apostrophe.

5. Some cases of elision are so common that the breath group would sound very strange or stilted if the vowel in question were not dropped.

6. Such cases involve:
   a) certain noun markers in the singular, as in: *un'italiana, l'ufficio,* "the office," *quest'ufficio* "this office," *quell'ufficio* "that office"
   b) certain pre-verbal items, especially with ┼*esserci,* as in: *c'è* or *ce n'è uno*
   c) expressions like: *che cɔs'è, dov'è, anch'io*

7. In addition to the above, you should learn the following:
   a) the feminine singular *buɔna* "good," like *una,* undergoes elision, but preferably only before a vowel sound-type (*not* before a semivowel).
   b) the feminine singular forms of ┼*questo* "this," ┼*quello* "that," and ┼*bello* "beautiful, handsome, fine" undergo elision *before a vowel sound-type;* the masculine singular of these words undergoes elision *before a vowel* or *semivowel.*
   c) ┼*grande* "big, large, great" frequently follows the same rule as for ┼*questo,* ┼*quello,* and ┼*bello.*

d) the masculine singular of ╪santo "Saint" undergoes elision *before a vowel sound-type;* the feminine singular does so, as a rule, only *before* a.

*8. In accordance with what was said in frame no. 7 (a), translate the following into Italian.
    a) "She's a good woman."   -_____
    b) "She's a good Yugoslavian."
        [use: *Iugoslava*]   -_____
    c) "She's a good teacher."   -_____
    d) "It's an Englishwoman."   -_____

*9. In accordance with what was said in frame no. 7 (b) and (c), translate the following into Italian. NOTE: "F" stands for "feminine" and "M" stands for "masculine."

F   "this student"   -_____
    "this Yugoslavian"   -_____
    "this teacher"   -_____

M   "this student"   -_____
    "this Yugoslavian"   -_____
    "this teacher"   -_____

F   "that student"   -_____
    "that Yugoslavian"   -_____
    "that teacher"   -_____

M   "that student"   -_____
    "that Yugoslavian"   -_____
    "that teacher"   -_____

F   "that good-looking student"   -_____
    "a good-looking Yugoslavian"   -_____
    "a good-looking teacher"   -_____

M   "a good-looking student"   -_____
    "a good-looking Yugoslavian"   -_____
    "a good-looking teacher"   -_____

F   "a big steak"   -_____
    "a big Yugoslavian"   -_____
    "a great Italian"   -_____

M   "a large lake"   -_____
    "a great man"   -_____
    "a great Italian"   -_____

*10. In accordance with what was said in frame no. 7 (d), translate the follow-
      ing into Italian.
      a) "Saint Mary"   -_____
         [use: *Maria*]
      b) "Saint Irene"   -_____
         [use: *Irɛne*]
      c) "Saint Anna"   -_____
         [use: *Anna*]
      d) "Saint Stephen"   -_____
         [use: *Stêfano*]
      e) "Saint Eugene"   -_____
         [use: *Eugɛnio*]
      f) "Saint Anthony"   -_____
         [use: *Antɔnio*]

11. Elision is normal with *ci*, as in *c'ɛra*. However, before the vowel letters *a, o,*
    ɔ, and *u* this elision is never shown by a written apostrophe, the reason
    being to reflect the proper pronunciation of the consonant (i.e., /Č/)Thus,
    ci andiamo "we are going there" normally stands for
    (/ČANDYÁMO/)X

12. As a rule, cases of elision other than those pointed out here do occur,
    especially in rapid speech, but they are not obligatory.

13. Remember that the guidelines given here refer to words in breath groups
    (see Unit 4). Consequently, elision is not normal after any *significant pause* or
    sharp pitch change.

14. When you are in doubt as to whether to make an elision or not, it is recom-
    mended you *not* make it!

                              * * * * *

15. Not to be confused with elision is another phenomenon called APOCOPA-
    TION.

16. APOCOPATION is the dropping of the final *unstressed vowel* or *unstressed*
    syllable of a word.

17. In a few cases such words have become very common and may occur with
    nothing following them.

18. One such word is *pɔ'*(short for *pɔco*), especially used in the combination *un pɔ'.*

   Repeat:

(un pɔ' di vino)X	"a little (amount of) wine"
(soltanto un pɔ')X	"just a little (amount)"
(aspɛtti un pɔ')X	"wait a minute"

19. Shortened words like *pɔ'* are written with an apostrophe.

20. However, there are certain words with which APOCOPATION occurs *only* immediately before another word in a breath group.

21. With such words, APOCOPATION is *never* represented in writing by an apostrophe.

22. Here are some examples of this kind of apocopation with words that you have had so far:

   a) ┼*uno* occurring as *un* in the masculine:
   (un animale)X
   (an uɔmo)X
   (un bambino)X

   b) ┼*buɔno* occurring as *buɔn* in the masculine singular:
   (buɔn americano)X
   (buɔn uɔmo)X
   (buɔn giorno)X

   c) ┼*signore* and ┼*dottore* occurring as *signor* and *dottor* respectively in the masculine singular:
   (signor Adams)X
   (signor Vegli)X
   (dottor Paglia)X

   d) *vuɔle* changing to *vuɔl* before an infinitive:
   (vuɔl aspettare)
   (vuɔl parlare)X

23. In most cases this kind of apocopation is optional and takes place with words of more than one syllable which end in *-e* or *-o* preceded by *n, r, m,* or *l.* Thus, one may say either:

   (Dĕvo fare la spesa.)X   or   (Dĕvo far la spesa.)X
        "I have to do my grocery shopping"
   (Arrivano domani.)X   or   (Arrivan domani.)X
         "They are arriving tomorrow."
   (Sôno sɛmpre pronto.)X   or   (Sôn sɛmpre pronto.)X
         "I am always ready."

(Fanno sɛmpre bɛne.)X   or   (Fan sɛmpre bɛne.)X
"They always do well."

24. To remember the *consonants* after which this kind of apocopation is normal, remember the consonant letters in the word "<u>n</u>or<u>m</u>a<u>l</u>."

*25. According to what you have learned so far, may apocopation take place before a consonant?

*26. According to what you have learned so far, may elision take place before a consonant?

*27. How is elision normally represented in writing?

*28. In which of the following two cases is apocopation represented in writing by an apostrophe?
   a) with shortened words that may occur with nothing following them
   b) with shortened words that occur *only* immediately before another word in a breath group

29. In certain cases apocopation is the norm and *should* be used. Such cases involve the following genderables:
   a) ~~grande~~, in the meaning of "great," "important," occurring as *gran,* especially in the masculine singular, but preferably *not* before *s + consonant, z, gn, pn, ps,* etc., nor in those cases (see frame no. 7(c)) in which *grand'* occurs.
   in the masculine singular
   b) *uno* and *buɔno* changing to *un* and *buɔn* respectively, but *not* before *s + consonant, z, gn, pn, ps,* etc. (see frame no. 22)
   c) *quello* and *bɛllo* changing respectively to *quel* and *bɛl* before consonant letters other than *s + consonant, z, gn, pn, ps,* etc.
   d) *santo* "Saint" changing to *san* before a semivowel or a consonant other than *s + consonant.*
   e) titles in *-ore* (like *signore*) changing to *or* before proper names or other titles. (see frame no. 22)
   f) the following titles used before Christian names:
   frate changing to *fra*   "Brother; Father; Friar"
   dɔnno changing to *dɔn*   "Don; Father"

in the feminine singular
g) the title *suɔra* "Sister; Mother," changing to *suɔr* before a Christian
   name.

*30. In accordance with what was said in frame no. 29(a), translate the follow-
     ing into Italian.
     a) "He's a great gentleman."   -_____
     b) "He's a great psychologist."   -_____

*31. In accordance with what was said in frame no. 29(b), translate the follow-
     ing into Italian.
     a) "He's a good American."   -_____
     b) "He's a good Yugoslavian"   -_____
     c) "He's a good doctor."   -_____
     d) "He's a good student."   -_____
     e) "He's a good uncle.   -_____

*32. In accordance with what was said in frame no. 29(c), translate the follow-
     ing into Italian.
     a) "that gentleman"   -_____
     b) "a handsome gentleman"   -_____
     c) "that handsome gentleman"   -_____
     d) "that student" [male]   -_____
     e) "that handsome student"   -_____
     f) "that handsome student"   -_____

*33. In accordance with what was said in frame no. 29(d), translate the follow-
     ing into Italian.
     a) "Saint Jacob"   -_____
        [use: *Iącopo*]
     b) "Saint John"   -_____
        [use: *Giovanni*]
     c) "Saint Zenone"   -_____
        [use: *Ženone*]
     d) "Saint Stephen"   -_____
     e) "Saint Andrew"   -_____
        [use: *Andrɛa*]

*34. In accordance with what was said in frame no. 29(e), translate the follow-
     ing into Italian.
     a) "Good morning, Mr. Jones."   -_____
     b) "Good evening, Dr. Russo."   -_____
     c) "Mr. Jones and Dr. Russo
        are here."   -_____

    d) "The gentleman is here."   -_____

    e) "I'm calling the doctor."   -_____

       [do *not* use: *medico*]

*35. In accordance with what was said in frame no. 29(f) and (g), translate the following into Italian.

    a) "Brother James was a good { monk brother"
       [use: *Giacomo*]

    b) "Sister Teresa was a good { nun sister"
       [use: *Teresa*]

    c) "Father Giovanni was a good priest." [use: *prete* for "priest"]

36. As a rule, cases of apocopation other than those pointed out here do occur, especially in rapid speech, but they are not obligatory.

37. Except for a few words like *pɔ'*, the guidelines for apocopation (like those for elision) given here refer to words in breath groups. Consequently, with the exception of the few words like *pɔ'*, apocopation is not normal after any *significant pause* or *sharp pitch change.*

38. When in doubt as to whether to make apocopation or not, do *not* make it!

* * * * *

The drills in frames no. 39 through no. 46 are designed to practice some important cases of elision and apocopation. In each drill you will hear a sentence followed by a cue word. Substitute the cue word for the last word in the sentence. As you do so, repeat the new sentence, making any other changes required. vows response will be confirmed each time. NOTE: If the cue word may be interpreted as *either* masculine or feminine (e.g., *insegnante*), it should be used as masculine or feminine in accordance with the gender of the word it replaces.

*39. Substitution Drill on ╪*grande* "great, important" (see frames no. 7(c) and 29(a))
    Model sentence: *È una gran signora.* "She's a great lady."

(1) amico	(6) monumento	(11) sbaglio
(2) cɔsa	(7) ospedale	(12) scɛna
(3) elemento	(8) poɛta	(13) signora
(4) giɔia	(9) pranżo	(14) signore
(5) irritazione	(10) preoccupazione	(15) uɔmo

*40. Substitution Drill on ⊬*grande* "big, large" (see frame no. 7(c))
Model sentence: È una grande città.   "It's a big city."

(1) ambasciata	(6) cɔsa	(11) stazione
(2) animale	(7) inflazione	(12) studio
(3) ażienda	(8) investigazione	(13) tạvolo
(4) città	(9) monumento	(14) ufficio
(5) consolato	(10) ospedale	(15) uɔmo

*41. Substitution Drill on ⊬*buɔno* "good" (see frames no. 7(a) and 29(b))
Model sentence: *È una buɔna dɔnna.* "She's a good woman."

(1) insegnante	(8) zio	(15) signore
(2) americano	(9) dottore	(16) inglese
(3) studɛnte	(10) uɔmo	(17) studentessa
(4) insegnante	(11) collɛga	(18) amico
(5) iugoslavo	(12) americana	(19) mɛdico
(6) dɔnna	(13) psicɔlogo	(20) zia
(7) inglese	(14) iugoslava	

*42. Substitution Drill on ⊬*questo* "this" (see frame no. 7(b))
Model sentence: *Mi piace questo libro.* "I like this book."

(1) programma	(7) pôsto	(13) libro
(2) uɔmo	(8) ufficio	(14) casa
(3) ambasciata	(9) studɛnte	(15) poɛta
(4) iugoslava	(10) intenzione	(16) città
(5) insegnante	(11) monumento	
(6) arrɔsto	(12) żona	

*43. Substitution Drill on ⊬*quello* "that" (see frames no. 7(b) and 29(c))
Model sentence: *Non mi piace quello studɛnte.*   "I don't like that student."

(1) studio	(4) żona	(7) żɔo
(2) città	(5) amica	(8) uɔmo
(3) insegnante	(6) ambasciata	(9) americano

(10) programma   (14) pôsto   (18) dɔnna
(11) amico   (15) studɛnte   (19) spɔrt
(12) iugoslava   (16) consolato   (20) libro
(13) intenzione (17) università

*44. Substitution Drill on ┼bɛllo "beautiful, handsome, fine" (see frames no. 7(b) and 29 (c))

Model sentence: È una bɛlla dɔnna.   "She's a beautiful woman."

(1) żona   (8) dɔnna   (15) stanza
(2) italiana   (9) nome   (16) città
(3) iugoslava   (10) ambasciata   (17) żɔo
(4) studio   (11) insegnante   (18) artista
(5) lago   (12) università   (19) giǫvane
(6) insegnante   (13) guardia   (20) programma
(7) uɔmo   (14) scɛna   (21) consolato

*45. Substitution Drill on ┼questo ┼bɛllo "this good-looking..." (see frames no. 7(b) and 29(c))

Model sentence: Questo bɛl libro?   "This beautiful book?"

(1) uɔmo   (5) pôsto   (9) bagno
(2) ufficio   (6) studio   (10) scɛna
(3) stanza   (7) studentessa   (11) vaso
(4) ambasciata   (8) libro   (12) sbaglio

*46. Substitution Drill on ┼quello ┼bɛllo "that good-looking..." (see frames nos. 7(b) and 29 (c))

Model sentence: Quel bɛl libro? "That beautiful book?"

(1) uɔmo   (5) libro   (9) bagno
(2) stanza   (6) scɛna   (10) studentessa
(3) pôsto   (7) sbaglio   (11) ambasciata
(4) studio   (8) vaso   (12) ufficio

* * * * *

47. In Unit 22 you were told of some of the different kinds of Italian gender-ables. Let's review the most important ones.

48. Certain genderables like +arrɔsto (masculine) and +persona (feminine) that belong exclusively to only one gender category may be said to *have inherent gender* as opposed to genderables like +italiano (with masculine and feminine forms) or +insegnante (masculine and feminine) that *do not have inherent gender.*

49. Those with inherent gender we will call GENDER-INTRINSIC and the others will be called GENDER-EXTRINSIC.

*50. Is +arrɔsto GENDER-INTRINSIC or GENDER-EXTRINSIC?

*51. What about +italiano?

*52. What about +poɛta?

*53. What about +turista?

*54. What about +persona?

*55. What about +guardia?

56. Except for genderables that can *never* refer to people or animals (e.g., +libro, +casa and hence are gender-intrinsic, it is not possible to predict whether a genderable that *may* be used to refer to animate beings (e.g., +persona, +turista) is gender-intrinsic or gender-extrinsic. This can only be learned through observation.

57. From what we have observed so far one may see that there are Italian genderables with one form, two forms, three forms or four forms.

58. Unit 25, frame no. 62 classifies most of those that have only *one form*. They are gender-intrinsic. Examples are: (sofà)X   (crisi)X

59. Those with *two forms* are either:
   a) gender-intrinsic, ending in unstressed -*o*, -*a*, or -*e* in the singular.

Examples:	**singular**	**plural**
masculine	(libro)X	(libri)X
	(programma)X	(programmi)X
	(nome)X	(nomi)X
feminine	(mano)X	(mani)X
	(persona)X	(persone)X
	(spɛcie)X	(spɛci)X

or b) gender-extrinsic, ending in unstressed -*e* in the singular.

Example:	**singular**	**plural**
masculine/feminine	(insegnante)X	(insegnanti)X

60. Important kinds of *three-form* genderables are those ending in *-ista* or *-cida* in the singular. They are gender-extrinsic.

Examples:

masculine/feminine singular	masculine plural	feminine plural
(artista)X	(artisti)X	(artiste)X
(süicida)X	(süicidi)X	(süicide)X
"suicide victim"		

61. The largest group of *four-form* genderables consists of those with dictionary forms in unstressed *-o*. They are gender-extrinsic.

Example:

masculine singular	feminine singular	masculine plural	feminine plural
(italiano)X	(italiana)X	(italiani)X	(italiane)X

62. Other kinds of four-form genderables should be thought of as exceptional. The forms cannot be predicted.

Examples:

masculine singular	feminine singular	masculine plural	feminine plural
(dottore)X	(dottoressa)X	(dottori)X	(dottoresse)X
(studɛnte)X	(studentessa)X	(studɛnti)X	(studentesse)X
(attore)X	(attrice)X	(attori)X	(attrici)X
"actor"	"actress"		

63. The following sums up the most important kinds of Italian genderables.

GENDER-INTRINSIC	GENDER-EXTRINSIC
Mainly two-form with the dictionary form ending in:	Dictionary form normally ends in:
unstressed *-o* (like +*libro*),	unstressed *-o*
unstressed *-a* (like +*persona*),	unstressed *-a*
or unstressed *-e* (like +*nome*).	unstressed *-e*.
	Most with dictionary form in *-o* have *four forms*, like (+*italiano*).
	Most with dictionary form in *-ista* or *-cida* have *three forms* (like +*artista* or +*suicida*).
	Most with dictionary form in *-e* have *two forms* (like +*insegnante*).

*64. Translate the following into Italian.

    a) "He's Italian"   - _____

    b) "She's American."   - _____

    c) "He's Belgian."   - _____

    d) "She's Yugoslavian."   - _____

*65. If in the four sentences listed in the preceding frame we had put "a" or "an" before the nationality word, would we have changed the basic meaning of the sentences?

*66. Therefore, would you say that the Italian translations given for frame no. 64 would be valid for the corresponding English sentences with "a" or "an"?

67. In Italian after the verb ╪*essere* a word classifying a person as to nationality, religion or political affiliation is often *not* preceded by the unit marker unless the word is accompanied by a descriptive word or phrase.

*68. Thus, translate the following into Italian.

    a_1) "He's a good American."   - _____

    a_2) "He's an American."   - _____

    b_1) "She's a good Anglican."   - _____

    b_2) "She's an Anglican."   - _____

    c_1) "He's a good Communist."   - _____

    c_2) "He's a Communist."   - _____

69. The same holds true for many (though not all) words indicating one's status, professional, occupational or titular. For example:

GENDER-EXTRINSIC 4-FORM GENDERABLE

    (È studɛnte.)X   "He's a student."

    (È un buɔno studɛnte.)X   "He's a good student."

GENDER-EXTRINSIC 4-FORM GENDERABLE

    (È dottore.)X   "He's a doctor."

    (È un buɔn dottore.)X   "He's a good doctor."

GENDER-EXTRINSIC 4-FORM GENDERABLE

    (È impiegato.)X   "He's an office employee."

    (È una buɔna impiegata.)X   "She's a good employee."

GENDER-EXTRINSIC 3-FORM GENDERABLE

    (È psichiatra.)X   "(S)he's a psychiatrist."

    (È un buɔno psichiatra.)X   "He's a good psychiatrist."

    (È una buɔna psichiatra.)X "She's a good psychiatrist."

GENDER-EXTRINSIC 2-FORM GENDERABLE
  (È statale.)X   "(S)he's a government employee."

MASCULINE 2-FORM GENDERABLE
  (È funzionario.)X   "(S)he's an $\begin{cases} \text{official} \\ \text{officer [non-military]} \end{cases}$

  (È un buɔn funzionario.)X   "(S)he's a good officer."

MASCULINE 2-FORM GENDERABLE
  (È ufficiale.)X   "(S)he's a military officer."
  (È un buɔn ufficiale.)X   "(S)he's a good (military) officer."

BUT:
  (È una spia.)X   "(S)he's a spy."
  (È una guardia.)X   "(S)he's a guard."
  (È una guida.)X   "(S)he's a guide."
  (È un agɛnte.)X   "(S)he's an agent."

70. When you are in doubt as to whether or not you should use the unit marker with words indicating status such as those of the preceding frame, it is advisable to use it!

71. Learn the following questions.

   (Di che nazionalità è X?)X   "What is X's nationality?"
   (Di che religione è X?)X   "What is X's religion?"
   (Che grado ha X?)X   "What is X's rank?"
   (Che lavoro fa X?)X   "What kind of work does X do?"
   (Che mestiɛre fa X?)X   "What is X's occupation?"
   (A quale partito politico $\begin{cases} \text{"To which political party} \\ \quad \text{does X belong?"} \\ \text{"What is X's political affiliation?"} \end{cases}$
      appartiɛne X?)

72. Learn the following Italian cognates of English words. They are all gender-extrinsic.

   (buddista)X   "Buddhist"   (buddista)X
   (cattɔlico)X   "Catholic"   (cattɔlico)X
   (ebrɛo)X   "Hebrew"   (ebrɛo)X
   (musulmano)X   "Moslem"   (musulmano)X
   (protestante)X   "Protestant"   (protestante)X

73. Learn the following cognates. They are all gender-extrinsic.

(democrạtico)X	"Democrat"	(democrạtico)X
(democristiano)X	"Christian Democrat"	(democristiano)X
(fascista)X	"Fascist"	(fascista)X
(repubblicano)X	"Republican"	(repubblicano)X
(socialista)X	"Socialist"	(socialista)X

74. Here are some military terms for you to learn. They are all grammatically masculine.

(colonnɛllo)X	"colonel"	(colonnɛllo)X
(generale)X	"general"	(generale)X
(militare)X	"soldier, one in the military"	(militare)X
(sergɛnte)X	"sergeant"	(sergɛnte)X

75. Learn the following of which only +cɔnsole is gender intrinsic (masculine).

(presidɛnte)X (masc.)	"president"	(presidɛnte)X
(presidentessa)X (fem.)		(presidentessa)X
(ambasciatore)X (masc.)	"ambassador"	(ambasciatore)X
(ambasciatrice)X(fem.)		(ambasciatrice)X
(cɔnsole)X	"consul"	(cɔnsole)X
(funzionario degli ɛsteri)X	"Foreign Service officer"	(funzionario degli ɛsteri)X
(cameriɛra)X	"waitress, maid"	(cameriɛra)X
(cameriɛre)X	"waiter"	(cameriɛre)X

76. Learn the following. They are all gender-extrinsic.

(cinese)X	"Chinese"	(cinese)X
(giapponese)X	"Japanese"	(giapponese)X
(russo)X	"Russian"	(russo)X
(spagnɔlo)X	"Spanish"	(spagnɔlo)X
(tedesco)X	"German"	(tedesco)

77. You will now be asked one of the questions of frame no. 71. Reply in two words by using è plus a translation of the English cue. Your response will be confirmed each time. NOTE: The words you will need to use are found in the following lists:

+cinese	+buddista	+colonnɛllo	+presidɛnte	+democratico
+giapponese	+cattolico	+generale	+ambasciatore	+democristiano
+russo	+ebrso	+militare	+console	+fascista
+spagnɔlo	+musulmano	+sergɛnte	+cameriɛre	+repubblicano
+tedesco	+protestante			+socialista

Questions		Cues
(1) Di che nazionalità è lui?	-	Russian
(2) Di che religione è lɛi?	-	Hebrew
(3) Che mestiɛre fa lɛi?	-	waitress
(4) Di che nazionalità è lɛi?	-	Japanese
(5) A quale partito polịtico appartiɛne lui?	-	Democrat
(6) Che lavoro fa lui?	-	ambassador
(7) Che grado ha lui?	-	sergeant
(8) Di che religione è lɛi?	-	Catholic
(9) Di che nazionalità è lui?	-	German
(10) Che lavoro fa lɛi?	-	consul
(11) A quale partito politico appartiɛne lɛi?	-	Republican
(12) Che lavoro fa lui?	-	in the military
(13) Di che religione è lɛi?	-	Protestant
(14) A quale partito polịtico appartiɛne lui?	-	Socialist
(15) Che mestiɛre fa lui?	-	waiter

78. The construction you used in the preceding drill changes to one with the unit marker when one is answering the question:

    Chi è X?   "Who is X?"

79. Thus, study the following contrast.

    a) (Di che nazionalita è quel signore?)X
       (È americano.)X
    b) (Chi è quel signore?)X
       (È un americano.)X

*80. You will now be asked a question like those of frame no. 71 *or* a *Chi* question as in frame no. 78. Answer accordingly, using a two-word response as in (a) above or a three-word response as in (b) above Your response should be a translation of the English cue given below and it will be confirmed each time. NOTE: The words you will need to know are either found listed in frames no. 69 and 77 or should be otherwise known to you.

Questions	Cues
(1) Di che nazionalità è quella signora?	Chinese
(2) Che grado ha lui?	colonel
(3) Chi è quella signora?	Yugoslavian
(4) Che mestiere fa quel signore?	actor
(5) Chi è quell'uomo?	Moslem
(6) Chi è quel signore?	priest
(7) Chi è quel giovane?	student
(8) Di che religione è quel signore?	Buddhist
(9) Che lavoro fa quella signorina?	actress
(10) Che grado ha lui?	general
(11) Chi è quella signorina?	maid
(12) Chi è quella donna?	sister [religious]
(13) Di che nazionalità è quel signore?	Spanish
(14) Chi è lui?	Belgian
(15) A quale partito politico appartiene lui?	Fascist
(16) Chi è quella signorina?	Foreign Service Officer
(17) Chi è lui?	government employee
(18) Chi è quella donna?	military officer
(19) Chi è quella donna?	agent
(20) Che lavoro fa lui?	guide

* * * * *

*81. Is the word ┼studente a two-form genderable, a three-form genderable or a four-form genderable?

*82. Is ┼studente gender-intrinsic or gender-extrinsic?

*83. In the first two examples of frame no. 69, what causes one to use the form studente rather than studentessa?

*84. When dealing with a gender-extrinsic word like ┼studente or ┼buono is it important to know what determines your choice of either a masculine form or a feminine form?

85. When dealing with gender-extrinsic words that are either *purely animate in reference* (like ⱡ*studɛnte* that only refers to people) or *marked* (like all of the examples in frame no. 69 marked by *un* or *una*), what determines the gender selection is the sex of the person or animal referred to.

86. Thus, we may say that the gender in such cases is determined by the *sex referent*.

*87. Study the following model.

S: Chi è quella spia?	"Who is that spy?"
R: È un americano.	"It's an American (male)."

This drill is designed to practice the gender-determinant rule of frame no. 85. You will hear a *Chi?* question involving a gender-intrinsic word like ⱡ*spia*. Reply as in the model with a marked genderable which should be a translation of the English cue given below. Your response will be confirmed each time.

Questions	Cues
(1) Chi è quella persona?	a doctor (male)
(2) Chi ɛra quel funzionario?	a young American (female)
(3) Chi è quell'agɛnte?	a Japanese (female)
(4) Chi era quella guardia?	a German (male)
(5) Chi ɛra quell'ufficiale?	a Russian (female)
(6) Chi è quella guida?	an Italian (male)
(7) Chi ɛra quel capo?	a young Frenchwoman
(8) Chi è quella spia?	a Belgian (male)
(9) Chi ɛra quella vittima?	a student (male)

88. When dealing with other kinds of cases involving gender-extrinsic words, however, the gender is determined differently.

89. For example, study the following sentences.

(Quella spia è americana.)X	"That spy is American."
(Quella guardia è simpatica.)X	"That guard is nice."
(Quella persona è scema.)X	"That person is stupid."
(Quella vittima ɛra zɔppa.)X	"That victim was lame."
(Quella guida è occupata.)X	"That guide is busy."

(Quel capo è americano.)X   "That boss is American."
(Quel funzionario non è   "That officer is not always
   sempre diplomatico.)X   diplomatic."
(Quell'ufficiale è fantastico.)X   "That (military) officer is fantastic."
(Quell'agente è occupato.)X   "That agent is busy."

90. In each of these examples the second word is a gender-intrinsic word —
spia, guardia, persona, vittima and *guida* are all grammatically feminine,
whereas *capo, funzionario, ufficiale* and *agente* are all grammatically masculine.

91. Notice how the last word in each sentence refers to the gender-intrinsic
word.

*92. Is the last word in each sentence gender-intrinsic or gender-extrinsic?

93. Notice how the last word in the first five sentences is grammatically feminine, whereas the last word in the last four sentences is grammatically
masculine.

94. In other words, the gender-extrinsic word that directly refers to a
gender-intrinsic word agrees with it in gender.

95. Said still another way, the gender of the gender-extrinsic word is *determined* by the gender of a gender-intrinsic word being referred to.

*96. Look again at the examples of frame no. 89. Do any of these sentences
show whether the person referred to is male or female?

*97. Does the gender of the last word in each of these sentences depend on the
sex referent?

*98. Now translate the following into Italian.
a) That (male) spy will be a *student* in Rome.

_____

b) That (male) spy is a young *American.* [use: *giovane* for "young"]

_____

*99. Of what gender are the equivalents of the underlined English words in
the two sentences you just translated?

*100. What determined the gender of these two words, the grammatically femi-
nine word *spia* or the sex referent?

*101. In frame no. 98, then, were the masculine forms *studente* and *americano* selected in accordance with what was stated in frame no. 85?

*102. However, while still talking about the same male spy, but without refer-ring to the word *spia* itself, which of the following ((a) or (b)) should you say?

a) *È americana.*
b) *È americano.*

*103. Thus, was the form of "American" here determined by (a) the word *spia* or (b) the sex referent?

104. What we have been trying to illustrate in frames no. 88 through no. 103 is the following rule:

When dealing with gender-extrinsic words other than those described in frame no. 85, the gender selection is based on:

1) the gender of a gender-intrinsic word that is being referred to and that *has in almost all cases been just mentioned* (frames no. 89 through no. 97), or

2) in the absence of the above, the sex referent (frames no. 102–103).

105. It is important that you remember frames no. 85 and no. 104 since these two frames tell you *what determines the gender of gender-extrinsic words.*

106. What is said in frames no. 85 and no. 104 regarding gender applies also to number.

*107. Thus, translate the following into Italian.

a) "Those (male) spies are students of Greek."

_____

b) "Those spies are American(s)."

_____

c) "They [referring to the male spies but without the word *spie* in mind] are American(s)."

_____

108. In determining the gender and number of a gender-extrinsic word, if no gender-intrinsic word is being referred to and there is no specific sex ref-erent, *the masculine singular form is normally used.*

*109. Thus, if you wish to refer to an American in general, which of the following should you say?

a) *un'americana*
b) *un'americano*

*110. How do you say, "What is that?" in Italian when you want to know the name of a particular object?

*111. Translate, "We speak Italian."

*112. Study the following model.

      S: Tre di questi capi sôno americani ed uno è italiano.
        "Three of these bosses is American and one is Italian."
   R-S: Soltanto un capo è italiano? Chi è?
        "Only one boss is Italian? Who is it?"
      R: Sonia Pinzan.
      S: ɔh, è italiana lɛi?
        "Oh, is she Italian?"
      R: Sì, è italiana.
        "Yes, she's Italian."

Imagine that someone is looking at a list of names. As in the model you will be given a statement about some people. Ask a question about the last part of the statement, using: *Soltanto un/una.......è.......? Chi è?* When given the name, you ask, surprised: *ɔh, ɛ.......lui/lɛi?* Your second question will then be answered in the affirmative. Your questions will be confirmed each time.—The purpose of this drill is to show how the same speaker (in this case, the student) may use a descriptive word like ~~*italiano*~~ once in its masculine form and another time in its feminine form, both times referring to the same person.

(1) Quattro di questi funzionari sôno cattɔlici ed uno è, ebrɛo .
    - Marįa Fɔrte.   - Sì, è ebrɛa.

(2) Tre di queste gaide sôno grɛche ed una è italiana.
    - Carlo Gąber.   - Sì, è italiano.

(3) Diɛci di questi agɛnti sôno scientįfici ed uno è diplomątico.
    - Bianca Tagliaferro.   - Sì, è diplomątica.

(4) Diɛci di queste persone sôno comuniste ed una è repubblicana.
    - Mario Lo Iɔla.   - Sì, è repubblicano.

(5) Due di queste guardie sôno russe ed una è tedesca.
    - Rudolf Rainer.   - Sì, è tedesco.

(6) Tre di questi capi sôno americani ed uno è italiano.
    - Sonia Pinzan.   - Sì, è italiana.

* * * * *

113. The word +uɔvo is one of a limited group of genderables that behave in a
     unique manner.

114. Such genderables are peculiar because they are MASCULINE in the SIN-
     GULAR, ending in -o, but FEMININE in the PLURAL, ending in -a.

• End of Tape 12A •

Tape 12B

115. Repeat and learn the following.

Masculine	Feminine
(Quest'uɔvo è fresco.)X	(Queste uɔva sôno fresche.)X
"This egg is fresh."	"These eggs are fresh."
(Questo paio è brutto.)X	(Queste paia sôno brutte.)X
"This pair is ugly."	"These pairs are ugly."
(Questo centinaio*è caro.)X	(Queste centinaia sôno care.)X
"This hundred is expensive."	"These hundreds are expensive."
(Questo migliaio* è cattivo.)X	(Queste migliaia sôno cattive.)X
"This thousand is bad."	"These thousands are bad."
(Quel miglio è esatto.)X	(Quelle miglia sôno esatte.)X
"That mile is exact."	"Those miles are exact."
(Quel braccio è lungo.)X	(Quelle braccia sôno lunghe.)X
"That arm is long."	"Those arms are long."
(Quel dito è corto.)X	(Quelle dita sôno corte.)X
"That finger is short."	"Those fingers are short."
(Quel labbro è grɔsso.)X	(Quelle labbra sôno grɔsse.)X
"That lip is { fat / big."	"Those lips are { fat / big."

*116. Study the following model.

    S: Quest' uɔvo è fresco.   "This egg is fresh."
    R: Anche queste uɔva sôno   "These eggs are fresh, too."
       fresche.

Follow the above model with the statements you will hear. Your response
will be confirmed each time.

(1) Questo centinaio è pronto.
(2) Questo braccio è buɔno.
(3) Questo paio è caro.
(4) Questo migliaio è buɔno.
(5) Questo dito è spɔrco.
(6) Questo labbro è grɔsso.
(7) Questo miglio è magnịfico.
(8) Quest'uɔvo è fresco.

*117. Study the following model.

S: Queste uɔva sôno fresche.   "These eggs are fresh."

R: Anche $\left.{\text{quest'} \atop \text{questo}}\right\}$ uɔvo è fresco.   "This egg is fresh, too."

Follow the above model with the statements you will hear. Your response will be confirmed each time.

(1) Queste centinaia sôno pronte.
(2) Queste paia sôno care.
(3) Queste dita sôno spɔrche.
(4) Queste miglia sôno magnịfiche.
(5) Queste braccia sôno buɔne.
(6) Queste labbra sôno grɔsse.
(7) Queste migliaia sôno buɔne.
(8) Queste uɔva sôno fresche.

*NOTE: The words ┼centinaio and ┼migliaio refer to approximate numbers.

(not recorded)

In accordance with the guidelines given in this unit, for each of the forms listed below, choose from the following items—*amica, amico, pôsto, studɛnte, studentessa, uɔmo*—that word which might occur immediately after it in a breath group. NOTE: In some cases, as in no. 2, more than one possibility exists.

1) buɔn'_____

2) buɔn_____; buɔn_____; buɔn_____

3) buɔno_____

4) buɔna_____

5) quest'_____; quest'_____; quest'_____

6) questo_____; questo_____

7) questa_____

8) quell'_____; quell'_____; quell'_____

9) quel _____

10) quello _____

11) quella _____

12) bɛll'_____; bɛll'_____; bɛll_____

13) bɛl_____

14) bɛllo _____

15) bɛlla_____

16) grand'_____; grand'_____, grand'_____

17) gran_____

18) grande_____; grande _____; grande_____

TEST B

(not recorded)

In accordance with the guidelines given in this unit, for each of the titles listed below, choose from the following items—*Agata, Antonio, Eugenio, Giovanni, Maria, Stêfano* that name which might occur immediately after it in a breath group. NOTE: In some cases, as in no. 1, more than one possibility exists.

1) Sant'_____; Sant'_____; Sant'_____
2) San _____
3) Santo _____
4) Santa _____
5) Fra _____; Fra _____; Fra _____; Fra_____
6) Dɔn _____; Dɔn _____; Dɔn _____; Dɔn_____
7) Suɔr _____; Suɔr_____

TEST C

(answers not recorded)

DICTATION: You will hear fifteen sentences. Write each one as you hear it, paying special attention to apostrophes.

1)_____

2)_____

3)_____

4)_____

5)_____

6)_____

7)_____

8)_____

9)_____

10)_____

11)_____

12)_____

13)_____

14)_____

15)_____

TEST D

(answers not recorded)

The instructions for this test are those of frame no. 80, but using the English cues given here.

1) Japanese   -_____

2) ambassador   -_____

3) waiter   -_____

4) Protestant   -_____

5) Christian Democrat -_____

6) consul   -_____

7) Russian   -_____

8) Republican   -_____

9) sergeant   -_____

10) doctor   -_____

11) spy   -_____

12) Hebrew   -_____

13) brother [religious] -_____

14) psychiatrist   -_____

15) in the military -_____

16) guard   -_____

17) Socialist   -_____

18) German   -_____

19) Catholic   -_____

20) Foreign Service Officer -_____

UNIT 29

(not recorded)

In each of the sentences below, fill in the blanks with the proper form of *+bɛllo*.

1) È un _____ americano.
2) Quella spia è_____.
3) È una _____ giapponese.
4) Maria è sempre _____.
5) Quel capo è_____.
6) Quel giovane è_____.
7) Quel _____ giovane è qui.
8) Quella giovane è _____.
9) Quelle guardie sôno_____.
10) Questi funzionari non sôno_____.
11) Quell'agɛnte è_____.
12) Quella vittima ɛra_____.
13) Quest'uɔvo è _____.
14) Quelle dita sôno_____ .
15) Questo _____ paio mi piace molto.
16) Queste uɔva non sôno _____.
17) Questo programma è _____.
18) Questa _____ radio mi piace.
19) Quelle guide sôno _____.
20) Questi vaglia sôno_____.
21) Quel _____ studɛnte mi piace molto.
22) Quel _____ sergɛnte è a Roma.

TEST F

(not recorded)

Next to each of the words listed put a check in the appropriate column according to whether the word is (a) GENDER-EXTRINSIC, (b) MASCULINE, (c) FEMININE, or (d) MASCULINE IN THE SINGULAR AND FEMININE IN THE PLURAL.

	GE (a)	M (b)	F (c)	M(sg) F(pl) (d)
1) ɟagente				
2) ɟambasciatore				
3) ɟamericano				
4) ɟanimale				
5) ɟartista				
6) ɟattore				
7) ɟbambino				
8) ɟbraccio				
9) ɟbuɔno				
10) ɟcameriere				
11) ɟcapo				
12) ɟcentinaio				
13) ɟcinese				
14) ɟcittà				
15) ɟcolonnello				
16) ɟcɔnsole				
17) ɟdemocratico				
18) ɟdito				
19) ɟdottore				
20) ɟfunzionario				
21) ɟgrande				
22) ɟguardia				
23) ɟguida				
24) ɟimpiegato				
25) ɟinsegnante				
26) ɟlabbro				
27) ɟlibro				
28) ɟmano				

	(a)	(b)	(c)	(d)
29) ┼miglio				
30) ┼migliaio				
31) ┼nome				
32) ┼occupato				
33) ┼paio				
34) ┼persona				
35) ┼presidɛnte				
36) ┼programma				
37) ┼protestante				
38) ┼psichiatra				
39) ┼sergɛnte				
40) ┼spɛcie				
41) ┼spesa				
42) ┼spia				
43) ┼statale				
44) ┼studɛnte				
45) ┼süicida				
46) ┼ufficiale				
47) ┼uɔmo				
48) ┼uɔvo				
49) ┼vino				
50) ┼vi̠ttima				

TEST G

(not recorded)

Translate the following thoughts into Italian by using *only* what has been presented so far.

1) That good-looking student doesn't study very much. He doesn't like to study.

_____

2) It's in the Garda, a large lake in the North.

_____

3) He's both a great gentleman and a great Italian.

_____

4) That beautiful studio belongs to Mr. Jones.

_____

5) That beautiful book is not Dr. Russo's.

_____

6) Who are those beautiful actresses?

_____

7) What kind of work does that man do here in Rome?

_____

8) Who is that guide? Is he an American?

_____

9) Is that guide American?

_____

10) He's a good employee but he talks a lot.

_____

11) Are you a Foreign Service Officer? I thought you were in the military.
   [NOTE: Put this idea into Italian in the form of a question.]

_____

12) Those women are Foreign Service Officers. They work at the American
   Embassy in London.

_____

13) There's a military officer on the {line. phone He'd like to speak with one of the agents.

_____

14) There are hundreds of mistakes here. Why are they always making mistakes?

_____

15) These three pairs are beautiful but I only want that pair over there.

_____

16) Those eggs aren't expensive and they are magnificent.

_____

17) They don't work for the government. They are priests.

_____

18) Is _he_ a priest? I thought he was a doctor. [SEE NOTE for no. 11]

_____

19) What is your nationality? Are you Spaniards?

_____

20) These waiters are always nice. I like them a lot.

_____

TEST H

(answers not recorded)

COMPREHENSION EXPANSION: You will hear a narrative in Italian. The narrative purposely contains several new items that were not introduced in previous units. After hearing it one or more times, write a résumé in English of all that you understood. Try to guess the meaning of the new items from their form and their context. The idea is to see how well you can guess. Indicate here how many times you listen to the narrative—_____times.

TEST I

(not recorded)

The meaning of some of the new items found in the narrative of TEST H can be easily guessed. Give the Italian equivalents (used in the narrative) of the following.

1) Christmas - _____

2) important - _____

3) decorations - _____

4) trepidation - _____

5) Santa Claus - _____

6) in general - _____

7) Epiphany - _____

8) tradition - _____

9) policemen - _____

10) government - _____

UNIT 29

TEST A ANSWERS

1) amica
2) amico - pôsto uɔmo
3) studɛnte
4) studentessa
5) amica - amico uɔmo
6) pôsto - studɛnte
7) studentessa
8) amica - amico uɔmo
9) pôsto
10) studɛnte
11) studentessa
12) amica – amino – uɔmo
13) pôsto
14) studɛnte
15) studentessa
16) amica - amico - uɔmo
17) pôsto
18) pôsto - studɛnte - studentessa

TEST B ANSWERS

1) Ạgata - Antɔnio - Eugɛnio
2) Giovanni
3) Stêfano
4) Marịa
5) Antɔnio - Eugɛnio - Giovanni - Stêfano
6) Antɔnio - Eugɛnio - Giovanni - Stêfano
7) Ạgata - Marịa

TEST C   ANSWERS

1) Sôn qui?
2) Non sɔ dov'ɛ.
3) È un buɔn agɛnte.
4) Non mi piace quel libro.
5) Hɔ una buɔn'amica in Italia.
6) È un grand'ażżardo.
7) Fra Antɔnio non ɛra un grand'artista.
8) Vorrɛi mangiare quest'uɔvo.
9) Lɛi sa chi è Sant'Andrɛa?
10) Conosce Dɔn Iạcopo Lɛi?
11) Non vuɔl andarci con il dottor Rossi.
12) Ce n'è uno lì ma è un pɔ' caro.
13) Suɔr Marịa è una buɔna suɔra.
14) Chi è quell'antropɔlogo?
15) È simpatico ma non è un bɛll'uɔmo.

TEST D   ANSWERS

Questions	Answers
1) Di che nazionalita è lui?	È giapponese.
2) Chi è lui?	È un ambasciatore.
3) Che lavoro fa lui?	È camerierɛ.
4) Di che religione è lɛi?	È protestante.
5) A quale partito politico appartiɛne lɛi?	È democristiana.
6) Chi è lɛi?	È un cɔnsole.
7) Chi è lui?	È un russo.
8) A quale partito polịtico appartiɛne lui?	È repubblicano.
9) Che grado ha lui?	È sergɛnte
10) Che mestiɛre fa lui?	È dottore. (or) È mɛdico.
11) Chi è lui ?	È una spia.
12) Di che religione è lɛi?	È ebrɛa.
13) Chi è lui ?	È un frate.
14) Chi è quel signore?	È uno psichiatra.
15) Che lavore fa lɛi?	È militare.
16) Chi è lui?	È una guardia.
17) A quale partito politico appartiɛne quell'uɔmo?	È socialista.
18) Di che nazionalita è quella dɔnna?	È tedesca.
19) Di che religione è quella signora?	È cattɔlica.
20) Chi è quella signorina?	È un funzionario degli ɛsteri.

TEST E   ANSWERS

1) bell'
2) bella
3) bella
4) bella
5) bello
6) bello
7) bel
8) bella
9) belle
10) belli
11) bello
12) bella
13) bello
14) belle
15) bel
16) belle
17) bello
18) bella
19) belle
20) belli
21) bello
22) bel

TEST F   ANSWERS

1) b	11) b	21) a	31) b	41) c
2) a	12) d	22) c	32) a	42) c
3) a	13) a	23) c	33) d	43) a
4) b	14) c	24) a	34) c	44) a
5) a	15) b	25) a	35) a	45) a
6) a	16) b	26) d	36) b	46) b
7) a	17) a	27) b	37) a	47) b
8) d	18) d	28) c	38) a	48) d
9) a	19) a	29) d	39) b	49) b
10) a	20) b	30) d	40) c	50) c

TEST G   ANSWERS

1) Quel bɛllo studɛnte non studia molto. Non gli piace studiare.

2) È nel Garda, un grande lago nel Nɔrd.

3) È un gran signore ed anche un grand'italiano.

4) Quel bɛllo studio è del signor Jones.

5) Quel bɛl libro non è del dottor Russo.

6) Chi sôno quelle bɛlle attrici?

7) Che lavoro fa qui a Roma quell'uɔmo?

8) Chi è quella guida? È un americano?

9) È americana quella guida?

10) È un buɔn impiegato ma parla molto.

11) È un funzionario degli Ɛsteri Lɛi? Non è militare?

12) Quelle dɔnne sôno funzionari degli Ɛsteri. Lavɔrano all' Ambasciata Americana a Londra.

13) C'è un ufficiale al telɛfono. Vuol ⎫
      Vorrĕbbe ⎭ parlare con un agɛnte.

14) Ci sôno centinaia di sbagli qui. Perchè fanno sɛmpre sbagli?
      (or) Perchè sbagliano sɛmpre?

15) Queste tre paia sono bɛlle ma vɔglio soltanto quel paio lì.

16) Quelle uɔva non sôno care e sôno magnịfiche.

17) Non sôno statali. Sôno prɛti.

18) È prɛte lui? Non è ⎰ mɛdico
                          ⎱ dottore?

19) Di che nazionalità siĕte? Siĕte spagnɔli?

20) Questi camerięri sôno sɛmpre simpạtici. Mi pịacciono molto.

TEST H ANSWERS

Giovedì sarà il 25 dicembre e il 25 dicembre è Natale.

In Italia questa festa è molto importante; ci sôno decorazioni in ogni casa e in ogni città.

Generalmente nel Nord, a Torino, a Genova, a Milano, i bambini aspettano con trepidazione Babbo Natale. Babbo Natale è un vecchio che arriva la sera tardi quando dormiamo e porta qualcosa per i bambini buoni.

A Roma, a Napoli, a Palermo e in generale nel Sud, i bambini aspettano la Befana che arriva il 6 gennaio, per l'Epifania. La Befana è una buona vecchia che il 6 gennaio porta qualcosa per i bambini buoni.

A Roma c'è una bella tradizione per l'Epifania: con la collaborazione di poliziotti, agenti, guardie e autorità del governo, ogni anno in piazza Navona c'è una gran festa per i bambini. In quel giorno anche un bambino povero può avere un po' di gioia.

The following is a *translation* of the narrative. Student résumés should reflect the information given here.

"Thursday will be December 25 and December 25 is Christmas.

In Italy this holiday is very important. There are decorations in every home and in every city.

Generally in the North (in Turin, Genoa, Milan) the children await Father Christmas (Santa Claus) with trepidation. Santa Claus is an old man who comes late in the evening when we are asleep and he brings something for the good children.

In Rome, Naples, Palermo and in the South in general, the children wait for the Befana who comes on January 6, on the day of the Epiphany. The Befana is a kind old woman who on January 6 brings something for the good children.

In Rome there is a beautiful tradition on the day of the Epiphany. With the collaboration of policemen, guards and government authorities, each year in Piazza Navona there is a great celebration for the children. On that day even a poor child can have a little bit of joy."

TEST I   ANSWERS

1) Natale
2) importante
3) decorazioni
4) trepidazione
5) Babbo Natale
6) in generale
7) Epifania
8) tradizione
9) poliziotti
10) governo

UNIT 30

*1. Do most Italian words end in a vowel, a semivowel or a consonant?

*2. When speaking Italian, which is more important, separating individual words or separating breath groups?

3. When one of the relatively few Italian words ending in a consonant comes in contact in a breath group with a following word beginning with a consonant, caution is in order.

4. Let us examine the case involving words ending in /L/. In Unit 15 you were told that for this sound-type the front part of the tongue almost always touches the upper teeth or the ridge directly behind the upper teeth.

5. Thus, in cases such as the following, be careful to pronounce the /L/ correctly.

(quel signore)X		(quel signore)X
(quel bɛl cane)X		(quel bɛl cane)X
(quel bɛl gatto)X	"that beautiful cat"	(quel bɛl gatto)X
(quel ristorante)X	"that restaurant"	(quel ristorante)X

6. In some cases such as in an -*ils*- combination, the /L/ sometimes disappears and the result resembles an -*ss*- combination. Listen carefully and repeat.

(Dov'ɛ il signor Riva?)X	(Dov'ɛ il signor Riva?)X
(Is sergɛnte parte domani.)X	(Il sergɛnte parte domani.)X

7. Be carefal, too, with words ending in -*n*. [See Unit 14.]

(un cane)X	(un cane)X;
(un figlio)X "a son"	(un figlio)X
(un bambino)X	(un bambino)X
(un ristorante)	(un ristorante)

8. With an -*nr*- combination as in the last example the preceding vowel is sometimes nasalized and the nasal consonant is dropped. Listen carefully and repeat.

(un ristorante)X	(un ristorante)X
(un buɔn ristorante)X	(un buɔn ristorante)X

9. Sometimes a word beginning with *s* + consonant is preceded by the letter *i*- after a word ending in a consonant. Thus, the items on the left may occur as on the right:

(in Scɔzia)	"in Scotland"	(in Iscɔzia)X
(in Spagna)	"in Spain"	(in Ispagna)X
(in Svɛzia)	"in Sweden"	(in Isvɛzia)X
(in Svizzera)	"in Switzerland"	(in Isvizzera)X
(per sbaglio)	"by mistake"	(per isbaglio)X

* * * * *

10. When the coming together of two words in a breath group brings two vowel letters together *no* complete pause should ever be present. Notice how in the following phrases the voice continues between the last two words.

(Ci sarà Anna.)X	*"Anna* will be there."	(Ci sarà Anna.) X
(Ci sarò oggi.)X	"I'll be there *today."*	(Ci sarò oggi.) X
(Ci sarà oggi.)X	"(S)he'll be there *today."*	(Ci sarà oggi.)X

*11. In each of the preceding examples, do the two vowel letters that are brought together represent stressed vowels?

12. In cases in which the vowel letters that are brought together do *not* both represent stressed vowels, *one* of the vowels tends to become a semivowel and in some cases (especially rapid speech) is lost.

*13. For example, listen to the following phrase. In how many syllables is it pronounced?

(diciotto italiani) "eighteen Italians"

14. What you just heard might be represented as follows, with the syllables separated. NOTE: The accent mark is used over the first /T/ to show that the consonant is TENSE. Repeat:

(/DI-Čɔ-T́OY-TA -LYÁ-NI/)X   (/DI-Čɔ-T́OY-TA-LYÁ-NI/)X

*15. In the preceding example which vowel became a semivowel, the /O/ or the /I/?

*16. Now listen to another pronunciation of the same phrase. In how many syllables is it pronounced?
(diciotto italiani)

17. What you just heard might be represented as follows with the syllables separated. Repeat:

(/DI-Čɔ-T́WI-TA -LYÁ-NI/)X   (/DI-Čɔ-T́WI-TA -LYÁ-NI/)X

*18. In the preceding example which vowel became a semivowel, the /O/ or the /I/?

19. In more rapid speech the same phrase might be pronounced as follows:
(diciotto italiani)

20. What you just heard might be represented as follows, with the syllables separated. Repeat:

(/DI-Čɔ-T́I-TA -LYÁ-NI/)X   (/DI-Čɔ-T́I-TA -LYÁ-NI/)X

*21. In the preceding example what happened to the final /O/ of the first word?

22. Frames no. 13 through no. 21 illustrate the principle explained in frame no. 12.

23. The vowel that either tends to become a semivowel or is lost is *always unstressed, often /I/ or /U/,* and *most often the first of the sequence.*

24. As closely as possible imitate the following phrases in which the two vowel letters in question are linked by‿. In the pronunciation of these phrases you will hear a full vowel only for the second of these two vowel letters.

   (Questi americani!)X
   (Queste americane!)X
   (Parla olandese ?)X   "Do you speak Dutch?"
   (Parla inglese.)X
   (Voglio una matita.)X   "I want a pencil."
   (Mi porti un libro.)X
   (Vado in Italia.)X
   (Parlo arabo.)X

25. In breath groups in which two like unstressed vowels come together, one vowel is usually formed, long or short.
   Repeat:

   (Tutti insieme;)X   "All together!" [said in 4 syllables] (Tutti insieme!)X

26. The importance of all that has been said so far regarding breath groups should not be underestimated. In order to sound pleasing to the ear and to attempt to imitate educated Italian speech you must strive for mastery of this material.

                              * * * * *

*27. Now let us turn to something else. So far you have had two individual words for "you," one used as a singular (to address one person) and the other used as a plural (to refer to the person you are addressing *plus* one or more people). What are these two words?

28. Besides these two words, Italian has other words for "you." The reason you were given *Lei* and *voi* first is that these two are the ones that an adult will more readily need to know. Their range of usage is quite large.

29. At this time, however, two new words for "you" will be introduced. These two words are much more limited in use and should be used with care.

30. In the plural, besides the word *voi*, Italians also use *Loro* (preferably capitalized).

31. Unlike *voi, Loro* is preferably used in highly formal situations such as when addressing two or more very important government officials or distinguished guests.

32. Although some Italians use *Loro* in situations in which other Italians would use *voi*, the distinction in the same speaker seems to be one of a more formal connotation for *Loro* as opposed to a less formal or an informal connotation for *voi*.

*33. Should you use *voi* or *Loro* in the following situation? You are speaking to several friends whom you have invited over for drinks at your home.

*34. Should you use *voi* or *Loro* in this situation? You are officially welcoming the Mayor and two other city officials.

35. Besides these distinctions, you should know that *voi* is the form generally used *to address the public* in a speech, an advertisement, etc.

36. Furthermore, *voi* is sometimes used as a *singular*, especially in written Italian as a translation of English "you" or French "vous" This is commonly done in magazine cartoons.

37. If ever you are in doubt as to whether to use *Loro* or *voi*, use *Loro*.

38. In the singular, besides the word *Lei*, Italians also use *tu*.

39. Unlike *Lei, tu* is preferably used in highly informal situations such as most of the situations in which you are addressing a person (adult or child) that you would call by his or her first name. It is also used (a) in prayers and (b) for animals.

40. In addressing adults it is best for you *not* to use *tu* unless the Italian asks you to do so. The Italian will normally do this by saying something like:

(Perchè non ci diamo del tu?)X   "Why don't we use 'tu' with each other?"

(Ci diamo del tu?)X   "Shall we use 'tu' with each other?"
(Diamoci del tu!)X   "Let's use 'tu' with each other"
(Mi dia del tu, per favore.)X   "Please use 'tu' with me."

41. Some conversations in which it is generally advisable for you to use *Lɛi*
    and not *tu* are between:

    a) boss and secretary
    b) employer and domestic
    c) customer and waiter/waitress.

*42. Should you use *tu* or *Lɛi* in the following situation? You are being intro-
    duced to the wife or one of your Italian co-workers.

*43. Should you use *tu* or *Lɛi* in the following situation? You are speaking with
    your friend Carla.

44. If ever you are in doubt as to whether to use *Lɛi* or *tu*, use *Lɛi*.

45. To review the important uses of the forms for "you,"study the following
    chart:

SITUATIONS	Singular	Plural
highly formal	Lɛi {	Loro
formal		voi (or) Loro
informal	Lɛi (or) tu	} voi
highly informal	tu	

46. In other words, the Italian forms for "you" might be labeled as follows:

    tu   -   informal, singular
    Lɛi -   not highly informal, singular

    voi -   not highly formal, plural
    Loro -   formal, plural

* * * * *

47. In Unit 28 you learned that Italian verbs generally have at least five forms in a tense like the PRESENT.

*48. Write the forms indicated of the PRESENT TENSE of ɟascoltare.

IO FORM - _____ NOI FORM - _____
                                 VOI FORM - _____
LEI FORM - _____ LORO FORM - _____

*49. In a situation in which you are addressing people as *voi*, which verb form should you use to address these people?

50. In a situation in which you are addressing people as *Loro* the verb form you should use to address these people is the LORO FORM.

*51. Thus, how would you say, "Are you well, gentlemen?" in a highly formal situation?

52. In a situation in which you are addressing someone as *tu*, a special verb form must be used that we will call the TU FORM.

53. In the PRESENT TENSE this form may be derived from the LEI FORM as follows:
    a) if the *LEI FORM ends in an unstressed vowel;* change the final vowel to -*i* (e.g. *parli, proponi, finisci*);
    b) if the *LEI FORM ends in a stressed vowel,* add -*i* to it (thus: *dai, fai, hai, puɔi, sai, stai, vai*).

*54. Write the PRESENT TENSE LEI FORM and TU FORM of the following verbs:

	LEI FORM	**TU FORM**
ɟascoltare	_____	_____
ɟdesiderare	_____	_____
ɟvedere	_____	_____
ɟdire	_____	_____
ɟcapire	_____	_____
ɟsenture	_____	_____
ɟavere	_____	_____
ɟandare	_____	_____
ɟfare	_____	_____
ɟstare	_____	_____
ɟsapere	_____	_____
ɟpotere	_____	_____
ɟtradurre	_____	_____
ɟbere	_____	_____

*55. Remembering the spelling rules explained in Unit 28, write the PRESENT
TENSE LEI FORM and TU FORM of the following verbs:

	LEI FORM	TU FORM
†cominciare	_____	_____
†mangiare	_____	_____
†studiare	_____	_____
†scïare	_____	_____
†giocare	_____	_____
†vspiegare	_____	_____

56. Exceptions to the rule given in frame no. 53 are the followin

	LEI FORM	TU FORM
†essere	(è)X	(sɛi)X
†esserci	(c'è)X	(ci sɛi)X
†volere	(vuɔle)X	(vuɔi)X

* * * * *

57. PRESENT TENSE TU FORMS end in -i. However, in Unit 24 you were
given some other verb forms that also end in -i.

58. For example, in Unit 24 you were given the following forms of regular -are
verbs:

(Scusi!)X
(Ascolti!)X
(Studi!)X
(Aspɛtti!)X
(Parli!)X

*59. What were such forms called in Unit 24?

*60. If they are FORMAL REQUEST FORMS, are they forms of tu or forms of
Lei?

*61. Make sure that you are able to distinguish between a PRESENT TENSE TU
FORM and a LEI REQUEST FORM of regular -are verbs. They both end in
what letter?

* * * * *

*62. What did we decide to call the words io, Lei, lui, lɛi, noi, voi and loro in Unit
28?

*63. What are two new BASIC IDENTIFIERS that you have seen in this unit?

*64. Like the other BASIC IDENTIFIERS, *tu* and *Loro* are also used for emphasis in cases like the following. Translate:

a) "The doctor is American, but *you* are Italians, aren't you?" [use: *Loro*]

_____

b) *"You* are an American, but they are Italians, aren't they?" [use -*tu*]

_____

65. The following responses to questions with *chi* are treated like other cases of emphasis and require a BASIC IDENTIFIER, usually *after* the verb. Repeat.

(Chi è?)X	- (è lui.)X
"Who is it?"	"It is *he*."
(Chi comincia?)X	- (Comincia lεi.)X
"Who is going to begin?"	"*She* is (going to begin)."
(Chi va a Milano?)X	- (Ci andiamo noi.)X
"Who is going to Milan?"	"*We* are (going there)."
(Chi abita lì?)X	- (Ci abitano loro.)X
"Who lives there?"	"*They* live there."

* * * * *

66. As we have seen so far, Italian verb forms must agree with their BASIC IDENTIFIERS. In talking about oneself as "being well," one says *stɔ bɛne* whether the word *io* is actually uttered or not; in talking about a third person as "being well," one says *sta bɛne* whether the word *lεi* or *lui* is actually uttered or not.

67. Similarly, in Standard English one does not say "I is well" or "I are well," but rather "I am well," since the word "I" in Standard English goes with "am" rather than with "is" or "are."

68. In a sense, then, a word like "I" in English or the BASIC IDENTIFIERS in Italian may be said to "govern" the form of a verb in a given tense since they make a speaker select a particular verb form from within a given tense.

69. Elements that *govern* this kind of selection may conveniently be referred to as VERB GOVERNORS.

70. Notice that Italian equivalents of the English "It is I," "It is you," "It is we," etc. have the verb form agree with the following *io, Lɛi, noi,* etc.

(Sôno io.)X   "It is I."

(Sɛi tu.)X }
(È Lɛi.)X }   "It is you." [singular]

(È lui.)X   "It is he."

(È lɛi.)X   "It is she."

(Siamo noi.)X   "It is we."

(Siĕte voi.)X }
(Sôno Loro.)X }   "It is you. " [plural]

(Sôno loro.)X   "It is they."

*71. Thus, the VERB GOVERNOR in these Italian sentences is *io, tu, Lɛi,* etc., but what is the VERB GOVERNOR in each of the English equivalents given?

*72. Notice that the English equivalents of the same sentences may also be, "I am (the one)," "You are (the one)," etc., in which case what is the VERB GOVERNOR in English?

*73. Observe the following model.

S: Chi sôno i signori White?   "Who are Mr. and Mrs. White?"
R: Siamo noi.   *"We* are."

You will now be asked questions with *chi.* Answer as in the model by using the English cues shown. Your response will be confirmed each time.

Questions	Cues
(1) Chi è signor White?	I
(2) Chi è Mario Colombo ?	He
(3) Chi sôno i signori Di Stêfano?	they
(4) Chi è Maria Guzzi?	she
(5) Chi sôno Silvio e Anna Riva?	we
(6) Chi è la signora Fɛrro?	she
(7) Chi è la signorina Smith?	I
(8) Chi sôno i signori Brown?	we
(9) Chi sôno Tɛresa e Gina Cristaldi?	they
(10) Chi è il signor Bizzi?	he

*74. A VERB GOVERNOR may be something that may be replaced by a BASIC IDENTIFIER. Thus, since in the following sentence *Maria e Rɔsa* may be replaced by *loro*, what is the VERB GOVERNOR?

(Maria e Rɔsa sôno italiane.)X

*75. On the other hand, what is the VERB GOVERNOR in each of the following sentences?

a) (Questa casa è grande.)X
b) (Ci sôno due cestini lì.)X

*76. What is the VERB GOVERNOR in the following sentences?

a) (Chi sôno io?)X	"Who am I?"
b) (Chi sɛi tu?)X	"Who are you?" [singular]
c) (Chi siamo noi?)X	"Who are we?"
d) (Chi siĕte voi?)X	"Who are you?" [plural]
e) (Chi sôno loro?)X	"Who are they?"
f) (Chi sôno i signori Croce?)X	"Who are Mr. and Mrs. Croce?"

77. The preceding frame illustrates that the VERB GOVERNOR is the *last element* in a construction consisting of:

chi + †*essere* +   BASIC IDENTIFIER (or)
                      something that may be
                      replaced by a BASIC
                      IDENTIFIER

78. However, if the element following *chi + †esssere* is something other than the above, the VERB GOVERNOR is *chi*, which is always grammatically *singular*, even though the corresponding English may be plural. For example:

(Chi è americano qui?)X	{ "Who is American here?" "Who are American here?"
(Chi non sta bɛne ɔggi?)X	{ "Who isn't well today?" "Who aren't well today?"
(Chi parla francese qui?)X	"Who speak(s) French here?"
(Chi è avvocato qui?)X	{ "Who is a lawyer here?" "Who are lawyers here?"

*79. Notice that in the first and last examples above, not only is the verb singular because of the singular *chi*, but so is another word. What is it?

*80. Study the following model.

>   S: I signori (garbled) sôno americani.
>   "Mr. and Mrs. (garbled) are American."
>   R-S: Chi è americano?
>   "Who are American?"
>   R: I signori Richwood sôno americani.
>   "Mr. and Mrs. Richwood are American."

You will hear a statement which is partially garbled, followed by a space. In this space ask a *chi* question as in the model. Your question will be confirmed and followed by a final response.

* * * * *

*81. What is the VERB GOVERNOR in each of the following?

>   a) (Vedo un cane.)X
>   b) (Chiamiamo il signor Russo.)X
>   c) (Non conoscete i signori Croce?)X
>   d) (Parli inglese?)X
>   e) (Ɔggi parli in inglese?)X

82. In addition to a VERB GOVERNOR, a verb may be used with something else that answers the question *Chi?* "Whom?" or *Che cɔsa?* "What?" in connection with the verb.

83. For example, observe the following in which the first four sentences listed in frame no. 80 appear as responses or suggestions.

>   a) Che cɔsa vede Lɛi? - Vedo un cane.
>   b) Chi chiamate voi? - Chiamiamo il signor Russo.
>   c) Chi non conoscete? Non conoscete i signori Croce?
>   d) Che cɔsa parli? Parli inglese?

*84. What element in each of the sentences on the right seems to answer the question *Chi?* or *Che cɔsa?*

85. Such elements will be referred to as DIRECT OBJECTS of the verb.

86. In the case of sentence (e) of frame no. 81, on the other hand, there is no DIRECT OBJECT of the verb since *inglese* there does not answer the question *Che cɔsa?* but rather *In che cɔsa?* "In what?"

*87. Do verb forms always have a DIRECT OBJECT?

*88. Do the verbs in the following sentences have any DIRECT OBJECT?

(Andiamo a Venezia.)X
(Sôno in ufficio.)X
(Parlo con la signorina Jones?)X

*89. According to the definition of DIRECT OBJECT that you have been given in this unit, what is the DIRECT OBJECT of the verb in the following sentences?

a) (Giącomo è italiano.)X
b) (Alfredo è attore.)X

(answers not recorded)

DICTATION: You will hear twenty utterances. Write each one as you hear it, paying special attention to word divisions.

1)_____

2)_____

3)_____

4)_____

5)_____

6)_____

7)_____

8)_____

9)_____

10)_____

11)_____

12)_____

13)_____

14)_____

15)_____

16)_____

17)_____

18)_____

19)_____

20)_____

TEST B

(not recorded)

For each of the following situations indicate the form of address (*tu, Lɛi, voi* or *Loro*) you should use. NOTE: If the situation tells you nothing about whether those being addressed are distinguished people *or* close friends of yours, do *not* assume so.

1) You are speaking to Mr. Rossi, a recent acquaintance of yours.
2) You are addressing a group of newspapermen at a press conference.
3) You are telling the porter at the airport where to take your luggage.
4) You are speaking to the ambassador and his wife.
5) You are a visa officer interviewing a visa applicant, a businessman in his forties.
6) You are inviting the Bianchis to your home for dinner. Mr. Bianchi is an old friend of yours with whom you use the "tu" form, but Mrs. Bianchi you have just met. How do you address both of them together?
7) You are speaking with Angelo who is eight years old.
8) You are escorting a group of Italian visitors on a tour of a USA exhibition at an international fair.
9) You are in a restaurant giving the waiter your order.
10) You are being introduced to two Italian senators.
11) You are addressing yourself saying something like, "You are an idiot, Jack."
12) You are asking your secretary to call someone for you.
13) You have just met and are talking to a twenty-year-old Italian girl.
14) You are chatting with Giacomo, a close friend of yours.
15) You are the desk clerk of a first-class hotel addressing two or more distinguished guests.
16) You are speaking to a sales clerk in a store.
17) You are a visa officer interviewing two visa applicants, husband and wife.
18) You are at a garage, asking the mechanic to check a few things in your car.

TEST C

(answers not recorded)

You will hear statements in the IO FORM. For each statement write out a question in the TU FORM, expressing surprise, as in the following example:

S: Abito a Washington.   "I live in Washington."
R: Oh, abiti a Washington?   "Oh. You live in Washington?"

1) Capisco l'inglese.   _____

2) Sento un uomo.   _____

3) Ho due penne.   _____

4) Vado a Firenze domani.   _____

5) Faccio sbagli.   _____

6) Sto a casa stasera.   _____

7) So due lezioni.   _____

8) Non posso venire.   _____

9) Traduco bene.   _____

10) Bevo vino.   _____

11) Mangio una bistecca.   _____

12) Studio religione.   _____

13) Scio con Teresa.   _____

14) Non salgo ora.   _____

15) Gioco a tennis.   _____

16) Spiego una lezione oggi.   _____

17) Sôno astrologo.   _____

18) Non ci sôno domani mattina. _____

19) Non voglio lavorare stasera. _____

20) Esagero.   _____

21) Importo birra.   _____

22) Abito a New York.   _____

23) Conosco il signor Salvo.   _____

24) Non dormo bene.   _____

25) Leggo molto.   _____

26) Parto ɔggi.   _____

27) Non ɛsco stasera.   _____

28) Non vinco mai.   _____

29) Non propongo niɛnte.   _____

30) Prenɔto due tạvoli.   _____

31) Sottraggo.   _____

32) Dĕvo ritelefonare.   _____

33) Non dico niɛnte.   _____

34) Telɛfono sạbato.   _____

35) Pɛnso di cominciare lunedì.   _____

TEST D

(not recorded)

For each of the following sentences identify the VERB GOVERNOR and the
DIRECT OBJECT OF THE VERB. If a sentence has no DIRECT OBJECT, leave
the second column blank.

	Verb Govenor	Direct Object
1) Maria e Roberto sôno italiani.	_____	_____
2) Ci sôno due cestini lì.	_____	_____
3) Vedo un cane.	_____	_____
4) Non mi piacciono quelle signorine.	_____	_____
5) A quale partito politico appartiene Carlo?	_____	_____
6) Chiamiamo il signor Russo.	_____	_____
7) Litiga sempre con la segretaria.	_____	_____
8) Parlo con la signorina Jones?	_____	_____
9) Non conoscete i signori Croce?	_____	_____
10) Vorrei una stanza per due giorni.	_____	_____
11) In questa città ci sôno centinaia di studenti.	_____	_____
12) Parli inglese?	_____	_____
13) In quell'ufficio parla sempre la segretaria del signor Jones.	_____	_____
14) Chima i signori Jones il dottor Russo?	_____	_____
15) Oggi parli in inglese?	_____	_____

TEST E

(not recorded)

Underline the VERB GOVERNOR in each of the following questions.

1) Chi è lɛi?
2) Chi è americano qui?
3) Chi non sta bɛne ɔggi?
4) Chi sôno i signori Rossi?
5) Chi chiamate voi?
6) Chi conɔscono quelle signore?
7) Chi sôno io?
8) Chi parla francese qui?
9) Chi è quell'uɔmo?
10) Chi è avvocato qui?
11) Chi c'è in ufficio?
12) Chi è Marịa Ricci?
13) Chi conosce i signori Brown?
14) Chi chiạmano Anna e Rɔsa?
15) Chi siamo noi?

TEST F

(not recorded)

Translate the following thoughts into Italian by using *only* what has been presented so far.

1) [addressing a child] Do you know where I might find a good restaurant?

_____

2) [addressing a waiter] Do you see that man over there? Do you know who he happens to be?

_____

3) [addressing a waiter] Waiter, bring me a salad. Wait! Make that two salads, please.

_____

4) [addressing a maid] Will you be able to work Saturday night?

_____

5) Shall we use "tu" with each other? - All right! Let's use "tu" with each other.

_____

6) [addressing a secretary] You can finish this this afternoon, if you wish.

_____

7) [addressing a boss] Are you busy? There is a lawyer here. He says that he would like to speak with you.

_____

8) [addressing a customer] You don't like these books? All right. Would you rather have this one?

_____

9) [addressing two co-workers] Where are you going? Aren't you supposed to work today?

_____

10) [addressing two distinguished guests] Are you leaving tomorrow? When do you plan to get there?

_____

TEST G

(answers not recorded)

You will hear a narrative in Italian followed by thirteen questions. On the lines below, answer each question in Italian by using more than one or two words.

1) Che cosa sôno lui e Maria?

_____

2) Ạbitano insieme?

_____

3) Dove lavọrano?

_____

4) Perchè preferiscono abitare in campagna?

_____

5) Vanno insieme in ufficio?

_____

6) Quando fanno le spese?

_____

7) Non ritọrnano mai a casa per pranżo? Perchè?

_____

8) Mạngiano sempre in ufficio con due colleghi?

_____

9) è sempre molto occupata Marịa?

_____

10) Che giorno è ọggi?

_____

11) Perchè vanno a casa più tardi stasera?

_____

12) Dĕvono lavorare domani?

_____

13) Che possono fare domani?

_____

• **End of Tape 12B** •

TEST A   ANSWERS

1) Questo consolato ha dieci uffici.
2) Mi porti una mela, un po' di formaggio e anche un caffè.
3) Non ha una penna?
4) Děve andarci oggi?
5) Questi agenti hanno un buon pôsto.
6) Voglio un po' di vino ora.
7) Non ha una copia Andrea?
8) Non c'è ogni giorno.
9) Giochiamo a tennis con due amici.
10) Studia arabo in un'università in Giordania.
11) Parlano italiano a casa
12) È occupato ora. Può aspettare?
13) È caro anche qui in campagna.
14) Io ho una soluzione.
15) Ci sôno dodici americani in ambasciata.
16) Quanto fa uno più uno?
17) Lɛi è in Ispagna.
18) Che cos'è una gru?
19) C'ɛra lui iɛri?
20) Potrěbbe aspettare un momento? Non è in ufficio ora.

TEST B   ANSWERS

1) Lɛi?
2) voi
3) Lɛi
4) Loro
5) Lɛ
6) voi
7) tu
8) voi
9) Lɛ

10) Loro
11) tu
12) Lɛi
13) Lɛi
14) tu
15) Loro
16) Lɛi
17) voi
18) Lɛi

TEST C   ANSWERS

1) ɔh, capisci l'inglese?
2) ɔh, sɛnti un uɔmo?
3) ɔh, hai due penne?
4) ɔh, vai a Firɛnze domani?
5) ɔh, fai sbagli?
6) ɔh, stai a casa stasera?
7) ɔh, sai due lezioni?
8) ɔh, non puɔi venire?
9) ɔh, traduci bɛne?
10) ɔh, bevi vino?
11) ɔh, mangi una bistecca?
12) ɔh, studi religione?
13) ɔh, scii con Terɛsa?
14) ɔh, non sali ora?
15) ɔh, giochi a tɛnnis?
16) ɔh, spiɛghi una lezione ɔggi?
17) ɔh, sɛi astrɔlogo?
18) ɔh, non ci sɛi domani mattina?
19) ɔh, non vuɔi lavorare stasera?
20) ɔh, esageri?
21) ɔh, impɔrti birra?
22) ɔh, abiti a New Yɔrk?
23) ɔh, conosci il signor Salvo?
24) ɔh, non dɔrmi bɛne?
25) ɔh, lɛggi molto?
26) ɔh, parti ɔggi?
27) ɔh, non ɛsci stasera?

28) ɔh, non vinci mai?
29) ɔh, non proponi niɛnte?
30) ɔh, prenɔti due tạvoli?
31) ɔh, sottrai?
32) ɔh, dɛ̌vi ritelefonare?
33) ɔh, non dici niɛnte?
34) ɔh, telɛfoni sạbato?
35) ɔh, pɛnsi di cominciare lunedì.

TEST D   ANSWERS

Verb Govenor	Direct Object
1) Marịa e Robɛrto	italiani
2) due cestini	—
3) io	un cane
4) quelle signorine	—
5) Carlo	—
6) noi	il signor Russo
7) lui (or)	—
lɛi (or)	—
Lɛi	—
8) io	
9) voi	i signori Croce
10) io	una stanza
11) centinaia	—
12) tu	inglese
13) la segretaria	—
14) il dottor Russo	i signori Jones
15) tu	

TEST E   ANSWERS

1) lɛi
2) chi
3) chi
4) i signori Rossi
5) voi
6) quelle signore
7) io
8) chi
9) quell'uɔmo
10) chi
11) chi
12) Marịa Ricci
13) chi
14) Anna e Rɔsa
15) noi

TEST F ANSWERS

1) Sai dov'è un buon ristorante?
2) Vede quell'uomo lì? Sa chi è?
3) Cameriere, mi porti un'insalata. Aspetti! Mi porti due insalate, per favore.
4) Può lavorare sabato sera?
5) Ci diamo del tu? - Va bene! Diamoci del tu.
6) Può finire questo questo pomeriggio, se vuole.
7) È occupato? C'è un avvocato qui. Dice che vorrĕbbe
   parlare con Lei.
8) Non Le piacciono questi libri? Va bene. Preferisce questo?
9) Dove andate? Non lavorate oggi?
10) Partono domani? Quando pensano di arrivare?

TEST G ANSWERS

Io e Maria siamo impiegati. Lavoriamo in un ufficio in città, ma abitiamo fuori città perchè è meno caro e ci piace la campagna. Ogni giorno andiamo in ufficio insieme e il giovedì quando ritorniamo a casa, facciamo le spese.

Non ritorniamo mai a casa per pranzo perchè preferiamo mangiare qualcosa in città. Spesso andiamo in un ristorante con due colleghi. Qualche giorno Maria è molto occupata e non può venire con noi.

Stasera andiamo a casa più tardi perchè vogliamo vedere un film in città. Domani è sabato, non dobbiamo andare in ufficio e possiamo dormire.

1) Lui e Maria sono impiegati.
2) Non sappiamo se abitano insieme.
3) Lavorano in un ufficio in città.
4) Preferiscono abitare in campagna perchè è meno caro e gli piace la campagna.
5) Sì, vanno insieme in ufficio.

6) Fanno le spese il giovedì quando ritornano a casa.
7) Nɔ, non ritornano mai a casa per pranzo perchè preferiscono mangiare qualcɔsa in città.
8) Nɔ, spesso vanno in un ristorante con due colleghi.
9) Nɔ, qualche giorno è molto occupata.
10) Ɔggi è venerdì.
11) Stasera vanno a casa più tardi perchè vɔgliono vedere un film in città.
12) Nɔ, non dĕvono lavorare domani.
13) Domani pɔssono dormire.

RECAPITULATION (Units 26–30)

Sound-Types

sound-types	written symbols	as in:	unit
/š/ (always TENSE)	sc [before ε, e, i] sci [elsewhere]	scεna, scemo sci scià, sciɔpero, sciupare	26
/T̂S/ (always TENSE)	zz [usually between vowel sounds] z [elsewhere]	razza zio, Lazio	27
/D̂S/ (always TENSE)	żż [usually between vowel sounds] ż [elsewhere]	rażża żεro, ażiεnda	27

Consonants Best Treated as Always Tense (Unit 27)

/Ň/	–	as in:	*bagno*
/Ľ/	–	as in:	*aglio*
/š/	–	as in:	*fascio*
/T̂S/	–	as in:	*Venεzia*
/D̂S/	–	as in:	*ażiendale*

Slack Version of /š/ for /č/ Between Vowel Sounds (Unit 26)

Between vowel sounds (as in the word *pace*), some speakers, especially Tuscans, may pronounce a slack sound similar to /š/ in places where other Italians pronounce /č/. Either pronunciation of *pace*, however, will differ from that of *pasce*.

The Letter Z (Unit 27)

The letter z (or zz) in Italian may stand for either /T̂S/ or /D̂S/. Conventional Italian spelling does not differentiate the two sound-types. Wherever this text has ż (or żż), the student should use /D̂S/. Wherever this text has z (or zz), /T̂S/ is always acceptable, although in some of these cases an Italian may prefer /D̂S/ instead.

Syllabication in Spoken Italian (Unit 28)

In spoken Italian, syllables are separated in such a way that a SYLLABIC BREAK occurs *before* one of the following:

a) a vowel that is preceded by another vowel - e.g., zi-o
b) a semivowel that is between vowels - e.g., l'A-ia
c) a single consonant sound-type - e.g., pa-pa
d) the last consonant of a group - e.g., ques-to

         or

the entire group when it is represented by: ʒɛ-bra

$$\left.\begin{matrix} p \\ b \\ t \\ d \\ c \\ g \\ f \\ v \end{matrix}\right\} \; + \; \left\{\begin{matrix} l \\ r \end{matrix}\right.$$

More on Vowel Length (Unit 28)

Stressed vowels that *end syllables* are usually longer than those that do not end syllables. Thus, of the examples given under SYLLABICATION IN SPOKEN ITALIAN, the stressed vowel in questo is usually pronounced shorter than the stressed vowel in each of the other Italian examples.

Syllabication in Written Italian (Unit 28)

In writing and printing, syllabication is important in order to know what to do when approaching the end of a line and there is only enough room for part of a word. In such cases, the syllabication rule given above for spoken Italian is generally followed. However, there are four important exceptions.

1) Combinations of vowel letters ($a,e,\varepsilon,i,o,ɔ,u$) are generally not separated. Thus, the vowel letters in either *zio* or *l'Aia* should not be separated.

2) Tense consonants represented by a symbol containing two like consonant letters or by -cq- show a syllabic break between the two consonant letters involved. Thus: raz-za, ac-qua

3) *S* before a consonant is normally not separated from the consonant it precedes.
   Thus: que-sto
4) Some writers separate a prefix from the rest of the written word.
   Thus: in-a̱-bi-le (prefix *in-*)

In addition, some writers or printers dislike having the last word of a line end in an apostrophe. Thus, either of the following may be found:

....una
artiste...

or

....un
artiste...

Elision (Unit 29)

The dropping of the *final vowel* of a word immediately before a vowel or a semivowel of another word is very common in certain breath groups and is referred to as ELISION. ELISION is normally represented in writing by an apostrophe. (see frames no. 6 and no. 7) For example, *un'italiana, c'è, anch'io.*

Apocopation (Unit 29)

APOCOPATION is the dropping of the final *unstressed vowel* or *unstressed syllable* of a word.

   a) Some such words may occur with nothing following them and a they are written with an apostrophe. For example, *pɔ'* (short for *pɔco*) as in: *aspetti un pɔ'.*
   b) Other such words have APOCOPATION *only* immediately before another word in a breath group and these words are never represented in writing with an apostrophe. For example, *vuɔl parlare* for *vuɔle parlare.*

Although APOCOPATION is generally optional*, it is normal to have it with words of more than one syllable which end in *-e* or *-o* preceded by *n, r, m,* or *l* (the consonant letters in the word "normal").

*See frame no. 29 for those cases in which APOCOPATION *should* take place.

Consonants Brought Together in Breath Groups (Unit 30)

A word ending in the letter *l* or *n* brought in contact with a following word beginning with a consonant results in some interesting sound combinations (see frames no. 5–8).

Sometimes a word beginning with *s* + consonant is preceded by the letter *i-* after a word ending in a consonant. Thus, *per sbaglio* may occur as *per isbaglio*.

Vowels Brought Together in Breath Groups (Unit 30)

When the coming together of two words in a breath group brings two vowel letters together, *no* complete pause should ever be present. In such cases, if the vowel letters brought together do *not* both represent stressed vowels, *one* tends to become a semivowel and in some cases (especially rapid speech) is lost. The vowel that does so is *always unstressed*, often /I/ or /U/ and *most often the first of the sequence*.

For example: *ci sarà Agata*   /CISARÁÁGATA/
diciotto italiani   /DIČɔ́TOYTALYÁNI/
or
/DIČɔ́TWITALYÁNI/
or
/DIČɔ́TITALYÁNI/ (rapid speech)

Compound Verbs (Unit 26)

A COMPOUND VERB is one consisting of a prefix (like *ri-*) plus a base verb (like *†vedere)*. Thus, *†rivedere* is a COMPOUND VERB.

Syncopated Infinitives (Unit 26)

A SYNCOPATED INFINITIVE is one that has become shortened from an earlier, archaic form which can be useful in remembering some of the other forms of a given verb. The Italian SYNCOPATED INFINITIVES are the following, together with their compounds:

bere   from an earlier, archaic *bevere*
dire   from an earlier, archaic *dicere*
fare   from an earlier, archaic *facere*
porre   from an earlier, archaic *ponere*
trarre from an earlier, archaic *traere*
and verbs ending in: *-durre,*
like *produrre* from an earlier, archaic *producere*

Verb Classes (Unit 26)

Italian has three VERB CLASSES defined according to the ending of the INFINITIVE. In the case of SYNCOPATED INFINITIVES, the VERB CLASS is determined by the earlier, archaic form. Thus,

CLASS I	CLASS II	CLASS III
┼ascoltare	┼vedere and syncopated infinitives)	┼capire

Verb Irregularities or Peculiarities (Unit 26)
Class I

Some verbs with infinitives of more than three syllables have their stress in the PRESENT TENSE SINGULAR forms (and the LORO FORM) on the *third vowel from the end* rather than on the second vowel from the end. (see frames no. 47 and 48)

Thus: ┼abitare - ạbito, ạbiti, ạbita, ạbitano

Class II

Some CLASS II infinitives are stressed on the second vowel from the end (like *vedere*) whereas most are stressed on the third vowel from the end (like *piɔvere*).

Most verbs with infinitives in -*cere*, -*scere*, or -*gere* have PRESENT TENSE IO FORMS AND LORO FORMS that only *look* regular in their written forms.

Thus: ┼vịncere   - *vinco, vinci, vince, vịncono*
       ┼conoscere - *conosco, conosci, conosce, conọscono*
       ┼leggere   - *leggo, leggi, legge, leggono*

In addition to the above, CLASS II contains many highly irregular verbs to be learned through observation.

Class III

Although most CLASS III verbs have forms like ┼capire *(capisco, capisci, capisce, capiscono)* a few (about twenty) have forms like ┼partire *(parto, parti, parte, pạrtono)*.

Basic Identifiers (Units 26, 28, and 30)

Words used to emphasize or clarify the idea of someone or something involved in the meaning of Italian verb endings are called BASIC IDENTIFIERS. Such words are *io, tu, Lɛi, lui, lɛi, noi, voi, Loro,* and *loro*.

IO Form, LEI Form, etc. (Units 26, 28, and 30)

Verb forms may be referred to by the BASIC IDENTIFIER that might occur with them. Thus:

IO FORM	- *ascolto*	NOI FORM	- *ascoltiamo*
TU FORM	- *ascolti*	VOI FORM	- *ascoltate*
LEI FORM	- *ascolta*	LORO FORM	- *ascoltano*

Formation of Present Tense TU Form (Unit 30) General Rule

If the LEI FORM ends in an unstressed vowel, change the final vowel to -*i*;
If the LEI FORM ends in a stressed vowel, add-*i* to it.

Thus:

LEI FORM	TU FORM
ạbita	*ạbiti*
sta	*stai*

Formation of Present Tense LORO Form (Unit 28) General Rule

If the LEI FORM ends in unstressed /A/, add -*no* to it;
If the LEI FORM ends in stressed /A/, add -*nno* to it;
If the LEI FORM does not end in /A/, add -*no* to the IO FORM.
Thus:

LEI FORM	LORO FORM
ạbita	*ạbitano*
sta	*stanno*
vede	*vẹdono*
capisce	*capịscono*

Verb Governor (Unit 30)

The element that may be said to "govern" the form of a verb in a given tense (since it makes the speaker select a particular verb form within a given tense) is the VERB GOVERNOR.

As a VERB GOVERNOR the word *chi* is always grammatically singular. Thus: *Chi è americano qui?* Who is American here? or Who are American here?

Direct Object of the Verb (Unit 30)

Something other than the VERB GOVERNOR, that answers the question *Chi?* "Whom?" or *Che cosa?* "What?" in connection with a verb is the DIRECT OBJECT of the verb.

Forms of Address (Unit 30)

SITUATIONS		singular	plural
highly formal			Loro
formal		Lɛi	voi (or) Loro
informal		Lɛi (or) tu	voi
highly informal		tu	

Relationship Between Certain Verbs, Words in -zione and Their English Cognates (Unit 27)

Many CLASS I verbs with infinitives of more than three syllables that have their stress in the PRESENT TENSE SINGULAR forms on the *third vowel from the end* have related forms in -*zione*. Furthermore, the Italian stress on the singular verb forms parallels the English stress on most of the corresponding cognates.

Thus:

INFINITIVE	ENGLISH COGNATE
abitare	inhabit

	IO FORM	LEI FORM
	abito	*abita*

WORD IN -ZIONE
abitazione

The I Rule (Unit 28)

Two *i*'s together are not normally found in the spelling of Italian words unless the first one stands for a stressed /I/.

Thus:

					(pronounced)
	mangi-	+	*-iamo*	= *mangiamo*	/MANǦÁMO/
	sci-	+	*-iamo*	= *sciamo*	/ŠIÁMO/
sg.					
bacio:	*baci-*	+	*-i*	= *baci*	/BÁČI/
zio:	*zi-*	+	*-i*	= *zii*	/T͡SÍI/
	(with stressed /I/)				

-ch- and gh- Before Certain Verb Endings and in Plural Genderables (Unit 28)

	gioc-	+	-iamo	=	giochiamo
	spieg-	+	-iamo	=	spieghiamo
sg.					
	pɛsca: pɛsc	+	-e	=	pɛsche
	vôga: vôg	+	-e	=	vôghe

Plural of Genderables in -co and -go (Unit 28)

a) Most singlar genderables ending in -co immediately following a stressed syllable form their plural in -chi.
Thus: (singular) fico - (plural) fichi

Exceptions are: (singular) - (plural)

amico	amici
grɛco	grɛci
nemico	nemici
pɔrco	pɔrci

b) Most singular genderables ending in -co not immediately following a stressed syllable form their plural in -ci.
Thus: (singular) mɛdico - (plural) mɛdici

c) Most singular genderables ending in -go form their plural in -ghi; however, the plural of words in -ɔlogo or -ɔfago that refer to people is generally in -gi.
Thus:

	(singular)	(plural)
	dïạlogo	dïạloghi
but:	astrɔlogo	astrɔlogi
	antropɔfago	antrɔpofagi

Gender-Intrinsic Versus Gender-Extrinsic Words (Unit 29)

Certain genderables like ┼arrosto (masculine) and ┼persona (feminine) that belong exclusively to only one gender category may be said to *have inherent gender* as opposed to genderables like ┼italiano (with masculine and feminine forms) or ┼insegnante (masculine and feminine) that *do not have inherent gender*. Those with inherent gender are called GENDER-INTRINSIC and the others are called GENDER-EXTRINSIC. (See frame no. 63 for important chart.)

Gender-Number Determinants and Gender-Number Agreement (Unit 29)

When dealing with gender-extrinsic words that are either *purely animate in reference* (like ‡*studɛnte* that only refers to people) or *marked* (like *un buɔn ufficiale*), what determines the gender selection is the *sex of the person or animal referred to*.

With other gender-extrinsic words, the gender selection is based on:
1) the gender of a gender-intrinsic word that is being referred to and that has in almost all cases been just mentioned, or
2) in the absence of the above, the sex referent.

Thus: *Quella guardia è americana.* (referring to a guard, whether male or female but: *È americano.* (referring to a male guard without referring to the word *guardia*)

In the absence of both a gender-intrinsic word being referred to and a sex referent, the *masculine singular form is normally used.* Thus: *Che cɔs'è quello?*

Omission and Use of the Unit Marker (Unit 29)

After the verb ‡*ɛssere*, a word classifying a person as to nationality, religion, or political affiliation is often *not* preceded by the UNIT MARKER unless the word is accompanied by a descriptive word or phrase. The same holds true for many words indicating one's status, professional, occupational, or titular.

Thus:　　È americano.
　　　　　È studɛnte.
but:　　　È un buɔn americano.
　　　　　È un buɔno studɛnte.

However, the UNIT MARKER *does* occur in the above cases when one is answering the question- *Chi è X?*
Thus: *Chi è quel signore? - È un americano.*

Masculine in the Singular and Feminine in the Plural (Unit 29)

(masculine singular)	(feminine plural)
braccio	*braccia*
centinaio	*centinaia*
dito	*dita*
labbro	*labbra*
migliaio	*migliaia*
miglio	*miglia*
paio	*paia*
uɔvo	*uɔva*

More on Uno (Unit 27)

The MASCULINE UNIT MARKER *uno* (and not *un*) occurs before words that begin with:

s + consonant	-	*uno studio*
gn	-	*uno gnɔmo*
z	-	*uno zio*
ż	-	*uno żero*

and the relatively few words that begin with *pn, ps, x* and any other consonant group not normally found at the beginning of an Italian word.

uno pneumạtico
uno psichiatra
uno xilɔgrafo
uno bdellịo

Cardinal Numerals Through Twenty

0 - *żero*	11 - *ụndici*
1 - *uno*	12 - *dọdici*
2 - *due*	13 - *tredici*
3 - *tre*	14 - *quattôrdici*
4 - *quattro*	15 - *quindici*
5 - *cinque*	16 - *sedici*
6 - *sɛi*	17 - *diciassɛtte*
7 - *sɛtte*	18 - *diciɔtto*
8 - *ɔtto*	19 - *diciannɔve*
9 - *nɔve*	20 - *venti*
10 - *diɛci*	

Adding and Subtracting (Unit 27)

1 più 1 fa 2.
7 meno 4 fa 3.

VOCABULARY

UNITS 1–10

VOCABULARY

c'è	- is in, is around, is present, is there, is here
chi?	- who (m)?
Chi ama?	- Who loves?
Chi è?	- Who is it? Who is (s)he?
chiama	- (s)he is calling
chianti	- Chianti [Italian wine]
düello	- duel
è	- it is, (s)he is, is
È Amanda.	- It is Amanda.
È Amanda?	- Is it Amanda?
jɔ-jɔ.	- yo–yo
lacüale	- laky
la quale	- she who, which
l'haïtiana	- the Haitian woman
lì	- there
mai	- (n)ever
nɔ	- no [meaning that a negative statement is true]
Nɔ?	- Isn't that so? Right?
non	- not
Non è Amanda.	- It is not Amanda.
Non c'è.	- (S)he is not in.
non........mai	- not........ever, never
paüroso	- fearful
qui	- here
sì	- yes [meaning that an affirmative statement is true]
Sì?	- Yes? Is that so?
spïava	- was spying

FOREIGN WORDS

Wạshington
watt
yacht
yankee

GIVEN NAMES

masculine	feminine
Cɔla	Agata
Luca	Alina
	Amanda
	Amina
	Augusta
	Bianca
	Bista
	Ɛva
	Fina
	Gina
	Lɛa
	Lia
	Lina
	Linda
	Lɔla
	Magda
	Mɛna
	Mina
	Nɛna
	Nina
	Nini
	Pia
	Sabina
	Savina
	Spina
	Tina

UNIT 11

VOCABULARY

colomba	- female pigeon, dove
colombo	- male pigeon, dove
Colombo	- Columbus
giôgo	- yoke
intŏnso	- uncut, unshaven
lombo	- sirloin
vôga	- vogue, fashion
vɔto	- void, vacuum, empty space [literary and popular word]
voto	- grade, vote, mark

GIVEN NAMES

masculine	feminine
Adɔlfo	Alda
Alano	Antɔnia
Aldo	Clɛo
Alfio	Colomba
Alfɔnso	Dina
Antɔnio	Donata
Augusto	Fabia
Beniamino	Fausta
Dino	Flavia
Donato	Giovanna
Ɛlio	Guendalina
Fabio	Lidia
Fausto	Livia
Flavio	Nanda
Gino	Pina
Giovanni	Saffo
Gosto	Silvia
Guido	Sɔnia
Lɛo	Tosca
Lino	
Livio	
Nando	
Nicɔla	
Nino	
Noè	
Pino	
Quinto	
Silvio	
Tano	
Tino	
Tɔnio	
Ugo	

UNIT 12

VOCABULARY

bébé	- baby [French word]
cede	- chick-pea
cemento	- cement
Êlba	- Elba [Italian island]
elemento	- element
pɛsca	- peach
pesca	- fishing, load of fish
tĕmpio	- temple

GIVEN NAMES

masculine	**feminine**
Adone	*Adɛle*
Bela	*Cice*
Cecè	*Clɔe*
Dante	*Dafne*
Felice	*Ɛbe*
Leone	*Ɛgle*
Napoleone	*Edvige*
Pasquale	*Elsa*
Samuɛle	*Fede*
Solone	*Lena*
Ulisse	*Selɛne*
Valɛnte	
Vitale	

UNIT 13

VOCABULARY

casa	- house, home
cassa	- case, box
*cestino	- basket, waste-basket
che?	
che cɔsa	- what?
cɔsa?	
Che cɔs'è	
questo?	- What is this?
cɔsa	- thing
*dɛnte	- tooth
*lupo	- wolf
*naso	- nose
questo	- this
*sasso	- stone
*sofà	- sofa
*tɔpo	- rat
un	- a(n)
*vaso	- vase

*These words may occur after *un'*.

UNIT 14

VOCABULARY

animale	- animal
bambino	- (male) child
bastone	- cane, stick
bɔsco	- woods, wooded area
cane	- dog
chimɔno	- kimono
cɔno	- cone
consolato	- consulate
conto	- account, (hotel or restaurant) bill
elefante	- elephant
fico	- fig
film	- film, movie
fuɔco	- fire
gɔlf	- sweater
italiano	- (male) Italian
mese	- month
monumento	- monument
ɔsso	- bone
ospedale	- hospital
pane	- (loaf of) bread
pilɔta	- pilot
poɛta	- (male) poet
ponte	- bridge
uɔmo	- man
uɔvo	- egg
velo	- veil
vino	- wine

(All these words may occur after *un'*.)

UNIT 15

VOCABULARY

*agosto	- August
*anglicano	- Anglican
Bolôgna	- Bologna [Northern Italian city]
*cognome	- surname, last name
fa .	- is doing
*giugno	- June
glandola	- gland
glɛba	- clod, lump
*glɔbo	- globe
glielo dà	- (s)he gives it to him
gli piace	- (it) is liked by him
*glutine	- gluten
gnɔmo	- gnome
la campagna	- the country [as opposed to city or town]
la Campania	- [region in Southern Italy]
la vigna	- the vineyard
le miglia	- the miles
l'Emilia	- [region in Northern Italy]
lieto	- glad
li taglia	- (s)he cuts them
l'Italia	- Italy
l'Ɔglio	- [affluent of the Po River]
l'ɔlio	- (the) oil
*luglio	- July
*maggio	- May
negligɛnte	- negligent
niɛnte	- nothing
non.....niɛnte	- not.....anything, nothing
*nome	- name, given name
nome e cognome	- full name, first and last names
*pôsto	- place
sôgna	- (s)he is dreaming
vogliamo	- we want
voliamo	- we fly

GIVEN NAMES

masculine	feminine
Emilio	Emilia
Giulio	Giulia
Giunio	Lavinia

*These words may occur after *un'*.

UNIT 16

VOCABULARY

bɛne	- fine, well
benino	- fairly well, pretty well
come?	- how?
così così	- so so
il sig. Vegli	- Mr. Vegli
il sig.	- [an abbreviation for: the gentleman]
la sig.a Segni	- Mrs. Segni
la sig.na Paglia	- Miss Paglia
male	- bad, ill
molto bɛne	- very well
non c'è male	- not bad, one can't complain
sta	- is [used to refer to health, as in:
Come sta?	- How is (s)he?
Sta bɛne.	- (S)he is fine.]

UNIT 17

VOCABULARY

B. G.	- [an abbreviation for the greeting or leave-taking expression: Good day]
B. S.	- [an abbreviation for the greeting or leave-taking expression: Good evening; Good night]
chiamo	- I am calling
ci sôno	- I am in
e Lɛi?	- and you?
faccio	- I am doing
g——	- [an abbreviation for: Thank you]
la sig.a	- [an abbreviation for: the lady (married)]
la sig.na	- [an abbreviation for: the lady (unmarried)]
piace	- is liked

gli piace - (s)he {(it) / is liked by him; he likes} {it / her / him}

le piace	- " " " her; she "
Le piace	- " " " you; you like "
mi piace	- " " " me; I "
sig.a	- [an abbreviation for: madam]
sig.	- [an abbreviation for: sir]
sig.na	- [an abbreviation for: miss]
sôgno	- I am dreaming
sôno	- I am
stɔ	- I am [used to refer to health, as in:
Stɔ bɛne.	- I am fine.]

UNIT 18

VOCABULARY

a d——	- [an abbreviation for: on the right]
a s——	- [an abbreviation for: on the left]
*campo	- field
*capitano	- captain
ce n'è uno $\begin{cases} lì \\ qui \end{cases}$	- there is one $\begin{cases} \text{there} \\ \text{here} \end{cases}$
*chilo	- kilogram
*chiɔdo	- nail
*chiɔsco	- kiosk, newsstand
*chiusino	- cover, lid [metal or stone]
*cubo	- cube
*cuɔco	- (male) cook
*cuɔio	- leather
*dove?	- where?
Dov'è....?	- Where is...............?
*gas	- gas
*ghetto	- ghetto
*ghigno	- grin
*ghiottone	- glutton
*guanto	- glove
*gufo	- owl
*quotidiano	- daily newspaper
schiusi	- I opened
scuɔla	- school
scusi	- excuse me [said to one person formally]
spaghetti	- spaghetti

*These words may occur after *un'*.

UNIT 19

VOCABULARY

c'ɛra	- was in, was around, etc.
c'ero	- I was in
ci sarà	- will be in, around, etc.
ci sarɔ	- I will be in
domani	- tomorrow
due minuti fa	- two minutes ago
ɛra	- was
ieri	- yesterday
ma	- but
mattina	- morning
non sɔ	- I don't know
ɔggi	- today
ora	- now
pomeriggio	- afternoon
questo pomeriggio	- this afternoon
sarà	- will be
sera	- evening
stamattina	- this morning
stasera	- this evening, tonight

GIVEN NAMES

masculine	feminine
Oliviero	Cɔra
	Dɔra
	Mara
	Nɔra
	Sara
	Vɛra

UNIT 20

VOCABULARY

ciancia	- groundless rumor
*cieco	- blind man
*cielo	- sky
ciɔcia	- sanda
*ciuco	- donkey
*deficiɛnte	- deficient (one)
*giacinto	- hyacinth
giɔia	- joy
igiɛne	- hygiene
società	- society
spɛcie	- kind, sort

GIVEN NAMES

masculine	feminine
Biagio	Alice
Bonifacio	Berenice
Cesco	Bice
Cino	Cecilia
Ciro	Celɛste
Cherubino	Chiara
Gaetano	Galatɛa
Genɛsio	Gɛgia
Giacinto	Ghita
Giuliano	Gigi
Giusto	Gilda
Guɛlfo	Giɔia
Gugliɛlmo	Gisɛlda
Lodovico	Glɔria
Luciano	Godiva
Lucio	Licia
Lüigi	Lodovica
Michɛle	Micaɛla
Sancio	Michɛla
Ughino	Ɔlga
Vigilio	Pelagia

*These words may occur after *un'*.

VOCABULARY

VERBS

†andare	- to go
†ascoltare	- to listen (to)
†avere	- to have
†bere	- to drink
†capire	- to understand
†chiamare	- to call
†cominciare	- to begin, start
†dare	- to give
†dire	- to say, tell
†domandare	- to ask (for)
†esserci	- to be in, be around, etc.
†essere	- to be [not to be confused with [stare]
†fare	- to do, make
†finire	- to finish, end
†fumare	- to smoke
†imparare	- to learn
†lavorare	- to work
†mangiare	- to eat
†piacere	- to be liked

gli piace   -   it ⎫ is liked by them; they like ⎰ it
                             (s)he ⎭   her / him

ci piace   -   "   "   "   us; we   "   "
vi piace   -   "   "   "   you; you   "   "

†sapere	- to know
†sentire	- to hear
†sognare	- to dream (of)
†spiegare	- to explain
†stare	- to be [used to refer to health, as in: *Come sta?*, *Stɔ bɛne.*]
†studiare	- to study
†vedere	- to see
†venire	- to come

UNIT 21

VERBS

†andare	- to go
va	- is going
vado	- I am going
†arrivare	- to arrive

OTHER

ad Ancona	- in Ancona, to Ancona
*americano	- (male) American
a Rio	- in Rio, to Rio
con	- with
di Roma	- of Rome, from Rome [= originating in Rome born in Rome]
molto	- a lot, a great deal
ogni	- each, every
quando	- when
spesso	- often

GIVEN NAMES

masculine	feminine
Renato	Rachele
Rico	Regina
Rinaldo	Renata
Rodolfo	Rina
Rolando	Rita
Romeo	Rosa
Rosina	

NAMES OF ITALIAN CITIES

Ancona	
Bari	
Cagliari	
Genova	- Genoa
Milano	- Milan
Napoli	- Naples
Perugia	
Riva	
Roma	- Rome
Torino	- Turin
Udine	

*This word may occur after *un'*.

VOCABULARY

UNIT 22

GENDERABLES

masculine		feminine	
antipasto	- hors d'oeuvre	acqua	- water
arrosto	- roast	aranciata	- orangeade
burro	- butter	birra	- beer
caffè	- coffee	bistecca	- steak
capo	- boss	donna	- woman
corso	- course	insalata	- salad
formaggio	- cheese	mela	- apple
gelato	- ice cream	pera	- pear
pepe	- pepper	persona	- person
sale	- salt		
sbaglio	- mistake		
tè	- tea		
tovagliolo	- napkin		
uovo sodo	- hard-boiled egg		

masculine/feminine

artista	- artist
cane/cagna	- dog
capitalista	- capitalist
capitano/capitanessa	- captain
comunista	- communist
dentista	- dentist
elefante/elefantessa	- elephant
gnomo/gnomide	- gnome
insegnante	- teacher
linguista	- linguist
poeta/poetessa	- poet
studente/studentessa	- student
turista	- tourist
un(o)/ un' / una	- a(n)

VERBS AND VERB PHRASES

†*desiderare*	- to wish, to want
Desidera?	- What to do wish?
Che desidera?	May I help you?
†*portare*	- to bring, to take (somewhere), to carry, to wear
Mi porti......	- Bring me......
vorrei	- I'd like

OTHER

arrivederci	- good-bye
arriverderLa	- good-bye [said to one person formally]
per favore	- please
per piacere	
un po' di......	- a little......

GIVEN NAMES

masculine	feminine
Alberto	*Berta*
Armando	*Carla*
Arturo	*Carmela*
Bernardo	*Marta*
Carlo	*Virginia*
Roberto	

VOCABULARY

UNIT 23

GENDERABLES

masculine		feminine	
costui	- that man	*banca*	- bank
est	- east	*cena*	- supper
giovedì	- Thursday	*chiesa*	- church
lunedì	- Monday	*città*	- city
martedì	- Tuesday	*classe*	- class
mercoledì	- Wednesday	*domenica*	- Sunday
nord	- north	*montagna*	- mountain
ordine	- order		
ovest	- west		
sabato	- Saturday		
sud	- south		
ufficio	- office		
venerdì	- Friday		

masculine/feminine

giovane	- young, young person

VERBS AND VERB PHRASES

†*dormire*	- to sleep
dɔrmo	- I sleep
†*fare la spesa*	- to do one's grocery shopping
†*fare le spese*	- to do one's shopping
†*giɔcare*	- to play [a sport, a game]
giɔco a tɛnnis	- I play tennis
†*pensare*	- to think
pɛnso	- I think
†*pensare di* + INFINITIVE	- to plan to......
†*stare*	- to stay

OTHER

avantiɛri	- the day before yesterday
ci	- [PLACE REPLACER]
ciɔ̀	- this thing, that thing
dopodomani	- the day after tomorrow
fuɔri	- out, outside
già	- already
in	- in
più	- more
qua	- here

GIVEN NAMES

masculine	feminine
Cɛsare	Cia
	Gia

Islands (that are preceded by *a* for "movement to" or "location in or at")

Corfù	
Cuba	
Haiti	
Ischia	[Italian]
Malta	
Taiti	- Tahiti

VOCABULARY

CITIES*

Addis Abeba	- Addis Ababa	Lagos	
Alcalà		Las Vegas	
Algeri	- Algiers	L'Avana	- Havana
Amman		Lisbona	- Lisbon
Ankara		Los Angeles	
Bagdad		Managua	
Bahia		Miami	
Baia	[Italian]	Monaco di	
Baltimora	- Baltimore	Baviera	- Munich
Bangkok		Mosca	- Moscow
Beirut		Nicosia	
Berlino	- Berlin	Nuova Delhi	- New Delhi
Bogotà		Padova [Italian]	- Padua
Boston		Palermo [Italian]	
Bucarest	- Bucharest	Pavia [Italian]	
Budapest		Pechino	- Peking
Buenos Aires	- Kabul	Porto Said	- Port Said
Cabul		Rabat	
Caracas		Saigon	
Catania	[Italian]	Santiago	
Città del		Siviglia	- Seville
Guatemala	- Guatemala City	Sofia	
Colonia	- Cologne	Tangeri	- Tangiers
Copenaghen	- Copenhagen	Tokio	- Tokyo
Cordova		Toronto	
Damasco	Damascus	Tunisi	- Tunis
Filadelfia	- Philadelphia	Varsavia	- Warsaw
Helsinki			
Kartum	- Khartoum		

*See note, p. 589

OTHER GEOGRAPHICAL PLACE NAMES*

NOTE: In this list, words in *-a* are feminine unless marked [m.] for masculine; all others are masculines

Abissinia	- Abyssinia		*Danimarca*	- Denmark
Afganistan	- Afghanistan		*Estonia*	
Alabama [m.]			*Etiopia*	- Ethiopia
Alasca	- Alaska		*Europa*	- Europe
Albania			*Finlandia*	- Finland
Algeria			*Florida*	
America			*Garda* [m.]	
Andalusia			*Georgia*	
Aquitania			*Germania*	- Germany
Arabia Saudita	- Saudi Arabia		*Ghana* [m.]	
Argentina			*Giappone*	- Japan
Arizona			*Giordania*	- Jordan
Arno			*Guatemala* [m.]	
Asia			*India*	
Atlantico			*Iraq*	
Barberia			*Iugoslavia*	- Yugoslavia
Bulgaria			*Kansas*	
California			*Kentucky*	
Cambogia	- Cambodia		*Libano*	- Lebanon
Canadà [m.]			*Liberia*	
Castiglia	- Castille		*Libia*	- Lybia
Cile	- Chile		*Liguria*	
Cina	- China		*Lombardia*	- Lombardy
Colombia			*Luisiana*	- Louisiana
Colorado			*Macedonia*	
Corsica			*Malesia*	- Malaysia

VOCABULARY

Manciuria	- Manchuria	Po	
Marocco	- Morocco	Polonia	- Poland
Maryland		Portogallo	- Portugal
Massachusetts		Romania	
Mauritania		Romania	- [the neo-Latin world]
Medio Oriente	- Middle East	Russia	
Mediterraneo	- Mediterranean	Sardegna	- Sardinia
Mississippi		Siberia	
Moravia		Sicilia	- Sicily
Nevada [m.]		Siria	- Syria
New York		Spagna	- Spain
Nicaragua [m.l		Sudan	
Nigeria		Tasmania	
Normandia	- Normandy	Tevere	- Tiber
Nord Dakota [m.]		Thailandia	- Thailand
Norvegia	- Norway	Toscana	- Tuscany
Ohio		Tunisia	
Pacifico		Turchia	- Turkey
Patagonia		Ungheria	- Hungary
Pensilvania	- Pennsylvania	Veneto	
Persia		Venezuela	
Piave		Vietnam	
Piemonte	- Piedmont	Virginia	

*NOTE: For some Italians, the Italian stress on some of the foreign place names given differs from that shown.

UNIT 24

GENDERABLES

masculine		feminine	
aprile	- April	*A. A.*	- [an abbreviation for: American Embassy]
Centralino	- [telephone exchange normally used in calling the telephone operator]	*guardia*	- guard
dicembre	- December		
memento	- moment		
novembre	- November		
numero	- number		
telefono	- telephone		

masculine/ feminine	
inglese	- English
pronto/pronta	- ready
segretario/segretaria	- secretary

VOCABULARY

VERBS AND VERB PHRASES

†aspettare	- to wait (for)
Aspetti!	- Wait!
Chi la desidera?	- Who shall I say is calling (her)?
Chi lo desidera?	- Who shall I say is calling (him)?
†dovere	- to have to, must
Děve lavorare?	- Do you have to work?
Děvo ⎫ Děbbo ⎭ lavorare.	- I have to work.
Dovrěbbe lavorare?	- Should you work?
Dovrei lavorare.	- I should to work.
†insegnare	- to teach
Mi dispiace.	- I'm sorry.
†parlare	- to speak, talk
†potere	- to be able to, can
Può lavorare?	- Can you work?
Posse lavorare.	- I can work.
Potrěbbe lavorare?	- Could you work?
Potrei lavorare.	- I could work.
Qui è l'ufficio....	- This is the office...
†sbagliare	- to make a mistake
Avrà sbagliato numero.	- You must have dialed the wrong number.
Sôno io.	- Speaking [= I am the one].
Vedo se c'è.	- I'll see if (s)he is in.
†volere	- to want
Vuol(e) lavorare?	- Do you want to work?
Voglio lavorare.	- I want to work.
Vorrěbbe lavorare?	- Would you like to work?
Vorrei lavorare.	- I'd like to work.

GIVEN NAMES

masculine	feminine
Alfredo	Cristina
Andrea *	Griselda

* Cognate of the English "Andrew."

GEOGRAPHICAL NAMES

masculine	feminine	
Brasile - Brazil	Africa	
	Australia	
	Brasilia	
	Francia	- France
	Grecia	- Greece
	Francoforte	- Frankfurt
	Londra	- London

OTHER

adagio	- slowly
al telefono	- on the phone
del signor White	- Mr. White's
della signora Smith	- Mrs. Smith's
di, d',	- of
uno studente	
d'italiano	- a student of Italian
il dottor Russo	- Dr. Russo
la guardia all' A.A.	- the guard at the American Embassy
prego	- [see frame no. 7 of Unit 24]
pronto	- hello [said on the phone]
sempre	- always
tre	- three

UNIT 25

masculine		feminine	
†affresco	- fresco	†acredine	- bitterness
†aggio	- premium	†ala	- wing
†aggravio	- load, burden	†arma	- weapon
†agio	- ease	†copia	- copy
†atrïo	- entrance hall	†coppia	- couple
†baco	- worm	crisi	- crisis
bar	- bar, coffee, counter	†fuga	- flight [= escape]
†bue	- ox	gru	- crane
†bufalo	- buffalo	†libbra	- pound
†camino	- chimney	†libra	- Libra
†cammino	- way, path	†mano	- hand
†carro	- wagon, cart	pala	- shovel
cinema	- movie-theater	palla	- ball
†fato	- fate	pappa	- pap
†fatto	- fact	pena	- penalty
†febbraio	- February	penna	- pen
†libro	- book	radio	- radio
†luccio	- pike	†replica	- reply; replica
†papa	- pope	università	- university
portacenere	- ashtray	virtù	- virtue
†programma	- program		
†quadro	- painting		
†scapolo	- bachelor, unmarried (male)		

GENDERABLES
masculine/feminine

†soqquadro	- confusion, disorder	†africano	- African
sport	- sport	†agrario	- agrarian
vaglia	- money order	†caro	- dear, expensive
		†dio/dea	- god/goddess
		†francese	- French, French person
		†occupato	- busy

VERBS AND VERB PHRASES

†*accreditare*	- to credit
accredita	- (s)he credits
†*amare*	- to love
†*applicare*	- to apply (something)
†*applica*	- (s)he applies (something)
†*cadere*	- to fall
†*cadde*	- (s)he fell
†*cade*	- (s)he falls
†*Dĕvo riferire*	
qualcɔsa?	- Would you like to leave a message?
	[literally: Do I have to relay something?]
†*fuggire*	- to flee, escape
†*fugga*	- flee
†*dire che......*	- to tell (someone) that....
gli dica che	- tell him that
le dica che	- tell her that
†*dire di*	
(+ infinitive)	- to tell someone to....
gli dica di	
telefonarmi	- tell him to phone me
le dica di	
telefonarmi	- tell her to phone me
ha telefonato X	- X telephoned
†*importare*	- to matter
non impɔrta	- it doesn't matter, that's all right
†*piɔvere*	- to rain
piɔve	- it rains
piɔvve	- it rained
†*raddrizzare*	- to straighten (something)
†*richiamare*	- to call back, call again
†*richiamarLa*	- to call you back
†*richiamerɔ*	- I'll call back
†*riferire*	- to report, relay, refer
†*riferirɔ*	- I'll relay the message
†*ritelefonare*	- to call back, call again
ritelɛfono	- I call back
†*ritornare*	- to return to [= to go back, come back]
se vuɔle	- if you wish
†*telefonare*	- to telephone
telɛfono	- I telephone
†*tornare*	- to return [= to go back, come back]
va bɛne	- O.K., all right, it's all right

VOCABULARY

GIVEN NAMES

masculine	feminine
Bacco - Bacchus	*Stella*
	Vanda

OTHER

Buffalo	- Buffalo [city]
fra X giorni	- X days from now
fra poco	- shortly [= a little while from now]
fuori città	- out of town
nel pomeriggio	- in the afternoon
ɔh!	- oh!
per	- for
più tardi	- later
qualche giorno	- a few days, one or more days
quattro	- four
soltanto	- only

UNIT 26

GENDERABLES

masculine		feminine	
lui	- he	†*ambasciata*	- embassy
†*pôsto*	- seat, place	*lɛi*	- she
sci	- ski	†*scɛna*	- scene
scià	- Shah	†*scïovia*	- ski-lift
†*sciɔpero*	- strike		
†*tạvolo*	- table		

masculine/feminine

†*cosciɛnte*	- conscious, aware
†*scemo*	- stupid; fool
†*scïente*	- knowing
†*scientifico*	- scientific

GIVEN NAMES

masculine	feminine
Mario	*Marịa*

OTHER

anche	- also, too
e	- and
ed Emilio	- and Emilio
io	- I
neanche	- neither
perchè	- why; because

VOCABULARY

VERBS

†abitare	- to live [= reside]
abito	- I live
†accelerare	- to accelerate
†accelero	- I accelerate
†addurre	- to adduce, *allege*
†adduco	- I adduce
†agevolare	- to facilitate
agevolo	- I facilitate
†apporre	- to affix, appose
appongo	- I affix
†aprire	- to open
†apro	- I open
†attrarre	- to attrac
attraggo	- I attract
†comporre	- to compose
†condurre	- to conduct, conduce
†conoscere	- to know [= be acquainted with]
conosco	- I know
†considerare	- to consider
considero	- I consider
†contrapporre	- to set against; oppose
†contrarre	- to contrac
†dedurre	- to deduct, deduce
†deporre	- to depose
†detrarre	- to detract, deduct
†disporre	- to dispose
†distrarre	- to distract
†dormire	- to sleep
dɔrmo	- I sleep
†esporre	- to expose
†imporre	- to impose
†indurre	- to induce
†interporre	- to interpose
†introdurre	- to introduce [= lead or bring in]
†lasciare	- to leave (some thing)
†leggere	- to read
leggo	- I read
†manipolare	- to manipulate
manipolo	- I manipulate
†opporre	- to oppose
†partecipare	- to participate
partecipo	- I participate
†partire	- to leave [as when going on a trip]
parto	- I leave
pascere	- to graze
pasco	- I graze
†porre	- to place
†posporre	- to postpone
†predisporre	- to predispose
†preferire	- to prefer
†prenotare	- to reserve
prenɔto	- I reserve

†*preporre*	- to place before
†*produrre*	- to produce
†*proporre*	- to propose
†*protrarre*	- to protract
†*ridurre*	- to reduce
†*ritrarre*	- to retract
†*salire*	- to go up (stairs)
salgo	- I go up (stairs)
†*sciäre*	- to ski
†*sciupare*	- to waste, spoil
†*scusare*	- to excuse
†*sedurre*	- to seduce
†*sottrarre*	- to subtract
†*supporre*	- to suppose
†*tradurre*	- to translate
†*trarre*	- to draw [= bring forth]
†*uscire*	- to go out
ɛsco	- I go out
†*vincere*	- to win
vinco	- I win

VOCABULARY

UNIT 27

GENDERABLES

masculine		feminine	
†aglio	- garlic	†aẓalɛa	- azalea
†aẓẓardo	- hazard, risk	†aẓiɛnda	- business firm
†bagno	- bathroom	†razza	- race [= breed, lineage]
†bdellio	- [name of a resin]		
†discórso	- speech	†razza	- skate [type of fish]
†fascio	- bundle	†salsa	- sauce
†indirizzo	- address	†stanza	- room
†pneumatico	- pneumatic tire	†zappa	- hoe
†pranẓo˙	- dinner [= most important meal of the day]	†ẓebra	- zebra
		†ẓɔna	- zone
		†ẓuppa	- soup
†psicɔlogo*	- psychologist		
†sɛnso	- sense		
†xilɔgrafo	- xylographer		
†xilɔfono	- xylophone		
ẓɛlo	- zeal		
ẓɛro	- zero		
ẓinco	- zinc		
†ẓɔo	- zoo		
†ẓúcchero	- sugar		

* Although listed in dictionaries as masculine, some words ending in -ɔlogo or -ɔfago may be heard with a corresponding feminine form in -ɔloga or-ɔfaga, respectively.

masculine/feminine

†*aziendale*	- of the business
†*nazista*	- nazi
†*psichiatra*	- psychiatrist
†*Arazzista*	- racist
†*zio*	- uncle/aunt
†*zitto*	- quiet, silent
†*zoppo*	- lame

words in -*zione* (feminine)

†*abitazione*	- habitation, place of residence	†*circonvallazione*	- circumvallation, circumferential road
†*accelerazione*	- acceleration	†*coalizione*	- coalition
†*addizione*	- addition	†*collaborazione*	- collaboration
†*adduzione*	- adduction	†*composizione*	- composition
†*adozione*	- adoption	†*concentrazione*	- concentration
†*affezione*	- affection	†*condizione*	- condition
†*agevolazione*	- facilitation	†*conduzione*	- conduction
†*alimentazione*	- alimentation	†*congratulazione*	- congratulation
†*ambizione*	- ambition	†*considerazione*	- consideration
†*applicazione*	- application	†*consolazione*	- consolation
†*aspettazione*	- expectation	†*contestazione*	- contestation, protest
†*assimilazione*	- assimilation	†*continuazione*	- continuation
†*attenzione*	- attention	†*contraddizione*	- contradiction
†*attrazione*	- attraction	†*contrazione*	- contraction
†*autorizzazione*	- authorization	†*coronazione*	- coronation
†*aviazione*	- aviation, Air Force	†*corruzione*	- corruption
†*azione*	- action	†*costituzione*	- constitution
†*benedizione*	- benediction	†*costruzione*	- construction
†*circolazione*	- circulation		

VOCABULARY

words in -*zione* (feminine)

†*deduzione*	- deduction	†*investigazione*	- investigation
†*deposizione*	- deposition	†*irritazione*	- irritation
†*detrazione*	- detraction	†*ispirazione*	- inspiration
†*dilazione*	- dilation, extension [of time]	†*legislazione*	- legislation
		†*lezione*	- lesson
†*direzione*	- direction, management	†*limitazione*	- limitation
		†*litigazione*	- litigation
†*disposizione*	- disposition	†*maledizione*	- malediction, curse
†*distrazione*	- distraction	†*manifestazione*	- manifestation, demonstration
†*dizione*	- diction		
†*emozione*	- emotion	†*manipolazione*	- manipulation
†*eruzione*	- eruption	†*motivazione*	- motivation
†*esagerazione*	- exaggeration	†*narrazione*	- narration
†*esportazione*	- exportation	†*nazione*	- nation
†*esposizione*	- exposition	†*opposizione*	- opposition
†*fazione*	- faction	†*orazione*	- oration
†*frazione*	- fraction	†*orientazione*	- orientation
†*giustificazione*	- justification	†*partecipazione*	- participation
†*importazione*	- importation	†*porzione*	- portion
†*imposizione*	- imposition	†*posizione*	- position
†*indicazione*	- indication	†*posposizione*	- postposition
†*induzione*	- induction	†*pozione*	- potion
†*infezione*	- infection	†*predisposizione*	- predisposition
†*inflazione*	- inflation	†*predizione*	- prediction
†*informazione*	- information	†*prenotazione*	- reservation
†*integrazione*	- integration	†*preoccupazione*	- preoccupation
†*intenzione*	- intention	†*preposizione*	- preposition
†*interruzione*	- interruption	†*produzione*	- production
†*introduzione*	- introduction	†*promozione*	- promotion

words in -*zione* (feminine)		VERBS	
╪*proposizione*	- proposition	╪*assimilare*	- to assimilate
╪*protrazione*	- protraction	*assimilo*	- I assimilate
╪*raccomandazione*	- recommendation	╪*collaborare*	- to collaborate
╪*ratificazione*	- ratification	*collaboro*	- I collaborate
╪*razione*	- ration	╪*esagerare*	- to exaggerate
╪*riduzione*	- reduction	*esagero*	- I exaggerate
╪*ripetizione*	- repetition	╪*esportare*	- to export
╪*ritrazione*	- retraction	*esporto*	- I export
╪*seduzione*	- seduction	╪*giustificare*	- to justify
╪*sensazione*	- sensation	*giustifico*	- I justify
╪*sezione*	- section	╪*importare*	- to import
╪*situazione*	- situation	*importo*	- I import
╪*soddisfazione*	- satisfaction	╪*indicare*	- to indicate
╪*soluzione*	- solution	*indico*	- I indicate
╪*sottrazione*	- subtraction	╪*integrare*	- to integrate
╪*spiegazione*	- explanation	*integro*	- I integrate
╪*stazione*	- station	╪*investigare*	- to investigate
╪*supposizione*	- supposition	*investigo*	- I investigate
╪*traduzione*	- translation	╪*irritare*	- to irritate
╪*trascrizione*	- transcription	*irrito*	- I irritate
╪*trasformazione*	- transformation	╪*limitare*	- to limit
╪*trazione*	- traction	*limito*	- I limit
╪*vaccinazione*	- vaccination	╪*litigare*	- to quarrel
╪*violazione*	- violation	*litigo*	- I quarrel
╪*volizione*	- volition	╪*preoccupare*	- to worry (someone)
		preoccupo	- I worry (someone)
		╪*ratificare*	- to ratify
		ratifico	- I ratify

VOCABULARY

NUMERALS

cinque	- five
sɛi	- six
sɛtte	- seven
ɔtto	- eight
nɔve	- nine
diɛci	- ten
ụndici	- eleven
dọdici	- twelve
trẹdici	- thirteen
quattôrdici	- fourteen
quịndici	- fifteen
sẹdici	- sixteen
diciassɛtte	- seventeen
diciɔtto	- eighteen
diciannɔve	- nineteen
vento	- twenty

OTHER

Firɛnze	- Florence [Italian city]
grazie	- thanks
Lazio	- Latium [Italian region]
meno	- minus, less
più	- plus, more
Quanto fa......?	- How much is......?
Venɛzia	- Venice [Italian city]

UNIT 28

masculine		feminine	
ǂantropɔfago*	- cannibal	ǂvacca	- cow
ǂantropɔlogo*	- anthropologist		
ǂarcheɔlogo*	- archeologist	**masculine/feminine**	
ǂastrɔlogo*	- astrologist	ǂabile	- capable
ǂbacio	- kiss	ǂamico	- friend
ǂdïalogo	- dialog	ǂbɛlga	- Belgian
ǂfilɔlogo*	- philologist	ǂcollɛga	- colleague
ǂgeɔlogo*	- geologist	ǂdiplomatico	- diplomat, diplomatic
ǂlago	- lake	ǂfantastico	- fantastic
ǂluɔgo	- place	ǂgrɛco	- Greek
ǂpɔrco	- pig	ǂinabile	- incapable
ǂstudio	- studio; study	ǂmagnifico	- magnificent
ǂteɔlogo*	- theologian	ǂmɛdico	- doctor; medical
		ǂnemico	- enemy
		ǂpolitico	- politician; political
		ǂsimpatico	- nice, pleasant
		ǂspɔrco	- dirty

OTHER

l'Aia	- the Hague
loro	- they, them
noi	- we, us
voi	- you [plural]

*See note, page 599.

VOCABULARY

GENDERABLES

masculine		feminine	
╪agɛnte	- agent	╪guida	- guide
╪colonnɛllo	- colonel	nazionalità	- nationality
╪cɔnsole	- consul	╪religione	- religion
╪dɔnno	- Don; Father [religious title]	╪suɔra	- Sister [religious title]
╪frate	- Brother; [religious title]		
╪funzionario	- officer; official [non-military]	**masculine in the singular and feminine in the plural**	
╪funzionario degli Ɛsteri	- Foreign Service Officer	╪braccio/braccia	- arm/arms
╪generale	- general	╪centinaio/centinaia	- about a hundred/ hundreds
╪grado	- rank; grade	╪dito/dita	- finger/fingers
╪lavoro	- work	╪labbro/labbra	- lip/lips
╪mestiɛre	- occupation	╪migliaio/migliaia	- about a thousand/ thousands
╪militare	- soldier; in the military	╪miglio/miglia	- mile/miles
╪partito	- party [as in "political party"]	╪paio/paia	- pair/pairs
╪prɛte	- priest	╪uɔvo/uɔva	- egg/eggs
╪sergɛnte	- sergeant		
╪ufficiale	- military officer		

GIVEN NAMES

masculine		feminine	
Eugɛnio	- Eugene	*Anna*	- Ann
Giạcomo	- James	*Irɛne*	- Irene
Iạcopo	- Jacob	*Marịa*	- Mary
Stêfano	- Stephen	*Terɛsa*	- Teresa
Zenone			

masculine/feminine

†*ambasciatore/* ambasciatrice	- ambassador
†*attore/attrice*	- actor / actress
†*bɛllo*	- good-looking, beautiful, handsome
†*brutto*	- ugly
†*buddista*	- Buddhist
†*buɔno*	- good
†*cameriɛre/* cameriɛra	- waiter / waitress, maid
†*cattivo*	- bad
†*cattɔlico*	- Catholic
†*cinese*	- Chinese
†*corto*	- short
†*democrạtico*	- Democrat; democratic
†*democristiano*	- Christian Democrat
†*ebrɛo*	- Hebrew
†*esatto*	- exact
†*fascista*	- Fascist
†*fresco*	- fresh
†*giapponese*	- Japanese
†*grande*	- big, large; great
†*grɔsso*	- big, fat
†*impiegato*	- (office) employee

VOCABULARY

‡iugoslavo	- Yugoslav, Yugoslavian
‡lunge	- long
‡musulmano	- Moslem
‡presidente/presidentessa	- president
‡protestante	- Protestant
‡quale	- which
‡quello	- that
‡questo	- this
‡repubblicano	- Republican
‡russo	- Russian
‡santo	- saint
‡socialista	- Socialist
‡spagnolo	- Spanish, Spaniard
‡statale	- government worker
‡süicida	- suicide victim
‡tedesco	- German

VERB

‡appartenere	- to belong
A quale partito politico appartiene X?	- To which political party does X belong?

UNIT 30

GENDERABLES

masculine		feminine	
†ristorante	- restaurant	Scozia	- Scotland
		Spagna	- Spain
		Svezia	- Sweden
		Svizzera	- Switzerland

masculine/feminine	
†arabo	- Arab, Arabic
†avvocato/avvocatessa	- lawyer
†figlio	- son/daughter
†gatto	- cat
†olandese	- Dutch

OTHER

tu	- you [informal, singular]
Loro	- you [formal, plural]
per (i) sbaglio	- by mistake
tutti insieme	- all together
Perchè non ci diamo del tu?	- Why don't we use "tu" with each other?
Ci diamo del tu?	- Shall we use "tu" with each other?
Diamoci del tu!	- Let's use "tu" with each other!
Mi dia del tu, per favore.	- Please use "tu" with me.